Trouble of the World

Zach Sell Trouble

of the World

SLAVERY AND EMPIRE IN THE

AGE OF CAPITAL

THE

UNIVERSITY OF

NORTH CAROLINA

PRESS

Chapel Hill

*This book was published with the assistance
of the Anniversary Fund of the University of
North Carolina Press.*

Set in Bulmer and Clarendon by Tseng Information Systems, Inc.
Manufactured in the United States of America

The University of North Carolina Press has been
a member of the Green Press Initiative since 2003.

Cover illustration: detail from *Carte Figurative Et Approximative
Représentant Pour L'année Les Émigrants Du Globe, Les Pays Dóu
Ils Partent Et Ceux Oú Ils Arrivent*, by Charles Joseph Minard et al.
(Paris: Charles Joseph Minard, 1858); courtesy Library of Congress,
Geography and Map Division.

Library of Congress Cataloging-in-Publication Data
Names: Sell, Zach, author.
Title: Trouble of the world : slavery and empire in the age of capital / Zach Sell.
Description: Chapel Hill : The University of North Carolina Press, 2021. |
Includes bibliographical references and index.
Identifiers: LCCN 2020038251 | ISBN 9781469661346 (pbk ; alk. paper) |
ISBN 9781469660455 (cloth) | ISBN 9781469660462 (ebook)
Subjects: LCSH: Slavery—Economic aspects—United States—History—
19th century. | Colonization—Economic aspects—History—19th century. |
Capitalism—History—19th century. | Imperialism—History—19th century. |
Great Britain—Colonies—Social conditions—19th century.
Classification: LCC E441 .S46 2021 | DDC 331.11/734097309034—dc23
LC record available at https://lccn.loc.gov/2020038251

Contents

Figures

Trouble of the World

Introduction Terrible Convergence

This book returns to the explosive era of capitalist crisis, upheaval, and warfare between emancipation in the British Empire and Black emancipation in the United States (1833–65) to address a long-standing trouble in the field of empire studies: the relationship between slavery and empire within capitalism. During this age of global capital, U.S. slavery exploded to a vastness hitherto unseen, propelled forward by the outrush of slavery-produced commodities to Britain, continental Europe, and beyond. Britain waxed fat from this outflow and helped finance U.S. slavery while looking toward its empire to meet the bar U.S. slavery set. As slavery-produced commodities poured out of the United States, U.S. slaveholders transformed their profits into slavery expansion. U.S. slavery provided the raw material for metropolitan Britain's explosive manufacturing growth and inspired new hallucinatory imperial visions of colonial domination that took root from the Atlantic world to Asia and the Pacific.

Passed in 1833 by Britain's parliament, the Act for the Abolition of Slavery ended the enslavement of 800,000 people across the British Empire from the Caribbean to Canada to Mauritius while exempting India, Sri Lanka, and Saint Helena from its provisions.[1] The act further resulted in the compensation of slaveholders with the extraordinary sum of £20 million.[2] Britain's abolition of slavery followed quickly on the heels of the largest slave rebellion in Jamaica, the Baptist War of 1831.[3] By 1865, enslaved people in the United States brought down slavery in the midst of the American Civil War, resulting in the immediate end of slavery for 4 million people. Because slavery regimes were being toppled and because colonial subjects and enslaved people from India to Jamaica to the United States revolted against colonial occupation and exploitation, this epoch was also defined by racist and imperialist reaction. Slaveholders, colonial bureaucrats, factory owners, rural settlers, politicians, and wage workers seeking protection in whiteness all struggled to extend capitalism's lease on lives.

There was a terrible convergence between U.S. slavery and British imperial expansion, providing a new proving ground for the elaboration of projects toward dispossession within the changing realities of global capitalism. U.S. slavery plantations provided raw materials that drove British manufacturing forward, with slaveholders responding to demands created by slavery's location in the world market. Liverpool shipping, Manchester manufacturing, and London finance all together sustained the demand for U.S. slavery–produced commodities. Across the British Empire, politicians, colonial officials, and settlers sought to reshape imperial rule and occupation to allow commodities to pour out of colonies to match or surpass the economic dynamism of U.S. slavery. Technological modifications in factories and on plantations responded to meet the demands of the world market. U.S. slaveholders and Britain's manufacturers relentlessly sought ways to maximize their profits globally. This terrible convergence was part of the increasingly integrated, coordinated world of global capitalism.[4]

Three interrelated tendencies within capitalism's production of, and operation through, racial domination and colonial occupation came to define this era. The first tendency entailed projects to perpetuate plantation society through the elaboration of new forms of coercion.[5] The second tendency involved the pursuit of all-white settler societies or white racial ethno-states based upon Indigenous dispossession and Black removal to make new white men's countries.[6] The third tendency was defined by projects to racially arrange, dispossess, and dominate work through the capitalist marketplace. This last tendency operated through the making of a false choice, drawn starkly in colonial and post-slavery contexts, between the compulsion to work for wages or produce commodities to sell on the marketplace or otherwise suffer from destitution. Together, these three tendencies were essential to mid-nineteenth-century capitalism and remain accumulated within the structures of everyday life.

An Imperial World

Such tendencies within capitalism spilled over national boundaries and flowed across empires, converging in the contradictory spaces of colonial projects. U.S. slavery itself was essential to the expansion of the United Sates as an empire-state.[7] During the nineteenth century, the United States grew into the largest site of enslavement in the modern world.[8] In 1830, the enslaved population of the United States was over 2.5 million people. By 1860, 4 of the 6 million people enslaved in the Atlantic world were enslaved in the United States. Slaveholders accumulated unprecedented power through continental imperialism and Indigenous dispossession. Aggressive territorial conquest in the United States was defined by the Indian Removal Act (1830) and the annexation of Texas (1845), the latter of which nearly doubled the size of the United States.[9] These state-backed settler projects enabled slaveholders to gain further political power through U.S. settler slavery, a racial, colonial, and class-based relationship of dominance.

At the same time, Victorian Britain asserted global economic dominance through the expansion of manufacturing and finance along with the growth of overseas trade.[10] But this era was about more than just the so-called imperialism of free trade.[11] Instead, the British Empire increased its reach through both the formal incorporation of territories and people along with the expansion of its informal imperial relations. The British used their empire and its settlers to force southern Africa into a dependent economic relationship, propelled by the imperial belief that the region should be subordinated and ruled for the expansion of metropolitan capital and for the benefit of white settlers.[12] In India, British colonial bureaucrats imagined the plantation and field as pillars for new economic dominance as supported through colonialism. They looked toward tea, indigo, and jute cultivation as guides to inform how further agrarian conquest could meet and surpass cotton, rice, and other U.S. slavery–produced commodities.[13] British manufacturers, politicians, and colonial officials were just some of those who drew lessons from U.S. slavery to understand how to try to make the empire work for them.

U.S. slavery expansion was supported by Britain's dominant position within global capitalism and by demand for slavery-produced commodities. By 1860, U.S. slavery accounted for nearly 75 percent of U.S. domestic exports, with much of these exports destined for Britain.[14] As nineteenth-century observers suggested, when the price of cotton increased in Liverpool, the demand for enslaved people in the United States went up, the violence against enslaved people intensified, and plantations grew.[15] This cotton sustained Britain's manufacturing dominance and enabled its growth into the "workshop of the world."[16] By 1851, there were roughly 527,000 textile workers in England and over 3.2 million enslaved people in the United States. In 1860, over 88 percent of British cotton came from U.S. slavery and half of the total U.S.-produced tobacco crop would be exported to Britain that year.[17] Carolina rice continued to remain the single-most-valued rice staple in Liverpool and London markets until the American Civil War. In the midst of the war, Sarah Parker Remond, a Black abolitionist from the U.S. lecturing in London, would describe the knotted relations that held enslaved people in the United States and English wage laborers together, stating "the free operatives of Britain are, in reality, brought into almost personal relations with slaves during their daily toil."[18]

U.S. slavery's booming but combustible growth and Britain's continued profits inspired new British imperial imaginations of what forms of colonial conquest were possible. British metropolitan society fashioned new obligations onto India, the British Caribbean, and Australia where colonial projects unfolded with aims to match or surpass the economic dynamism of U.S. slavery without replicating settler slavery itself. Colonial India was meant to be remade into both Britain's cotton field and rice swamp.[19] Workers who could not find jobs in Britain's shuttered factories were expected to become settlers in Britain's colonies where they were to grow cotton, buy textiles, and remain forever. Yet, British colonial projects and fantasies of unbridled success encountered limits set by U.S. slavery's structural advantages within nineteenth-century capitalism. These limits frustrated Britain's capitalists, settlers, and merchants, who all saw their profits set back by U.S. slavery's dominance. The limits to empire further disappointed Atlantic abolitionists who promoted the possibility of emancipation through capitalism based upon increased colonial commodity production to outstrip U.S. slavery. U.S. slaveholders feared diminished significance should a part of the British Empire surpass their cotton or rice plantations as occurred with the shift in indigo cultivation from South Carolina to eastern India.

The relationships that spiraled out of the terrible convergence between U.S. settler slavery and the British Empire were about much more than the circulation of slavery-produced commodities alone. These relationships were also about wringing value through the making and management of racial difference.[20] Race management practices moved globally.[21] U.S. slaveholders scanned across the British Empire from southern Africa to the Straits Settlements in Southeast Asia to inform their perspectives on colonization and plantation organization. U.S. slaveholders and overseers traveled throughout the British Empire to British Honduras, Egypt, India, and beyond to manage colonial projects and plantations.[22] British colonial planters moved between slave plantations in Mississippi and South Carolina and instructed slaveholders about colonial techniques for plantation management. The trans-imperial circulation of these projects makes it impossible to organize these histories of capitalism as constituted through white supremacy, slavery, and colonialism according to discrete nation-states or empires.

U.S. slaveholders and British colonial planters engaged in furious debate over indentured, enslaved, and wage work to provide ideological support for their race management tactics. While abolitionists argued that U.S. slavery was a unique form of violence, U.S. slaveholders consistently argued that "coolie slaves" and "white factory slaves" within the British Empire were more exploited than enslaved people.[23] In 1859, the Virginia slaveholder Edward Alfred Pollard advocated for the reopening of the Atlantic slave trade, stating that he had seen the "hideous slavery of Asia" in the form of Asian indentured labor.[24] At the same time, however messy, there were real racial and colonial fault lines during this era. In 1857, a Virginia slave owner could identify with the British Empire during the Indian Uprising of 1857 while colonial subjects such as the Bengali antiquarian Rajendralal Mitra could criticize English indigo planters as "men whose like can be had only in the slave owners of Virginia."[25]

In standard accounts, such as Karl Polanyi's *The Great Transformation*, this era falls in the middle of 100 years of peace.[26] In reality, this was an age of war and insurgency against slavery and empire characterized by constant upheaval. These uprisings included Nat Turner's Rebellion in Virginia (1831), the Baptist War in Jamaica (1831–32), the first Afghan War (1839–42), the Indian Uprising of 1857, the Indigo Revolt in Bengal (1859), the Jamaican Morant Bay Rebellion of 1865, and the American Civil War (1861–65).[27] This *Pax Britannica* was defined by colonial, anticolonial, race, and slavery-based wars. W. E. B. Du Bois recognized this when he noted, "There was not a single year during the nineteenth century when the world was not at war."[28]

Anticolonial and antislavery uprising interrupted the smooth operation of power. At the same time, capitalist crisis, Black freedom, and suffering became increasingly coexpressed through the circuits of capital. Beginning in 1860, a devastating famine in India's North-Western Provinces resulted in deaths that were estimated at more than 1 million people. This famine lit the fuse for a capitalist crisis in metropolitan Britain that would detonate far beyond metropole and colony alone. The crisis was further intensified by the onset of the Civil War with the Union Army blockade of Confederate ports, limiting the export of slavery-produced commodities. Soon, in Britain, more than 400,000 factory workers would be unemployed or have their hours cut.[29] This crisis became known as the Lancashire cotton famine, a name that suggested that unemployed workers suffered from famine due to the inaccessibility of slave-produced cotton, a type of deprivation equivalent to death from starvation as occurred in the North-Western Provinces. In reality, this crisis and its management revealed the hierarchical ordering of the world within capitalism and the structural advantaging of the metropolitan worker.

As slavery regimes toppled, new racial and colonial projects were built. A white U.S. observer in Britain reflected back in the midst of the Civil War, "The anti-slavery sentiment of Great Britain, which had hitherto been regarded abroad as a great and solid fact upon which all the world might lean, has come to seem, after all, to be of 'such stuff as dreams are made of.'"[30] This was part of a deeper reality made clear in the midst of Black emancipation in the United States. Capitalism during this era was defined by the refashioning of global racial and colonial projects.

Capital, Slavery, Empire

It was from this world of crisis, contradiction, and upheaval that Karl Marx's critique of capital emerged. Marx would write drafts of all three volumes of *Capital* and *Theories of Surplus Value* in London during the midst of the American Civil War.[31] He also wrote extensively about colonialism in India as a way to theorize noncapitalist social relations. His analysis of settler colonialism in western Australia and the United States at the conclusion of *Capital* was essential to his account of the emergence of capitalism through primary or so-called primitive accumulation.[32] Yet, the perspective and categories that Marx fashioned through looking toward slavery and colonialism reveal critical limits in his understanding of domination in capitalism.

Despite the realities of mid-nineteenth-century capitalism as existing through slavery and colonialism, *Capital* itself is written principally as a critique of "enslavement to capital," a relation whereby the appearance of freedom conceals an abstract form of domination.[33] *Capital* most often addresses not the realities of capitalist slavery but rather deploys representations of slavery to understand abstract domination, what Marx elsewhere calls "indirect slavery."[34] When Marx describes capitalist domination through the selling of labor-power, he writes that the patriarchal male wage laborer resembles a slave trader, selling both himself and his family. According to Marx, "now the capitalist buys children" and advertisements for children to be sold to work in English factories resemble "the inquiries for Negro slaves that were formerly to be read among the advertisements in American journals."[35] Through an account of factory labor recruitment's resemblance to racial slavery, Marx offers a perspective on how capitalist domination operates.

Yet, Marx's description of domination through resemblance cannot address the reality of capitalism as produced through slavery and empire. In the nineteenth century, 1 million enslaved people were moved from the Upper South to the Lower South through the emergence of a new internal slave trade. This mass dispossession was facilitated by prosaic newspaper advertisements that read, "Cash will be paid for likely young negroes from the age of 18 to 25 years."[36] This internal slave trade depended directly upon Black women's reproductive labor, which sustained the perpetuation and expansion of slavery. This internal trade, in turn, sustained the demand for factory work in metropolitan Britain by supplying factories with raw materials.[37] Breaking these histories apart through an account of resemblance is a critical limit in Marx's conceptual account of domination in capitalism. This is part of a larger pattern in Marx's writing that cannot account for the racialization of capital let alone what Cedric Robinson named as *racial capitalism*.[38]

Another limit to Marx's concept of domination is his separation of colonialism from capitalism. In his writing on colonialism in India, Marx describes England's looting of the subcontinent as producing conditions for the revolutionary emergence of capitalism.[39] As Marx writes, "Whatever may have been the crimes of England she was the unconscious tool of history in bringing about that revolution."[40] In this account, colonialism had a progressive character because the transition to communism passed through capitalism. Elsewhere, Marx's concept of the Asiatic Mode of Production sought to account for the realities of Asia through the description of non-feudal, non-slavery-based social relations that were also not part of capital. In the process, Marx fashioned an orientalist concept of Asia.[41] While Marx abandoned the Asiatic Mode of Production in *Capital*, he would nonetheless continue to insist that Indian society in particular was static and characterized by "unchangeability."[42]

The separation of colonialism from capitalism is at the heart of the end of *Capital*. There, Marx provides an account of primary accumulation based upon an analysis of "systematic colonization," or what now would be referred to as settler colonialism, to clarify the emergence of capitalist social relations through colonial dispossession.[43] Marx situates primary accumulation as the prehistory of capitalism's origins rather than depicting primary accumulation as a recurrent part of capitalism or rendering colonialism as capitalism itself.[44] Marx's analysis draws upon a study of failed settler colonization in the Swan River colony of western Australia and suggests that it was in the political economy of the New World (here including Australia) where a secret of the Old World was discovered, that the capitalist mode of production and accumulation rests upon "the expropriation of the worker."[45] But by not rendering colonialism as capitalism, Marx misses how metropolitan societies were stabilized by settler colonial projects through the reallocation of work and bodies.[46]

Against the limits of Marx's concept of domination, Black radical and anticolonial critique revealed how a focus upon abstract domination and the expropriation of the worker misrecognized the realities of how dispossession and race structure capitalism.[47] The landmark scholarship of C. L. R.

James reconfigured domination in capitalism based upon a relativization of factory exploitation, as Sylvia Wynter recognized.[48] This relativization of factory production reconfigured the factory and wage as only one aspect in a broader structure of capitalist domination that moved through and depended upon race, slavery, and empire. This reconceptualization of capitalist domination was realized most fully in James's landmark study of the Haitian Revolution, *The Black Jacobins* (1938).[49]

Further, Eric Williams's *Capitalism and Slavery* (1944) and W. E. B. Du Bois's *Black Reconstruction* (1935) were both essential to refiguring slavery and empire as part of capitalism. In *Capitalism and Slavery* (1944), Williams identifies how slavery in the British Caribbean contributed to the profits and industrialization of the British capitalist economy.[50] Yet, as manufacturing-based industrial capitalism came to dominate the British economy, Caribbean slavery diminished in significance. However, as Williams continues, the baton of slavery in the British Caribbean was ultimately passed forward to the United States during the early nineteenth century. In *Black Reconstruction*, Du Bois reconfigures Marx's critique based upon a historical account of capitalism through a consideration of slavery and emancipation in the United States. In this account, Black emancipation, brought about through a general strike of enslaved people, was followed not by freedom but the ultimate global emergence of a "new imperialism" after the end of slavery. Together, this was part of a much larger mid-twentieth-century radical anti-capitalist current focused upon the critique of the racial and colonial realities of capitalism.

Following the 2008 financial crisis, there has been continued interest in the relationship between slavery and capitalism, most prominently through the paradigm of "the New History of Capitalism."[51] This scholarship has focused most directly upon slavery's capitalism in the United States and has been characterized especially by concern for understanding the messy empirical realities of American capitalism. While this work has offered important historical analysis in consideration of capitalist slavery, it has also produced a binary between the new and the old in the study of capitalism and in the process unintentionally distanced itself from the radical tradition of the critique of capitalism. In addition, commodity histories centered upon jute, cotton, sugar, tea, indigo, and tobacco to reframe capitalism in global perspective.[52] In addition to engagement with these histories, this book is especially inspired by the critical histories of race, colonialism, and capitalism across fields including the work of Tracey Banivanua Mar, Anthony Bogues, Madhavi Kale, Lisa Lowe, Walter Johnson, Manu Karuka, Kris Manjapra, Jennifer Morgan, and Andrew Zimmerman.[53] This scholarship has focused upon formations of race and empire as the analytical foundations for the critique of historical capitalism. Together, this work informs my approach to capitalism as structured by race and colonialism beyond any given national or imperial boundary.[54]

Capitalism since the global financial crisis has been defined by a decade of more austerity, more killer cops, relentless land grabs, and unrelenting projects of enclosure. This capitalism has also put forth new miseries: new forms of authoritarian populism and new racist regimes. In the present, a new conjunctural crisis is defined by pandemic, capitalist breakdown, police murders of Black people, unemployment, and mass dispossession and displacement. The present crisis is also very much itself about the refashioning of capitalist domination. This project of extending capitalism's lease on lives is not untethered from the nineteenth-century world. At the same time, the global uprisings against this horrible reality, from the Movement for Black Lives to protests against the Citizenship Amendment Act in India, reveal possibilities for another world.

Troubled World

Trouble of the World is organized to clarify histories, structures, and lives made and unmade across what C. L. R. James once referred to as the "tangled skein" of the world. To do so, it relies upon multi-sited archival research in Australia, Belize, Britain, India, and the United States. Across chapters, the perpetuation of plantation regimes, the pursuit of all-white settler societies, and the colonial and racial formation of new market coercions come into focus.

The book is divided into four sections to reveal different dimensions in the racial and colonial histories of capitalism. The first section, "Making Capital through Slavery," demonstrates U.S. slavery's formation in relation to the British imperial world. Chapter 1 positions U.S. settler slavery as part of a global regime of accumulation through consideration of W. E. B. Du Bois's insistence that slavery itself was defined by the "reduction" of Black humanity to real estate. Real estate was central to both slavery and territorial expansion in the nineteenth-century United States. Chapter 2 examines how the dispossessions produced through U.S. slavery converged with the pursuit of free-trade policies between Britain and the United States. U.S. slaveholders joined with Britain's capitalist manufacturers and free traders in aggressive pursuit of tariff reduction policies during the mid-nineteenth century. This movement reached a new height following the annexation of Texas in 1845. The next year, a series of free trade policies strengthened the relationship between U.S. slaveholders and British manufacturers. Free trade through slavery and empire revealed shared interests between British imperial liberalism and U.S. slaveholding.

The second section, "An Immense Accumulation of Commodities," examines the history of three different plantation export commodities — Bengal indigo, Carolina rice, and U.S. cotton staples — to reflect upon the location of U.S. slavery within capitalism. Taken together, these commodity histories offer insight into the different textures of relations of power as U.S. slavery and British imperialism converged. From the perspective of slaveholders, British colonial planters, and abolitionists, the shift of U.S. slavery-based indigo cultivation from South Carolina to eastern India seemed to provide raw material for fashioning expectations for transformation in both the United States and India. In South Carolina and Georgia, slaveholders looked at the shift in indigo production to colonial India to make sense of their place in the world. British planters imagined cotton following this global shift in indigo production while abolitionists saw the possibility for the production of Black freedom through this shift.

In contrast, projects to introduce Carolina rice and U.S. cotton staples in India revealed a different reality, one defined by U.S. slavery's expansion and persistence. Throughout the first half of the nineteenth century, Carolina rice was singularly valued within European markets. In response to expanding demand after 1830, the East India Company and the Agricultural and Horticultural Society of India sought to introduce Carolina rice cultivation across colonial India. Yet, these projects largely failed. Despite their limits, the demand for Carolina rice created expectations for colonial India to match U.S. slavery. The final chapter in this section returns to the history of U.S. plantation overseers who traveled across colonial India to introduce U.S. cotton staples from 1839 to 1849. These projects especially exposed not just the different realities between slavery-based and colonial smallhold production but also divergences within colonialism between the United States and India. Together, these colonial commodity projects reveal how U.S. slavery, metropolitan Britain, and colonial India were coproduced through one another and within global capitalism.

The book's third section, "Crisis," examines the formation of global capitalist crisis from the late 1850s through the 1860s to elaborate upon the meaning of both Britain's dominance within the global economy and its relationship to U.S. settler slavery. Chapter 6 examines this crisis through the colonial and racial bifurcations in suffering that were produced through ideas of famine. Visions of U.S. slave revolt destroying capitalism, followed by "cotton famine" in England, were part of deeply engrained anxieties over British industry's dependence upon slave-produced cotton from the

United States. These fears bloomed with the outbreak of the American Civil War, culminating in the belief that social fallout from disruption in the circuit of textile production was a "Lancashire Cotton Famine." Yet, the social and economic circumstances for the emergence of this crisis went beyond the Atlantic world and were inextricably bound to social conditions in India's North-Western Provinces. How this crisis unfolded was related to the hierarchical and colonial ordering of the world extending from U.S. slavery through Metropolitan Britain to colonial India and beyond.

Chapter 7 explores the expectations that U.S. slavery created within British colonial projects to transform cotton production and exchange across colonial India in the midst of this crisis. Manufacturers demanded that India surpass U.S. slavery-produced cotton in quantity and quality as emancipation unfolded in the United States. When India was seen to have failed to meet these demands, British capitalists and bureaucrats fashioned new disciplinary projects for colonial India just as the crisis in the British textile industry was displaced onto India. In this era, the colonial obligation for India to become Britain's cotton field was set by British manufacturers, merchants, and workers who saw this in relation to their dependence upon U.S. slavery.

Chapter 8 examines the colonial project to build a white man's country in Queensland, Australia, to relieve the suffering of unemployed British factory workers as supported by white settler factions who believed that Black, Asian, and Indigenous presence degraded white work. These white settlers drew this perspective from consideration of the condition of white nonslaveholding southerners in the United States. To provide white bodies to support settler colonization, immigration officials looked toward unemployed factory workers to settle and grow cotton to stabilize the crisis in Britain's textile industry. When this plan broke down, settlers seeking to become planters turned toward bringing migrant labor from the South Pacific to Queensland. This turn depended upon building a new plantation society defined by white supremacy, a model that itself was connected to practices of racial domination emerging from the United States.

The last section, "Slavery's Pathways," examines the colonial legacies of Black emancipation in the United States connecting British Honduras to the post-slavery United States. Chapter 9 considers how during the 1860s Chinese indentured labor, African American emancipation, contested Maya sovereignty, and white southern plantation settler colonization all converged in the Central American colony. Landholding companies first sought to bring formerly enslaved people to the colony based upon knowledge that the republican government of the United States was committed to Black removal projects. When this project failed, there was a turn toward Chinese indentured labor, which first arrived in British Honduras in 1865. Colonial planters believed that there would be a seamless development of the plantation through Chinese indentured labor. However, when this vision was not realized and Chinese migrants resisted, the colonial government sought to bring former slaveholding planters from the United States to settle and manage plantations. Against such unfolding histories of plantation violence, Chinese migrants resisted, abandoning plantations and joining the Santa Cruz Maya. This was just one instance of the unexpected small fires that defined anticolonial disruption during this era. These fires burned imperial boundaries.

The final chapter, "Keeping Real Estate White," considers how the land struggles of formerly enslaved people and ideas to transform the United States into a white-racial ethno-state collided in the post-slavery American South. This chapter considers how Black freedom and white demands for Black removal were part of the colonial legacy of U.S. slavery, with crucial linkages to ideas of settler colonization in Australia. Enslaved people themselves set limits to these projects. The book concludes with consideration of the long shadow that these histories have cast into the present.

The slave song "Trouble of the World" described enslaved people's "trouble" as a result of the world. From Du Bois's perspective, slave songs with their sorrow "spoke to the world." In this case, the song spoke to the world as it was: troubled. At the same time, enslaved people spoke to their world of slavery and its ends. With lyrics "I wish I was in Jubilee," the song expressed a desire to be free beyond this world. With lyrics "Roll, Jordan Roll," the song further presented one route to an end of this troubled world through escape. Ultimately, "Trouble of the World" depicted the brutality of slavery as a product of the world and demanded a different way of living, one that would be partially realized and tragically betrayed, through the world, at the end of this era.

PART I : : : **Making Capital
through Slavery**

1 : : : Real Estate Questions

An enslaved person described only as a "young boy" escaped from E. C. Briscoe in South Carolina in 1857. Briscoe was based in Port Gibson, Mississippi, when he sought assistance from the Charleston, South Carolina, slave trader Ziba B. Oakes to recapture the fugitive child. Briscoe requested that Oakes hire someone who "makes a business of ketchin [sic] negroes" so that Oakes could either sell the recaptured person in South Carolina or place him aboard a ship destined for New Orleans.[1] During the nineteenth century, New Orleans, Charleston, and Port Gibson were brought together through the internal slave trade, which unified the Upper South of the United States with a territorially expanding Lower South and resulted in the forced relocation of approximately 1 million enslaved people.[2] For Oakes, Briscoe's request was just one part of his sprawling business based upon the slave trade. While Oakes primarily depended upon speculation in enslaved people, he was also deeply invested in speculation in plantation land.[3]

Historical scholarship on the United States has often described the internal trade as guided by "the chattel principle" and defined the predicament of enslaved people across the United States in relation to chattel property.[4] However, in *Black Reconstruction*, W. E. B. Du Bois emphasized not the chattel character of U.S. slavery but its real estate character. As Du Bois wrote, "No matter how degraded the factory hand, he is not real estate."[5] This perspective located slavery's violence not only in the degradation of forced work but also in the operation of real estate as a principle based upon the slaveholder trade in and accumulation of enslaved people.[6] As Du Bois's correspondence shows, his choice of "real estate" as a basic category to understand U.S. slavery was neither a mistake nor incidental. In a letter to Harcourt, Brace and Company written just before the publication of *Black Reconstruction*, Du Bois insisted that the legal status of enslaved people was real estate, not personal property, writing that a proofreader change of "real estate" to "property" throughout the manuscript was done "without knowing the facts."[7]

Throughout the history of slavery in mainland North America, the legal status of enslaved people moved between chattel and real estate in ways that were part of incoherent legal fictions.[8] While in Port Gibson and Charleston an enslaved person's legal status was as personal or chattel property, in New Orleans the legal status of an enslaved person was as real estate. According to a strictly legal definition, while in Louisiana and Kentucky enslaved people were classified as real estate, more generally throughout the United States enslaved people were classified as personal or chattel property.[9] Yet, to dismiss Du Bois's observation as an error limits the possibility for considering real estate as a critical concept rather than as a legal category alone.[10] Critical concepts in *Black Reconstruction*, from the wages of whiteness to the general strike, have often worked against commonsense definitions.[11] From this perspective, Du Bois's use of real estate to describe slavery provides insight into a U.S. manifestation of the form of slavery-value introduced by the Atlantic slave trade, or what Sylvia Wynter has called the *pieza* framework that operated in the writing of C. L. R. James.[12] Within the *pieza* framework, the sixteenth-century enslaved African man became part of a general equivalent of value that defined ways that non-enslaved labor would be exploited within capitalism while also establishing principles that enabled the operation of the slave trade. In the context of the nineteenth-century United States, Du Bois's concept of real estate reveals ways that slavery-value and slave trading shaped the territorial and expansionary dynamics of the nineteenth-century United States as an empire.

Removed from a strictly legal definition, slavery real estate can be better understood in relation to definitions used for post-slavery real estate. In his study of Jim Crow South Florida, Nathan Connolly defines real estate as "land turned into property for the sake of further capital investment" and notes that this real estate "served as one of the chief vehicles for the development and continuance of anti-Black racism."[13] In *Black Reconstruction*, enslaved real estate gave property value by making enslaved people themselves a form of capital investment and accumulation.[14] At the same time, as *Black Reconstruction* reveals, this operation of slavery real estate was directly related to landed real estate, and through this relationship real estate established conditions for Black dispossession after slavery.

Du Bois's insistence that real estate was central to structuring the predicament of enslaved people is also part of the history of the United States as an empire. As Vine Deloria Jr. once observed, U.S. treaties with Indigenous nations have been consistently interpreted by the United States as real estate contracts.[15] Du Bois's concept of slavery real estate was shaped by real estate's other basis in the transformation of Native sovereign territory into property for investment and accumulation, something that slave traders like Ziba B. Oakes made an essential part of their business. More generally, throughout the nineteenth century, slavery increased the value of plantation land, which grew in relation to the availability of enslaved people for purchase, a reality that made slaveholders at once concerned with land speculation and slave trading as essential to a geographically expanding plantation economy.[16] Commodities produced through U.S. plantation slavery accounted for nearly 75 percent of U.S. domestic exports by 1860.[17] As cotton, tobacco, and rice were sold in Atlantic markets, the profits from these sales were transformed into the further accumulation of slavery and landed real estate in the sense outlined by Du Bois. The majority of white capital held in the southern United States was in enslaved people and land. Considering together the making and holding of real estate connected to the export-orientation of the slaveholding U.S. economy provides a way to consider how the United States as a slavery-based settler empire emerged in relation to Britain's dominance within global capitalism.

Taking Real Estate

The American Revolution was a revolt led by British North American settlers and slaveholders and an experiment in the establishment of what Aziz Rana has called a *settler empire*.[18] As a settler empire, the United States was characterized by the hierarchical differentiation of territory and people through enslavement and Indigenous dispossessions.[19] The establishment of the United States as an independent, slavery-based settler empire challenged the extent of British imperial overseas rule. The British Empire depended upon a system of imperial trade and taxation that connected South Asia, China, Britain, and the Caribbean to mainland North American colonies for British imperial advantage.[20] Within the era, there was a series of experiments with new forms of British settler and colonial property. The systematic English settler colonization of Australia commenced following the formation of the colony of New South Wales. White Englishmen declared the continent terra nullius, a status that sought to claim that Aboriginal people had no property rights in the land (1788).[21] In colonial Bengal, the Permanent Settlement of 1793 established a new set of colonial property relations that the British envisioned would create new conditions for capitalist agriculture.[22]

Protection of slaveholders' ability to operate freely across imperial space unfolded against the immediate backdrop of earlier colonial North American slaveholder resistance to perceived limits placed upon slavery within the British Empire. In 1772, the *Somerset v. Stewart* ruling limited slavery as a form of possession within the British Empire. In this case, James Somerset, born in West Africa, was brought to colonial Virginia aboard a slave ship in 1749. Somerset was sold to merchant Charles Stewart, who moved to London in 1768. In London, Somerset left Stewart's house and refused to return, challenging his enslavement.[23] In the court case that followed, the King's Bench placed modest limits on re-enslavement in Britain, declaring Stewart's claim to Somerset's enslavement invalid. As the lawyer who represented Somerset argued, the moment an enslaved person "put their foot upon English Ground that moment they become free."[24] The subsequent decision that Somerset could not be re-enslaved in England placed imperial limits on slavery and territorially fixed spaces of slavery and non-slavery.[25]

In breaking away from the British Empire, settlers and slaveholders in the North American colonies created an independent state that enabled often unrestrained slave-ownership and territorial expansion. The U.S. Constitution provided what sociologist Moon-Kie Jung has described as the framework for the United States as both an empire-state and as a state of white supremacy.[26] The U.S. Constitution enabled territorial expansion while protecting the interests of slaveholders, particularly against slave revolts and abolitionist movements. It directly supported slavery in Article I, Sections 2, 8, and 9, and Article IV, Section 2 (the Fugitive Slave Clause).[27] Article I, Section 2, granted political power to slaveholders and declared that the total members of the House of Representatives would be determined by the slave population of the United States, who would count as "three fifths of all other persons." The so-called Three-Fifths Compromise emerged from earlier principles of taxation determined in relation to land, houses, and racially differentiated populations during the 1787 Constitutional Convention.[28] This was a constitutional mechanism that transformed enslaved people into slaveholder political power and capital according to a territorial logic, conditions that enabled the realization of slave and landed real estate together.

The U.S. Constitution enshrined a relationship between Native land and the adherence of capital in the form of Black life as real estate while allowing for the consolidation of white political power through this adherence. The Constitution thus enabled historically unique forms of settler, slave-owning power. In the new United States, the Constitution protected the Atlantic slave trade for at least twenty years, preventing a ban until 1808. The Constitution also enabled settler territorial expansion and colonization. As the Constitutional Convention deliberated, the passage of the Northwest Ordinance (1787) transformed land west of the Appalachian Mountains and between the Mississippi and Ohio Rivers and Great Lakes into the Northwest Territory. Article 3 of the Northwest Ordinance declared that "good faith" should be demonstrated toward Indian nations and that neither land nor property could be taken "without their consent," a declaration consistently suspended for conquest. As Roxanne Dunbar-Ortiz further notes, the Northwest Ordinance established principles for annexation, occupation, and statehood while making land sales a base for wealth and power.[29] While Article 6 of the Northwest Ordinance banned slavery in the territory, it also made the continuation of slavery possible by mandating the return of any enslaved "fugitive" who sought refuge, setting forth a principle that would subsequently make the entirety of the United States slavery territory.[30]

In the early United States, a new set of territorial relations to define slavery emerged, protecting the rights of slaveholders across the entire settler empire, even as individual states passed laws for the gradual abolition of slavery.[31] Efforts to define states as "free soil" existed alongside the consistent national affirmation of slaveholder rights throughout the United States, rights with constitutional support. The Constitution's Fugitive Slave Clause established the national basis of slaveholder power, declaring, "No person held to service of labor in one state, under the laws thereof, escaping into another, shall, in consequence of any law or regulation therein, be discharged from such service or labor, but shall be delivered up on claim of the party to whom such service or labor may be due."[32] The Fugitive Slave Clause established the entire United States as slavery territory that would consistently expand with the annexation of territory. The status of the entire United States as slavery territory was repeatedly upheld by the Supreme Court in rulings such as *Prigg v. Pennsylvania* (1842) and given further legislative power nationally through the Fugitive Slave Act of 1850.[33] U.S. founding documents enabled a unique expression of slavery's real estate character through protecting slaveholder accumulation and slave trading without limits.

Differences in plantation slavery between British colonies and the United States meant that the slave trade ban strengthened the real estate basis of U.S. slavery as a means to accumulate capital. Legal restrictions on the slave trade in the North Atlantic world following the U.S. Act Prohibiting the Importation of Slaves (1807) and the British Slave Trade Act of 1807 influenced the demographic character of plantation slavery in both the United States and the Caribbean. However, from the closing of the Atlantic slave trade to the United States until the American Civil War, the enslaved population in the United States increased from 1.19 million to nearly 4 million.[34] In Latin America and the Caribbean, enslaved deaths often outpaced births, leading to dependence upon the Atlantic slave trade to provide enslaved labor for sugar plantation production. Within the British Caribbean, the abolition of the Atlantic slave trade was followed by general enslaved population decrease.[35] While the demographic violence of sugar plantation production curtailed Black life expectancies, in the United States, so-called natural decrease was offset in the sugar-producing parishes of Louisiana by the internal slave trade.[36] Within sugar-producing regimes in the British Caribbean, Black survival was an unnecessary part of a plantation system that expected Black death and disposability; reproduction of labor was instead dependent upon the Atlantic slave trade.[37] In mainland North America, and particularly in the post–Atlantic slave trade United States, slavery and the accumulation of slaveholder power relied increasingly upon Black women's reproduction directed toward enslaved population expansion as the basis of slaveholder real estate and political power.[38]

The growing territoriality of slavery within the United States gave new meaning to the possibility of slaveholder real estate accumulation.[39] In the early United States, the largest landmass expansion occurred through the Louisiana Purchase, which doubled the size of the United States by incorporating 828,000 square miles.[40] The incorporation of continental North America as U.S. territory—as real-estate-in-waiting—was made possible through European finance. Bonds totaling $15 million to finance the Louisiana Purchase were issued to the United States by the British merchant bank Barings Bank and the Amsterdam Hope and Company.[41] Thomas Jefferson, president during the acquisition, wrote that the Louisiana Purchase would enable "the future spread of our descendants" with a population that would double or triple the size of the United States.[42] He envisioned the future U.S. as a white racial ethno-state and was committed to Black removal and replacement by whites as necessary to the realization of this vision. For him, Louisiana offered a place to experiment with his vision of Black territorial diffusion—to move enslaved people across the United States in order to decrease Black population density and therefore the possibility of Black revolution against slaveholders, something he was acutely fearful of in the midst of the Haitian Revolution.[43] Jefferson proposed that only states that did not participate in the Atlantic slave trade could participate in the internal slave trade, and Louisiana itself could not rely upon the Atlantic slave trade.[44] Together, this might limit the extent of U.S. dependence on racial slavery while maintaining a settler empire. In reality, the Louisiana Purchase enabled not just territorial but also slavery-based expansion, facilitating the transformation of the Mississippi River valley into land for slaveholding planters, resulting in both the expanded accumulation of real estate in the form of enslaved people and land and also greater slaveholder political power through this accumulation.

The expansion of U.S. slavery itself was driven in part by the British industrial demand for commodities produced through slavery. The Mississippi River valley, seized through the Louisiana Purchase and the Indian Removal Act of 1830, would be demographically transformed during the nineteenth century with the spread of slavery and settler colonization and remade into a plantation complex where cotton would feed, at an ever increasing rate, the factories of Britain, Europe, and the northeastern United States.[45] By 1841, slavery-produced cotton accounted for 10 percent of British manufacturing.[46] Slave owners in the Upper South supported the extension of slavery into the Mississippi valley and U.S. territorial incorporation because of a regional dependence upon slavery and slave trading. Territorial expansion created a larger internal market for the Upper South–controlled slave trade. Slave owners in the Lower South supported the interstate slave trade as a means to develop the slavery basis of the region. Following the Louisiana Purchase, white Louisianans demanded access to enslaved people sold through the internal slave trade.[47] Louisiana's sugar barons invested in enslaved people both as real estate and as workers to grow sugar that would be sold for money, and that money would be used to further invest in enslaved people and land. Cotton, rice, and tobacco planters engaged in the same process but depended directly upon the export economy to sustain and increase the value of enslaved people and plantation estates in the process. Slavery and territorial expansion were sustained through this and defined by a logic of real estate as drawn by Du Bois.

Holding Real Estate

The holding and transfer of real estate assumed a unique form in the context of the formation of the United States as a slavery-based settler empire. Slaveholders from the Upper South looked toward their sons as men who would colonize land in the Lower South and through slavery and the slave trade establish and extend their slaveholding families. Scholar of settler colonialism Lorenzo Veracini has described the characteristic form of settler colonial possession as the surveying plat and the deed as indispensable for enabling "intergenerational transfer."[48] Yet this perspective on the conveyance of land to white settler families is removed from an account of the relationship between the deed, the bill of sale, and other mechanisms for enacting slavery-based possession. In such contexts, deeds served as a central instrument for the intergenerational transfer of land real estate to settlers. But in the context of U.S. slavery, deeds not only transferred land to non-slaveholding settlers but also transferred enslaved people to settlers and land to slaveholders and often both to the children of slaveholders.[49]

Real estate was fused to slaveholding familial genealogies and the structure of capital accumulation.[50] Slaveholder genealogy informed the structure of the intergenerational transfer of enslaved people and land to white children and was part of what Katherine McKittrick has described as the logic of "plantation futures."[51] Formerly enslaved people offered acute insight into this process in narratives while also seeking to disrupt this practice of white possession by noting its violence and challenging white control of this knowledge.[52] Charles Ball wrote that following the death of the owner who claimed his family, he, his mother, and his several brothers and sisters were sold to different slave owners. Ball was about four years old when this happened, and he never saw any members of his family again. Sojourner Truth's narrative begins with this intergenerational passing of her enslaved family to Colonel Ardinburgh's son, Charles.[53] These transfers following death could be governed differently by the law based upon the status of enslaved people as real estate or chattel, as determined by states. However, regardless of legal statuses, these inheritances enabled the continuation of slaveholder family–based accumulation and, through this, the continuation of the plantation. Future plantation inheritances were promised in bills of sale for enslaved people that declared enslavement of "heirs and assigns forever."[54]

The wills of slaveholders provided legal instructions governing the allocation of genealogical inheritance in a racial and colonial social order obsessed with familial relations.[55] These wills formed the specific basis for the reproduction of slavery through the intergenerational transfer and division of enslaved people and land to white children. When a slaveholding planter died, families sought to ensure the future operation of the plantation through the inheritance of enslaved people and land, while enslaved people were also sold to pay for the debt of the deceased.[56] Beyond the future operation of the plantation, the familial transfer of enslaved people ensured the nursing and rearing of the children and family of the dead slaveholder and facilitated the resolution of outstanding debt.[57] White racial inheritance through real estate promised future stability for slaveholding families.

If the plantation could not continue to function or if the family fell into debt, the sale of enslaved people provided a mechanism for stabilizing the foundations of the white family. Enslaved people also served as security for slave owners to receive bank loans.[58] Debt-based sales of enslaved people occurred as a form of division within white inheritance and often meant breaking Black families apart for white familial economic stability.[59] As Harriet Jacobs wrote, "Notwithstanding my grandmother's long and faithful service to her owners, not one of her children escaped the auction block."[60] Henry "Box" Brown described the sales of enslaved people as "heart-rending separations" while trying to envision a different form of relation between enslaved people, where "a slave's friends are all he possesses that is of value to him."[61] However, struggles for self-possession were made against a dominant regime of value defined by slaveholder accumulation of slave-based real estate.

Wills were further essential for securing future real estate holding. In general, wills sought to ensure that enslaved people would continue to be enslaved to perpetuate the good order and functioning of the deceased slaveholder's plantation. Wills sometimes manumitted enslaved people, particularly of slaveholders' so-called shadow families, a euphemism for the enslaved women forced into sexual relations by slaveholders and the children of such racialized, gender-based violence.[62] Wills secured the continued enslavement of the children of enslaved women to the children of the deceased slaveholder and allowed white children to inherit money through the subsequent sale of enslaved people. Wills enabled whites to enact and realize familial stability through real estate.[63]

The intergenerational transfer of enslaved people and land through fictions of possession was driven by racialized obsession with legacy and inheritance and therefore U.S. settler expansion. The U.S. statesman Henry Clay gave the Lexington, Kentucky, Ashland plantation to his wife along with "all my slaves," intending that both enslaved people and the plantation would be inherited by their children.[64] Henry Clay had eleven children; seven died during his lifetime. His remaining three sons inherited and together divided the enslaved people and land that made up Ashland plantation. Far from the supposed frontiers of U.S. expansion, the realities of U.S. empire shaped the character of plantation inheritance.

The white slaveholding family and the U.S. settler empire were tied together with a broadening base of slaveholding and territory emerging between 1820 and 1860.[65] The white family as slaveholders and settlers was maintained through relations establishing enslaved people and colonized land as real estate while serving also as the basis for U.S. power. The term "father" as used to describe the architects of U.S. colonialism and slaveholding emerged among the second generation of U.S. white elites sometime in the 1820s and 1830s, around the time of Jefferson's death. White men such as Andrew Jackson considered their role in the inheritance of the U.S. empire-state as the children of these fathers and engaged in the aggressive expansion of slavery with Jackson himself serving as the architect of Indian removal. Central to this new empire was a material investment in relentless expansionism with white settler psychologies forged in relation to land speculation and enslavement.[66] Jackson's will stated, "All my negroes that I may die possessed of, with the exception hereafter named, with all their increase after before recited debts are fully paid, with all the household furniture, farming tools, stock of all kind, both on the Hermitage tract farms, as well as those on the Mississippi plantation," would be transferred to his adopted son, Andrew Jackson Jr., "and his heirs forever."[67] Andrew Jackson had no biological children but adopted two—his white son, Andrew Jackson Jr., and Lyncoya (Creek)—while providing for more. Lyncoya had been seized by white soldiers during an attack on the Upper Creek and sent to Jackson. As historian Dawn Peterson has written, "In adopting Creek children, Jackson tied his familial household to his violent forays against the Creek" while he was at the same time engaged in wars to expand the territory for white plantation households.[68] Jackson Jr. inherited Jackson's plantation, the Hermitage, and nearly all of the more than 100 enslaved people, with 4 enslaved women given to Andrew Jackson's wife, Sarah.

Estate books in Kentucky, Louisiana, and parts of North Carolina record dual dispossessions characteristic of U.S. slavery, records of sales of enslaved people and of colonized land transformed into real estate. These records document the seriality of enslaved dispossession made possible through what W. E. B. Du Bois described as the "reduction of a human being to real estate."[69] In 1852, the sale of Mary and her one-year-old daughter, Sarah, from J. F. E. Hardy to Isaac McDunn is recorded in a bill of sale for $200.[70] The bill notes that Hardy had purchased Mary from Patton and Burg in 1849. The bill makes no mention of the child's father. In 1855, a deed from Buncombe County, North Carolina, records "May" and her four-year-old child "Sally's" sale by Isaac McDunn to John W. Ballew. May and Sally were the only enslaved people McDunn owned, and this sale was in resolution of his debt.[71] These sales together are part of the serial dispossession characteristic of racial slavery with future violence structured in. This was a series of instances defined by several white men buying and selling a Black woman, her young daughter, and their "future increase" as real estate in the Du Boisian sense. The bill of sale records the relationship between May and Sally, yet no father is mentioned. Whose child was being sold to pay off McDunn's debt? In a white supremacist regime obsessed with documenting family relations, white-enforced silences about sexual violence were backed by direct physical violence and the state.

Silences about white paternity of the children of enslaved women were central to this regime of real estate. On the one hand, there is a meticulous listing, ordering, and fixing of white descendants of male slaveholders to ensure inheritance while at the same time an erasure of the descent of enslaved children of the same white male slaveholders. Harriet Jacobs described the life-altering chain of events that followed when enslaved men and women made it known that a white man was the father of an enslaved woman's child—physical violence, followed by the breaking apart of enslaved people through sale. As Jacobs writes, she "had forgotten that it was a crime for a slave to tell who was the father of her child."[72] Deeds, wills, bills of sale, and genealogies all conveyed enslaved people as real estate while at the same time functioning as part of an epistemological project based upon the forgetting of white male parentage, a forgetting central to the perpetuation of this regime. In settler colonial contexts, deeds and wills conveyed land, but in the context of nineteenth-century U.S. empire, deeds and wills also conveyed enslaved people.

Estate books recording the sale of May and Sally also document land transactions, part of the intertwining of slavery and settler colonialism. The territory now called Buncombe County became salable as real estate through transforming territory seized from the Cherokee in a centuries-long settler process of land colonization and occupation dating from the sixteenth century. Cherokee dispossession remained part of an ongoing white colonial project into the nineteenth century. Following the Treaty of New Echota in 1837, the Cherokee, along with the Creek, were forcibly and systematically removed from western North Carolina.[73] The recording and ordering of such transfers was part of the U.S. formation of real estate through enslavement and occupation, based upon the assumption that land would be forever occupied and future generations of enslaved people would remain enslaved with both conveyed "to have and to hold" forever. In the age of capital, slavery real estate would also be driven forward by the slaveholder pursuit of free trade as a means for both territorial and slavery expansion.

2 ::: Slavery, Empire, Free Trade

In November 1845, Frederick Douglass addressed a crowd gathered in Cork, Ireland, to speak against the U.S. annexation of Texas.[1] According to Douglass, slaveholders who led the policy of annexation were not just "rotten at heart but a band of dastards."[2] He declared that Britain should have interfered against the plot for southern slavery's expansion. As Douglass later wrote from Edinburgh in July, U.S. northerners' acquiescence to plunder through the U.S.-Mexico War (1846–48) was "like sharks in the bloody wake of a slave ship."[3]

The annexation of Texas doubled the size of the United States, facilitating the expansion of U.S. slavery and precipitating a central U.S. imperial war.[4] With annexation, slaveholders increased their territorial domain and their political power through Texas statehood. The first Texas senators, Thomas Rusk and Sam Houston, were both slaveholders. In the period Douglass decried, U.S. and British expansionary pursuits aligned through increased economic integration enabled by a series of tariff reduction policies.

Karl Marx thought of immigrating to Texas in 1846, believing that settler access to land pressed "inevitably on to communism."[5] He also saw the 1846 passage of tariff reduction policies between Britain and the United States as momentous, serving as a "guiding star" that signaled the arrival of the millennium.[6] For Marx, these laws heightened the contradictions within capitalism. These free trade laws consisted of the repeal of the Corn Laws in Britain, the U.S. proslavery Walker Tariff, which reduced cotton taxes, and the equalization of sugar duties through the British Sugar Duties Act.

Together, these tariff reduction policies were part of a broad liberalization of the mid-nineteenth-century economy between Britain, British colonies, the United States, and the slaveholding sugar economies of Cuba and Brazil. This liberalization enabled greater economic integration across imperial, colonial, and oceanic space while creating conditions for expanded access to enslaved labor and the accumulation of capital and territory through U.S. settler slavery.

After the American Revolution, U.S. slavery was, as the historian Eric Hobsbawm observed, "extended and maintained by the insatiable and

Richard Caton Woodville, *War News from Mexico* (1848).

rocketing demands of the Lancashire mills."[7] U.S. independence posed challenges to British commercial dominance but witnessed the emergence of an era of trade liberalization policies between Britain and the United States from the 1780s. The continuation of trade between Britain and the United States enabled the general perpetuation of relationships that made the United States a primary producer of raw materials, particularly through plantation slavery, and a significant outlet for British manufactured goods.[8] Before American independence, British colonial trade with mainland North

American colonies supplied provisions for plantations in the British West Indies—horses, soap, candles, and, most importantly, food—enabling British Caribbean planters to concentrate plantation production in sugar.[9] In July 1783, Britain established principles for trade with the United States enabling British products to be imported into the United States and most American products to be imported into Britain. Further, the important provisioning trade was extended in revised form; now only British vessels could bring American manufactured goods to Britain's Caribbean colonies.[10] Yet, if the revision in trade policies may have had what some have argued to be an unanticipated and negative impact upon plantations in the British West Indies, the fact that this trade continued was part of a broader trend where pre-Revolutionary patterns of trade generally continued after the American Revolution.[11]

There were exceptions, particularly between 1807 and 1814, when a series of tariff protectionist movements sought to limit trade with Britain. Further, throughout the pre–Civil War United States, northeastern manufacturers often aggressively advocated for trade protectionism, as occurred most dramatically in 1828 with the protectionist legislation that John C. Calhoun would name the "Tariff of Abominations." Throughout the era, slaveholders aggressively advocated for trade liberalization policies, succeeding most dramatically in 1846. In general, between the American Revolution and the American Civil War, slaveholding advocacy for trade liberalization supported the expansion of slavery by facilitating the exportation of plantation commodities to Britain and continental Europe.[12]

Trade relationships between Britain and the United States assumed increasing importance as slavery-produced cotton became central to the expansion of British manufacturing and as other U.S. plantation–produced commodities such as tobacco and rice remained significant. Further, the British were involved in the colonial re-exportation of other import commodities such as tea and indigo to the United States. Throughout the nineteenth century, the economic relationships created within the North Atlantic world, with expanding U.S. plantations exporting raw materials and other commodities to Britain, created a new economic dynamism within the North Atlantic world. A rapidly industrializing Britain was dependent upon U.S. plantation production as well as on continued access to colonial and foreign markets, often stabilizing political disputes despite contradictory political and territorial interests.[13]

If pre- and post-independence trade patterns between Britain and the United States did not undergo fundamental transformation, the American Revolution created a new set of relationships between political power, slaveholding, and territorial conquest. The Revolution marked an end to a strictly British mercantilist trade system and inaugurated an era of expanded trade between Britain and the newly formed United States. In the new country, white settlers were defined by a capacity to own rather than merely occupy, a capacity attached directly to the dispossession of Native nations through the transformation of enslaved people and land into real estate. In the United States, slaveholders had seized power and created a new nation based upon the spread of slavery and the continental expansion of the newly formed nation, an action that ensured and enshrined the perpetuation of slavery and territorial growth.

The production of raw materials—of indigo and cotton, of food like rice, and of mild stimulants like sugar and tobacco—was only one element of plantation production. Plantation production was dominated by the process of realizing capital through real estate in the form of enslaved people and land. This process was not analogous to factory production, even as techniques of factory production emerged through slavery. The cotton, cane, and tobacco fields, the rice swamps, and indigo vats made relentless demands upon enslaved people's work and lives. Managerial and technological practices emerged through slavery and were transformed within industrial factory production. The plantation's expansionary drive— for slaveholders to increase the family, to develop the estate—depended upon the production of commodities that could be transformed into the greater accumulation of capital as real estate in the form of enslaved people and land.

In the midst of the American Revolution, Jefferson was dependent upon prices set in the London markets for the tobacco that enslaved people would cultivate on his Virginia plantations. In 1785, Jefferson would note that "[England] can do too well without all our commodities except tobacco, and we cannot find elsewhere markets for them."[14] While Jefferson would transform and diversify his plantation practices in the late eighteenth century, increasingly shifting toward wheat and grain cultivation along with nail manufacturing, the export dependence that he outlined continued to characterize the U.S. slavery–based economy.

This general relationship was strengthened through tariff reduction policies established to enable greater economic integration between Britain and the United States. Economic integration caused inter-imperial political strife between Britain and the United States to subside. Along with British opposition to the annexation of Texas, tensions had been inflamed in border disputes over Oregon and Maine. While Britain's secretary of state Lord Aberdeen explored the possibility of military intervention against

U.S. annexation, Prime Minister Robert Peel believed the strategic value of an independent Texas was nothing when compared with the possibility of war with one of the largest consumers of British manufactured goods.[15] For slaveholders, the export economy enabled expanded access to markets for raw materials and through this, ultimately, the further accumulation of capital in the form of enslaved people and land.

The British repeal of the Corn Laws—tariffs on imported grains— established a free trade policy that also secured the United States' role as an important market for British manufactured goods and as a supplier of agricultural commodities. The repeal of the Corn Laws enabled the importation of cheap grain from the western United States. The repeal was a particular triumph of Anti-Corn Law League organizing, a group led by Richard Cobden that had formed close working relationships with abolitionists in the North Atlantic world. Cheap food for factory workers and cheap raw materials for factories meant reduced wages and production costs for British manufacturers.

In the United States, the annexation of Texas was quickly followed by the passage of the Walker Tariff in July 1846. The Walker Tariff ushered in an era of pro-free trade policy advanced particularly by U.S. slaveholders.[16] The passage of the tariff was delayed until the U.S. Congress received notification of Britain's repeal of the Corn Laws. The tariff's primary architect was the slaveholding Mississippi Democrat and treasury secretary Robert J. Walker. In the midst of the U.S.-Mexico War, Walker wrote to the College of William and Mary that a toast should be made to commerce and mankind: "They will be most prosperous and happy when the products of every nation and of every clime shall be freely exchanged without tax or restriction."[17]

The British Sugar Act of 1846 was passed at the same time as the repeal of the Corn Laws and reduced tariffs on imported sugar. This made less expensive sugar produced through slavery in Cuba and Brazil available to British consumers. The equalization of sugar duties resulted in a drastic 56 percent decrease in sugar exports from Calcutta between 1846 and 1848. In the critical essay "Novel and History, Plot and Plantation," Sylvia Wynter elaborated upon the meaning of this economic integration for formerly enslaved people in the Caribbean: "Liberal free trade rhetoric, the rhetoric which freed the slaves, compensated the masters and set the slaves free in a world dominated by commercial relations, to fend naked for themselves, was the first sketch of monopoly capitalism."[18] From this perspective, the "nakedness" of formerly enslaved people is a description of the direct, unmediated violence made possible through economic integration that occurred in the post-slavery British Caribbean. British metropolitan consumers demanded enslaved produce. Gesturing toward decreased imports between 1844 and 1846, characterized by low sugar yields, the Liverpool sugar refiners Macfie and Sons wrote to Prime Minister Peel that it was "perfectly evident that erelong the refineries will be forced to reduce their workings for want of raw material, unless new sources of supply are opened."[19] Here "new sources of supply" served as a euphemism for expanded access to sugar produced through slavery in Cuba and Brazil.

Before emancipation within the British Empire, a common antislavery refrain was that free labor was economically more efficient than slavery but that the slaveholding British Caribbean planter aristocracy had been unnaturally established and artificially maintained through protective tariffs.[20] If followed by the ending of protective tariffs, free trade would enable the proliferation of free labor economies operating together in harmony. Yet, the idea of a progressively developing economy moving from unnatural landholding and restricted trade to a natural economy of free trade and free labor did not reflect the realities of the underlying dynamics that made slavery embedded within and essential to the mid-nineteenth-century capitalist economy. Instead, the dynamics that sustained slavery in capitalism could not be resolved through tariff policies, even as both protectionism and trade liberalization had anti-Black characters. However, the focus upon tariff policy as a means for abolition relocated a relation of racially structured social violence within capitalism to the domain of the economy alone.

Emancipation within the British Empire had different meanings among colonies.[21] The territoriality of slavery existed within a world where British imperial possession had progressively become defined in terms of a putative liberal freedom, a process that also made the United States an increasingly singular site of racial state terror through slavery, a form of terror supported through British imperial possession. After emancipation within the British Empire, U.S. slavery's existence through the intergenerational accumulation of capital in the form of slaveholding and landed conquest, particularly in the mid-nineteenth century, had a character that existed in singular relation to the British imperial world. Compensated emancipation of £20 million paid to slaveholders affirmed the historical legitimacy of property claims in Black lives while also marking an end to British slavery. In the mid-nineteenth-century United States, real estate and inheritance became sites for white self-actualization through slaveholding. This real estate was an increasingly unique characteristic of the making of capital through settler slavery following emancipation within the British Empire.

After this emancipation, Britain's manufacturing class, led ideologically by the Lancashire textile manufacturers Richard Cobden and Joseph Hume, advocated for the primacy of free trade while challenging new emerging abolitionist demands for antislavery protective tariffs. A dominant tendency in free trade ideology was access to slavery in the most direct and unobstructed form possible. Such ideas were put forth especially by Joseph Sturge, founder of the British and Foreign Anti-Slavery Society. The free trade fundamentalism of Cobden and Hume would prioritize free trade in relation to the demands of slaveholders. This free trade fundamentalism had a twofold anti-Black character: anti-Black once in the perpetuation of slavery and anti-Black again in the ascription of failure to Black freedom in the British Caribbean when freedpeople did not produce sugar in quantities equal to enslaved people in Cuba and Brazil. This anti-Blackness was articulated across lines of slavery and post-slavery. However, protectionist tariffs did not offer an alternative to racial slavery, even as the era of post-1846 free trade enabled slaveholders to continue to assert particular dominance over the economy through reduced tariffs in Atlantic world trade. If, as Eric Williams argued, the British Caribbean colonies were "forgotten" after 1846, this forgetting was the product of the continuing significance not just of sugar plantation production based upon slavery but of relations of conquest and slavery more general, a pattern of relations that was defined by the relationship between U.S. settler slavery and slavery in Cuba and Brazil.[22]

Beyond the British Caribbean, in the southern African Cape Colony, emancipation across the British Empire enabled the deepening and extension of colonial capitalist power. In Cape Town, compensation for indebted slaveholders was transferred to merchants who put these funds in the wool economy.[23] These transformations were simultaneous within an increasingly integrated global economy dominated by the British Empire as linked to U.S. settler slavery.

Following emancipation within the British Empire, new antagonisms among abolitionists over free trade emerged, with debates centering free trade's role in the reproduction and abolition of slavery. In 1841, Cobden wrote to Sturge stating he would never join an antislavery society if it supported tariffs against plantation slavery–produced sugar.[24] In 1843, Cobden and other Anti–Corn Law League members attended the General Anti-Slavery Convention organized by Sturge's British and Foreign Anti-Slavery Society to argue against protective tariffs on slavery-produced commodities, deriding these tariffs as imperial protectionism. Sturge would ultimately shift his position on protective tariffs to argue that all protections should be eliminated and that the equalization of sugar duties would ultimately benefit not Cuba and Brazil but putatively "free" labor, producing sugar beyond the British Empire.[25] However, this belief in reality primarily supported the slaveholding sugar producers of Cuba and Brazil.

A year after the Anti–Corn Law League disrupted the antislavery convention, the chairman of the league wrote to John C. Calhoun, the proslavery white supremacist and ardent advocate for free trade, to express "admiration" for Calhoun's "able and consistent advocacy of Free Trade with all nations."[26] This approving letter caused some antislavery members of the league to resign in disgust.[27] Calhoun wrote in reply, stating his belief in the civilizational and racial nature of free trade between Britain and the United States and asserting common cause through advocacy for a proimperial and proslavery free trade led by Britain and the United States:

> I regard free trade, as involving considerations far higher, than mere commercial advantages, as great as they are. It is, in my opinion, emphatically the cause of civilization & peace — of wide spread civilization & durable peace among the nations of the earth. It belongs to England and the United States to take the lead in this great cause, and I hope that day is not distant, when they will set the noble example to the rest of Christendom of freeing commerce of every shackle & imposition.[28]

Ideologies of free trade enabled new exchanges and relations between slaveholders and manufacturers, especially after 1846. Free trade liberalism enabled the articulation of new Atlantic world racisms through appeals to a belief in shared white civilizational dominance and advancement led by U.S. and British empires. Anglo-Saxon blood gave rise to convictions about shared Atlantic world racial histories. When asked about the annexation of Texas, Horsley Palmer, director of the Bank of England, stated, "It would be a signal benefit to the world at large if the Anglo American or 'Anglo Saxon' 'race' as it is call'd had possession of the whole of N. America especially that region over from our Mississippi Vall[e]y to the Pacific."[29] Rather than being in opposition, free trade policy enabled and sustained the dynamism of a simultaneously racial and imperial economy forged through an alliance led by Atlantic world slaveholders and British manufacturers. The persistence of a territorially expanding U.S. slavery extended beyond trade policies, protectionist or free. But trade liberalization unlocked new possibilities for the spread of slavery as a form of accumulation for planters by providing greater access to global commodity markets.

In Britain, U.S. lobbying organizations such as the American Chamber of Commerce of Liverpool argued that trade liberalization would improve the condition of the English working class, particularly through the reduction of tariffs on cotton. The organization noted U.S. textile manufacturers concentrated in the Northeast enjoyed a structural advantage through "the place of production of the cotton" being within the United States. Such advocacy generally euphemized the slavery that the export of cotton depended upon.[30]

The shared pursuit of liberal free trade policies between the United States and Britain further implied a different configuration of exposure to the violence of the economy with implications for not just the Caribbean but also India. Northeastern textile manufacturers in the United States sought to convince U.S. southern slaveholders that developed U.S. manufacturing through protectionist tariffs would benefit the expansion and stability of U.S. slaveholders. Abbott Lawrence of Boston wrote to Calhoun that Britain's efforts to improve the quality and quantity of cotton exported from India made protective tariffs necessary. Lawrence maintained that protective tariffs would enable domestic manufacturers to develop and increase consumption of southern cotton. In this argument, for both northeastern manufacturers and southern planters, competition with Britain reduced the market value of cotton and textiles.[31] In this protectionist vision, the U.S. settler empire would create protected trade zones where recently colonized territory would be used to economically develop manufacturing and compete with a British Empire "improving" colonial agriculture for export.[32]

Dominated by the export of cotton, grain, and sugar, trade liberalization in the 1840s was broadly advocated for and supported by southern slaveholders. In 1846, longstanding disputes over tariffs on U.S. exported rice staples were partially resolved. Before the American Civil War, U.S. slaveholders led the production of cotton, rice, and tobacco within export-oriented economies. U.S. cottons, Carolina rice, and Virginia tobacco remained benchmark commodities within British commodity markets. This ensured that slaveholders would continue to dominate the production of some of the most profitable raw materials and agricultural commodities until the U.S. Civil War. However, U.S. slaveholders' position within the global economy was also affected by the character of Britain's empire in this period. Significant agricultural commodities exported from India to Britain between 1846 and the U.S. Civil War—tea, indigo, jute, and opium—largely did not compete in Liverpool and London markets with U.S. plantation staples. U.S. slaveholders debated and often feared the implications of Britain's expanding empire for the future of U.S. slavery.

In Britain, the free trade movement also sought to secure unrestricted free trade with India. Belief in free trade corresponded with commitment to the necessity of colonial transformation, in antagonistic relation to the East India Company.[33] John Bright fiercely opposed East India Company rule and became interested in colonial India as a site for the production of cotton. Free traders looked at efforts conducted earlier by the East India Company to introduce U.S. cotton cultivation and other plantation staples (see chapters 4 and 5) and organized a select committee to inquire into the limits of these projects in January 1847.[34] For free traders like Bright, the limits of colonial Indian cotton cultivation were located in the failures of the East India Company.[35] This was accompanied by a dramatic increase in textile exports between 1846 and 1856, with the value of exports growing by an estimated 60 percent.[36]

Abolitionists and Lancashire textile manufacturers interested in the expansion of cotton cultivation worked together for India reform through the establishment of organizations such as the British India Society, founded in 1839. The British India Society, along with later organizations such as the Indian Reform Society (1853), sought the extension of English colonization in India—through the language of reform—as a means to ensure the production and export of raw materials from the country.[37] Further, Lancashire's interest in an empire-based cotton supply also sought the introduction of British settlers to India.

While textiles manufactured from cotton produced by enslaved people in the United States were exported to Calcutta, along with other Indian cities, to be sold throughout colonial India, raw materials produced in colonial India and imported to the United States included jute and indigo. Jute-made gunny cloth was exported from Calcutta to the United States and used in plantation production. Jute gunny sacks, manufactured from Bengal jute, were used in the southern plantation economy primarily as cotton bagging but also in some instances as provisions for enslaved people as blankets and clothing. As Jenny Proctor, enslaved as a child in Alabama, remembered, on Sundays when clothing was getting washed, children were given only "gunny sacks wid holes cut for our head and arms."[38] The gunny sack made from Bengal jute also enabled the reallocation of enslaved labor from the production of hemp for bagging and toward the production of more valuable export plantation commodities.[39] Not just northern states such as Rhode Island but also colonial India were part of the provisioning of plantations.[40]

U.S. slaveholders consumed gunny and sometimes sought to produce homespun hemp and cotton bagging through slavery in response. However, despite slaveholder ideals of economic independence, the importation of gunny sacks did not economically challenge U.S. planters' mid-nineteenth-century position within the global economy but rather facilitated expanding profits by enabling the concentration of enslaved labor within the most economically profitable forms of plantation production.[41]

Rather than a competition between free and enslaved labor, trade policies, social relations of production, and territorial conquest held together the character of mid-nineteenth-century capitalism as it existed between slavery and non-slavery. While the character of slavery was affected by trade policies and economic liberalization, the focus upon trade policy alone and commodity regimes removed attention from slavery's deep embeddedness within the global economy. While slavery had an economic logic that was structured by trade policies, it was undermined by neither free trade nor protectionism. At the same time, economic integration and market liberalization shaped the ways that U.S. settler slavery would influence and be influenced by colonial relations across the British Empire, particularly colonial India.

PART II : : : **An Immense Accumulation of Commodities**

3 ::: **Blue Past and Future**
Bengal Indigo and the American South

In 1862, the Thalassery-based British merchant Francis Carnac
Brown reflected upon the global history of colonial raw material production. Looking to the success of the "English indigo of Bengal"
and the declining production of "slave indigo of the United States,"
Brown suggested that "the English indigo of Bengal" extinguished
slavery-produced indigo from colonial America. In light of this history,
Brown drew broader conclusions about slavery, empire, and capitalism:

> Bearing this fact in mind, and surveying the globe as we now behold
> it—witnessing in every various and distant region the Englishman trans-
> forming in a score of years, and in climates widely different from his
> own, the wildest wastes into great, wealthy, and prosperous communi-
> ties—no unprejudiced man can doubt, when he also beholds English
> enterprise supplying the world with Indian sugar, and with Mauritius
> sugar, grown by natives under Englishmen, and sees it beginning to
> supply the world with Indian tea and Indian coffee, for the coffee of
> Ceylon is grown by them with Indian labourers; no man can doubt that
> if English enterprise had been permitted to have free access to the cotton
> marts of India eighty years ago . . . that not a pound of American Cotton
> would ever have seen the light; and that the vast wealth which has cre-
> ated America would, in its natural course, have been spread, first, over
> the face of India by Englishmen calling into action, as they are doing, the
> industry and intelligence of the natives, next distributed over the face of
> manufacturing England.[1]

For Brown, the transformation in indigo cultivation from Carolina
slavery plantations in North America to smallholder production in colonial India served as part of a usable past that would help make sense of
Britain's textile industry, India's position within the British Empire, and
Britain's dependence upon U.S. slavery. Writing in 1862 in the midst of
the Lancashire cotton famine, a global economic crisis that had a shock-
ing impact on Britain's textile industry, Brown argued that the systematic
colonization of India by the English would ameliorate the economic crisis

impacting manufacturing across the North Atlantic world and enable colonial India to supply Lancashire's manufacturers with cotton.[2]

Brown was not the only one seeking to explain global political economy through indigo's slave and colonial histories in the mid-nineteenth century. British merchants, manufacturers, U.S. slaveholders, and abolitionists tended to focus on one element of that history in particular—that indigo, once produced in South Carolina, was now produced in eastern colonial India—to understand shifting relationships between U.S. slavery and the British Empire. Brown stood out, however, for his argument that metropolitan consumption emerged through colonial relations of racial dominance—"natives under Englishmen"—which was a socially structured relationship different from U.S. slavery. Brown asserted that Englishmen "calling into action" the "natives" could have allowed for the shared expansion of Britain and colonial India.[3]

Commodity histories like Brown's reflections on indigo were efforts to explain the mid-nineteenth-century global economy in which patterns of accumulation drew the United States and India into relation, particularly through Britain's global dominance in manufacturing. This dominance depended upon U.S. slavery–produced cotton and colonial markets in India, particularly the North-Western Provinces. The history of indigo was used to narrate partially the circumstances of this convergence during an era when the violence of U.S. racial slavery expanded as a settler colonial project and colonial agrarian projects across India placed intensifying demands on peasant cultivators through exposure to unstable prices in global commodities markets. For planters in both eastern colonial India and the southern United States, such comparisons emerged to differentiate and describe the character of enslaving and colonial projects, projects already connected through global patterns of trade, production, and accumulation.

U.S. Indigo in Decline

Indigo had been cultivated by enslaved people in British North America, particularly in the mid-Atlantic, since the seventeenth century.[4] From the 1740s, indigo cultivation became a defining feature of Carolina plantation slavery. But after over fifty years of fluctuating exports and staple quality, slavery-based indigo cultivation in early republic America rapidly dissipated as slaveholding planters shifted toward the production of more valuable plantation commodities, particularly cotton, while participating in the growing internal slave trade.[5] During the nineteenth century, northern U.S. textile manufacturers depended upon indigo re-exported from Britain and originally produced in eastern India, a dependence that marked a definitive shift from the patterns of production and consumption that defined the second half of the eighteenth century. By the late 1820s, indigo was systematically cultivated only in Orangeburg District, South Carolina, in the United States, while eastern colonial India and its reorganized indigo industry dominated global exports. Between 1839 and 1847, just as U.S. slaveholders embarked on projects of economic diversification and entertained the possibility of re-engaging in indigo production, indigo experienced a global price slump. This decline in indigo prices, part of a broader commercial crisis, placed new pressures and miseries upon cultivators in eastern India.[6] Combined with the sustained value of U.S. slavery–produced cotton, the slump served to curtail sustained engagement in the experimental reintroduction of indigo cultivation within the slaveholding United States.

The near-simultaneity of the fluctuation of price and demand for indigo within London markets, the shift in nineteenth-century U.S. slavery away from indigo and toward cotton, and the massive expansion of U.S. slavery during the nineteenth century demanded an explanation. Many sought it in indigo's history, which at times came to be used to describe the dynamics of accumulation that characterized the era. Beyond explaining shifts in production, the U.S. slaveholders, North Atlantic abolitionists, and British colonial officials who told indigo's history also used the commodity as a metonym for understanding U.S. slaveholding futures and the futures of the British Empire, particularly the colonial export orientation of the South Asian economy.[7] In accounts of the experiences of those who engaged directly in the work of indigo cultivation, seemingly discrete life histories become entangled through global patterns of capital accumulation.

In 1840, at the beginning of the indigo price decline, the U.S. abolitionist Wendell Phillips observed that the cultivation of indigo in colonial India offered historical precedent for the revolutionary character of free trade in India.[8] In Phillips's telling, as the sugar beet in France caused demand for the sugar of French Caribbean planters to disappear, indigo, once the product of enslaved labor in the United States, was transformed into a commodity of "freedom" within the British imperial world. Once indigo began to be cultivated by so-called free labor in India, an antislavery transformation occurred: "the moment a free hand touched any article, that moment it fell from the hand of a slave."[9]

This movement of commodities between the hands of free and enslaved people posited a vision of a rational economy whose logic of accumulation oriented toward freedom and against slavery. It was a vision Phillips and many others wanted to believe in, but it did not reflect the social realities of mid-nineteenth-century colonial or slavery-based capitalism.

In the mid-nineteenth century, U.S. slavery defined the political economy of South Carolina just as it had from the founding of Carolina as a colony with *The Fundamental Constitutions of Carolina* (1669), which assigned "absolute power" over enslaved Africans. Planters sustained their rice cultivation, increased cotton and tobacco cultivation, and maintained their participation in the internal slave trade, a trade that systematically relocated over 1 million enslaved people from the Upper to the Lower South during the nineteenth century. Following the shift of indigo cultivation to eastern India, slavery actually expanded across the United States. In 1800, there were 900,000 enslaved people in the United States; by 1860, nearly 4 million. The global economy moved through transformations within Atlantic world slavery and patterns of colonial agrarian relations in India. Capitalism took form across the British imperial world in dynamics structured through relations that went beyond any single agricultural commodity, even as observers looked to indigo to make sense of this history.[10] While abolitionists hoped colonial agrarian projects in India would disrupt slavery, often with disregard for the impact that these projects had upon those who would be expected to perform the work of empire, U.S. slavery continued to expand during the period between 1838 and the outbreak of the American Civil War.[11]

The one remaining district of indigo cultivation as of 1828, Orangeburg, South Carolina, became particularly significant for U.S. slaveholders who reflected on the possibility of revitalizing the crop in light of competition from colonial eastern India.[12] Writing on Orangeburg indigo, prominent Georgia slaveholder Thomas Spalding calculated profitability in reference to the "hand," an enslaved person as an abstract laboring unit, as a way to theorize the productive capacities of enslaved people in the U.S. South in relation to global commodity prices. Besides rendering enslaved people into an abstraction with a fungible relation to other commodities, profit "to the hand" allowed planters to consider *which* commodities produced by enslaved people would enable the greatest accumulation for slaveholders.[13] Calculating profit to the hand of indigo and cotton, Spalding argued that cultivation of indigo could indeed be profitable in the future but determined that such pursuits must be calibrated according to global profitability.

There was a considerable difference between Phillips's historical description of indigo and Spalding's. Phillips's metaphor of commodities shifting through hands — not between enslaved and enslaver but between enslaved and so-called free colonial subjects — offered an incomplete vision of transformation within the global economy. It implied a conception of justice through transformed commodity production. As global economic integration proceeded, the supposedly free hand in colonial India and the enslaved hand in the United States would grow more interrelated. The colonial economy would provide a means for the accelerated production of "freedom" in the United States and also future liberties in colonial India. For slaveholders such as Spalding, this economic integration meant pursuing the most profitable forms of cultivation in relation to global market prices and returns. This meant making plantations as profitable as possible to strengthen and expand slavery through calculations of profits to the hand.

Not just slaveholders but abolitionists, too, became preoccupied with colonial commodity production. George Thompson was an abolitionist whose work frequently focused on the interrelationship between slavery in the United States and colonialism in India. Thompson would travel between the United States and India during this era and also form close working relationships with indigo factors in Bengal and the prominent Bengali zamindar Dwarkanath Tagore.[14] In 1840, the English abolitionist George Thompson delivered a series of lectures on India. In one lecture, Thompson argued that it was only with indigo that a competition between enslaved and free labor had been "fairly tried." The expansion of "free labor" cultivation had "advanced with such rapidity in the East, that it is now estimated to employ nearly 500,000 free persons, and the article has ceased to be cultivated by slaves," according to Thompson. This process, "by a silent but sure operation, has effected the entire destruction of the slave trade and of slavery, and may be justly considered, at the present moment, to have saved 500,000 human beings, amounting to nearly two-thirds of the whole male population of our West India colonies, from a cruel and degrading bondage."[15] For Thompson, the "free labor" of tenant indigo cultivators in India was necessary also for the production of Black emancipation. Such assessments sat uncomfortably alongside the experiences of tenant smallholders who were forced to focus upon indigo cultivation and were exposed to repeated indigo price crashes.[16] Some abolitionists went further, envisioning colonial expansion as setting limits to the extent of slavery and the Atlantic slave trade. John Sturge, the prominent advocate for free trade, abolitionism, and transformed colonial relations in India, noted that three years after the first importation of indigo from colonial India, the Carolinas closed ports for the slave trade.[17] While conceding that the expansion of cotton cultivation meant that slavery persisted, Sturge continued, "It may fairly be estimated that several hundred thousand Africans have been saved from the horrors of slavery, in consequence of the cultivation of Indigo by free-labour [in India]."[18]

All of these abolitionist assessments saw a transformation taking place through the shift between enslaved people's work in the United States to "free" colonial smallholding producers in eastern India — though the actual experience of these supposedly free smallholding producers did not enter into these interpretations. In Bengal and Bihar, where cultivation was concentrated, indigo growers' experiences varied according to several systems of relations between land, capital, cultivator, landlord, and planter, each with differing balances of power. Whether cultivating according to *nij* cultivation controlled by European planters or according to *raiyati*, where peasants claimed land as their own, credit relations allowed planters and landholders to level extreme demands on cultivators' households.[19] Across eastern India, the varying systems all relied on coerced non-slavery work, often characterized by direct violence and unmediated exposure to global price fluctuations.[20] When planters contracted cultivators, the use of violence was often direct, one of many realities that complicate comfortable nineteenth-century abolitionist support for free labor as anything that was not racial slavery. Further, accounts such as Sturge's demonstrate little concern for the conditions of non-enslaved Black life in the United States in an era when a series of white supremacist laws led to the curtailment of Black rights and citizenship.[21]

Indigo's history was laden with different meanings for British capitalists intrigued by the possibility of further transforming colonial agrarian production in the mid-nineteenth century.[22] For British manufacturers and sugar refiners, it seemed that if barriers to free trade were removed, the cultivation of sugar and cotton in India would be realized, as was the case with indigo.[23] Later, these same manufacturers would become ardent advocates for the application of criminal contract law to bind cultivators to indigo cultivation as a means of enforcing indigo production and exportation.[24] For manufacturers, colonial production promised an expansion of freedom of a sort, but unlike the abolitionist vision of free labor spreading like a contagion to the United States, colonial exploitation offered a means for freeing themselves from the constraints of fluctuations in prices and supply. Despite ideologies of free trade and laissez-faire, manufacturers sought to exert consistent pressure on the colonial state to expand the availability of raw materials and plantation commodities to produce freedom in this sense, a freedom that also entailed further exposing smallholding cultivators in potential export commodity–producing regions across colonial India to ever-greater risk of price collapses.

Abolitionists' vision of the expanded colonial production of freedom was further confounded as British indigo importers and European planters based in South Asia became interested in applying the lessons of colonial indigo to strengthen U.S. slavery. Francis Bonynge, who described himself as a planter based in India and China for fourteen years, visited the United States and throughout 1851 surveyed slaveholder plantations, arguing in *The Future Wealth of America* (1852) that the agrarian base of U.S. slavery could be transformed in ways influenced by South Asian agriculture.[25] He imagined that slavery could last forever. Bonynge wrote that colonial India could supplant cotton cultivation in the United States just as it had supplanted U.S. indigo. He then argued that southern slaveholders should return to indigo cultivation to diversify their production and strengthen the foundations of U.S. slavery. Such shifts, along with the introduction of new plantation commodities such as tea, would preserve slavery in the United States by deepening its significance within the global economy.

Demonstrating their confidence in the future of U.S. slavery, some former English indigo manufacturers became directly involved in slavery. William Partridge had owned an indigo dyeing establishment in the west of England and had purchased slave-produced indigo for his factory before moving to the United States in 1808 to attempt to restore slavery-based indigo production. He corresponded with Wade Hampton (then among the largest slaveholders in the United States) in 1809 and would draw upon these correspondences much later as he pursued this slavery-based indigo production.[26] Partridge would write in 1830 that it was necessary to improve the value of indigo produced in the United States through the improvement in indigo quality, stating that the first object of U.S. southern indigo manufacturers would be to "make their indigo equal in quality to the best Bengal, and the second to go as far beyond them as is practicable."[27] This project of staple improvement seemed to mirror contemporaneous British colonial projects in India to replicate and surpass the quality of slavery-produced cotton staples.

While numerous U.S. slaveholders and their supporters explored the possibility of increasing indigo production, many were concerned about indigo's possible harms while also fearing that they might not be able to match Bengal indigo cultivation in quality and quantity. Eighteenth-century indigo slaveholding planters had found indigo to be an "unhealthy" plant that led to the death of enslaved people. For slaveholders invested in an economy governed by the value and accumulation of enslaved people as much as by the production of any single raw material, these impressions contributed to a reluctance to introduce the plant.[28] In plantation management journals such as *Southern Cultivator, Farmers' Register, American Cotton Planter*, and *De Bow's Review*, slaveholders recounted the harms the crop caused to enslaved people and to animals, describing streams full of dead fish.[29] They argued that the lives of enslaved people in the United States generally improved following the end of indigo cultivation, writing that they would feel sorry to see "the beautiful culture of cotton" exchanged for indigo "known to be unhealthy as well as . . . disgusting."[30] By comparison, they found cotton to be "so remarkable for its freedom from the concomitants of tobacco and indigo culture, and comparatively so light, neat, and agreeable in its handling."[31] This evaluation, of course, removed the deep anti-Black violence that characterized cotton plantation slavery.[32] To address the destructive effects upon physical health that characterized indigo cultivation, some slaveholders examined transformations in the production process in Bengal; for example, "the more intelligent indigo makers" prevented heaps of fermenting indigo plants to be kept near the houses of peasants who processed indigo, something that would reduce the perceived danger of indigo cultivation.[33] These reflections were meant to be implemented on South Carolina plantations to expand indigo cultivation.

For some white supremacist supporters of slavery, the history of the shift in indigo cultivation, contrary to Wendell Phillips's understanding, was not a potential cause of the end of slavery but a *result*. This interpretation gestured toward the Haitian Revolution, after which indigo cultivation came to an end.[34] As one author argued, the end of slavery in the British Caribbean gave India a monopoly on the sugar trade; by the same logic, the end of slavery in the United States would provide colonial India with a dominance in global cotton production.[35] This description ignored the realities of shifts in production related to their relationship to slavery and also slavery-based commodity production's relationship to global commodities markets, particularly in Liverpool and London. While formerly enslaved people in Haiti refused to cultivate indigo after the revolution, a shift away from indigo had already unfolded in response to the greater profitability of Caribbean sugar and coffee during the eighteenth century.[36] Even so, this explanation supported contemporaneous pro–U.S. slavery arguments, which played upon fears of British imperial economic transformation bringing about the economic end of export-dependent southern planters. Such arguments bolstered slaveholders' aggressive pursuit of free trade and tariff reduction policies throughout the mid-nineteenth century.

While U.S. slaveholders saw themselves as dominating Liverpool and London markets in the price and quality of their tobacco, rice, and cotton, indigo revealed a different reality. In Orangeburg, the one district where indigo was cultivated, "the prices received by the Orangeburg planters in

Charleston, are thus about the prices of the lowest Bengal quality."[37] To address this, some slaveholders pursued the distribution of Bengal indigo seeds for cultivation. As Donald B. Jones wrote, "I have for the last six or eight years been an Indigo planter, and although the crop has not been a very profitable one, for the last two years, I do not feel disposed to abandon it, for I still think that, in our pine land, it is as profitable, if not more so, than a cotton crop; and I think, too, that a great deal depends on the kind of seed we plant. . . . I feel anxious to try the Bengal seed."[38] These efforts for indigo improvement did not succeed in transforming the new foundations of U.S. cotton production in U.S. slavery, but they did reveal the ways that some slaveholders looked to global markets and cultivation methods.

Race, Indigo, and Imperial Culture

Commodity production brought together seemingly disparate regions, from colonial eastern India to South Carolina. For Carolina slaveholders, British colonial officials, and manufacturers, the success of commodity production also promised the smooth functioning of social and racial orders within a world characterized by disruption and transformation. Ideas and histories of indigo production were always about more than just the production of commodities alone and instead also offered a way to imagine different forms for stabilizing racial domination and imperial rule. During the mid-nineteenth century, U.S. slaveholders sought to transform the basis of their plantations by looking toward colonial India, just as British manufacturers and colonial officials more commonly looked toward U.S. slavery to imagine the agricultural and economic transformation of colonial India. As these connections proliferated, a series of disparate techniques for the management of race and empire traveled globally.

New colonial and slavery commodity projects were often formed in response to breakdown and uprisings. Following the Indian Rebellion (1857–58), terms of anti-Black racism proliferated among British colonial elites and in metropolitan discourse as part of the transformation of imperial racism expressed against formerly enslaved people in the British Caribbean, enslaved people in the United States, and colonial subjects in India.[39] This emergent racism was also articulated in relation to an expanding commitment to Anglo-Saxon whiteness that produced a new, shared whiteness between Britain and the United States.[40] In the Bengali play *Nil Darpan* (1860), the antagonistic pressures of cultivating rice and indigo work against one another with the death of cultivators as the most likely consequence. In the play, Mr. Wood twice uses the word "nigger," first before ordering Amin to attack Ray in the first act and later in the fourth act before Wood attacks

Gopi.[41] The context of planter racial hatred can also be seen in the lieutenant governor of Bengal J. P. Grant's response to the Indigo Commission report, authorized immediately following the Indigo Revolt. In his response, Grant wrote, "Now, if one remembers that these Ryots are not Carolina slaves, but the free yeomanry of this country, and indeed, strictly speaking, the virtual owners of the greater part of the land in the old cultivated parts of Bengal, so heavy a loss as this will fully account to us for the strength of the opposition to Indigo cultivation which we have just experienced."[42] In referencing Carolina slavery, Grant attempted to maintain a distance between indigo production in India and the historical precedent of slavery-based production in Carolina. Yet, U.S. slavery and indigo cultivation in colonial India converged through the proliferating violence of planters and the uprising of tenant cultivators even as the relations of tenant cultivation and racial slavery differed.

The general shift in production away from indigo in the American South toward cotton and rice also affected the lives of people enslaved in South Carolina, though the shift would have disappointed abolitionists hoping for colonial cultivation to have a humanitarian effect. In 1853, the *Southern Literary Quarterly* published a critique of Charles Ball's *Slavery in the United States*, first published in 1837, which offered an account of the author's decades of enslavement in Maryland, South Carolina, and Georgia, along with the daily violence that characterized the lives of people enslaved on plantations. Indigo first appears in Ball's narrative in a recollection of the last time he saw his mother, whom he was separated from through a sale. As Ball writes, he had no doubt his mother was sold to Carolina, where she "toiled out the residue of a forlorn and famished existence in the rice swamps, or indigo fields of the south."[43] After Ball is once told by a man about the suffering of enslaved people who worked on cotton and indigo plantations, he loses sleep.[44]

In 1806, Ball was sold and enslaved on the plantation of Wade Hampton, where he was forced to cultivate indigo. Ball remembered, "Notwithstanding its location on dry ground, the culture of indigo is not less unpleasant than that of rice," likening its smell to parsley. However, once indigo was "ready to cut the troubles attendant upon it have only commenced." Ball transferred indigo into a steeping vat, where it underwent fermentation, before transferring it to a pounding vat. The work, which entailed the repetitive process of refilling, "continued without interruption." He stirred the water in a bucket with holes in the bottom. This was followed by the ultimate drying of the indigo and its pressing into cakes. After pressing the indigo, enslaved people were forced to wash the tubs, work that was "exceedingly unpleasant, both on account of the filth and the stench arising from the decomposition of the plant."[45]

Plantation-based indigo cultivation had nearly ceased in the United States by the time that Ball cultivated indigo on a small part of a plantation mostly dedicated to other commodity production. But, that plantation continued and so, too, did Ball's enslavement for another thirty years. Wendell Phillips's notion of colonial cultivation transforming one crop and thereby challenging slavery as a whole proved to be a fantasy. Slavery's relationship to commodity production always extended beyond the production of any single commodity, a reality that was part of the resilience of slavery itself.

The mid-nineteenth-century narration of the economy through indigo as told by abolitionists, slaveholders, manufacturers, and colonial officials provided a way of describing plantation and colonial futures through the simplified history of a single commodity.[46] At the same time, tenant cultivator struggles and the accounts of enslaved people who were forced to cultivate indigo are part of the interrelated histories of export-oriented economies that were connected through patterns of accumulation that went beyond any single commodity. The interrelationships produced through this economic orientation were often represented as history through indigo, but this mode of historical narration through indigo also served as a way to ensure the further entrenchment of U.S. slavery and colonialism in eastern India or, in antislavery form, often informed projects that prioritized shifts in commodity production against direct confrontation with slavery and colonialism itself. As slaveholders imagined their futures through indigo, British manufacturers and colonial officials across India looked toward U.S. slavery–produced commodities as a few sought to transform colonialism within the British Empire through lessons learned from U.S. slavery.

4 ::: Limited Growth
Carolina Rice and Colonial India

amuel Tayler was one of the over 1 million enslaved people sold through the internal slave trade in the United States. He was taken from his family in Georgetown, South Carolina, and moved to Mobile, Alabama, in 1835. In 1838, following the Panic of 1837, the price of cotton crashed and Tayler's "price" dropped.[1] In a letter to Elizabeth Blyth, the slaveholding rice planter who had sold him, Tayler made the case that declining prices meant that Blyth might profit by repurchasing him.[2] "My mind is always dwelling on home, relations, and friends which I would give the world to see." He closed his letter, "Remember me also to Sarah, my ma-ma, and Charlotte, my old fellow servant, and Amy Tayler."[3]

The reality of slavery in the United States created conditions where enslaved people such as Tayler were systematically and serially separated from kin.[4] Tayler wrote, "I beg you will tell me how all my relations are," and while pleading for information about the family Blyth had severed him from, Tayler insisted that he would be "happy" to "serve" her and her descendants. As U.S. slavery transformed geographically and in relation to different regimes of commodity production, the lives of enslaved people living in the Upper South changed. In the letter, Tayler makes the case that transformations in capitalism made it possible and profitable for him to be reunited with his family. Yet, it is also possible that the man who purchased Tayler ventriloquized him and used the specter of his and his family's pain to profit from his return sale. In the face of perpetual hereditary-racial slavery, the language of the letter sent to Tayler's former owners was the type that troubled slaveholders across the South—one of a global racial capitalism that emphasized concern for profits through slavery and indifference toward Black suffering.

Tayler's lifeworld was structured in relation to settler slavery's position within the global economy. The systematic movement of enslaved people through the internal slave trade was driven by the rapid settler expansion of cotton plantations in the United States. The internal slave trade enabled Upper South planters in states like South Carolina to profit through speculation in enslaved people along with rice, cotton, and other plantation staples. This allowed slaveholders to gain through the trading of enslaved people while profiting from plantation agricultural enterprise, a form of life that W. E. B. Du Bois noted had "curious psychological effects" upon whites.[5]

Global commodities markets intersected with the valuation of Black life and were at the same time structured by the controlled mobility of enslaved people. The unique qualities, prices, and volumes of commodities exported from the United States, particularly cotton, tobacco, sugar, and rice, shaped the internal dynamics of settler slavery expansion and the character of the global economy simultaneously. An 1852 handbill directly connected enslaved people and the production of plantation commodities, advertising the sale of a "Gang of 25 Sea Island Cotton and Rice Negroes" in Charleston, South Carolina, purchasable through a combination of money and mortgages.[6] Such trading was the product of valuations that economically rendered enslaved people as laboring, exchangeable, and accumulable commodities whose value was backed by the legal regulation of U.S. slavery.

The importance of U.S. slavery was clear to British observers. Carolina rice, grown extensively in the Low Country of South Carolina and Georgia, was a significant export to England from the early eighteenth century on. In Liverpool markets, by the nineteenth century, Carolina rice served as the benchmark for all mid-nineteenth-century rice staples. By the mid-nineteenth century, British demand for Carolina rice was accompanied by a series of projects to introduce Carolina rice cultivation in colonial India. A former East India Company official argued that peasant smallholding cultivators could accomplish far more for the British Empire than anything settler slavery could do for the United States.[7] As Francis Bonynge wrote, "It may be supposed that a poor man in that condition could not contend with the planter of Carolina with his hundreds of slaves, but that is not the case; the naked Indian has the advantage through the combination of all the planters in a district."[8] However, colonial projects to introduce Carolina rice in India did not reflect a direct competition between labor in colonial India and the United States in the ways Bonynge imagined when making such comparisons. Instead, such projects were part of the interrelationship between U.S. settler slavery and colonial India and between colonial transformation and plantation slavery.

The economic dynamism of U.S. plantation slavery, as imagined through U.S. cotton staples, Virginia tobacco, and Carolina rice, depended upon an anti-Black fetishism of commodities and enabled projects for colonial transformation beyond the Atlantic world. In the United States, white settler anti-Black racism existed through enslavement and land-grabbing backed by the U.S. empire-state in a form buttressed by an export-oriented economy. Projects to introduce Carolina rice cultivation in colonial India were informed by the possibilities of colonial agrarian transformation that could be understood in relation to the realities of U.S. slavery and through interpretations of U.S. slavery's position within the North Atlantic economy.

Beginning with an examination of the role of Carolina rice within North Atlantic markets, this chapter considers the transforming realities of enslaved people who cultivated Carolina rice in the mid-nineteenth century, situating enslaved lives in relation to Atlantic world transformations in rice milling. It concludes with a series of colonial projects to introduce Carolina rice cultivation in India between 1830 and 1870. Through these overlapping histories, the social, cultural, and economic production of Carolina rice emerges as part of a global colonial and slavery-based project that exposes the reach of slavery and anti-Blackness within nineteenth-century capitalism. Together, enslaved cultivation of rice in South Carolina and Georgia, the transformation of milling, and colonial projects to introduce Carolina rice into India reveal overlapping realities where racial slavery in the United States, wage labor in Britain, and multiple sets of agrarian relations across colonial India converged. The British colonial pursuit of Carolina rice in India would ultimately fail, but it is a revealing product of the imagining of future possibilities for empire, which were imagined through U.S. slavery's role within the global economy.

The Demand for Settler Slavery

The mid-nineteenth century was characterized by the persistent demand for slavery-produced plantation commodities including not just sugar, tobacco, and cotton but also rice. Brazilian, Carolina, and "East Indian" rices were among the most common staples sold in British markets from 1830 through the Civil War. Rice staples from Brazil were likewise the product of slavery and exported to Britain and continental Europe. Additionally, rice from British Burma would become increasingly important for importation to British and European markets, especially after 1850, with further impetus following the U.S. Civil War.[9] Yet, until Black emancipation in the United States, Carolina rice dominated England's market. In general, it met the highest demand, sold in the highest volumes, and commanded the highest prices until the disappearance of the staple from British and European markets following Black emancipation.

The very name of Carolina rice marked the staple as a product of U.S.

slavery. In the magazine *Household Words*, Charles Dickens observed the fetishism characteristic of European demand for Carolina rice:

> It must not be supposed by European readers, that rice, in the larger acceptation of the word, is represented by "the finest Carolina," or even "the best London Cleaned Patna." There is no more affinity between those white artificial cereals, and the "real, original" staple food of India and the East, than there is between a sponge-cake and a loaf of genuine farm-house bread. The truth is, people in this part of the world, have no conception of what good rice is like. If they had, there would not be such a lively demand for the produce of the Southern American States. But such is prejudice, that if a merchant were to introduce into any port of Great Britain, or Ireland, a cargo of the real staple food of orientals, he would not find a purchaser for it, so inferior is it in appearance, in its colour, shape, and texture, to the better known and tempting looking grain of South Carolina.[10]

In this assessment, Dickens brought together and compared global rice staples according to racial and colonial logics. Dickens at once observed that the demand for the produce of enslaved people in the United States had no basis in reality while at the same time noting that it persisted nonetheless.

Rice was not the principal staple of English households, even though it was widely consumed and might be used as an ingredient in puddings, flours, rice cakes, fritters, custards, and ground rice milk.[11] In an 1863 survey of working-class households (conducted at the moment of Black emancipation in the United States), the surveyor noted that rice was most commonly consumed among that population in winter "to supply the place of vegetables" and that small quantities of rice were consumed in 58 percent of cases in almost every county.[12]

Enslaved people in the United States and metropolitan Britons were connected through Carolina rice in a social relation that stretched beyond the world of textile production. The supplementary position of rice within the mid-nineteenth-century English diet reflected a demand for a filling meal as well as a need to reproduce labor power at the lowest cost possible. While this may have been suggestive of commonalities between the enslaved and the English working class, analogies between English workers and enslaved people distorted fundamental differences in lived experiences, especially noted by Black abolitionists. When formerly enslaved people visited England, they took note of the difference in experiences between English laborers and enslaved people bound to rice plantations. In 1855, the Black abolitionist William Wells Brown wrote that he had often been told that "the English labourer was no better off than the slave upon a Carolina rice-field. I had seen the slaves in Missouri huddled together, three, four, and even five families in a single room not more than 15 by 25 feet square, and I expected the same in England. But in this I was disappointed."[13]

The demand for Carolina rice in England alongside other rice staples offered English consumers the opportunity to make decisions about preferences in relation to the perceived character of commodities produced by enslaved labor versus those produced by colonial smallholders in sites of imperial rule such as India—yet the results of these choices disappointed abolitionist observers. The British abolitionist George Thompson commented upon English consumers, "Ask the frugal housewife, who prepares the dish of rice for her household, or her guests. These are the buyers, the rewarders, the upholders of Slavery."[14] Thompson's comments drew upon the politicization of the household in metropolitan Britain that had emerged, particularly with earlier antislavery sugar boycotts that depended upon similar language.[15]

Beneath such appearances, North Atlantic shipping networks facilitated the dominance of U.S. slavery–produced commodities within British and continental European commodities markets, and avowed taste preferences bolstered this dominance.[16] At the 1851 Great London Exhibition, the Carolina rice produced by U.S. slaveholder Edward Heriot received an award for the best rice staple. Judges praised the rice as "magnificent" and compared it against the "slovenly character of the native commerce" of colonial India.[17] Such comparisons were ideological, offering little description of the intrinsic or sensorial character of rice, but nevertheless contributed to the perpetuation of Carolina rice's unique valuation within British and European commodity markets.

U.S. slaveholders like Heriot were well aware of slavery-produced commodities' popularity within British and European markets and insisted that through commodities like Carolina rice, any blow to slavery would redound onto the larger world. Heriot argued that if U.S. slavery was destroyed,

> the agricultural productions, and the whole civilized world would be shook to its very center—Europe would feel it much more than we would—the manufacturing interests would be overturned, and destitution and nakedness of the working classes would amount to famine. Think of the cotton, rice, sugar, Indian corn, wheat, and other exports from the country consumer in different portions of the world, and

the manufacturing of some of them giving employment to millions of people, what if all were cut off—and recollect that free white labour cannot be substituted—it is a monstrous question . . . it is now interwoven with the relations of the world.[18]

Heriot's observations did not account for the complex political economic relations that made settler slavery so pervasive within global capitalism. Nevertheless, he was correct about the sheer market dominance that planters had achieved. Planters like Heriot had realized themselves globally through their relationship to slavery as slaveholders and to land as settlers—two relationships that had come about only through enormous violence over time within mainland North America.

The Transformation of Carolina Rice

Throughout the nineteenth century, the demand for Carolina rice persisted, but the relations of rice production and exportation transformed. This transformation intensified the violence constitutive of the labor process, particularly worsening enslaved people's work experiences as they were increasingly confined to the brutal plantation labor involved in producing rice. At the same time, the practice of milling Carolina rice gradually relocated to Liverpool, London, and continental Europe, incorporating the work of British and continental European workers in the process of rice production.

Rice cultivation was the most complex and differentiated process of plantation agriculture in the United States before the Civil War. Thoroughly shaped by enslaved knowledge of rice planting, cultivation, and milling practices, these labor practices were regulated in part by enslaved people even as they were dictated by the demands of slave owners.[19] This push and pull can be seen in the process of rice milling through pounding, a task that was essential but also among the most labor-intensive processes of plantation production in the Low Country. Manual pounding involved beating rice with a mortar and pestle and relied particularly upon enslaved women's work. Pounding rice yielded four products: market rice, small rice, rice flour, and chaff. Flour, chaff, and small rice were partially allocated as provisions for enslaved people.[20] Small rice was distinguished from Carolina rice and classified as the "imperfect grains" that emerged from the pounding process. Over the course of their struggles to exercise control over their work and lives, enslaved people would at times reappropriate some of this rice, selling it or consuming it to supplement deficient plantation rations.[21]

A stereoscope of a South Carolina rice field (1850–1930).
(The Miriam and Ira D. Wallach Division of Art, Prints and Photographs,
New York Public Library)

Low Country rice cultivation was often but not exclusively organized according to the task system, with considerable variation in cultivation practices among individual plantations.[22] Rice fields could be made from drained swamps, surrounded by ditches for irrigation. The digging of these ditches was brutal work that freedpeople often refused to perform following emancipation.[23] In cultivating, enslaved people would first chop the ground, mixing layers of soil roughly two to three inches deep. After chopping, the ground would again be hoed.

When seed planting commenced in March, enslaved people would quickly and evenly trench a field with great precision and evenly distribute rows. On some plantations, enslaved women would then cover seeds using wooden beaters.[24] Enslaved men and women would then plant a field in a single day so that it could be flooded for the first time, for a period of between one and two weeks. Afterward, the water was drained from the field and enslaved people would weed and hoe before a second flooding. Planters and drivers demanded unrelenting and physically destructive work from enslaved people.[25] During the second flooding, enslaved people would be forced to wade through flooded rice fields, picking volunteer rice, an inferior rice that reduced the staple's market value. This meticulous attention to staple quality was characteristic of U.S. plantation slavery.[26]

Following the final draining of rice fields, enslaved people cut rice with a sickle and then placed cut stalks out to dry in stacks.[27] In harvesting, overseers placed different demands on cutting by enslaved people, exactions that varied based upon the distance required to carry cut rice stalks and the demands made by individual planters. Ben Horry, enslaved as a youth, remembered that cutting rice was an "awful job" and that the task of cutting rice was one-half acre a day—sometimes twice as much.[28] When an assigned task was not met, overseers and drivers deployed direct physical violence against enslaved people.[29]

Enslaved people would then tie rice in bundles.[30] Across all stages, including cutting, enslaved people struggled to place limits on planter demands and regulate the work process. As one planter complained, Black rice cultivators were "cunning enough to remember that what they are harvesting they will have to thresh, & will tie as small sheaves as they can."[31] Such efforts were part of the daily struggle over the intensity of plantation extortion managed and maintained by planters, overseers, and drivers.

Carolina rice production rested not only upon the labor of enslaved people but also on the knowledge of enslaved cultivators in South Carolina and Georgia, which was turned into commodities uniquely valued when sold for export, a form of valuation that reflected back upon enslaved people themselves. Black knowledge and skill about rice cultivation emerged through the African diaspora and the pathways of a productive process that tied the rice-producing South Carolina and Georgia Low Country to practices of West African rice production in Upper Guinea.[32] Enslaved people knew not just more about the process of rice cultivation but also more about the daily management and day-to-day operation of plantation work, knowledge that could produce intense oppositions between Black drivers and field laborers.[33] Planters evinced a pronounced anxiety about rice cultivation because it depended upon enslaved people working beyond direct supervision. Besides knowing little about the daily practice and process of rice cultivation, rice planters were often absent, leaving their plantations for up to sixth-month periods beginning in spring or early summer out of fear of disease and returning in November after rice harvesting.[34] Black drivers' knowledge about rice cultivation was often essential to operations.[35] As one planter responded when asked about rice planting techniques, "[I] will barely suggest, (and in this instance only) the propriety of your consulting the driver, being an old rice planter."[36] The response put to words the known but rarely stated.[37]

The processes of threshing and milling rice underwent significant transformation in the North Atlantic during the first half of the nineteenth century, with implications for the British imperial world. After cutting, rice was generally threshed and winnowed before pounding. Threshing relied particularly upon bondwomen's labor and entailed flailing rice stalks with a wooden staff that had a second wooden staff bound to it.[38] This process separated the rice from the stalk. Flailing was so labor-intensive and demanding a process as to effectively impose a limit on expanded production.[39] By the 1850s, on the largest plantations, threshing might be done by enslaved people using a threshing machine, introduced in the 1830s. Yet often throughout this period, threshing continued to be performed by hand, accompanied by enslaved peoples' efforts to take control of the work. As the once enslaved Maggie Black remembered of threshing, the process of rice cultivation was accompanied by songs, which in part regulated the pace of work on rice plantations.[40]

If threshing was the most labor-intensive part of rice processing, the milling of rice placed consistently high demands on enslaved labor. Throughout the nineteenth century, the labor-saving mechanization of milling enabled expanded theoretical possibilities for accumulation by slaveholding rice planters. In the early nineteenth century, the mechanization of rice pounding became increasingly common.[41] This mechanization first took place directly upon South Carolina and Georgia plantations, including two mills in Charleston owning over seventy enslaved people each. The West Point Mill claimed ownership in eighty-nine enslaved people.[42] Steam engines and millstones for some of these rice mills were manufactured in Britain and shipped from Liverpool to South Carolina.[43]

In the process, new geographical distance was created between mills and plantations while further connecting the process of production across the North Atlantic. Elizabeth Blyth, the slave owner who had sold Tayler away from his family, would sometimes send her rice to be milled at the mills of Jonathan Lucas in Charleston.[44] The Lucas family had accumulated considerable capital through slavery, the construction of mills, and the milling of rice and took part in the Atlantic world transformation of rice milling that was already underway. From 1817, the milling of Carolina rice transformed as Carolina rice was increasingly exported from the United States in unmilled, paddy form. In 1819, Jonathan Lucas partnered with London merchant Henry Ewbank to establish a patent for a rice cleaning machine in Britain.[45] In the early 1820s, Lucas's son, Jonathan Lucas Jr. of South Carolina, was involved in the construction of rice mills in England capable of processing over 300,000 bushels of rice.[46] Lucas Jr. facilitated the construction of three rice mills in Liverpool and one in Rotherhithe near London. By 1823, the first shipment of rough rice (known as unmilled or paddy rice) was exported from the United States to Britain. In 1828, a slave-owning southern rice planter could see that the building of mills would ultimate lead to paddy rice being exported more often than milled rice.[47] By 1850, that transformation was nearly complete, as most rice exported from the United States was paddy rice.

Transformations in rice milling relocated a crucial part of the work process that had long been conducted by enslaved people to wage laborers in the English cities of Liverpool and London as well as to mills in continental Europe. This caused plantations to redouble their efforts to contain enslaved people, an action that was particularly urgent in light of fears about enslaved flight and insurrection. In 1822, during the trial of Denmark Vesey, Bram and Richard, two enslaved people owned by Lucas, had been charged with involvement in the conspiracy. They were acquitted, but Charleston's white supremacist planter class was nonetheless shaken.[48] One rice mill owner experienced a near shutdown after five enslaved people fled from the mill.[49] The relocation of rice milling to England and continental Europe structurally concentrated enslavement in rice production to plantations.

The Atlantic world transformation of milling was calibrated according to increasing profitability, shipping logistics, consumer desires, and the perpetuation of U.S. slavery. One South Carolina rice planter noted that continued dependency upon enslaved labor for rice milling would have made it impossible to produce and "prepare for market anything like the number of barrels now produced. But, by the application of steam, and improvement of Machinery, the Rice-mill has been introduced into Europe, paddy exported there in the rough, and offered freshly prepared to consumers, thereby enhancing its value and increasing its consumption."[50] One British observer who traveled between South Carolina and London reflected, "I have frequently, since my return, eaten rice managed in this way by Messrs Lucas and Ewbank of London, as fresh in taste and in appearance as any I met with in South Carolina."[51] These transformations enabled the persistence of slavery on rice plantations in the South Carolina and Georgia Low Country.

Shifts in rice milling to England reshaped the character of slavery in the United States. Mechanization reduced the ratio of enslaved labor on colonized land, making the profitable production of Carolina rice part of an intensification of the labor process for enslaved people. Through tariff policy, Britain further encouraged the exportation of unmilled rice from the United States while offering a reduced tariff for the importation of rough rice from West Africa. Tariff disputes were resolved in 1846, just as the pro-slaveholder Walker Tariff in the United States and the repeal of the Corn Laws in Britain established a proslavery free trade policy between the United States and Britain.[52] Slaveholding mill owners and family members moved between South Carolina and England with ease, writing one another about their thoughts concerning one another's countries and discussing diasporic families, while Atlantic relations of production in rice milling and the consumption of rice shifted in proslavery ways.

Slave owners' meticulous control of the process of production exacted through slavery was crucial to their competitive advantage and profitability — as such, some feared the loss of control implied by the movement of milling. Some Carolina rice planters worried it would ultimately enable the displacement of Carolina rice from European markets by South and Southeast Asian staples.[53] Yet other planters saw this as only enhancing the advantage that U.S. slaveholders had over India and Southeast Asia because the increased weight of unmilled Carolina rice improved the shipping advantages of South Carolina over colonial India.[54] In any event, the demand for slavery through the consumption of Carolina rice continued unabated through the Civil War.

Though slave owners' fears went unrealized, the concentration and extension of Carolina rice milling in Liverpool and London and across Europe led to a much larger change, enabling a racialized transnational and trans-imperial reorganization of labor. The Atlantic shift of milling degraded plantation labor for enslaved people, reduced the amount of labor required on land, and made it further possible for rice planters to profit through the internal slave trade. Subject to global market fluctuations, enslaved people were now increasingly concentrated on rice fields, where they produced rice primarily for export.

Though the elementary components of the work process remained unchanged, the labor process transformed through the intensification of work itself. Black women's hand milling of rice had been exacting and demanding, but the shift to machine milling had numerous negative ramifications on a larger scale. Laboring in rice swamps was singularly damaging to the health of enslaved people. Ned, an enslaved man who labored in a mill on a Georgia plantation, attributed his own relative health to the fact that he had not been tasked with working the rice fields.[55] The removal of milling from the labor process meant that enslaved people were forced to spend even more time in these swamps.[56] What is more, the shift also expanded the territorial domain of rice cultivation on transatlantic and imperial scales, enveloping workers from London and continental Europe. Black people were now consigned to the particularized work of plantation slavery, enclosed in the plantation Low Country rice fields of South Carolina and Georgia.

One white plantation observer stated that "humanity rejoices" because of mechanization. He claimed that mechanization transferred to water and steam work that was "exhausting to the human as well as to the animal frame—and in this feeling we are confident every planter deeply sympathises."[57] Despite these proclamations of sympathy, which simultaneously degraded enslaved people through "zoological" language, the introduction of milling technologies ultimately freed up enslaved labor time for the slaveholder rather than for those enslaved.[58]

As rice milling became the work of wage laborers in Britain and continental Europe, the winter season on plantations was transformed, recentering Black work toward the maintenance of rice fields. While the workforce extended to include English factory workers, U.S. enslaved labor was concentrated on field and plantation maintenance, clearing land, and preparing manure.[59] This meant that those enslaved upon rice plantations would work longer in swamps, places planters imagined would lead to death from the very act of being in such places. The physically destructive nature of plantation labor upon white bodies had a palpable hold on the dominant imaginations of plantation work in the nineteenth century.[60] With the outsourcing of milling and the concentration of field work, "premature death" in the global circuits of Carolina rice plantation production and consumption showed its pronounced anti-Black character.[61]

The Colonial State of Carolina Rice

In 1841, the *British Indian Advocate* described a vision of emancipation through the free market. The world's commodities would be placed in competition with one another, and commodities produced through slavery would be forced out of the market because of price: "Produce a sufficient quantity of the same commodities at as cheap a rate, or at a cheaper rate, by means of free labour, and American slavery will receive its death blow."[62]

Throughout the nineteenth century until Black emancipation in the United States, the cultivation of Carolina rice through U.S. slavery was driven by British consumption and unimpeded by such a logic. Slavery may have been abolished across the British Empire, but it remained in the United States, Brazil, and Cuba and in the global plantation system. The liberal free trade rhetoric that infused the reaches of the world where slavery was abolished nevertheless depended upon the disciplining of formerly enslaved people within the British Empire to the market economy with its stark choice presented as work or die and a reality that often entailed work that exposed formerly enslaved people to premature death. This plantation dominance, in Sylvia Wynter's telling, also demanded the disciplining of Indian peasants as occurred in the colonial planter suppression of the Indigo Revolt of Bengal in 1859. It was in this world that peasants who resisted "growing indigo as a commercial crop for the English, had to be taught a lesson. The world had to be kept safe for the market economy," Wynter writes.[63]

Capitalism's violence built upon slavery's example. Indeed, the forms of domination introduced through Atlantic world plantation slavery established principles for imperial and colonial domination through capitalism stretching beyond the Atlantic and after slavery. The movement of indigo cultivation from Saint Domingue and Carolina to colonial Bengal during the late eighteenth century sketched out an earlier schematic of this dynamic. By the mid-nineteenth century, the imperial reuse of U.S. slavery's forms would become even more explicit.

Colonial projects to introduce Carolina rice cultivation in colonial India revealed the interconnections between U.S. slavery and peasant- and plantation-based agrarian production in colonial India. These abided by a disciplinary logic that depended upon liberal principles of free trade that not only failed to oppose slavery but were shaped in relation to it.

Projects to introduce Carolina rice into colonial India emerged sporadically throughout the mid-nineteenth century during an era marked by Atlantic emancipation within the British Empire and the end of slavery in the United States. Frequently situated in the Bengal and Madras Presidencies, they proceeded according to colonial ideas about imperial market-making — in India, the colonial state pursued export agriculture under the belief that the export trade was crucial to capital accumulation.[64] Such colonial agrarian projects drew upon the arsenal of plantation slavery in the United States and directed this arsenal toward what Neeladri Bhattacharya calls agrarian conquest.[65] Importantly, these colonial projects did not depend upon the direct replication of U.S. settler slavery. Still, they emerged *through* slavery and reveal how anti-Blackness and U.S. settler colonialism informed British colonial agrarian projects in India.

In these colonial projects, it becomes clear that the ideologies of British imperial liberalism were preoccupied by the economic dynamism of U.S. settler slavery. As one colonial official observed, "The statement frequently appears in the history of our attempts to acclimatize this [Carolina] rice, that the people would not eat it even if they could grow it. I take the liberty to doubt this; but were it even true, and the grain grown for export only, the experiment is of great importance. The people do not eat jute, but they are glad to grow it for all that."[66] This perspective depended upon peasant smallholding cultivators disciplined according to the logic of market relations and production for export. Yet, the dependence of such projects upon producing a structure that depended upon compelling cultivators to make "decisions" to grow Carolina rice also revealed emerging differences between U.S. settler slavery and the articulation of a non-enslaving colonial liberalism. The abstract belief that introducing structures of choice would make the cultivation of rice inevitable through the colonial economy existed in the same historic conjuncture as the belief that U.S. settler slavery enforced enslaved cultivation of Carolina rice. While in British India the colonial state struggled to induce the expanded cultivation of Carolina rice among smallholding peasant cultivators, in the South Carolina and Georgia Low Country, asymmetrical struggles between enslaved people and planters occurred over the labor process and the realities of enslavement upon plantations where Carolina rice cultivation was entrenched.

Within the British Empire, the Slavery Abolition Act of 1833 legally declared the end to the centuries-long history of slavery except in India, Sri Lanka, and Saint Helena. Former slaveholders were compensated £20 million by Britain's parliament; formerly enslaved people experienced post-slavery rule characterized by continued colonialism. In metropolitan Britain, the pursuit of free trade policies enabled continued profits through slavery in the United States, Cuba, and Brazil. Not only did Lancashire textile manufacturers depend upon U.S. cotton produced through slavery, but also the equalization of sugar duties enabled the expanded consumption of slave-produced sugar imported from Brazil and Cuba, something that itself led to a decrease in demand for northern India–produced sugars.[67]

While abolition in the British Empire resulted in a "swing to the East" and even the movement of some former Caribbean slaveholders to British India, India was not characterized by a powerful class of white slaveholders in the same way.[68] The 1833 Slavery Abolition Act had exempted India and Mauritius, but the Indian Slavery Act of 1843 legally declared the end of slavery in India. To be sure, British colonial law was often indifferent to caste-based bondages that did not, as Rupa Viswanath writes, directly depend upon or emerge through colonial legislation but were instead reproduced through "local power and state authority." The colonial state protected the relationship between landed caste elites and Dalit laborers as something that was "mutually beneficial," even as Dalit laborers sought means to challenge and escape caste oppression.[69]

European planter and merchant power were dominant, but the British Empire did not pursue a regime of accumulation predicated upon white planter permanent settlement coinciding with racial slavery. Violent relations defined the British planter class's dominance within indigo and tea production. The tea gardens of Assam existed through what Jayeeta Sharma has termed an "extractive economy" undergirded by violence and colonial racializations.[70] Yet, as Rana Behal and Prabhu Mohapatra have noted, plantations in India had no history of production through slavery.[71] Outside of tea and indigo, the colonial state's power to create and sustain agricultural production for export was often limited.[72] Global commodities markets produced and enabled structured indebtedness within colonial India with deep repercussions. The small latitude provided to smallholders carved out in relation to what commodities might be introduced set limits to the colonial state's ability to transform agrarian relations toward the export of experimental cultivation in projects like those to introduce Carolina rice and U.S. cotton staples.

To match U.S. settler slavery's capacity to produce and export commodities like Carolina rice and U.S. cotton staples, more drastic changes to colonial configurations of labor and land seemed necessary. Experimental projects occurred on the landholdings of Bengali zamindars (landholders), in jails in the Madras Presidency, and at colonial gardens.[73] As such, the introduction of Carolina rice into India had much in common with broader liberal colonial projects of agricultural "improvement." Yet as much as efforts to introduce Carolina rice took advantage of coercive institutions such as the jail or figures such as U.S. overseers brought to India, these projects still depended upon decisions made by cultivators and landholders. This diverged from the realities of U.S. settler slavery where bondpeople could struggle over the process of production yet had no control over the staples cultivated. The project to induce demand was about the making of colonial techniques of economic coercion intended to induce market-based transformations that would make the extensive production of Carolina rice for export inevitable.

Colonial officials and invested zamindars ultimately proved unable to introduce Carolina rice, revealing a number of essential realities of enslavement and enslaved people that made the growth of Carolina rice possible in the United States but not in colonial India. The Bengali zamindar Radhakanta Deb was a leading voice within the Agricultural and Horticultural Society of India (AHSI), a British colonial–dominated agricultural institute with membership that also included members of Bengal's Zamindari Association.[74] Deb's observations on rice cultivation in Bengal reflect a belief that the introduction of different staples in India could emerge from drawing upon techniques and seeds from the United States and reformulating these practices in relation to "native process." According to Deb, "European experience" would introduce "the methods of culture" while "taking so much from the native process adopted in this country as will

Frederick Fiebig, *Print of the Jail, Calcutta* (1851). The Fiebig Collection,
© The British Library Board (Photo 247/2[6]).

serve the objects of science."[75] Such projects involved systematic efforts to
introduce U.S. overseers, seeds, gins, implements, modes of assessment,
and sometimes direct physical violence. Yet colonial aspirations to produce
Carolina rice in India confronted repeated limits that proved impossible to
overcome.

Rice cultivation and consumption had deep cultural, economic, and
social significance within India during the mid-nineteenth century. Rice
served as the principal food grain in many parts of the subcontinent. Radhakanta Deb's "On the Culture of Paddy in Twenty Different Districts,"
an inquiry into these practices for the colonial AHSI, describes the staples
cultivated in Bengal and exported to England as "rough and inferior,"
sometimes commanding less than half the value of Carolina rice.[76] The
AHSI would write the South Carolina Agricultural Society as early as 1831
inquiring into the purchase of Carolina rice, frequently orchestrating shipments of Carolina rice from South Carolina to Liverpool and from Liverpool to Calcutta.[77] Yet, the East India Company and the AHSI failed to

disembed the production of Carolina rice from the contradictions that defined U.S. settler slavery and made Carolina rice uniquely valued in the North Atlantic.

At times, colonial officials believed that their inability to grow rice was the result of the climate and experimented with cultivating Carolina rice in different locations. In the Sundarbans, mangroves in the Bay of Bengal, colonial officials repeatedly sought to introduce Carolina rice, with no success.[78] When one project failed, an official wrote, "I feel confident that this failure cannot be attributed to want of care on the part of the Ryots [cultivators]."[79] The language of agrarian failure itself offers insight into the projects made in relation to colonizing visions of "successful" agricultural transformation as defined by colonial officials. In Odisha, another colonial observer stated that he believed it would be difficult or impossible to introduce Carolina seed there: "Those who have grown the seed refuse to eat the grain, and besides, there is no local demand for it, and until such demand arises cultivators will never be introduced to substitute the cultivation of Carolina rice for their own staple crop. If the Carolina mode of cultivation is absolutely necessary to ensure good results, the Ooryas will not adopt it, and will, therefore, never succeed in raising a crop which will secure for them the large profits that are anticipated."[80] Such a perspective, even as it was based upon export cultivation, also recognized the importance of peasant smallholding cultivators' decisions and practices of consumption. Left to the imagination was the implied solution: direct intervention through force.

In Bihar in 1840, an indigo planter reflected upon a decade of projects to introduce Carolina rice. According to the planter, he distributed Carolina seeds within the district with results that were largely satisfactory. The amount "far exceeded anything the Ryots had ever been accustomed to witness from their ordinary crops." The planter suggested that zamindars in the district should introduce Carolina rice on an "extensive scale amongst the ryots." After four years, he believed it had been cultivated to a considerable extent, noting that with "efficient machinery under proper management," the staple could compete with Carolina rice sold upon the European market and "command a much higher price than any of the best descriptions hitherto imported from Bengal." This made him advise zamindars in the region of the efficacy of introducing the staple also for increased yields.[81] However, despite these observations, this project was not pursued.

Between 1839 and 1849, an extensive project focused particularly upon the introduction of U.S. cotton and rice staples entailed relocating U.S. plantation overseers to colonial India.[82] While this project primarily focused upon cotton cultivation (see chapter 5), it secondarily focused upon Carolina rice. In 1839, an East India Company official named Thomas Bayles traveled from Bristol to New York en route to the American South, where he would recruit overseers and planters knowledgeable about the process of plantation production, focusing both upon rice and cotton cultivation. Bayles first visited South Carolina, where he examined Carolina rice plantations, observing methods of cultivation. Bayles reported confidently that he would be able to introduce and reproduce these techniques across India. In Savannah, one of the largest cotton markets in the South, Bayles met the wealthy plantation owner Charles Harris, who owned Upland and Sea Island cotton plantations in Georgia and Jefferson County, Mississippi.[83] Bayles would send cotton seeds, implements, and 250 bushels of Carolina rice to India.

In general, white planters and overseers involved in the rice plantation economy were reluctant to relocate with Bayles. For one, their livelihoods in the American South were simply too lucrative to leave behind. One overseer who would have been willing to relocate requested from Bayles an annual salary of $2,500, an amount Bayles could not provide.[84] These planters and overseers valued their own knowledge of the production process highly, positing white supremacy as a commodity and making demands in keeping with its perceived price on the global market. Because Bayles could not pay as demanded, he took extensive notes on the process of southern rice cultivation. Stating that he was "particularly struck" by the advantages of introducing South Carolina styles of rice cultivation to India, he recorded the "whole process" of enslaved rice cultivation in South Carolina and Georgia.[85]

Despite difficulties securing the aid of white planters and overseers involved in the rice economy, Bayles recruited two overseers who claimed knowledge about cultivation, John Blount and James Morris. Blount would be placed in the Bengal Presidency, while Morris would be located in the Madras Presidency. Morris's efforts to introduce the so-called American system of rice cultivation at Erode in the northwestern Madras Presidency reveal that even when directed by white plantation overseers from the United States, cultivators' choices had the power to disrupt the colonial pursuit of Carolina rice in India.

Morris arrived in Madras on 20 October 1840. While the majority of Morris's attention focused upon cotton, he also attempted to introduce rice cultivation between 1841 and 1843 at Erode. In 1841, Morris described the failure of his rice field as "certainly the most provoking and discouraging of any thing I have ever met with in the whole course of my life."[86]

The East India Company Board of Revenue, along with local revenue collectors, sought an explanation for the project's failure. While Morris insisted that he could have been successful, the district tahsildar (revenue collector), Rangasamy Naik, disputed any such claim: "The American mode of cultivation is unprofitable in every respect. The American ploughs are too large and heavy to be of any use and cattle of sufficient strength to work them with are not procurable in this part of the country. This difficulty may be overcome by the employment of additional coolies but as the system itself is not in any way advantageous, the ryots of this talook [revenue district] are not willing to follow it."[87] The refusal of peasant cultivators to follow Morris's method of rice cultivation was part of a set of already existing colonial agrarian relations in India that simply could not accommodate the introduction of forms of rice cultivation emerging from U.S. settler slavery.

The capital investment required for the purchase of implements used in the cultivation of the so-called American system seemed too great for the Erode District to meet the revenue demands of the colonial state.[88] The structure of colonial contradictions and the contradictions of U.S. settler slavery were not the same. And peasants' ability to refuse to follow the demand for the growth of rice had no equivalent in the United States, slaveholders and enslaved peoples' oppositional struggles notwithstanding. But instead of explaining his economic and agricultural failure in these terms, Morris reverted to the language of white supremacy, condemning the people of Erode as a "treacherous indolent race of beings."[89] However, Morris was also not alone in a racial explanation of the project's failure. Where Morris saw indolence, British colonial officials described Indian cultivators' usual "influence of the prejudice with which the introduction of new systems is usually regarded."[90] What is striking is not so much the difference between colonial and slavery-based racial explanations but their seamless cohabitation.

In the face of Morris's white supremacist commitments but without the relations of U.S. settler slavery, he failed to introduce any comparable form of export rice cultivation in India. He knew little about rice cultivation and did not possess the means of violence and expropriation that characterized the South Carolina and Georgia Low Country plantation economy. In 1845, Morris wrote a letter to his brother and reported that he was in "good health." A year later, Morris was dead of cholera in Ballari. His grave reads, "cotton planter of Natchez, Adams County, Mississippi, U.S.A."[91] The Arkansas-born Morris was neither a cotton planter nor from Natchez, Mississippi.

Besides relying upon U.S. overseers, projects to introduce Carolina rice drew upon practices of colonial incarceration.[92] These projects continued in colonial India following Black emancipation in the United States. On 30 July 1868, several barrels of U.S. rice seed were forwarded to the director of the Chengalpattu jail, located in the northern part of British India's Madras Presidency, part of a plan for introducing Carolina rice to the region developed by the jail's superintendent, Dr. Thompson. Thompson's experiments were rooted in a belief that Carolina rice would be easily grown by a "great body of convicts" in the jail.[93] Thompson thought that a large-scale system for the introduction and proliferation of Carolina rice cultivation could lessen the cost of colonial jails by forcing prisoners to grow their own food. Even more ambitiously, Thompson believed former convicts would bring positive reports of Carolina rice to their villages, choosing of their own free will to replicate their experience of carceral labor and helping Carolina rice to proliferate across India. Plans to introduce Carolina rice cultivation through jails depended upon the fortification of jailing practices and the exertion of greater control over the biological functions and social reproductive capacities of prisoners. The Chengalpattu jail would need to be expanded from 177 to 450 prisoners for such purposes. This jail expansion, Thompson calculated, would be funded through a single crop of Carolina rice. Seeking ever greater control over the biological functions of prisoners in service of rice cultivation, Thompson went so far as to calculate the "average quantity" of human excrement that would be used to fertilize land. Thompson's recommendations met enthusiastic interest among colonial administrators, but the plan was not generalized after a season of experimentation.

Both Thompson's and Morris's projects may have gone bust, but they were revealing failures even so. These colonial agrarian projects drew from the possibilities represented by U.S. settler slavery's position within global capitalism. Their efforts to force Indian cultivators to submit to the demands of the global economy were limited by market relations within colonial India, a different configuration of colonial space, and the impracticality of dictating prisoners' post-incarceration lives through carceral discipline. U.S. settler slavery would continue to exert a powerful influence globally, especially as global capitalism became increasingly entrenched through the production of colonial and racial domination.

In his 1970 overview of slavery and the Atlantic slave trade, C. L. R. James noted that slavery triumphed through the "negative recognition" of enslaved people "in every work sphere."[94] For James, negative recognition characterized the impossibility of white acceptance that enslaved people could also be gifted artisans. The constitutive violences of slavery went far beyond work alone, making the structuring violences of slavery at times unrecognizable.[95] The negative recognition James outlines was part of a generalized anti-Black hostility toward enslaved people that defined the nineteenth century with implications for capitalist social relations, characterized by the making and multiple passages of global capital through slavery.

In the U.S. South, social, cultural, and economic connections made through the world of rice cultivation created situations where U.S. slaveholders racially imagined differences between peasant smallholding cultivators and enslaved people. These imaginations produced contradictory conclusions about capitalist markets and were characterized by the state of "negative recognition" James described. One U.S. rice planter recalled the arrival of Bayles in the United States, describing ways that the settler economy of rice cultivation seemed to emerge from thin air against a colonial imagination of India outside of history. As the planter wrote, "Here, then, was an embassage from the banks of the Ganges — a spot where rice has been cultivated probably for twenty centuries, to inquire into the method of cultivation and preparation of a people amongst whom the grain had no existence one hundred and sixty years ago."[96] Such a racialized territorial imagination was ignorant of the history of rice cultivation through the African diaspora while also reproducing a settler slaveholder myth of North America as terra nullius.[97]

The failure of projects to transform staples across colonial India exposed ways that colonial power in South Asia and U.S. settler slavery could be brought together, particularly through the demands that slavery introduced into the global economy through its commodities. The contradictions that structured settler slavery in the United States diverged from those that defined colonial agrarian relations in colonial India. The "negative recognition" of enslaved people within the growth of Carolina rice in the mid-nineteenth century, along with violent histories of dispossession that characterized settler slavery, made this reality unrecognizable for those who sought to transform the economy and remake themselves through Carolina rice. Projects to introduce Carolina rice in colonial India reveal both the Atlantic particularities of racial slavery, which introduced possibilities and imaginations for social, cultural, and economic transformations, while also revealing how those particularities extended far beyond the Black Atlantic. Even in their failure to draw upon settler slavery to introduce Carolina rice or to leverage carceral logics to shape the life choices of the formerly incarcerated, these projects show that colonial visions for free market economic transformation within India were formed *through* plantation slavery in the United States. They reveal a deep-seated commitment to exposing smallholding peasant cultivators to the unmediated violence of the capitalist economy—and though Carolina rice cultivation in colonial India may have faltered, this larger project was by no means over. U.S. slavery exerted its influence most powerfully over colonial imaginations of India as a site for transformation through the introduction and exportation of U.S. cotton staples.

5 ::: White Overseers of the World
U.S. Cotton and Colonial India

For the radical theorist of racial capitalism Cedric Robinson, capitalism has been characterized by chaos that cannot be captured by unifying language.[1] If that is the case, it is not for lack of trying. In the mid-nineteenth century, abolitionist discourses sutured diverse geographies together in an effort to interpret the world through dichotomies of slavery and freedom. While this imagination enlivened abolitionist struggles against slavery in and beyond the United States, it also elided the forms of colonialism and expropriation that visions of free labor rested upon.[2]

In the first half of the nineteenth century, settler slavery in the U.S. South combined the colonization of Cherokee, Creek, Chickasaw, and Seminole lands with the forced migration of enslaved people to produce a new "Cotton Kingdom." These expropriations would provide a material base for the Lancashire textile industry.[3] As one observer would later reflect, "every new factory built in Lancashire creates a demand for slaves on the banks of the Mississippi."[4] This perspective fixed enslaved and wage labor in relation to one another through the expropriation of Indigenous land. For W. E. B. Du Bois, aggressive territorial conquest appeared to create conditions for a new slavery where plantations assumed the most extreme possibilities of the factory form itself.[5]

The explosive nexus between Lancashire and the slaveholding United States, combined with British colonial policies in India, facilitated the dismantling of Bengal's handloom textile industry. By the 1830s, India had become a net importer of Manchester goods, while British colonial interests sought to transform the export economy based upon agricultural productions.[6] The dismantling of handloom production in India was an ongoing process brought about through correspondences between the English factory and the cotton-producing slave South. By 1828, Bengal no longer exported textiles to England.[7] Followed by the Agra famine of 1837–38, settler slavery and social catastrophes created conditions for abolitionists to imagine new worlds of "free" cotton cultivation in India.[8] Visions of free Indian cotton were put forth at the first annual meeting of the British India Society in Manchester (1840). The British India Society comprised manufacturers

Power loom weaving in a Lancashire textile mill. (Edward Baines,
History of the Cotton Manufacture of Great Britain [London, 1835])

and abolitionists and encouraged the growth of non-slave-produced cotton
in India as an abolitionist project.[9] Founding member George Thompson
hoped to hear every textile factory owner and worker ask, "Why do not the
natives of British India, dying of famine by hundreds of thousands, produce all the Cotton we receive from America?"[10] As a boy, John Bowring
recalled seeing Indian handloom manufactures in English markets, but by
1840 everything had changed, a direct result of Lancashire's dominance
of Indian markets: "You have driven the poor weavers of India to starvation. Your Cotton stuffs monopolise the India markets; and will you not
enable them to furnish you with the raw material, of which those stuffs are
made?"[11] In such moments, the Lancashire textile invasion was presented
as destroying the foundations of colonial India, making it possible to imagine fundamental transformations in agrarian relations.

Such British metropolitan perspectives on connected histories of colonialism and emancipation suggested that it was the British Empire's duty
to enable "free" Indian cotton, universalizing "free" labor in the process.[12]
Some abolitionists further connected this universalization of free labor
with the expansion of settler colonialism in the United States. As Wendell
Phillips wrote, "To you [the British], to the sunny plains of Hindostan,
we shall owe it, that our beautiful prairies are unpolluted by the steps of a

slave-holder; that the march of civilization westward will be changed from the progress of the manacled slave coffle, at the bidding of the lash, to the quiet step of families."[13] From this perspective, not just the abolition of slavery but also the "free" colonization of the American West depended upon the cultivation of a cotton staple in India suitable for metropolitan industry. Phillips's claim for abolition was part of a set of visions where emancipation and colonization were bound together as part of a global process irreducible to a single empire or territory yet connected through a commitment to the expansion and transformation of the capitalist economy. This expansion was informed by a vision of free labor described not by economic autonomy but by economic dependency characterized by the need to work for others.[14]

In such moments, abolitionists relied upon divisions that marked slavery and freedom as diametrically opposed. Left unexamined were those forms of expropriation and dispossession that fell outside of this dichotomy.[15] As Chickasaw scholar Jodi Byrd observed, "Asia, Africa, and Europe all meet in the Americas to labor over the dialectics of free and unfree, but what of the Americas themselves and the prior peoples upon whom that labor took place?"[16] With a history of plantations and slaveries but without plantation slavery, expropriation in India toward the export production of U.S. cotton staples would assume a different form, emerging through the ongoing projects of agrarian conquest unfolding across the subcontinent.[17] George Thompson and East India Company officials each noted that indigo, once cultivated in South Carolina and Central America before shifting toward India, could serve as an instructive model.[18] Further, the particularity of the British India Society itself seemed to reflect new possibilities for expropriation. The British India Society grew directly from the Aborigines Protection Society, of which Cherokee chief John Ross was an honorary member, and set out to address the particularity of colonial subjects in India.[19] Despite interests in the specificities of colonial India, abolitionist visions of "free" Indian cotton rarely accounted for the multilayered nature of village agrarian relations nor for the realities of conquest that the export production of cotton would depend upon.[20]

The project that brought Morris and Thompson to India was also the most sustained effort to transform cotton cultivation in India before the U.S. Civil War, bringing together U.S. settler slavery and rural agrarian conquest in colonial India. This project depended upon the deployment of white U.S. plantation overseers to India to introduce an "American system" of cotton cultivation capable of competing in "quantity and quality" with the United States.[21] While India already cultivated cotton, the introduction of an "American system" was meant to produce U.S. staples according to the needs of British industrial capitalists.[22] Abolitionists from Charles Lenox Remond to Thomas Clarkson regarded this project as the concrete future end of U.S. slavery. In excised remarks from his speech at the first World's Anti-Slavery Convention in London (1840), Clarkson described the East India Company as "providentially engaged" in cultivating cotton in India. Calculating the difference between enslaved African American and "free" Indian cultivation, Clarkson noted that labor in India was valued at between one penny and three and a half pence per day, while slave labor never estimated under twenty-five cents. Clarkson asked, "What slavery can stand against these prices?"[23] Such reflections persisted in imagining the condition of colonial labor to be "free," even as the laborers themselves were transformed into objects instrumentalized for abolitionist ends that depended upon continuing to match the production of cotton as introduced to the world through settler slavery in the United States. By foregrounding what Jairus Banaji has called the "incoherence" of free labor in the telling of the East India Company's efforts to once again introduce an "American system" to India, this chapter considers the ways that projects to universalize free labor resulted in the proliferation of connections between colonialism, enslavement, and the domination of labor rather than through a global competition between slavery and free labor.

The British East India Company colonial project to relocate U.S. plantation overseers to India has attracted renewed attention, including in recent writing by Christopher Florio and Alan Olmstead. For Florio, the cotton projects in colonial India were characterized by an effort to push the status of colonial subjects in India from impoverished toward enslaved, particularly through the transference of slavery's labor practices. In contrast, for Olmstead, the British East India Company was implausibly engaged in a project of colonial uplift "to improve the conditions of farmers" despite dependence upon U.S. slavery's overseers.[24] In this chapter, I examine this project from a perspective that foregrounds the ways that slavery-based settler colonialism in the United States was again brought into relation with colonial projects in India. While these projects were not based upon the reproduction or introduction of hereditary racial slavery into colonial India, they formed part of the broader pattern of mid-nineteenth-century capitalism within which practices of colonialism were informed by the bar that U.S. slavery set for colonial economic transformation. While U.S. slavery organized the social domination of labor in accordance to a settler colonial form that depended upon the reduction of humanity to real estate, colonial projects to introduce cotton served as a theater in a broader battle for agrarian conquest in India through colonialism. When the U.S. overseers involved in these projects survived and returned to the United States, they reflected upon their participation in this field of conquest, looking back toward missed fortunes and viewing the realities of slavery-based colonialism in the United States differently.

Overseeing the World

In *The World and Africa*, Du Bois described the work of "the white masters of the world" in producing race and empire, destroying the possibility of something that might have been called humanity in the process.[25] Essential figures in this process of transformation were overseers—white supremacists responsible for the daily physical and psychological terrorization of enslaved African Americans in the U.S. South. Overseers were also integral to the colonization of southeastern Indian territory in the Cotton Kingdom. On slave plantations, overseers managed labor through direct, physical confrontations, stripping, flogging, and killing enslaved African Americans.[26] When an overseer died, some who were enslaved thought of this death as an act of "merciful providence."[27]

From 1839 to 1849, overseers traveled throughout India. Initially, the East India Company sent three to the Bombay Presidency, three to the Madras Presidency, and four to the Bengal Presidency and from there to the North-Western Provinces. In the initial stages of the project, overseers in the North-Western Provinces were central to the pursuit of cotton cultivation.[28] There, overseers found themselves trying to carve out plantations from a world of colonial agrarian relations where zamindars (landholders), *asamis* (tenant-at-will cultivators), and raiyats (smallholding cultivators) all struggled to produce within a depressed agrarian economy stressed by colonial land taxation.[29] Overseers worked as planters, managing experimental cotton plantations where they controlled land and the means of production with implements brought from the United States.[30] Yet, the object was not to reproduce U.S. settler slavery but rather to introduce cotton cultivation through experimental plantations. These plantations would serve as models for landholders and tenants alike.[31]

On experimental plantations, euphemistically referred to as experimental farms, overseers improvised with means of coercion including violence, terror, and techniques of racial management, believing that they would succeed at cotton cultivation in the process. According to Thomas Bayles, the East India Company official who brought the overseers from the American South, overseers should be allowed to organize cotton cultivation according to their own judgment: "They have all been reared on Cotton planta-

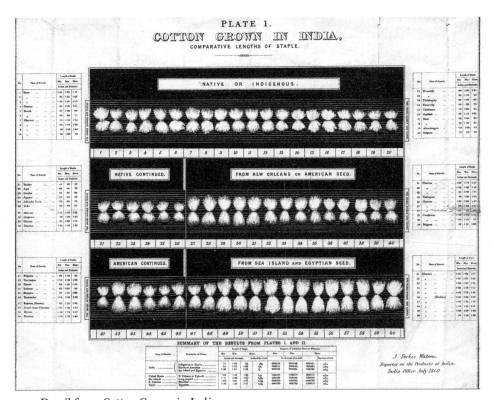

Detail from *Cotton Grown in India*.
(Henry Ashworth Papers, Lancashire Archives, Preston)

tions: from my knowledge of their character, I believe, were any other system pursued, it would decidedly check their zeal."[32] These were arguments for a "southern turn" toward colonizing India. This path did not center on the management of enslaved African Americans by white overseers but centered instead on white Americans' ability to draw upon those techniques to rearrange colonial relations of cotton production in India, a rearrangement that deployed race and direct violence but that was also subject to constant disruption and interruption.[33]

Thomas J. Finnie was the U.S. plantation overseer most central to the project to introduce an "American system" of cotton cultivation. Finnie managed two cotton plantations owned by widows in Natchez, Mississippi, the heart of the Cotton Kingdom.[34] Introduced to Bayles by another planter in Natchez, Finnie facilitated the recruitment of the other nine overseers who would travel to India. Though Finnie would not receive salary equivalent to his work in Mississippi, he agreed to the project because of a "conviction of realizing in the East an independence for himself" unobtainable in the American South.[35] This independence was inextricably bound to the extension of self through the domination of others. During their time in India, overseers attempted to move vertically within a global plantation hierarchy to become not just planters but something more. As one overseer reflected following the failure of the project and his return to the U.S. South, "Had success been within our reach I might now have been a Nabob in India . . . instead of a very humble cotton planter in the low lands of Louisiana."[36] Overseers imagined themselves leaving U.S. settler slavery to transform Indian cotton cultivation. Instead, they failed within already existing agrarian relations, either dying in India like Morris or returning to the United States unsuccessful.

Finnie was part of the group of four overseers who would ultimately travel to the Bengal Presidency and North-Western Provinces. This group left the center of cotton cultivation in the slaveholding South to go first to the center of textile manufacturing in Lancashire, England. They met with cotton brokers, spinners, manufacturers, and members of the Court of Directors and tested gins purchased from the United States before a gathered crowd of nearly 150, including East India Company officials and prominent members of the Liverpool and Manchester bourgeoisie. Samples of ginned cotton were graded, and the price that each would "fetch in the market" was told to overseers for future guidance in India.[37] They then traveled to Egypt to examine Egyptian cotton cultivation techniques before finally making their way to the Bengal Presidency and the North-Western Provinces.[38]

While in Egypt, Finnie had purchased a whip for flogging laborers made from hippopotamus hide. The whip, along with a developing terminology of white supremacy, was essential to overseers' visions of making cotton plantations in India. In the North-Western Provinces, overseers learned terms such as *zabardasti*—meaning "violence," "force," "oppression"—but were unable to commence cotton cultivation through the use of such techniques. Finnie attempted to introduce the "American system" of cotton cultivation in the North-Western Provinces along the Yamuna River, first in Kotra Makrandpur and later in Agra. After failures in the North-Western Provinces, Finnie resettled in southeastern India, where he struggled to grow cotton in Tirunelveli from 1845 until he ultimately left India in 1849.

Finnie's early failures in the North-Western Provinces provide insight into the malleability of notions of "free" labor and the centrality of violence and coercion in his plan to introduce the so-called American system of cotton cultivation. In Kotra Makrandpur, Finnie managed contracted labor while also instructing cultivators growing cotton on both zamindari and raiyati land. Following the East India Company's seizure of Bundelkhand and the Ganges-Yamuna Doab, the region where Finnie first struggled to establish cotton cultivation underwent environmental devastation. In 1837–38, the Agra famine had left behind widespread devastation.[39] Finnie dreamed of commanding capital similar to that of American planters in service of a cotton monoculture, believing he would "turn the Doab into one vast Cotton field."[40] Yet in Kotra Makrandpur that dream confronted a skein of colonial agrarian relations that defied Finnie's control. Finnie's failure reveals an inability to manage and make sense of differences between U.S. settler slavery and colonial agrarian relations in the North-Western Provinces.

Outlining his first year of cultivation for the *Journal of the Agricultural and Horticultural Society of India* (1842), Finnie offered a concrete vision of the North-Western Province's plantation future: "Although I am in the jungles where I see no one but 'natives' . . . when I ride over my plantation and see the beautiful prospect of a crop I cannot realize the fact that I am so far from my native land." He continued, "From a jungle I have given this something the appearance of a Mississippi plantation, and it looks so natural that it almost has the effect to cause me to forget that I am not on the banks of the 'Father of waters' in the new world, instead of on the Jumna in the old." By transforming the Doab into the banks of the Mississippi, Finnie would create an unparalleled form of pleasure: "If there is anything I would give the preference to as the most beautiful in nature, it is a *well regulated plantation*, and if there is any pleasure connected with the business of life that deserves to be classed above all others it is to manage that plantation."[41] Saidiya Hartman has written that the fungibility of the enslaved in the slaveholding South enabled a set of relations of power, pleasure, and possession that enabled masters' extension through "embodiment in external objects and persons."[42] In the North-Western Provinces, Finnie imagined comparable configurations of power, pleasure, and possession in his new position as a planter. But colonial India was not the U.S. South.

For all his dreams to remake the North-Western Provinces into a new Cotton Kingdom, Finnie failed to manage differences within colonial agrarian relations. This is clear in the new racial vocabulary and forms of management he confronted and made in his attempts to make white supremacy work. Finnie was confident that only subtle differences existed in the techniques of racial management he would deploy: "The only difference between a Coolie and a [N]egro is this: the first we can make work out of our sight by operating upon his fears, but the latter we must persuade and drive together which answers very well as long as we are present, but has no effect as soon as our backs are turned."[43] This statement contradicted his earlier contention that only one "servant" was willing to work when he was not in sight.[44] Despite the incoherence of Finnie's observation, it is a reminder that in some form, psychological terror always accompanied the whip. Finnie elsewhere centered the necessity of racially improving "coolies" to work as much as enslaved African Americans.[45] In such moments, the management and racial development of "coolies" was placed at the center of cotton production in the North-Western Provinces. As a planter, Finnie's own role was to oversee the realization of the productive capacity of racialized labor, just as masters and overseers imagined themselves doing in the slaveholding South.[46]

If Finnie believed he erred in seeking to manage "coolies" as if they were Black, he also repeatedly confronted multilayered agrarian relations within which he was nothing more than a fledgling observer.[47] Finnie's engagements with zamindars, raiyats, and contracted cultivators reveal a wealth of differences between U.S. settler slavery and agrarian relations at Kotra Makrandpur. Finnie hated the landholding zamindars who worked together to subvert his efforts. He resented that he had no control over them and saw them as "tyrannical" in their use of force, caste, and obligation to coerce cultivators—the very tactics Finnie tried and failed to use in his own attempts to introduce cotton cultivation. Finnie's efforts to convince raiyats to cultivate cotton repeatedly failed in the face of everyday forms of resistance. As one raiyat responded to Finnie's attempts to convince him to cultivate cotton, "*Sahib*, we are poor and meager, what Ram does will happen."[48] This response made it clear that Finnie could do nothing, that the U.S. overseer was powerless to get his way. The possibility of peasant choices here emerged through a language of powerlessness that also served to disrupt Finnie's own project.

Finnie clumsily tried to make sense of overlapping caste, land, and revenue relations and to envisage the possibility of transforming them to make cotton cultivation possible. Finnie stated that asami cultivators were "a worse race" than their neighbors and that Thakurs and Brahmins were "the poorest race alive as agriculturalists." For Finnie, instead, "the low-caste . . . if properly taught" would be the "regenerators of India."[49] In this vision, society was fundamentally divided between the planter-as-colonizer and the cultivator-as-colonized-labor. However, in putting forth this vision, Finnie revealed his own incapacity to instantiate such relations.

Finnie also struggled to negotiate new colonial relations around the payment of labor and the work of expropriation. After the first year of planting failed and the second year promised to do the same, a holiday on 11 August

1842 set Finnie up for a failure of a different kind. On that day, he noted that he was expected to give cultivators a customary payment or baksheesh to compensate them for a day's labor, despite not requiring work. In response, Finnie wrote, "They say they will acknowledge no other Chowdry hereafter but me; so I am promoted."[50] Finnie imagined that by giving this baksheesh, he might instill obedience and subvert the authority of the *chaudhari* ("Chowdry"), who was in this case the head of the cultivators, essential to determining the conditions and terms of work.[51] This illusion was soon shattered.

Just a few weeks later in September, Finnie observed that he could not get hoe-hands to work and that laborers were "as independent of me as a newly liberated negro in America, and if I pretend to hurry them they will not now come at all; they are too rich."[52] Finnie responded by attempting to renegotiate the terms of work through a combination of economic, physical, and psychological coercion. He first cut laborers' pay. Against this, cultivators engaged in work stoppages, flight, and soldiering, making the faltering project to introduce cotton cultivation in the North-Western Provinces impossible. Such difficulties caused Finnie to reflect, "The drought, the flood, and the rascality of these free 'niggers,' will cut my operations much shorter than I wished."[53] In racializing cultivators as simultaneously free and Black, Finnie indexed not just the centrality of white supremacy to his project but also his inability to achieve the work of expropriation upon which cotton cultivation rested. In racial assessments such as this, the degrees of dispossession between free and Black and "coolie" also mark Finnie's own failure to exert the forms of control he saw necessary for a functioning plantation.

The crucial differences between the U.S. South and the North-Western Provinces that emerged in daily confrontations revealed that introducing the American system would be impossible. As Finnie wrote, it was becoming increasingly apparent that a disruption was unfolding on his Kotra Makrandpur plantation.[54] Self-assured that the laborers had no cause for real dissatisfaction, Finnie turned to what Frantz Fanon called the settler's "zoological" mode of description, referring to cultivators engaged in a work stoppage for wage increases as "animals": "It is the nature of the animal to grasp, and the more he gets the more he wants."[55] Demanding a raise, laborers refused their pay, confronting Finnie in the evening to "frighten" him into their terms, which he refused. The following night, cultivators insisted that they were entitled to a pay increase and would leave if not given a raise. Finnie attempted to deploy a paternalist rhetoric of mutual dependence and mutual ruin, but cultivators refused to concede.[56] Without labor,

Finnie's plantation-making project would be ruined. In an everyday action, cultivators applied pressure to Finnie when he was at his most vulnerable.

Finnie addressed this insurgency through violence, boxing the ears of the one he believed to be the leader of the work stoppage.[57] From Finnie's perspective, the use of violence "humble[d]" the cultivators and caused those resisting to hold him in an "exalted" position. He justified this through his own understanding of village agrarian relations, writing, "They are so much accustomed to the exercise of arbitrary power among themselves, the high over the low, that, unless it is exercised occasionally, they begin to think they are forgotten and neglected."[58]

While Finnie relied upon physical violence, he also attempted to use economic coercion, withholding pay to ensure that laborers would be available and leave only with his "consent." He then woke one morning to find that all laborers had left his plantation. Finnie sent for them in the village, "but every man, woman and child of the working class had fled to the jungles."[59] When he inquired about the reasons, he was informed that it was because he had slapped a man the day before. Finnie was unconvinced that laborers would directly challenge his use of violence by leaving his plantation, instead writing that laborers wanted a raise and sought to exploit his vulnerability to such pressure: "They have taken advantage of my situation to demand and force me to pay them very high wages; and as my allowance would not justify me in employing a greater number of regular Coolies than I have got, there is no alternative but to give it to them, as they have me completely in their power."[60] Finnie had once imagined that he was in the process of making a Mississippi plantation on the Yamuna; now he was failing, unable to make sense of or transform the agricultural relations he confronted. Finnie's misapprehension of what he thought was a pliant labor force — in this case contracted so-called coolie labor — upended Finnie's pursuit of power.

In response, Finnie and several hired men tried to catch cultivators, bringing roughly twenty back to the fields to work. As Finnie continued, "These poor people have been driven to this by the Chowdree, who lays up and never works any himself, but makes each man of his clan give him part of their earnings every day. I have been under the necessity of letting him feel the weight of my old Egyptian 'Cawbash' [whip] before, for interfering with my business, and when I catch him now, I will venture upon the assertion that he does not interfere with my arrangements again."[61] Finnie again struggled against the chaudhari who was essential to determining the conditions of labor on the plantation. After attacking laborers on his "Mississippi Plantation" without success, he turned toward beating the man whom he had employed to engage them. Despite Finnie's previous recourses to violence, the chaudhari continued to subvert his efforts, revealing again the tenuous nature of Finnie's claims to power.

Difficulties with the work of expropriation saturated Finnie's white supremacist reflections on laborers' idleness. In his journal, Finnie suggested that day laborers would not even work for a few days before beginning to "luxuriate in their usual idleness," causing him to constantly employ new laborers.[62] Finnie drew upon the language of white supremacy, calling colonial cultivators free "niggers" who enjoyed "liberty."[63] By using this language, he described cultivators as the opposite of what he imagined African American enslavement meant. Though the social positions of raiyat, chaudhari, asami, and zamindar within agrarian relations at Kotra Makrandpur were unique, all undercut Finnie's project in different ways to introduce new techniques of cotton cultivation.

Finnie returned to the United States in 1849, his failures mirroring the experience of other overseers in India before him. Though some "improved" cotton staples were introduced by overseers in southwestern India, the project failed to introduce the American system. Overseers proved incapable of disrupting and transforming agrarian relations. John Stuart Mill would later reflect that while the project generally failed, it resulted in a "complete body" of information on cotton cultivation in India.[64] Although the overseers' project shaped the future course of efforts to transform Indian cotton cultivation, Mill made no extended remarks about the political economic lessons to be drawn from the project. Instead, Mill's observations formed part of the more general tendency of British colonialism characterized by the management, control, and organization of detail and information.[65]

"The Modern Theory of Colonization," the final chapter of the first volume of Marx's *Capital*, does not reckon with colonialism in India, nor is it meant to address settler slavery in the United States (though it cannot entirely avoid it).[66] Marx clarifies that he is attempting to deal only with "true colonies" where free immigrants colonized virgin soils—itself a settler myth. He is concerned with these colonies only to the extent that they reveal something about capitalism in the "Old World."[67] According to Marx, Edward Gibbon Wakefield discovered something about that capitalism in the colonies—in particular, that money, machines, and implements of production were not the same as the social relation of capital. In response to the efforts of Thomas Peel to establish capitalism in Western Australia, Marx noted Peel had brought everything to the Swan River Colony except

"English relations of production."[68] As the last paragraph of *Capital* reads, in the political economy of the New World, a secret of the Old World was discovered, that the capitalist mode of production and accumulation rests upon "the expropriation of the worker."[69]

One observer would later recall that Finnie arrived with American plows and hoes and "endeavored to introduce here precisely the same kind of cultivation as that pursued in America."[70] In that sense, Finnie emerges as a corresponding figure to Peel and the colonialisms unconsidered at the end of *Capital*. Finnie's failures serve as a reminder of the foundational and continuing dispossessions and expropriations through which "the worker" existed. Industrial capitalism itself rested upon the dual expropriations of Native land and enslaved African American labor.[71] Finnie participated in a failed effort to reimagine and reroute this history through other expropriations.

Finnie's reflections upon the experience of overseers in India provides a critical vantage for thinking in relation to the expropriations that capital existed through, registering the crucial difference between settler slavery in the U.S. South and colonial projects at Kotra Makrandpur and Agra. In 1854, the prominent white supremacist physician and proslavery theorist Samuel Cartwright wrote that the East India Company was a "true" slaveholder and that this violence lacked the progressive developmental qualities of patriarchal slavery in the United States. According to Cartwright, the U.S. overseers in India "left in disgust not having the inhumanity to make laborers work whose masters failed to furnish them the food and necessary clothing."[72] The purpose of Cartwright's observation was to proclaim the value of white supremacist mutual obligation, that the patriarchal enslavement of African Americans was a noble alternative to East India Company despotism. However, in a response signed "Brahminee Bull," Finnie disputed these characterizations, challenging Cartwright's statement and suggesting that colonial cultivators and enslaved African Americans could not be thought of analogously.[73] The crucial difference between colonialism in India and U.S. slavery was in the colonialism of the Cotton Kingdom itself: "Do we when we take the Indian Territory, take upon ourselves to feed and clothe the Indians?," Finnie asked. In asking, Finnie pointed to the dual expropriations that the slave South existed through and to the "Indian" dispossessions that did not occur in India. Finnie presented his failure in terms of the forms of colonial difference, which made settler slavery in the U.S. South singular. These were expropriations that industrial capitalism existed through, expropriations without equivalence.

PART III : : : **Crisis**

6 : : : **Kindred Distress**
Famine, Commodities, and Convulsion

It seems that the Anglo-Saxon race needs disaster.
—A. C. Brice, *Indian Cotton Supply, the Only Effectual and Permanent Measure for Relief to Lancashire*

The wolf is at the door!
—Dadabhai Naoroji, *Address on the Cotton Supply*, Lancashire (1861)

In an address to English textile workers written between the Indian Rebellion (1857–58) and the American Civil War (1861–65), a spokesperson for Britain's textile manufacturing capitalists argued for the necessity of an Indian cotton supply. Gesturing toward the possibility of capitalist collapse, the author called forth burning cotton mills and warned that there were "sparks among the cotton." John Brown's raid on Harpers Ferry had been an attempt "to fan the flame of negro insurrection from the sparks which lie thickly scattered over the cotton fields of the United States!" Such an insurrection was commensurable to the Indian Rebellion, which the English paid for in "rivers of the blood of our bravest heroes." Because the cotton trade depended for "*five-sevenths* of its employment upon the slave States of America for prosperity," war or "general insurrection" would ruin employers and "*famine* would stalk abroad among the hundreds and thousands of workpeople." This collapse would serve as a lesson for the British Empire for not promoting colonial cotton cultivation grown by the "*free labour of our fellow-men.*"[1]

Such visions of slave revolts destroying capitalism and bringing on famine in England reflected deep anxieties about textile mills' dependence upon U.S. slavery. These anxieties were bound to the perception that the British Empire was incapable of an equivalent system for cotton cultivation. The image of the factory as the apex of social, civilizational, and racial development gave way to anxiety over the fragile foundations and convulsive dynamics upon which the factory rested.[2]

At a gathering of Lancashire factory owners on the eve of the American Civil War, Dadabhai Naoroji, the prominent India reform advocate and later originator of the drain theory of wealth, expanded upon this relationship. Eliding Britain's own history of enslavement, Naoroji foregrounded the moral superiority of imperial abolitionism and argued that dependence upon American slavery weakened an otherwise morally righteous, liberal empire: "Look at the spectacle of men, who emancipated slaves, becoming the slaves to slaves; for what are we more than mere slaves to those very slaves when we depend upon them? A single disease among them, — a single revolution among them, — is enough to strike us all down here as effectually as they themselves and their oppressors."[3] For Naoroji and for factory owners, this was the wolf at the door: the factory's dependence upon African American enslavement exposed capitalism to systemic failure, triggered by the end of Black enslavement in the United States.

While the profits of Manchester's capitalist class largely rested on U.S. slavery, individual textile mill owners rarely invested in alternative sources of cotton production and made little headway in securing a replacement for U.S. slavery before or during the American Civil War.[4] As a class, the Manchester capitalists' most concerted effort to secure a cotton supply amounted to the formation of the Cotton Supply Association in 1857. Yet the encouragements of the Cotton Supply Association notwithstanding, Manchester capitalists rarely invested directly in cotton cultivation. To do so would expose industrial capitalists to the risks of direct competition between British colonial possessions and the slaveholding or post-slavery U.S. South.

Fears surrounding singular dependence upon U.S. slavery became alarmingly real with the outbreak of the American Civil War and the Confederate blockade of southern ports, culminating in the belief that the social disaster within the circuit of textile production was a "Lancashire cotton famine." Structuring this vision of a Lancashire cotton famine was a chain of equivalences between slave labor and raw material costs, between raw material costs and the cost of production, between the cost of production and the necessity of textile workers' labor, and between the workers' labor and the capacity to sustain oneself through food purchased by wages. Disruption at the beginning meant famine at the end. Disruption in the supply of raw materials — the availability of slave-produced cotton — destabilized the entire system and would ultimately destroy the English working class and the English factory owner alike. This collapse was the obverse of the earlier observation that the building of new factories in Lancashire led to an expansion of slavery in the United States.[5] Every destroyed or inaccessible plantation sapped the demand for factory labor in Lancashire and resulted in unemployment and declining profits.

Yet fears of industrial collapse did not reflect the entire social reality or deep structural problems of the textile industry during the 1860s. While the supply and price of cotton affected the cost of production for Manchester industrialists, Manchester capitalists were ultimately dependent upon their ability to realize the value of Manchester goods within domestic, foreign, and colonial markets, especially India.[6] The sale of these goods fundamentally depended upon the displacement of locally produced textiles and goods that enabled the expansion of metropolitan production.[7] After 1843, the primary English exports to India were Manchester goods made from slave-produced cotton from the American South.[8] Lancashire manufacturers received Indian textiles to imitate and produced jaconets and shirtings specifically for Indian markets.[9] By 1859, India formed one-third of the total export market for cotton goods and over one-quarter of the cotton yarns export market. Within India, the North-Western Provinces were regarded as the most significant outlet for Manchester goods.[10] A circuit of global capital began with U.S. slave plantations, continued to Lancashire textile factories, and concluded in the North-Western Provinces. This circuit depended simultaneously upon the differential exploitation of Black labor and factory workers and upon what Irfan Habib has called the "colonization of the Indian economy."[11] The circuit brought together plantations, factories, and bazaars while valorizing capital through colonial consumers.[12] The circuit—and the circulation of Manchester goods in general—did not depend upon the vertical integration of spaces of production but rather upon interlinked, independent arrangements and combinations of production, sales and purchases, and finance.[13] In particular, the export of textiles to colonial markets such as India's North-Western Provinces could often depend upon "adventuring," or the practice of shipping textiles on consignment in the hope that the textiles would eventually be purchased.[14]

The circuit further depended upon the physical movement of cotton from slave plantations to the Mississippi River and then on to ports in New Orleans. From New Orleans this cotton would eventually cross the Atlantic to arrive at Liverpool and then from Liverpool arrive in Manchester, where it would be worked upon in factories and transformed into textiles. From Manchester, textiles would be sold internally in domestic markets or exported to India, China, or Australia or back to the United States. In India, textiles would most frequently arrive in Calcutta to be loaded on bullock carts and shipped down dirt roads to bazaars in cities in the North-Western Provinces such as Kanpur, Faizabad, and Allahabad.

While classical political economy imagined supply and demand equilibrated by an invisible hand, expanded accumulation in the textile industry depended upon interlinked spaces that could be affected by disruption and disaster at any time.[15] In addition to Black freedom (a potential economic disaster even for Manchester industrialists who supported emancipation), textile warehouses could burn down before goods could be sold.[16] Dock strikes at ports could interrupt and delay the circulation process. Ships could be stranded at sea with Manchester goods aboard.[17] Monsoons could make roads impassable. Textiles shipped from Lancashire could be rotten when taken out of packages in the North-Western Provinces—a widespread problem following the outbreak of mildew in 1865.[18] White ants could eat through packaging, and leaky warehouses could cause water to drip onto textiles, destroying them. Hindu and Muslim holidays, a constant source of irritation for English merchants, guaranteed frequent "disruptions" from the perspective of British merchants, factory owners, and colonial officials. Annually, what Marx called the "salto mortale" (the death leap where anything could happen) taken by textiles in their transformation into money was suspended mid-air in the Bengal Presidency, and by extension the North-Western Provinces, for much of October during Durga Puja.[19]

The disasters and failures within the textile industry are what brought together and defined U.S. slavery, the English textile industry, and the North-Western Provinces in the 1860s. Picking up on a long-standing and extensive historiographical debate over the so-called Lancashire cotton famine, the following pages foreground the composite social histories of Manchester goods—the textile commodities produced by workers in Britain's factories—to argue that this crisis was in fact inextricably bound to the social histories of colonial markets in India's North-Western Provinces, and demand that the "Lancashire cotton famine" be understood as also part of a racial and cultural logic of empire.

The Global Crisis

What has come to be called the Lancashire cotton famine has been the subject of numerous historical arguments over the century and a half since the 1860s. Perhaps most prominently, in *Empire of Cotton*, Sven Beckert argued that the so-called Lancashire cotton famine represented the world's first raw materials crisis caused by a shortage of cotton due to the American Civil War. The American Civil War thus gave birth to new networks of labor, capital, and state power in India and elsewhere while marking India's hour of arrival within global capitalism.[20] Cotton kings followed a strengthened state, furthering a "double process of creative destruction," with merchants fully integrating an ever-larger swath of the "global countryside" and transforming the "Indian countryside" in the process.[21]

Such an interpretation is based upon a unidirectional exertion of colonial power and leaves unconsidered the significance of colonial markets within India to the textile industry during the period.[22] Metropolitan manufactures did not supersede the limits of capital. Instead, as Sabyasachi Bhattacharya argued in his important *Financial Foundations of the British Raj*, "the cotton boom [in India] was a temporary phenomenon."[23] After 1865, India lost the British cotton market. From this perspective, rather than creating new, permanent expanded networks of capital, this period instead was based upon the logistics of managing capitalist crises through empire and characterized by the failure to realize the colonial model of empire-based cotton cultivation.[24] The American Civil War established the importance of U.S.-produced cotton to the manufacture and sale of English piece goods in colonial markets.[25] The vision of a completed circuit of capital within the British Empire, which began with cotton produced in colonies and ended with textiles sold in these same colonies, failed not least because of the actions of colonial subjects in India. Yet, the efforts of metropolitan capital to realize an imperial circuit left a trail of wreckage as it cut through abstract principles of price and through crisis displacement techniques, bringing together the colonization of the Indian economy with the travestying of African American freedom.

This is not to deny that the textile industry could also flourish through disaster. The English textile industry profited greatly in the aftermath of the Indian Rebellion.[26] The failure of cotton crops in India following the rebellion and the disruption of domestic manufacture within the North-Western Provinces led to significantly increased demand for Manchester goods.[27] Following the mass destruction and closing of the textile trade that attended the rebellion, the textile industry boomed. The value of imports from 1858 to 1860 was the value of imports from the previous two-year period between 1855 to 1857.[28]

In 1859, the Bengal Chamber of Commerce warned that this increase in demand was temporary and that in 1860 the prices would be "as much below the average of late years as they have lately been above it."[29] Such views of cyclical crisis did little to prepare for the disruption ahead. At an 1860 meeting of the Manchester Chamber of Commerce, the textile factory owner and capitalist Henry Ashworth noted that the textile industry enjoyed unequalled prosperity in business due to free trade policy, prosperity that the Manchester capitalist Edmund Potter noted was directly related to the sale of textiles in India and China.[30] Ashworth remarked that the textile industry's extraordinary increase could not continue. The expansion of the trade would sooner or later produce a "natural" crisis.

The limits to capital and plummeting demand proved far greater than what either the Manchester or Bengal chamber of commerce could have anticipated or what the language of natural crisis suggested. A severe famine in the North-Western Provinces broke out in 1860 and extended into 1861, marking or exacerbating the bursting of the bubble of the Calcutta trade in Manchester goods and contributing to a lingering recession with reverberations through the 1860s. The famine, the product of rapid local increase in grain prices following the destruction of agricultural land during the rebellion as well as rainfall and crop failure, disproportionately impacted weavers, who were especially vulnerable because of the encroachment of Manchester goods in the North-Western Provinces following the Indian Rebellion. With the outbreak of the cotton crisis following the famine, weavers in the North-Western Provinces continued to be severely affected by the depression in the textile trade, resulting in migration to Mauritius and Guiana through the "coolie trade" for some. While weavers and other textile workers in Lancashire were impacted by a decreased demand for textiles in the North-Western Provinces and by the increased high price of cotton, metropolitan factory workers and colonial handloom weavers were differentially exposed to global economic disaster.

When global crisis within industrial capitalism, centered on the textile industry, assumed the name the "Lancashire cotton famine," this name focused attention upon the suffering of English weavers while foreclosing consideration of the broader imperial impact of the crisis. In conceiving of this crisis as a cotton famine, a colonial problem—famine—seemed to travel home to metropolitan society while assuming a form unique to the conditions of industrial capitalism. Decreased demand for labor within the textile industry combined with the outbreak of the American Civil War to create a belief that English textile workers suffered from cotton famine.[31] In England, cotton, as the basis for industry, became equivalent to food in the colonies, and the absence of cotton created circumstances for starvation and death. Through this, as explored below, the conditions of those affected by famine in the North-Western Provinces and of Manchester workers hit by capitalist crises were rendered equivalent, with famine relief funds redistributed from the former to the latter. This occurred just as the redirection of flows of cotton away from the North-Western Provinces and toward Lancashire severely impacted weavers in the North-Western Provinces.

When the language of cotton famine tied the scarcity of cotton to suffering and fixed this suffering spatially in Lancashire and structurally in relation to the English working class, it made the global crisis's particular bearing upon weavers in India unthinkable. During the famine in the North-Western Provinces and throughout the crisis in the textile industry, handloom weavers in India were disproportionately affected by both increased textile prices and the redirected flows of cotton. By 1864, not only had cotton that once flowed north from the Central Provinces ceased to flow in that direction, but cotton produced within the North-Western Provinces itself flowed south to ports for export.[32]

If the economic crisis was determined by the inability to sell textiles rather than by a raw materials crisis alone, the logistical crisis in cotton supply brought about by the American Civil War seemed to create conditions of possibility for the remaking of the cotton supply chain around the colonies within the British Empire. From the perspectives of many manufacturers, abolitionists, and even Naoroji, empire offered a means of bringing multiple, imperial locations and actors together through free trade and for mutual benefit. During the Civil War, cotton exports from Bombay increased significantly. This increase provided cotton to Manchester's textile industry in crisis where production had become stagnant.[33] Lancashire's textile industry depended upon Indian cotton staples such as Dharwad, Dhollerah, Hinganghat, and Oomra to meet decreased demand within the textile industry and also to be re-exported. This cotton was shipped from India's interior and sent from Bombay and Bengal.[34] Western India's Dharwad and Central India's Hinganghat became seen as two promising staples for Manchester industry during this period.

Yet Indian cotton and American cotton were not interchangeable. Because of their shorter staple and perceived "dirty" quality in comparison with cotton from the American South, in Lancashire and throughout England all varieties of Indian cotton often became referred to simply as Surat.[35] Surat cottons were hated by English textile workers, who sang songs about the poor quality of Surats and blamed these varieties for their suffering and sickness.[36] In vernacular English, Surat came to mean "muck" or anything adulterated or of inferior quality: "*Surats*, in Lancashire, has become a term indicative of everything bad, from beer to theology."[37] As the pro-Union English *Spectator* reported, " 'Surat' is not the cotton they [English mill workers] like and in whatever quantity it may come, they will still regret their shipments from the South [India], but brown bread is far better than starvation."[38] In Lancashire, a story of a Methodist spinner was sometimes told after the crisis. The spinner interrupted prayers for cotton, crying out, "But not Surat, O Lord!"[39]

Through organizations such as the Manchester Cotton Supply Association and the Manchester Chamber of Commerce, Manchester's textile factory-owning capitalists pressured the government of India to invest in infrastructure for the exportation of cotton. They hoped to transform "waste lands" in the North-Western Provinces into areas of expanded European settlement to oversee the cultivation of cotton.[40] The Lancashire industrialists' most concerted effort involved an initiative by the Manchester Cotton Supply Association to facilitate the development of infrastructure for cotton cultivation through the construction of a port at Sedashegar (near the major cotton-producing region of Dharwad). This project was conducted through collaboration between the colonial government and the Manchester Cotton Company (formed by members of the Cotton Supply Association). The project failed. The port was never built, and before the Civil War's end, the company ceased operating in India.[41] Efforts to refashion the global cotton supply chain within the British Empire with India at its center collided with a dramatic limit.

For all of the structural changes and advocacy before, during, and after the crisis, the capitalists of Lancashire continued to withhold direct investment in the cultivation of cotton in India or in other British colonies. Rather than seeking vertical integration through direct investment in cotton cultivation, Manchester industrialists invested in the abstract operation of price. In the process, mill owners sought to distribute the risk of falling prices to cotton cultivators themselves.

At times, cultivators resisted this burden. In a letter to the liberal Stockport member of parliament John Benjamin Smith in December 1863, Rochdale textile factory owner John Bright wrote, "I think importation of East India Cotton especially hazardous—for nobody will want it if American is to be had at any price. It is adulterated beyond all former example, and the loss is ruinous and workpeople will not have it at any wages when the mills are generally at work, with American cotton to be had."[42] In 1870, the Anglo-Indian historian Charles Crosthwaite captured the logic behind this resistance, writing that such investments would mean that direct investment in cotton production would mean Britain "would then have to share the risk. . . . No doubt, as a matter of immediate self-interest, Manchester is right. It is far better to throw the risk of any fall in price on the producer of the raw material, so far as may be."[43] Cutting against such efforts to "throw the risk" upon colonial producers, officials in both India's North-Western Provinces and Berar complained that economic incentives were often insufficient to encourage expanded cotton cultivation. Even increased prices did nothing to insulate producers from fluctuations in crop yield that could result in famine.[44]

Around the world, the Britain-dominated textile industry displaced risk through colonial crisis management techniques—this meant that when the crisis arrived, it would be widespread. In India, risk was shifted toward cultivators in cotton-producing regions such as Berar and Dharwad, toward Bombay merchants, and toward weavers, who depended upon Indian-produced cotton shipped to Manchester at increased prices. Instead of massive increases in cultivation, Bombay merchants responded by exporting cotton hitherto consumed within India. During the Civil War, they profited greatly.[45] After the war, the bubble burst. As one observer later reflected, at the end of the Civil War, "merchants, banks, and financial companies toppled over in a mass of hopeless wreckage."[46] The impact of this distribution of risk following the war can be seen in the dramatic fluctuation of colonial commodity prices.[47] In Cuba, a commercial crisis flared up after the United States resumed exports of cotton and tobacco. In Egypt, the collapse of cotton prices in 1867 caused a "terminal wound" for Egyptian finances.[48] In West Africa, the American Civil War brought first a cotton boom followed by a cotton bust.[49]

The liberal belief in the smooth, permanent supersession of cheap, free labor in India against the expense of slavery in the United States was tempered by failures in cultivating long-staple, foreign cotton to replace the cotton produced in the United States. As J. Talboys Wheeler concluded in his *Madras versus America*, "India will never produce a reliable and permanent crop of Cotton equal to the New Orleans variety"—the cotton staple that formed the foundation of the Manchester trade.[50] While the southern United States did not immediately produce cotton at the war's conclusion, a radical reworking of race and coercion led to cotton once again becoming foundational to the southern economy, and to the southern economy in turn resuming its foundational role in the British textile industry. By 1870, it had become increasingly clear to factory owners and metropolitan observers that the United States would assume the role of the world's primary cotton producer, with English industry as its major consumer and colonial markets such as India the continued outlet for England's textiles.

While some observers called this state of affairs "suicidal," individual manufacturing interests in England regarded investment in cotton cultivation outside of the American South as the truly suicidal option. Dependence upon the sale of Manchester goods in India and competition with Indian weavers caused Manchester's capitalists to express concern over the competitive advantage India's handloom industry would gain over Manchester mills if cotton were widely cultivated in India, given high carriage costs. If cotton of a superior cotton variety were cultivated in India, what would prevent consumers in regions such as the North-Western Provinces from simply purchasing Indian manufacture instead? The status quo was preferable—English factory-owning capitalists thrived and failed through simultaneous and differentiated access to a global division of labor within capitalism depending upon both U.S. slavery and colonial markets. The drive of U.S. slaveholders for the accumulation of capital through settler slavery had lowered metropolitan production costs and reduced the cost of metropolitan labor power.[51]

Famine and the Colonial Lives of Commodities

If, as C. L. R. James noted, the mid-twentieth-century United States enabled the grandiose manifestation of the commodity devouring the world, where "all peoples are entangled in the net of the world market," the nineteenth-century economy dominated by the British Empire exposed the world to that possibility.[52] While the vision was always for commodity relations to resemble the smooth ordering of the warp and the weft, the reality was often a tangled skein. The Manchester good, in its variety and dullness, was the exemplary commodity for mediating desires and aspirations of industrial capitalism. Plain white, cream, or gray, perhaps in the form of a jaconet, sometimes with a piece of silver thread, the Manchester good as textile obscured the relations of catastrophe, empire, and terror that it existed through. The Manchester good could be thread itself to be sold and turned into fabric. As thread or plain textile, the Manchester good was a creeping form of encroachment within the global economy, everywhere and often unnoticed.

In 1861, the Bengal Chamber of Commerce provided a brief history of the previous decade of Manchester goods in the North-Western Provinces. For the chamber of commerce, selling Manchester goods in Upper India was the most significant concern for Lancashire and for Calcutta. From 1850 to 1860, this trade had developed "on a scale of remarkable magnitude," giving Manchester goods access to India's "immense consuming population" and causing English manufacturing to be "fully employed." This "progress," of selling textiles in the North-Western Provinces, continued uninterrupted until the Indian Rebellion. Following the rebellion, the textile industry "revived with unparalleled activity" until "a desolating famine in the populous districts of Hindostan paralysed the ordinary commerce of the country."[53] The Bengal Chamber of Commerce's history identified four distinct phases in the 1850s: (1) increase until the Indian Rebellion, (2) disruption caused by the rebellion, (3) renewed increase, and (4) disruption caused by famine in the North-Western Provinces. The economic, social, and cultural significance of these phases is worth dwelling upon, especially regarding the famine's larger implications.

The Indian Rebellion was central to the creation of a bubble in the export of Manchester goods to India. Focal points of revolt in the North-Western Provinces—Fatehgarh, Kanpur, Agra, and Delhi—were centers for the sale of Manchester goods. Nearly half of the Manchester goods shipped to Calcutta were sent to the North-Western Provinces. In 1857–58, textile imports decreased greatly because of the rebellion. However, in 1859–60, imports reached an unprecedented volume. This bubble was partially the result of the destruction of textiles, as possibly £750,000 worth of textile goods were destroyed during the rebellion, according to one estimate. In Kanpur, nearly all warehouses were destroyed and goods were stored outside.[54] In Mirzapur, for example, Old Company's Mark Grey Shirting rose 33 percent, from six rupees to nine rupees after the rebellion. Through the destruction of so much capital in the form of accumulated commodities, the rebellion led to the increase in the value of Manchester goods and also to the increase in exportation and sale in the North-Western Provinces.[55]

Colonel Richard Baird Smith, a central figure in the suppression of the Indian Rebellion, was sent to the North-Western Provinces in 1860 to inquire into the declining demand for Manchester goods. During the rebellion, as Baird Smith wrote, the destruction of Manchester goods was widespread:

> The largest marts for cotton goods were the centres of the mutiny, and very little of what was in transit escaped destruction. At the close of the mutiny, the stocks in the North-West were therefore exceedingly low, not merely from the interruption of the regular supply, but from actual destruction: hence prices rose very high, trade between Calcutta and the North-West was stimulated, and a great demand continued till the merchants in the North-West were again supplied with the large stocks which they are accustomed to hold.[56]

This destruction of capital presented English manufacturers a unique opportunity to expand value through the production of more textiles to replace what was lost. An economic boom lasting for two years ensued.

At the same time, social crisis set limits on the realization of capital in these colonial markets. Though grain was also likely destroyed during the rebellion, it did not follow the same trajectory as Manchester goods.[57] While the destruction of textiles led to increased demand and an increase in textile production for the benefit of Manchester industry, the suppression of the rebellion led to agricultural displacement and the destruction of agricultural land. This was followed by two years of deficient rainfall and a monsoon failure in 1860, creating conditions for social catastrophe — a rapid increase in grain prices.[58]

In 1860, Bholanauth Chunder, a Bengali member of the Royal Asiatic Society, traveled throughout the North-Western Provinces to observe the impact of the rebellion, visiting Benares, Allahabad, Kanpur, Agra, Mathura, and Vrindavan. Chunder published accounts of his travels in the Calcutta-based *Saturday Evening Englishman*. In early September, on the road between Kannauj and Mainpuri, Chunder noticed signs of oncoming famine. Long trains of oxen along with camels and donkeys, sometimes fifty or sixty together, carried grain along the beaten-down road. Travelers could hear the ringing of bells tied to bullock necks, moving in a line of traffic extending half a mile:

> There was a meaning in the portentous hot haste to transport grain from one district to another. The annual rain-fall has failed, and there has not fallen a drop in the last forty days. The drought has parched up the earth. The fields have got embrowned. The wells have fallen sixty to seventy feet deep. The crop on the ground has lost the green of its verdure. The price of food-staples has risen nearly fifty per cent and the prognostications of an inevitable famine are in everybody's mouth. Hence the *Brinjarees* are taking care to provide against the day of need and distress, by housing and laying in stores of corn.[59]

Along the way, Chunder observed a woman from Delhi whose husband had died during the rebellion. She was traveling from the city to meet with a distant relative and had been begging along the way. After seeing her, Chunder reflected, "How many such there are, whom the recent mutiny has made homeless and penniless! And how many more such there will shortly be, whom the famine shall make restless vagrants in search of food they cannot find!"[60] Chunder's observation highlighted local preparations for famine in September 1860. Yet shortly afterward, the lieutenant governor of the North-Western Provinces claimed that measures for relief would not be necessary.[61]

Severe famine accompanied the continuing increase in grain prices in the North-Western Provinces, Punjab, and Rajputana through October 1861.[62] Displacement and death were widespread, most dramatically affecting an area corresponding with the territory of the 1857 rebellion.[63] An editorial in the *Bombay Times* suggested, "We are probably below rather than above the mark—if we make the sum total of dead, or suffering, two millions of people."[64] Estimates suggested that mortalities were over 200,000 with some as high as 500,000.[65] In Ballabhgarh, Delhi District, roughly 4 percent of the population had died of starvation by the end of January 1861.[66] Large numbers of migrants moved in search of famine relief works organized by the government, which resulted in exposure to extreme climate and other hardships.[67] Survivors were hobbled not only by malnutrition but also by the psychological trauma of witnessing famine's effects.[68] The famine rendered humans surplus within the North-Western Provinces and contributed to emigration within the "coolie trade"—in 1860 over 30,000 migrated to Guiana, Mauritius, and elsewhere.[69]

Songs about the famine, also known as the *Sattrah Akal*, declared that in some districts the famine was more severe than the famine of *Chalisa* (1783–84)—during this famine one-third of villages in the Delhi territory had been abandoned and remained so forty years later.[70] In parts of western Rohilkhand and Meerut, the pits of mangoes were turned to for food, and their price increased drastically.[71]

Statistics, which the British obsessed over, transformed famine into a matter of numbers, which it both was and was more than. A popular poem and a song about the famine convey differing social perspectives on how class, community, and caste confronted the famine.

Parte Kal Jullahe Mare (poem):

Parte Kal Jullahe mare
aur bich men mare Teli,
Utarte kal Baniye mare;
rupiye ki rahgai dheli
Channa chironji ho gaya,
aur gehun ho gae dakh
Sattrah bhi aisa para Chalisa ka bap

In the beginning weavers died
and in the middle Oil Makers died,
Last Baniyas [merchants] died;
the value of the rupee decreased
Channa sold at the price of chironji,
and wheat sold at the price of dakh [raisin]
The *Sattrah* famine was the father of the *Chalisa*

Bodi Bhagar ki Laliya Bol (song):

Bodi bhagar ki laliya (lagakar) bol,
Baniyon ne kar diya mahunga mol
Tut gae takri phat gae bat,
Ji gae Baniya, mar gae Jat;
Tut gai gadhi, mar gae bail;
Be muklawa ho gae gail.

The traders collected old and bad grain,
And sold it for an enormous price
The beam of their scales broke and their weights were worn away
    from constant use,
The trader lived and the Jat died;
The carts were broken and the oxen died;
Brides went with husbands without *muklawa* [gifts exchanged
    to family][72]

Together, the poem and song segments reveal the uneven impact of the famine. The poem places the *Sattrah* famine within the historical chronology of great famines, declaring this one to be more severe than the famine of Chalisa.[73] The song further puts the class dynamics of death in motion according to caste and occupation—*jullahas*, Muslim handloom weavers, die first, *telis* next, and *baniyas* last. The song captures the collapsing value of the rupee and the increasing price of grain. While the value of the rupee decreases, dal and wheat assume the rarity of delicacies.

The song foregrounds merchant profiteering from grains with even bad grains selling at high rates. The scales' weights wear away from constant use, further increasing the price of grain. Merchants live and cultivators die. The famine affects traditional wedding practices within which the bride was given to live with the husband's family without *muklawa*—a marriage exchange during which the husband's family gave gifts of money to the bride's family as she went to the husband's family's house. During the famine, these practices were disrupted.

In noting that *jullahas* died first, the song highlights these weavers' position within the global supply chain. Their exposure was directly related to the proliferation of Manchester goods within colonial markets in the North-Western Provinces at that time.[74] This was inextricably bound to the colonization of the Indian economy, during which Indian weavers became an externality as global exports destroyed the worldwide market for Indian textiles and Lancashire textiles invaded India's bazaars.[75]

A similar dynamic can be seen in the history of several cities. In Azamgarh District in 1836, 4,000 looms were in operation in a district where only the wealthiest residents wore clothing of English manufacture. By the time of the famine, the majority of people in the district wore English cloth.[76] Weavers' condition and suffering was offered as a justification for the revolt itself. As Firoz Shah noted in his Azamgarh proclamation, "The introduction of English articles into India, have thrown the weavers, cottondressers, the carpenters, the blacksmiths, and the shoemakers, &c., out of employ and have engrossed their occupations, so that every description of native artisan has been reduced to beggary."[77]

The dire situation of handloom weavers before the revolt became exacerbated during the famine. Weavers were now exposed to the violence of the abstract operational logic of capital tied to the realization of the value of Manchester goods and became, along with agriculturalists, the most common residents of relief projects. According to Baird Smith, "So completely dead is their trade for the moment, that I have heard of cases of their wandering about with supplies of their handiwork, offering it in exchange for a meal for their women and children, though its value under ordinary circumstances would be tenfold what they were content to take for it."[78] But the damage was not only borne by the weavers—the colonization of the Indian economy made it possible for a colonial social crisis to catalyze a metropolitan economic crisis as well.

While the famine was a matter of life or death for the weavers in the North-Western Provinces, for the Manchester textile industry the decreased demand brought about by the famine resulted in the bursting of a bubble, exacerbating the overaccumulation of capital and precipitating a crisis in the textile industry. In the final months of 1860, possibly as little as one-half of the ordinary quantity of Manchester goods was consumed in the North-Western Provinces. The famine resulted in the partial closing of the "most important outlet for British manufacturers" and an accumulation of stock in the hands of importers who were unable to sell goods despite a 10 to 25 percent decrease in nominal price.[79]

The textile industry's difficulties in selling Manchester goods were directly connected to the purchasing trends of "people fleeing from starvation," as Baird Smith noted. He continued to note that local merchant interest shifted to grain speculation, which had become more profitable than the importation of Manchester goods: "It is to the state of things thus described however; to the complete absorption for the time being of all available capital, and all available means of transport in the local grain trade, and to the wide area over which the spirit of speculation in grain spread that I am disposed to attribute that sudden check in the imports of Manchester goods from Calcutta which had arrested attention some months prior to this inquiry being set on foot."[80] In Alwar, the famine gained the name *ath sera* because grain reached the extraordinarily high price of one rupee per eight *seers*. The profitability of grain exceeded the profitability of the textile trade.[81]

The shifting profitability of textiles, grain, and cotton constituted a knot differentially entangling Manchester workers and colonial subjects in the North-Western Provinces. As Thomas Metcalf has noted, India was not just a laboratory for the experimentation of liberalism but also a place where these principles were made.[82] For colonial officials and Manchester Men, the answer to disaster within free trade, which disrupted what should have been self-regulating market mechanisms, was continuing adherence to the belief in technology and the economy to reorder the world.[83] According to Baird Smith and many Manchester capitalists, the "free spread" of Manchester goods depended upon communications — the infrastructure for the movement of people and things — as did the prevention of famine. English cloth was sold along the best roads and rivers, and the interest of Manchester was "direct and personal" in the condition of Indian roads and rivers.[84] The years 1860 to 1880 marked a period characterized by the rapid extension of communications networks within India.[85] According to Baird Smith, Manchester goods in the bazaars of the North-Western Provinces would reach agricultural and "poorer" nonagricultural classes who had not become customers of Manchester goods only if infrastructural projects were properly pursued. In practice, this infrastructure facilitated the export of textiles from England and grain from India.[86]

For British industrialists, the experience of the 1860–61 famine would become a key justification for establishing principles of free trade. These would support both valences of colonial capitalism through the opening of the Indian market, the development of raw materials, and the demand for a permanent land settlement.[87] For Baird Smith, exaggerated land revenue contributed to the famine in the North-Western Provinces, and famine relief entailed the temporary reduction of land revenue. The future, fixed, and permanent settlement of land revenue would safeguard against future famines by encouraging economic progress and development. From a utilitarian perspective, land revenue would intensify the cultivation of land without increasing the price of colonial commodities such as cotton, sugar, silk, and tobacco.[88] Baird Smith argued that the development of transportation infrastructure through railroads would alleviate famine by enabling the movement of grains from districts in the Central Provinces and enable a system where "pressure" in any one district could be alleviated by the swift flow of produce from another, which "guarantees against the evil effects of future Droughts."[89] According to Baird Smith, the "free circulation of Trade" would eliminate high famine food prices brought about by regional droughts.[90] Yet the history of the late Victorian period, characterized by a series of colonial famines, demonstrated the exact opposite.

The absence of overseas capital investment in infrastructural improvement caused the effects of such development to exacerbate rather than ameliorate such conditions. Railroads increased grain prices and decreased availability while enabling exports to countries in Europe that could purchase grains at higher prices.[91] The permanent settlement of the land revenue and improvements in transportation through roads and railways were primary goals through which merchants sought to transform the subcontinent into a site for the export of raw materials, especially cotton. Arguments for the permanent settlement of land revenue and the development of transportation in India were strongly made by members of the Manchester Chamber of Commerce and the Cotton Supply Association.[92]

Yet, often massive colonial infrastructure projects failed to realize their intended results. As W. Balston wrote of the famine in the North-Western Provinces, "Even when we hear of half a million of people starved to death through the misconstruction of a canal, and another half million reduced to pauperism by the want of cotton, which Indian canals, if properly constructed would have provided in abundance—even when these disasters become notorious, nobody cares to inquire what has been done with the many millions of money which have been spent ostensibly for the purpose of preventing famine, and promoting the cultivation of the soil."[93]

In 1871, Dadabhai Naoroji would draw upon the example of the famine in the North-Western Provinces to reflect on the violence of the colonial economy: "Now, what better proof can you have than that when in the year 1861, while British India exported to the United Kingdom alone, at the distance of thousands of miles, more than 3,000,000 cwt. of rice . . . the North West Provinces lost a quarter of a million of lives and immense property by famine."[94] While respondents would note that Naoroji's response collapsed distant spaces of rice cultivation, it is nevertheless the case that ending the famine by flooding the market with grain or rice was an option but was never pursued. The economy thrived through the ideological pursuit of free markets that ran through rather than against death from starvation and enslavement.

Kindred Distress

An' th' Indians are helpin' an' o;
Aw reckon they're grateful for th' past,
So they'll give us a bit of a lift,
For helpin' them eawt when they'rn fast.
—Samuel Laycock, "God Bless 'Em, It Shows They'n Some Thowt"

The famine in the North-Western Provinces had a broad social impact that disrupted the textile trade, becoming entangled with the American Civil War and the emerging discourse about the suffering that English factory workers endured as result of the famine's impact on metropolitan industrial capitalism. The crisis in the Lancashire textile industry came to be known as a "kindred distress" to the famine, and in time the crisis in the Lancashire textile industry simply became the "Lancashire cotton famine."

This rendering of the textile crisis as kindred to colonial famine reveals affinities between dissimilar social processes. As Mikhail Bakhtin has observed, when words are selected and deployed, they are not taken from language in dictionary form but are chosen from other utterances that are "kindred" in genre theme, composition, or style.[95] Through this kinship, famine relief collected to support colonial subjects in the North-Western Provinces was redirected toward workers in Lancashire's textile industry. In the process, colonial death through starvation and economic crisis in metropolitan Britain became somehow commensurate.

The differences between metropolitan and colonial subjects were made and reinforced through this commensurability. Within the unacknowledged knot of industrial capitalism in which the factory is dominant, the condition of food scarcity experienced by colonial subjects in the North-Western Provinces emerged as an analogy for the condition of the Lancashire working class. A closer focus on this structural and ideological bind, along with its origins, highlights a host of colonial, racial, and economic fault lines that divided and organized metropolitan and colonial subjects. This same form of division was also bound to the circumstances of Black emancipation in the United States.

In the wake of the Indian Rebellion, India was increasingly seen as incapable of meeting liberal visions of the world, if it was even worthy of such visions at all. While the dialect of Lancashire's working class was viewed as a significant cultural object offering England a living connection to Anglo-Saxon racial heritage, after the Indian Rebellion Britons increasingly used the slur "nigger" against colonial subjects in India as they had done and continued to do against Black people.[96] Such global racial alignments formed the preconditions through which famine in the North-Western Provinces and unemployment in Lancashire industry could be imagined as kindred. The racialized devaluation of colonial subjects' lives made famine and unemployment comparable. This emergence of famine analogies to describe the experience of the English working class has been lost amid the complex contours of race and colonialism that emerged after the Indian Rebellion and alongside the Civil War and Black emancipation.

The 1860s marked a point of rupture within global formations of race, class, and capital. Dominant renderings of this era have often followed Marx, who suggested that within the cotton crisis Manchester workers rallied in support of the northern United States, signaling the English working class's arrival as a rising social and moral force. The U.S. Civil War spurred English workingmen to demand the vote and enfranchisement again.[97] However, that very demand further forced the divide between citizen and subject, especially following the Morant Bay Rebellion (1865) in Jamaica. Nearly 200 accused Black subjects were executed following the uprising in a period of brutal colonial repression. English male enfranchisement following the Indian Rebellion and Morant Bay marked the difference between colonial and metropolitan workers and subjects.[98]

During the Lancashire crisis, manufacturers and social reformers lauded the moral superiority of the English working class, praising workers for not rising up and for waiting for better days. While workers and factory owners often supported the Confederacy and its white supremacy in particular, others supported Black emancipation in the United States— a stance whose racial and class implications beg to be untangled. If crisis in the textile industry did not emerge directly from the Civil War and the rerouting of cotton imports, African American emancipation created conditions for imagining shared miseries between English workers and factory owners who suffered together for liberal principles. As Henry Ashworth and Murray Gladstone of the Manchester Chamber of Commerce wrote to William Gladstone, "The deplorable struggle in which the two sections of the great American republic are now engaged has fallen like a blight upon the industry of our manufacturing districts. . . . Nevertheless, the noble attitude of patient endurance assumed by our operatives cannot be too highly eulogised."[99] In some retellings, factory owners and Lancashire workers imagined themselves as suffering together for liberal principles of African American freedom. As factory inspector Alexander Redgrave reported in 1861, "I am informed that there is now the best feeling between manufacturers and operatives, for the latter are convinced that the momentous question of the supply of cotton justifies whatever has been done by the former."[100] In his *Principles of Political Economy*, John Stuart Mill made the case that the proliferation of newspapers made possible a working-class enlightenment that had a positive impact upon the consciousness of workers: "During the cotton crisis, in the case of the Lancashire spinners and weavers, [they] have acted with the consistent good sense and forbearance so justly applauded, simply because, being readers of newspapers, they understood the causes of the calamity which had befallen them, and knew that it was in no way imputable either to their employers or to the Government."[101] As Mill declared, Civil War caused the calamity in the textile industry and workers acknowledged that this calamity was beyond the control of either factory owners or government.[102]

In some moments, English textile workers challenged this prevailing interpretation of their relationship to African American enslavement and the question of cotton supply. As Janet Toole has written, the Weavers' Committee worked to produce statistics and arguments to demonstrate that overproduction was the primary source of crisis and the American Civil War a pretext.[103] At times, south Lancashire "plebian radicals" combined antislavery with antagonism to liberal economics.[104] Workers disrupted the status quo in riots in Stalybridge, Dukinfield, Ashton, and Hyde. Fears of riots throughout Lancashire proliferated among the English elite.[105] Yet, overt expressions of anti-capitalism often blurred with defenses of slavery.[106]

The interlinkages between English workers and the cotton crisis assumed a variety of transnational dimensions. English workers' suffering was addressed through international organizations such as the American International Relief Committee, which sent grain to Lancashire and reminded English workers of homesteading opportunities following the passage of the Homestead Act in 1862.[107] Other organizations like the American Emigrant Company of New York City recruited Lancashire factory workers to work in the New England textile industry.[108] In 1862, an American antislavery advocate spoke to the Lancashire Relief Fund about the origins and history of the American Civil War, praising workers for starving rather than accepting the justness of American slavery: "All honor to those noble fellows who would rather starve than by any word or deed of theirs recognize a vile confederacy, based upon the eternal bondage of millions of their fellow-men."[109] Abraham Lincoln's 19 January 1863 letter of address to the workingmen of Manchester praised England's workers for their "sublime Christian heroism," noting that their dedication provided "re-inspiring assurance of the inherent power of truth, and of the universal

This flour barrel was filled with flour sent to support unemployed factory workers in Lancashire. The barrel reads: "I am one of the thousands that were filled with flour, and sent by the Free States of America, in the ship George Griswold, to the starving people of Lancashire, whose miseries were caused by the aggressive and civil war of the slave-owners in 1862-3-4." (Touchstone Rochdale)

In this cartoon about the Lancashire cotton famine, Britannia banishes starvation by collecting private charity for mill workers unemployed due to the blockade of southern ports during the American Civil War. (John Tenniel cartoon from *Punch*, London, 1862)

Richard Ansdell, *The Hunted Slaves* (1861). This painting of an enslaved woman and man escaping slavery in the Great Dismal Swamp of North Carolina was purchased by the Liverpool banker Gilbert W. Moss, with all proceeds going to the Lancashire Famine Relief Fund to support unemployed Lancashire factory workers. Earlier, in January 1836, the Moss family received over £40,000 in compensation for claims made on 805 enslaved people.

triumph of justice, humanity, and freedom."[110] In February 1863, Abraham Lincoln sent 15,000 barrels of flour to Liverpool to be distributed among factory workers.[111]

This spirit of charity for the Lancashire workers connected metropolitan Britain to settler colonization in Australia. In Queensland, Australia, unemployed Lancashire workers were given land to settle and cultivate cotton upon, a project that brought over 2,000 laborers to the colony and imagined a white circuit of capital that, from cotton to textile mill, was meant to draw upon only Anglo-Saxon labor on colonized land.

The structure and experience of relief in Lancashire was also tied to the administration of famine relief and its aftermath in North India and the North-Western Provinces. The 1860–61 famine in the North-Western Provinces marked the first time the colonial state was directly involved in the organization of famine relief.[112] By January 1861, famine relief projects were directed by a central relief committee established at Agra, with other local regional aid committees emerging in other cities including Lahore. Richard Baird Smith estimated that half a million people received benefit from relief houses, works, and public projects out of a total of between 1.25 and 1.5 million afflicted by the famine.[113]

Paradoxically, relief was pursued in relation to dedication to laissez-faire principles. While a contemporary observer argued that relief should take the form of "pouring grain from the abundant into the starving districts," the colonial state did not intervene to control prices or financially encourage the importation of grains.[114] Famine relief was instead guided by the project to inculcate rational work discipline in sufferers and prevent theft or remuneration without work.[115] When a project on the Ajmer Road in Rajputana began, colonial officials observed that it was difficult to induce people to work because food was being "gratuitously distributed" from the local relief kitchen. However, the numbers increased steadily until the conclusion of relief because "the more able-bodied were denied relief except in payment for labor."[116]

In England, the relationship between labor and relief was modified to support English workers. Relief through the poor laws ordinarily entailed a labor test to confirm the recipient's ability or inability to work, which was modified in the case of the "distressed famine operatives." Stockport, Lancashire, workers met with J. B. Smith to discuss and complain about the labor test.[117] Eventually, the labor test was modified or suspended in manufacturing districts such as Preston, Stockport, and Blackburn. Further, the forms of labor required from those who performed the labor tests were modified to include public works, moving away from stone-breaking and oakum-picking as previously required.[118] Ultimately, nearly 25 percent of Lancashire received public assistance, and additional relief was shifted toward educational projects to instruct unemployed factory workers.[119]

At the center of these transformations was an argument for the dignity of the working class against the degradation that textile workers experienced at the hands of unemployment and certain forms of manual labor. For one observing reverend, the dignity of the English working class made the Lancashire distress different from colonial famine: "The Irish famine has been more than once contrasted with this distress; but extreme as it undoubtedly was, it was altogether without that element of painful sensitiveness which so affectingly aggravates the present calamity."[120] This painful sensitiveness the reverend alluded to amounted to the dignified comportment of the English worker who did not want to accept charity or to be considered poor. Colonial subjects, begging for relief, lacked this dignity.

These approaches to relief marked a sharp break with earlier principles of relief as had been pursued throughout the North-Western Provinces,

Punjab, and Rajputana. "The Rules for the Relief of the Helpless" in 1860–61 established a set of eleven principles for relief. According to the rules, no "able-bodied" person capable of carrying a "basket of earth" was to receive relief without labor: "All such will be sent off to a laboring gang."[121] Those deemed helpless could apply for a once-daily ration of cooked food.[122] Sub-committees responsible for the administration of relief were to be composed of "a respectable member of the Native community" alongside a "trustworthy officer of government."[123] Relief houses were the major venue for prominent members of society in the North-Western Provinces to provide aid. Sayyid Ahmed Khan, founder of the Aligarh movement, facilitated the operation of a prominent famine relief house in Moradabad.[124] Local relief works distributed food for labor instead of wages because it was feared that those in need of relief would not travel to larger public relief works farther away from cities or village homes. As one official explained, "No native who could obtain an *anna* and a half a day within easy reach of his own door, would go to a distance for a like or even for a larger wage were that allowable and the acceptance of cooked food was moreover a fair test of distress, which it was necessary to maintain on general grounds, no less than on the particular grounds adverted to."[125] In response to such colonial anxiety, John Strachey devised the practice of supplying cooked food for relief to those confined in workhouses in order to place a "check" on "professional mendicants."[126] At relief works, it was believed that the daily wage should be kept at the lowest rate possible—"the object being to save the people from starvation, not to attract those who could obtain employment elsewhere."[127] Attention to work discipline and fraud emphasized supervision and often made administering relief impossible.

Relief recipients were divided into two categories: first the helpless, and then the able-bodied poor whose relief depended on a labor test and the performance of work for relief. The helpless poor included women, children, and orphans deemed unfit for outdoor labor. The able-bodied poor also included women and children but only those who could work.[128] Labor was to be concentrated as much as possible "to make supervision easy and economical."[129] The largest relief projects included work at the Bulandshahr branch of the Ganges Canal, where 14,258 workers were employed for famine relief on one day in July; at a special works in Agra, where 13,567 were employed; and at Mohan Pass, where between 18,000 to 26,000 people labored to build a stone causeway connecting Mussoorie and Landour to the plains.[130] Relief work projects often facilitated the improvement of communications for commerce and corresponded with Mill's expressions on the necessity of such state projects to remove all barriers to the expansion of the economy.[131]

Prevailing ideas about the proper, natural operation of the economy clashed with the provision of relief, which inherently violated this natural operation.[132] The opinion of Lord Canning, who served as both lieutenant governor of the North-Western Provinces and governor general, was summarized by the secretary of the government of India: "The object of the Govt. is to prevent people from starving, to alleviate distress, and it is impossible to believe that, if people are really starving, and unable to get employment elsewhere, they will refuse to receive a wage which will provide them with subsistence. It is essential, this Honor thinks, that the rate of wages should be kept as low as possible that it should not be higher than what will enable the people to buy food sufficient to sustain life, and strength to labour."[133]

Delhi maintained three major famine asylums: at Eidgah, near Delhi Gate, and at Qudsia Bagh. The largest was the Eidgah project, where 6,000–8,000 would receive one meal of chapati and dal daily. Those receiving aid had a ticket bound to their wrists to ensure that none would receive food twice. This food was given only after it was determined that they could not perform work. At Delhi Gate, the famine asylum had been made from the poorhouse, which had long existed there, and approximately 3,000 or 4,000 would gather there.

Robert Montgomery traveled to all three asylums in February 1861 and found the situation most dire at Qudsia Bagh, destroyed by the English during the rebellion. Many of those receiving aid were on the verge of death. Approximately 800 attended the Qudsia Bagh relief works during Montgomery's visit. He reported that those who received food were famished to such a degree that many died from the mere effort at eating. Disturbing as this was, "the hideous and repulsive aspect of these cases is utterly lost in the unbounded sympathy felt, as well as the request that more cannot be done, to arrest the scythe of the destroyer." Montgomery reflected upon the compassion that the assistant of the treasury, Mr. De Gruythers, showed in organizing relief:

Many hundred imploring beings owe their lives to the humane and disinterested exertions of one who had to flee from the infuriated mob at the first mutiny, and for weeks suffered every privation and misery with his family in the jungles. Is there any sense of shame or gratitude among the Asiatics? Will the spectacle of returning good for evil in this, and many other instances, on the part of the British community, and a Government though only a few years after a city, and district were doomed to retributive justice and confiscation for the greatest crimes, coming forward with sympathy and aid in the cause of common humanity, fail to rescue its inhabitants from misery?[134]

In his invocation of "the cause of common humanity," Montgomery crystallized the racial divide that separated colonial subjects from English citizens. This appeal to common humanity indicted colonial subjects for their failure to reciprocate or demonstrate the humanity that the English had demonstrated so fully. The inability of colonial subjects to meet the liberal designs of the British Empire and industrial capitalism meant that their relief projects required severe supervision. This vision also amplified visions of English Christian charity as selfless in the face of perceived Native depravity.

Funding for relief works was raised by a series of famine relief organizations operating in India and Britain, such as the London Famine Relief Committee, which donated £30,000. Money from London came from a variety of sources, including an unappropriated balance from the Huddersfield Mutiny Fund.[135] In May 1861, Liverpool had contributed Rs 50,000 and Edinburgh Rs 17,100.[136] Dublin and Manchester sent direct and government-contributed money equivalent to donations raised within India but not those from England or elsewhere abroad.[137]

The mayor of London and head of the London Famine Relief Committee, William Cubitt, explained the principles of imperial charity:

> The present crisis has done much to create an interest here in Indian affairs, and it will certainly prove, that having in the providence of God, been called upon to conduct the Government of that Country, we are not indifferent to the well-being of the people, and I cannot keep thinking, that this fact, will contrast favorably with the conduct of previous Rulers, will lead to a consolidation of our power, and thus not only reconcile India to our control, but cause our improvement in the religious aspect of that Country, and by an Extension of the Christian religion, conduce to the eternal happiness of the people.[138]

Donations were meant, as Cubitt noted in a letter to Lord Canning, to make "known to our fellow subjects in India that Her Majesty, and the Royal Family, the Nobility, Merchants and entire population of the United Kingdom deeply sympathise with them on the present deplorable occasion." Cubitt further hoped that such donations represented the "ties which unite India to this Country."[139] Liverpool's mayor, S. R. Graves, noted that donations were disproportionate to the magnitude of the famine while also firmly believing that the "free will offering" of Liverpool would be appreciated by "the suffering natives" and also "lead them to trust more earnestly henceforth to the generous principles which always actuate the people of England towards their fellow subjects."[140] These views formed part of an emerging imperial humanitarianism that enabled power over life through a system of exchange that attempted to recognize an equivalence between colonial rule and famine relief, between Native trust and colonialism — exchanges fundamental to colonial rule after the rebellion.

By mid-July the most severe impacts of the famine in the North-Western Provinces had waned. After five months, famine relief concluded in the middle of 1861.[141] The total amount of relief contributed was generously estimated at Rs 13,68,363.[142] Rs 3,85,286 remained in the hands of the Agra Committee after relief projects concluded. Such a large remaining surplus despite widespread suffering gestures toward the frugality that limited the aid's administration.[143]

Soon enough, debates erupted within the colonial government and among donors on potential uses for the surplus. Some proposed that remaining funds be used to provide seed and plows to districts in the North-Western Provinces. Grain was given as charity, and it was to be decided by district officers whether cattle would necessitate repayment.[144] Others argued the money should be capitalized in order that principal and interest would be available for future famine relief. Others argued that an orphanage should be created for children who had lost their parents.[145] D. McLeod, commissioner for the Punjab Famine Relief Fund, wrote that a portion of the remaining balance should be donated for a famine memorial hospital and poorhouse in Delhi.[146] The commissioner further proposed that half a lakh be given to support 100 orphans. The remaining balance could be invested in a permanent famine memorial fund. The government of the Punjab agreed that a support fund for Indian orphans could be established but should not exceed Rs 10,000. Further, it was proposed that surplus funds be invested in government securities to establish a permanent famine fund because by this the objects of the original contribution would be fulfilled.[147] Indeed, such an investment in a permanent relief fund was seen as desirable by the lieutenant governor, who proposed that "the whole should be invested as a Permanent Relief Fund for the Population of India."[148]

"Famine orphans" — children whose parents had died during the famine — received assistance from missionary organizations, though the extent of future support was unsettled. George Couper, secretary to the government of the North-Western Provinces, wrote about the colonial policy of extracting labor from starving children, stating that even children as young as seven who were "capable of carrying a basket of earth" should be forced to work to receive relief. Those young people older than twelve who did not work should not be allowed to receive any relief from "surplus" famine funds, according to the government of India.[149]

The course of the surplus famine funds remained undecided by the time the crisis in the Lancashire textile industry broke out. The crisis disrupted the manufacturing districts of Lancashire, Cheshire, Derbyshire, and Yorkshire. In 1860, approximately 440,000 persons were employed in cotton factories.[150] By late October 1862, 208,621 people within the district were receiving relief aid from the crisis, an increase of nearly 400 percent from the previous year.[151] During the crisis, 60 percent of spindles and 58 percent of looms ceased operations. The remaining 40 percent were used for only part of the week. Some 50,000 cotton workers were supported by the Poor Law, and 135,625 people were employed at what Friedrich Engels called "starvation wages" on public works and in sewing schools.[152]

In 1863, surplus famine relief funds were redirected to distressed sufferers in Lancashire. The language facilitating the fund transfer emphasized commensurability between cotton famine as experienced by Lancashire workers and famine in the North-Western Provinces. On 2 January 1863, William A. Rose, mayor of London, wrote a letter of appreciation to the governor general of India acknowledging that all surplus funds from the Indian Famine Relief Fund would be redirected for "the relief of our suffering fellow-subjects in Lancashire."[153]

In Alwar, part of Rajputana, an area also affected by the famine of 1860 and a site of major relief operations, funds were also awarded to weavers in Lancashire who were "suffering the greatest distress." A *kharita*, or official letter, issued by the Shivdan Singh Raja Rao, the official ruler of Alwar who was only twelve at the time, revealed the ways in which the language of shared suffering marked differences. The letter stated:

> Seeing that the British Govt. and nation always take a lively interest in the happiness and prosperity of the people of India, for they evinced their sympathy with the Indian sufferers from the last famine by most munificent and liberal donations for their relief, it is now time for us to respond to such liberal gifts of charity. I have learnt from the newspapers that the weavers in Lancashire of England are suffering the greatest distress, and that money contributed by the people of India for their succor is being remitted for their relief. I feel much for the poor suf-

ferers, and wish to aid them; and therefore earnestly desire that you will be so good as to sanction the expenditure of Rs. 15,000 for this charitable purpose, and to remit the amount to the Relief Fund Committee at Calcutta. I trust your good will towards me will not allow you to deny me this pleasure.[154]

When the Bengal Chamber of Commerce declared that funds from Indian famine relief should be applied to relieve "kindred distress in the mother country," the chamber elaborated on this connection:

> But a short time since a part of the people of India, through no fault of their own, were suffering the deepest distress from a deficient supply of food: England came to their aid and gave generously and largely; so largely that much more was given than required, and a large sum remains undistributed: now in their turn, and equally through no fault of their own, a part of the people of England are deprived of that work which has hitherto enabled them to buy to buy food; the Lancashire operatives are suffering distress which they are supporting with the noblest courage and fortitude.[155]

This language tied famine in the North-Western Provinces to crisis in the textile industry, positing commensurability. In the process, colonial death and working-class unemployment came to be rendered as kindred distresses.

Lancashire's workers did not starve, even during the most extreme stages of the crisis in late 1862 and early 1863. Instead, they spent savings, sold furniture and clothing, and purchased meats less often.[156] As *Cookery for the Lancashire Operatives* noted, ingredients beyond workers' present means were to be omitted "until better times."[157] Daniel Noble's "Fluctuations in the Death Rate," given before the Manchester Statistical Association in 1863, presented an overview of the impact that cotton famine had upon the Lancashire working class.[158] Noble stated that some had argued that there had been a reduction in the death rate because mothers were better able to attend to their children and the working classes drank less. Others suggested that there had been a diminution in working-class deaths because of less cotton fiber in the air, which in turn diminished bronchitis and lowered mortality rates. From Noble's own perspective, no "actual physical destitution" occurred during the crisis.[159] Instead the main impact of the famine upon health could be located in increased anxiety in the upper classes and a reduction of comfort and luxuries for the working class.

While the famine in the North-Western Provinces and the crisis in Lancashire were rendered equivalent, the process of relief and the ideologies of labor upon which it rested remained fundamentally different. In the North-Western Provinces, famine relief was implemented in relation to the disciplining of subjects and directed toward the inculcation of labor discipline. In Lancashire, such principles of relief defined by the Poor Law were modified or suspended.

The establishment of kindred relation between famine in the North-Western Provinces and cotton famine in Lancashire enabled famine relief support for colonial subjects in the North-Western Provinces to be redirected toward workers in Lancashire's textile industry. However, this redirection was about much more than the movement of money from India to Lancashire alone. It was instead part of a much deeper set of colonial and racial relations whereby colonial death through starvation and economic crisis in metropolitan Britain could be seen as commensurate. Through this commensurability, the differences between metropolitan and colonial subjects in the experience of disaster were made and reinforced. Without access to U.S. slavery–produced commodities, Lancashire's workers suffered from famine equivalent to death from starvation in colonial India.

7 ::: U.S. Slavery's Colonial Obligations

> The failure of India has allowed a deep cloud of misery
> to settle down on the cotton manufacturing districts of England.
> —*Friend of India* (1862)

In the midst of ongoing global economic crisis, British capitalists, workers, and colonial bureaucrats together placed a series of imperial obligations onto the future of colonial India. At the heart of these obligations was the expectation that India would produce cotton that surpassed the quantity and quality of U.S. slavery–produced cotton.[1] During this period of crisis, metropolitan Britain assessed colonial India based upon understandings of U.S. slavery and fastened new obligations onto their colony in relation. When metropolitan Britain came to believe that colonial India did not meet its imperial obligation to surpass U.S. slavery, India's weavers, merchants, and peasants were judged as failures who required further imperial intervention—discipline and domination—while the burden of ongoing capitalist crisis was further displaced from Britain and imposed onto the subcontinent.

This chapter documents how U.S. slavery created expectations for British colonial projects to transform cotton production and exchange across colonial India. It further considers the impact that the increased exportation of Surat cottons from western India to Lancashire had upon weavers in the North-Western Provinces still recovering from the impact of famine. Weavers struggled in the face of both increased cotton prices and market competition from Manchester goods. At the same time, as Surat cottons entered Britain's factories, workers complained bitterly about their quality. Together, British manufacturers, merchants, and workers, created a colonial obligation for India to become Britain's cotton field based upon their dependence on U.S. slavery.

At Least 4 Million

In 1862, the secretary of the Manchester Cotton Company, G. R. Haywood, put forth a vision of the supersession of American slavery by cotton cultivation in India.[2] Haywood presented the possibility for Indian production overwhelming, or at the very least matching, the productivity of the slave-holding United States: "Out of 180 millions of population, at least four millions—equal to the population of the American Slave States—could certainly be found for the cultivation of cotton."[3] This perspective overlayed the 4 million people enslaved in the United States onto colonial India and suggested that it would be possible to extort from the 180 million people living in India at least an equivalent amount of work. For Haywood, industrial capitalist production depended upon carving out an American South in India—different, but nonetheless equivalent. With all of what colonial officials imagined as surplus people and wasteland, India was obligated to meet these expectations.

In the guise of the newly formed Manchester Cotton Company, Manchester industrialists mounted a sustained effort to directly extract colonial cotton from India. Through collaboration with the Indian government, the company sought to transform the logistic space of cotton in India by building roads into the cotton-producing region of Dharwad and through building a port at Sedashegar. While the company directed most of its efforts toward India, it also sought to systematically settle white factory workers in Queensland, Australia, for the cultivation of cotton.

The U.S. colonization of the American South was part of a relentless settler colonial project that seized Indigenous land and infrastructure while depending upon the internal slave trade to systematically relocate enslaved people toward the plantation-based production of export commodities, particularly cotton. The seizure of land and enslaved people was central to the economic revitalization of both U.S. slavery and the propulsion of Britain's textile industry. British imperial officials drew inspiration from this relationship as they imagined colonial projects across the British Empire. Abolitionists also participated centrally in this project of imagination. In 1862, George Thompson, the longtime abolitionist and India reform advocate, encapsulated a world-making vision of antislavery free trade imperialism. Thompson suggested that while the British Empire was "to a certain extent" responsible for slavery in the United States, an empire-based cotton supply drawn from Queensland, western Africa, and Jamaica, along with the "vast plains of India," could remake the circuits of cotton supply through mechanisms of price, restating a vision of the project that he had been working toward since 1840. Through this imperial field, the British Empire would "be able to read the planter of the Southern States a lesson of political economy in the price currents of the day." This lesson would thwart the slave trade and undercut U.S. slavery. Thompson continued: "If a new era was inaugurated in America, English manufacturers would not get from free labour the amount of cotton hitherto produced by slavery; because that could only be done by robbery, cruelty, and the gradual extermination of a race of human beings."[4] For Thompson and many factory owners, an imperial textile circuit began with a colonial cotton supply—produced under a malleable definition of freedom—to undercut slave-produced cotton. In such readings, colonial "free" labor became more efficient than slave labor, even though the violence of U.S. slavery was singularly efficient in producing cotton in the American South. This amounted to a revision of the abolitionist position on the exploitability of colonial labor, drawing lessons from past failures to cultivate cotton in colonial India and recognizing the distance between abolitionism and the logics of industrial capital. If the coercion of formerly enslaved people could not match the economic output of the slavery-based cotton plantation, the colonial transformation of India became even more pressing in order to make up the difference and support metropolitan demand. Imperial circuits subordinated to the operation of price would open up new fields to stabilize industrial capitalism against singular dependence upon U.S. slavery.

Those interested in creating an imperial circuit of textile production dependent upon a colonial-based cotton supply spent little time reflecting upon the possible side effects for colonies identified for cotton cultivation. The complex agricultural visions of colonial cultivators were considered aberrant to liberal capitalism. The abolitionist argument for a world structured by cotton price currents against slavery did little to reflect upon the social damage that the price currents would continue to hide—as they hid in making U.S. settler slavery's cotton the cheapest and highest quality in global markets.[5] For manufacturers, increased cotton supply coupled with decreased prices would lower textile production costs. Increased cotton supplies from many markets governed by price would also rearrange risk, displacing crises in cotton supply toward cotton cultivators rather than toward manufacturers.[6] Thompson simultaneously claimed that price would undercut slavery and that the U.S. South would not return to produce quantities of cotton if slavery were abolished.

Yet such claims did not address the reverse possibility of the violence of the price current. If the U.S. South resumed cotton cultivation, cotton-producing colonies would face economic ruin while manufacturers would benefit from any collapse in raw material prices. Similarly, if a single colony outpaced cultivation elsewhere, those in pursuit of cotton monoculture would feel the greatest impact, while metropolitan capital would be insulated from risk. Manchester could benefit from the expansion of cotton cultivation and attendant reductions in price. However, if demand for cotton decreased in Manchester, this impact would be felt in cotton-producing colonies with smallholding cultivators left with unwanted cotton and no capacity to purchase grain. From this perspective, cotton cultivation on an expanded scale was a project to rearrange disaster and displace crisis.[7]

The potential disruptive impact of this reconfiguration of risk for cotton cultivation in India could be seen in W. Nassau Lees's *Tea Cultivation, Cotton and Other Agricultural Experiments in India* (1863). The study described differential exposures to risk between Indian cotton cultivators and English mill owners. According to Lees, the Civil War threatened the "annihilation" of English textile workers because England's colonies had not sufficiently supplied the Manchester textile industry with cotton. As Lees continued,

> Speculating on peace, England has denied India even the guarantee that she will take what is grown at a *fair* price; and the result has been quite in accordance with those sound principles of Economic Science which *ordinarily* regulate the laws of production and consumption. Manchester and Lancashire have been loud in their demands on the Home and Indian Governments to encourage the cultivation of Cotton,—nay even to compel the Indian *ryot* to undertake it. But Manchester and Lancashire, having reserved to themselves the right of buying in the cheapest and best markets of the world that may be open *at the moment*, have no just ground of complaint against India, or any other country that refuses to grow any staple for which circumstances may have created a *spasmodic* demand—that prefers certain to uncertain profits.[8]

This spasmodic demand was exactly what stoked cotton manufacturers' reluctance to invest directly in cotton cultivation. In 1863, the "bearing" of the market—speculating on a fall in cotton prices—reached an unprecedented level.[9]

Though Manchester manufacturers generally did not invest directly in cotton cultivation, organizations such as the Manchester Cotton Supply Association offered a platform for some manufacturers to work to encourage the extension of cotton cultivation throughout and beyond the British Empire, seeking to reorganize the "logistic space" of the textile industry and improve the quality of cotton.[10] Despite this, during the American Civil War, these efforts rarely materialized in improved cotton staples or permanent alternative cotton supplies. While English manufacturers compulsively stated the necessity of securing cotton from multiple sources, especially from within the British Empire, this recognition was often not met by action. This led to complaints that Manchester "said a great deal, but did little" to invest in alternative sources of cotton.[11] This itself reflected structural realities where economic liberalization instrumentalized the functional linkage between U.S. settler slavery and the British imperial economy, militating against the potential profitability of such investment.

Singular dependence upon cotton from the United States exposed Manchester manufacturers to seasonal fluctuations and variations that promised little certainty over the availability of cotton from year to year.[12] Individually, Manchester's capitalists rarely invested directly in cotton cultivation outside of the United States. Direct investment in alternative cotton supplies would have exposed individual capitalists to fluctuations within the market and placed manufacturers in direct competition with the American South. Even as capitalists as a class exposed themselves to the possibility of systemic failure, Manchester's capitalists collectively did not exert their full powers to secure alternative sources of cotton before African American emancipation. Even so, Manchester textile factory owners engaged in sporadic efforts to create logistic space for cotton supply, bringing British colonies and the U.S. South into a singular field of cotton supply. In the process, manufacturers and companies like the Manchester Cotton Company drew lessons from what they saw as Anglo-Saxon conquest through U.S. slavery as an indication of their own failures to profit through colonial rule in India.

In the face of disrupted supplies of U.S. slavery–produced cotton, members of the Manchester Chamber of Commerce griped that the Indian government had done too little. In his 28 February 1861 resolution on the "Supply of Indian Cotton to England," Lord Canning stated that the government would neither act as private capitalist, cultivator, or speculator nor interfere with private enterprise.[13] Canning further stated that government had already directed all possible energy toward the internal improvement of roads, railways, and canals. Not even the disruption in access to U.S. slavery–produced cotton could transform the British Raj's involvement in the expansive transformation of India toward the export of cotton cultivation. While the Indian government would consider transforming land tenure to encourage direct European capital investment in India's cotton districts, this investment and its results would not provide relief right away. Manufacturers insistently demanded that the empire work for them, and this meant matching or surpassing U.S. slavery.

Instead, Canning stated, to immediately increase cotton supply to England, the state would proliferate information about greater demand. The colonial state would further work toward improving the means for bringing cotton to ports, and central government would encourage local governments to examine the conditions of roads and fix these roads to whatever degree possible.[14] The textile manufacturer and chairman of the Manchester Cotton Company Thomas Bazley noted that roads and rivers should be developed first, and the railroad could then be developed to facilitate the expansion of internal trade in India, as it had in the United States.[15] Within such a vision for India, infrastructure was meant to connect cotton-producing regions such as Dharwad with waterways, railroads, and roadways linked to harbors to transform the logistical space of cotton within India. Plans during 1860–61 to repair and improve interior communication lines to facilitate the exportation of the following season's cotton were paired with plans of construction so that this infrastructure might be prepared for the following cotton season.[16] Such projects, however, fell short of their goal.

The effort toward the reconfiguration of colonial space that manufacturers struggled to realize during the period would depend upon drawing on dynamics that made the U.S. South hitherto singular in the cultivation of cotton through settler slavery. In India, infrastructure would enable the free flow of cotton, extending access to colonial labor imagined as "cheap" and to colonial textile consumers imagined as "bare" and "limitless." Rivers, steamboats, and railroads traversing colonized land made the exploitation of enslaved people's work possible in the slaveholding U.S. South. As W. E. B. Du Bois wrote, "The giant forces of water and of steam were harnessed to do the world's work, and the Black workers of America bent at the bottom of a growing pyramid of commerce and industry."[17] While the United States was connected by a vast network of rivers, roads, and rails traversed by carts, steamboats, and trains that moved cotton to ports, from the perspective of British manufacturers, India lacked such infrastructure—a limit to the smooth export of cotton and import of textiles. Colonial conquest in the United States gave slave-owning planters undisrupted claims to cotton-producing territory along the Mississippi River following Chickasaw removal in 1832, especially significant because cotton in the U.S. South was overwhelmingly transported by water.[18] In contrast, one English observer noted, "The States have their Mississippi and magnificent rivers; our Indus and Ganges avail us little in the matter of cotton supply."[19]

Britain's manufacturers signed and circulated the petition "Where is Cotton to Come from to Keep the Mills At Work" and again imposed comparison with U.S. slavery to demand that India absorb the burden of colonial cotton cultivation by meeting or surpassing U.S. slavery–produced cotton. The petition claimed that "Anglo-Saxon energy, skill and intelligence have directed the slave labour of the American Cotton States, while from India Anglo-Saxon enterprise has been almost excluded."[20] The petition further noted that slave-owning cotton planters enjoyed freehold land tenure while Indian cotton growers were compelled to farm upon leases and that, because the United States afforded security to capital, the U.S. South was connected through land- and water-based transport infrastructure. The interior of India lacked comparable securities and infrastructure for the rapid movement of commodities, and therefore cotton was less readily available for export. At the same time, this "Anglo-Saxon energy, skill, and intelligence" would have to assume a different form because of the colonial differences between the U.S. South and India. As the prominent factory owner Henry Ashworth stated, "We cannot populate the country out of a race such as we belong to."[21] While the manufacturers did not as yet intend to systematically settle India for white colonization to expand cotton production, they demanded that colonial India meet their demands for vast supplies of cheap, quality cotton.

The Manchester Cotton Company was central in the plan to transform the logistic space of India for direct trade between British capitalists and cotton growers in western India. The company first met in September 1860, when it was recommended that nine-tenths of its energy be put toward India and one-tenth toward Australia.[22] The company was chaired by Bazley who would also direct his attention toward the colonization of Australia. G. R. Haywood served as secretary and special commissioner of the company to India. In July 1861, Haywood left England for Egypt and India. In Egypt, Haywood met with Egypt's viceroy Sa'id Pasha where a boom in cotton prices would result in many peasant farmers shifting to cotton cultivation only to be followed by devastating credit crisis in 1865 at the end of the American Civil War. Haywood would next travel to Bombay and then on to Sedashegar with cotton commissioner G. F. Forbes.[23] Haywood investigated the practice of cotton growing in Dharwad while also examining Bombay's cotton trade.[24]

At Sedashegar, Haywood reported on the harbor while seeking to arrange for the purchase the highest quality cotton, which he was to export to Liverpool. Central to the Manchester Cotton Company's project was access to what they imagined as cheap peasant labor in Dharwad. As the Manchester Cotton Company stated in its instructions to Haywood, "Nearly £10,000,000 sterling is therefore being annually paid to rivet faster the chains upon the American slave, while the ryot of India can grow cotton for us more cheaply and in freedom."[25] As Haywood noted, the company did not intend to grow cotton but to manage its growth because "the natives knew sufficiently well how to grow cotton; all they required was European direction."[26] Rather than engage in direct cultivation, the Manchester Cotton Company sought to engage with peasant farmers as a buyer, presser, and exporter to "supersede that system of infinitesimal sub-agencies which is the present curse of Indian cultivation."[27] Essential to gaining access to peasant farmer–produced cotton was the establishment of infrastructure such as railroads to facilitate the uninterrupted movement of cotton from Dharwad to England. This initiative, coupled with the restructuring of relations of buying and selling, would reform and regenerate colonial India, transforming its economic basis to raw material exports to meet the demands of metropolitan society.

Collaboration between the colonial state and manufacturing interests never approached the extent that Manchester's capitalists dreamed of. If anything, attempts at collaboration revealed the impossibility of realizing their grand vision. In one notable example, the colonial state and the Manchester Cotton Company worked together in an attempt to build a harbor at Sedashegar that would be connected to Dharwad, the significant cotton cultivating region in the southern Maratha Territory of the Bombay Presidency. The current system of cotton necessitated moving it over 200 miles from Dharwad to Bombay, where the sale was controlled by both Indian and English merchants. This harbor would have significantly reduced that distance.[28] However, English cotton traders based in Bombay would soon raise questions about the role of the colonial state in such a project suggesting that it violated principles of free trade.[29]

While Manchester placed new imperial obligations for India to look more like the United States in its infrastructure for cotton export, the Manchester Cotton Company failed to realize its vision to build a harbor at Sedashegar to facilitate the direct purchase of cotton from peasant farmers.[30] As Manchester merchants envisioned a system where purchasers would work directly with producers toward the cultivation of cotton regulated by global price currents, their proposed revolution of logistic space would include not only plantations in the U.S. South connected to the Mississippi River but also the cotton-producing region of Dharwad connected by new roads to the harbor at Sedashegar, Queensland, Australia, as well as beyond. In India, the company sought to establish six cotton presses that could press one bale of Dharwad cotton per minute to facilitate the rapid export of cotton purchased from cultivators. But this effort to produce logistic space founded on direct connection between peasant producers and British capitalists utilizing the infrastructure built by the colonial state was not to be. The project to purchase and export cotton through its agents persistently confronted limits and on 18 August 1864, the Manchester Cotton Company dissolved.[31]

The vision of revolutionized logistical space put forth by Manchester capitalists failed to facilitate the transformation of the colony into a "field" capable of harnessing "cheap" peasant work to produce cotton that surpassed U.S. slavery. Despite this, throughout the U.S. Civil War, India supplied England's manufacturers with significant quantities of cotton—though the opinion of metropolitan Britain regarding the quality of this cotton was another story.

The Business of Quality

As the Manchester Cotton Company compared the geography of colonial India to the geography of U.S. slavery, cotton traders seeking to increase cotton exports from India sought to explain differences in cotton staple quality through discourse about regimes of racial and colonial domination, constantly comparing enslaved people in the United States and peasant cultivators in colonial India. These comparisons most often passed through a discourse about cotton quality. Criticism of the quality of cotton exported from colonial India provided another basis for placing future obligations upon colonial India to occupy the place of U.S. slavery within global capitalism. British discourse about cotton quality set again an imagination of the positive dimensions of racial slavery for producing cotton and sought to match these dynamics through colonialism in India.

Cotton destined for Britain's textile factories was generally sent from Dharwad and the Central Provinces to Bombay. British traders and manufacturers saw the cotton that arrived in Britain as damaged and adulterated. According to cotton commissioner G. F. Forbes, "The whole business of a merchant is to buy in the cheapest and sell in the dearest market. And if he believes that taking price into consideration, he will reap a higher profit from the purchase of adulterated saw-ginned cotton than he will from the finest Broach cotton, he will purchase the adulterated in preference to the pure article."[32] The belief that Indian traders adulterated cotton to take advantage of English brokers and merchants was contrasted with their belief in the effectiveness of U.S. slavery in producing pure, white cotton to meet the demands of Britain's textile industry.

The liberal Liverpool cotton broker and textile factory owner Samuel Smith traveled in India in 1862–63 to explore the capacity of the subcontinent "as a cotton-field" to match the United States.[33] Smith had just earlier traveled to the United States, beginning in 1860, where he observed the on-going confederate blockade-running trade that continued to connect New Orleans to Liverpool during the American Civil War. He then resolved to travel to India to observe how cotton production and exportation from India might take the place of the United States. His reflections on India's cotton trade set expectations for colonial India based upon his observations of slavery.[34]

For Smith, turning India into Britain's new cotton field relied upon a practice of looking and assessment honed through his earlier examinations of U.S. slavery's processes including the "great emporium" of New Orleans, where he spent two months "studying the cotton business."[35] Smith arrived in Bombay in the midst of a boom in cotton trading that provided the city's merchants led by Premchand Roychand and Jamsetjee Jeejeebhoy with an unprecedented expansion of capital accumulation. However, Smith looked toward how to make this trading work to the advantage of Britain's cotton traders and manufacturers, in part by undercutting their profits.

Smith looked on and described this trade not in terms of its tremendous if unstable growth but rather as defined by poor cotton quality, a perspective informed by his study of U.S. slavery. Slaveholding cotton planters sold ginned cotton to factors and provided slaveholders with both credit and commercial goods.[36] In colonial India, English merchants purchased cotton for export from Indian merchants by purchasing cotton already cultivated and in markets or by contracting with traders for future delivery.[37] This trade depended especially upon colonial networks with Bombay's merchants who were essential to the export trade. When cotton arrived in markets from Dharwad and the Central Provinces, purchasing agents from English merchant houses would send an English buyer ("selector") to the "green," a large open yard where cotton was held and traded upon its arrival. A sample would be drawn from a parcel on the green and presented to the buyer. Often, on the first day, this buyer would reject everything and return the following day. The same process would be repeated. The English house, through the selector, would threaten the dealer with a legal notice if the contract was not fulfilled. After this, the merchant house would receive a promise from the dealer, who would state that he was expecting additional cotton from the interior in the next few days with a new parcel arriving of quality that was still unacceptable from the perspective of the selector. Smith continued to describe this negotiation noting that in the back-and-forth exchange the selector would grow "wearied and disgusted" from the amount of "inferior" quality cotton that Indian brokers sought to sell him. In this process of trade, English buyers found it impossible to get the quality they demanded and would often accept cotton at a lower quality and higher rate than what was expected.[38]

The contempt that English traders had for Bombay trading practices was attended by a belief that, from the perspective of selectors and merchant houses, the larger the quantity of cotton purchased, the greater reduced its quality would be. The fact that white businessmen had to work and contend with Indian merchants, brokers, and laborers exacerbated their racial anxieties about control and quality. These fears extended to the everyday operation of the green itself, where, Smith commented, "The coolies, who sample and mark the cotton on 'the green,' cannot be trusted beyond arm's length."[39] The contempt that Smith evinced for cotton trading in Bombay stood in direct contrast to his perspectives on cotton trading in the United States, where trade between white men, bound together by Anglo-Saxon blood, represented a tremendous advantage over the realities of trade in India.

In the United States, slaveholders dominated the process of production and exchange, much to Smith's admiration. For English merchants, this dominance propelled U.S. slavery's cotton regime forward and sustained its quality for the benefit of Britain's capitalists, something Smith saw as absent in the export of cotton from India which was dependent upon Bombay's merchants and western Indian peasant cotton growers.

Smith's gaze toward improved cotton quality extended beyond the green and looked toward slaveholders' plantation management and used this management to contrast with cotton cultivation in colonial India. He saw the great productive advantage that U.S. slavery had over colonial India, where he saw peasant cotton growers as "slovenly":

> The picking [in India] is chiefly done by old women and children who gather a few apronfulls in a day, probably not more than one-sixth or one-tenth of what a well trained negro would do in America.
>
> Indeed it cannot be conceived by Europeans who have not visited the country how feeble and wasteful the labour of India is; though the cotton production is not half that of America, it is probable that four or five times as many persons are engaged in manipulating it.
>
> When these facts are borne in mind, the fallacy will be apparent of judging of India by arithmetical data, and looking for any abrupt and enormous development of the cotton trade.[40]

Smith's expectations for colonial India were informed by a belief that the abstract operation of price alone could not fundamentally transform the production and exchange of cotton in the way that Britain's capitalists demanded. Such beliefs saw that price mechanisms could not break the racially unchangeable "laziness" of peasant cotton growers, especially those who worked beyond direct white control or supervision.

Without direct oversight or the establishment of a U.S. slavery–style plantation system or a system that matched the colonial export triumphs of indigo and tea cultivation, colonial officials and British cotton traders looked on aghast at the inability of the mechanism of price to compel small-holding peasant producers to grow cotton for export. In reality, single-commodity production dependency was antithetical to preparations for famine which often depended upon the distribution of risk beyond any single crop. Yet, in the face of this, British merchants increasingly demanded that new mechanisms of coercion be introduced to make Indian peasant producers *feel* Britain's demands. As G. H. M. Batten complained of the North-Western Provinces,

> And herein lies the difficulty of persuading the people to extend their Cotton sowings. Accustomed to great and constant fluctuation in the market rates, they have learned by immemorial experience not to regard the rate which prevails at the time of sowing as any index of what it will be when the harvest is gathered. The home demand exercises but a vague and inappreciable influence upon the crops. It has long ceased to be felt directly by the people.[41]

By 1863, such indifference or resistance to cotton cultivation caused an observer to note that belief in the capacity of India had been dampened by the previous two years — "the stimulus of high price has been freely applied, but India has failed to respond effectually."[42] In an unsigned letter from Bombay written on the Indian cotton trade, its author argued,

> The ryot will not neglect the raising of food for the sake of cotton, however high its price may be, for in so doing he runs the risk of starvation. . . . During the famine in the North-West Provinces two years ago, half a million of people are said to have died from starvation, while in most of India the crops were not deficient, but so wretched were the means of internal communication, and so little was the trade in breadstuffs organized, that supplies could not be thrown into the famished districts in time to avert this awful calamity. It is not then to be wondered that the natives are reluctant to diminish their food crops in order to turn their land into cotton.[43]

Yet despite such acknowledgments of the devastating effects of the famine in the North-Western Provinces, the colonial state struggled to extend cotton cultivation in the North-Western Provinces in the immediate aftermath of famine, exposing those still living through its impact to new risks in a period of cotton boom that would soon be followed by bust.

Rather than based upon the rapid expansion of cotton cultivation, the export of cotton during this era was made possible through the reworking of the cotton supply chain. Cotton was taken out of circulation from India and exported to metropolitan Britain from western India, the Central Provinces, and Berar.[44] Despite colonial focus upon staple quality, particularly Berar's Hingunghat cotton, the staple quality was not substantially improved during this era from the perspective of Britain's manufacturers and workers.[45]

In order to improve the quality and quantity of cotton exported from colonial India, a series of inquiries were conducted into the possibility of the settlement of British capitalists who would advance money to cultivators, oversee the cultivation and picking of cotton, and import cotton producing implements. When asked about the prospects of such a plan, colonial officials and indigo planters stated that such a system would be different from American slavery or indigo and tea cultivation in the Doab because, as P. Saunders stated, "every man, woman, and child in the country would steal [cotton]." Saunders explained his position: "All agricultural produce that the natives can eat or use, such as grain or cotton, can never be grown on a large scale by Europeans."[46] Indigo planters settled in the Doab were asked if the extension of the cotton trade in the North-Western Provinces or the settlement of capitalists and agents would "result in the establishment of slavery in India as tyrannical as that of the negroes in America."[47] A planter replied that "ryots understood their rights" as well as Europeans, making it impossible to "force them to work against their will, or take their produce at one farthing less than the stipulated contract price. . . . No European could carry on business in this country who attempted such illegal and violent acts." He further added that only the government could compel peasant producers to do business and give opium on its "own terms."[48] Together these observations were informed by a belief that colonial India could not fulfill its obligations to Britain to export cotton. British traders, manufacturers, and merchants obsessively looked toward the transformation of colonial India in the terms of matching or surpassing expectations set by U.S. slavery and demanded transformations when these expectations were not met.

One part of this project entailed comparisons between peasant production in India and slavery-based cotton production in the United States. As Samuel Smith concluded, "It would never pay the ryots, however, to gather their cotton with as much nicety as is done in America, nor could Indian cotton, as a mass, ever equal American in cleanliness."[49] Slavery in the nineteenth-century United States was defined by an unrelenting and obsessive project based upon standardization and increased efficiency through the plantation-based production of cotton.[50] Wes Brady, a former slave, described the pain that was characteristic of cotton plantation production: "The rows was a mile long and no matter how much grass was in them, if you leaves one sprig on your row they beats you nearly to death."[51] Looking toward racial slavery in the United States informed Britain's expectations for colonial India.

Slave-produced cotton in the United States was based upon an obsessive attention to reducing the exposure of cotton staples to elements. As historian Walter Johnson has described, from the moment of cotton's blooming, techniques for protecting and ensuring the cleanliness of cotton against exposure were embedded in slave driving and the system of cotton cultivation in the United States. The longer that bloomed, unpicked cotton remained in the field, the more its value decreased,[52] so cotton was constantly monitored to ensure that its quality would not be degraded as the raw material traveled from cotton plantations to factories.[53] As cotton was ginned, its purity continued to be obsessively examined to make sure it was free from any adulteration, including bloodstains.[54] White obsessions with improved staple quality were based upon a commitment to profiting from the quality of cotton itself, which was ensured through the production process by the violent, meticulous, and relentless management of enslaved people by overseers and planters.[55]

The persistent British reference to slavery was part of a colonial logic that envisioned Indian cotton production through U.S. slavery. This envisioning was a critical part of the project to force India to take the place of America as Britain's cotton field. In trying to figure out a process for this to occur, Britons imagined how their empire could and must develop new techniques to exploit, dominate, and extract work from those they sought to rule over.[56]

As the American Civil War came to an end, the demand for cotton in India decreased, investments were lost, and cultivation became increasingly unprofitable.[57] In Dharwad, Sandip Hazareesingh has shown that following the Civil War, the Dharwar-American cotton bubble burst, with cultivators suffering losses.[58] In the Central Provinces and Berar, a cotton department was founded after the Civil War and led by Henry Rivett-Carnac, who would claim, in 1867, that "the seed of improvement has been sown."[59] Yet, this grand vision would be scaled back in later years with the closing of the department. Rivett-Carnac would reflect upon the inability to transform cotton cultivation in the Central Provinces and the limits of the colonial state in that transformation through Alfred Lyall's orientalist poem "The Old Pindaree," which described the limits to the extension of colonial cotton cultivation, documenting the gap between colonial visions of domination and the realization of those visions:

> There comes a Settlement Hákim to teach us to plough and to weed,
> (I sowed the cotton he gave me, but first I boiled the seed)
> He likes us humble farmers, and speaks so gracious and wise
> As he asks of our manners and customs; I tell him a parcel of lies.[60]

According to Rivett-Carnac, this was one of the "most picturesque and faithfully descriptive pieces in Anglo-Indian literature."[61] This colonial distrust and hatred for peasant cotton growers also reflected a disrupted and disturbed demand for domination of the economy and its producers by the colonial state.

Sparks in the Factory

In The Poverty of Philosophy (1847), Karl Marx made some of his earliest observations on the significance of slavery as part of capitalism, writing, "Without slavery you have no cotton; without cotton you have no modern industry," and continuing, "Wipe out North America from the map of the world, and you will have anarchy—the complete decay of modern commerce and civilization."[62] Marx's observations in both phrasing and concern reflected a perspective much earlier put forth by the English novelist and slave trade defender Daniel Defoe, who observed that English trade with West Africa and British Caribbean colonies would unravel should either this trade or the slave trade be interfered with: "The Case is as plain as Cause and Consequence: Mark the Climax. No African Trade, no Negroes no Negroes; no Sugars, Gingers, Indicos, &c. no sugars, & c. no Islands; no Islands, no Continent; no Continent, no Trade; that is to say, farewell all your American Trade, your West-India Trade, for it is that I am speaking of, it is all gone at once."[63] Marx himself extended these observations to consider not only how disruptions to slavery would have devastated world trade but also metropolitan manufacturing. Together, these were part of consistent observations on the transforming centrality of slavery to world commerce and global capitalism across centuries. In mid-nineteenth-century British metropolitan imaginations, it was Britain's colonies that were obligated to prevent economic disaster by doing the work of slavery.

During the American Civil War era, the majority of cotton supplied to England from India was grown within 300 miles of Bombay.[64] Britain's factory workers, traders, and capitalists saw these staples as the opposite of everything that slavery-produced cotton represented. For textile factory owners, workers, and colonial bureaucrats, Surat cottons exported from India lacked the standardized quality and long staple that Lancashire industry had learned to expect from U.S. slavery. While Surat cottons were meant to provide raw materials and alleviate the metropolitan demand for cotton, the arrival of Surat cotton in Britain's manufacturing districts was attended by bitter complaints about quality. Surats forced a reduction in the speed of machines, and the mass of fiber was diminished greatly during the production process, which lessened the mass of finished product and resulted in a reduction in workers' wages.[65] The speed of machines and the quality of finished textiles had been unlocked by U.S. slavery–produced cotton. In contrast, the perceived dirtiness of Surat cotton made the cleaning, preparing, and spinning of yarn increasingly back-breaking and grinding. The quality of yarn produced by Surat cotton was in turn affected by temperature; threads frequently snapped in production.

English textile workers reported nausea upon opening bales of Surat cotton.[66] Jesse Leach conducted research into the bodily impact that Surat cotton had upon English workers, writing for a prominent medical journal that working with Surats was "more damaging to the constitutions of the operatives employed."[67] Surat fibers filled the factory air causing workers to spit out blood from their lungs and to suffer from spasmodic coughing, sore throats, and asthma. In an attempt to get Surat cotton fibers dislodged from their lungs, workers chewed tobacco, drank gin, and smoked; "teetotalers use tea and coffee in lieu of these for the same purpose."[68] Surat cotton caused mixers' arms and hands to break out in rashes as a result of sand from Surat cottons. The short fiber cut up, "destroy[ed]," and irritated skin, making workers look "pale and sickly."[69] The process of textile production entailed weavers' "kissing the shuttle," a technique where weavers pulled thread through the eye of a shuttle with their mouths. Surat cotton frequently broke the weft, causing workers to digest the thread and cotton fibers making workers nauseous.[70] Some workers claimed they broke out in fever upon the arrival of cotton shipped from India.[71] Simply put, Surat cotton was seen as making the English working class suffer.

Surat cottons seemed to lack the standardization and reliability necessary for uninterrupted factory production, a process made possible through access to slavery-produced cotton. In 1864, the *Spectator* reported, "The calamities of Lancashire would be coming to an end if the Surat cotton were at all like the American, or even the Dharwad cotton, which is quite as good. As it is, it is said that it comes to hand so dirty that it positively affects the *health* of the operatives, and gives out a foetid smell,—and so rotten that no quantity of it can restore the trade."[72]

Surat cottons forced the speed of machinery to slow and demanded harder work for less money.[73] The 1863 *Annual Report of Factories* noted that the diminished availability of food from lack of income and the extra labor required to work with Surat cotton caused factory workers to be "generally thinner."[74] The slowdown in the pace of production caused by working with Surat cotton was believed to be the cause of reduced wages for spinners, carders, and weavers who worked by piece.[75] In Rawtenstall, a medical official noted that he had seen workers as patients "who were physically unable to bear up under the greater exertion required in the working [of] Surat cotton."[76]

Lancashire's textile weavers wrote poetry, sang songs, and told stories about how much they hated Surat cotton—a hatred that led to Surat becoming a synonym for muck. Songs including Samuel Laycock's "Shurat Weaver's Song," William Billington's "Th' Surat Weyver's Song," and "Surat Warps" by a Rossendale based writer all bemoaned the quality of Surat cotton and the difficult experience of working with it. "Th' Shurat Weyver's Song" concludes "To hell wi o' Surat."[77] "Surat Warps" described the difficulties of working with Surat warps: they caused bombshells to fly across the shed, breaking and knocking everything over in the factory. The factory master would see such horrible cloth and become angry, leaving only two possibilities: ripping the cloth or firing the weaver. This difficult position made the weaver shiver and "go queer," with nothing to do—"It makes me fit to hang myself!"[78] In May 1863, a Clitheroe mill owner reported that if the American Civil War ended, popular hatred would cause workers to refuse to use cotton from India, no matter how fine a quality of the staple.[79]

This hatred for Surat cotton became tangled with perceptions of the dishonesty of colonial Indian peasant cotton growers and a belief in their failure to meet the obligations that they as colonial subjects must bear in supporting metropolitan Britain. R. Arthur Arnold echoed such a perspective of colonial India's incapacity when he noted that the saw gin, a product of Eli Whitney's mechanical genius, "was not much used by the Hindoos," who instead relied upon "rude processes" that did not separate "the valuable export and the worthless refuse."[80] Britain's capitalists believed that Indian merchants cheated English buyers by weighting down and adulterating cotton with pebbles and stones. Arnold further wrote that this dishonesty, which inspection had begun to slightly curb, made Indian cotton unprofitable and could destroy textile machines or cause a factory fire.[81] Such complaints led to the passage of the Cotton Frauds Act of 1863.[82] However, the act made little difference in the perception that cotton arrived adulterated. As the deputy commissioner of Amravati (Oomraotee)—Berar home of the eponymous "Oomra" cotton—wrote in 1867, "Practically the act has, in my opinion, been a dead letter, and its effect has been neither beneficial nor otherwise."[83] The Manchester Chamber of Commerce seemed to share this opinion of the ineffectual nature of the act when it was revised in 1869, forming a subcommittee to point out the "hardships and defects of the Act" in 1870.[84] The subcommittee would ultimately declare that the act was unnecessary because eventually the benefits of legitimate and fair commerce would change the practices of Indian merchants.[85] From this perspective, some British capitalists still believed that the force of the economy would provide a powerful form of colonial tutelage, forcing traders to meet their demands. Further, rather than resulting in higher quality cotton, the subcommittee concluded that it would be "impossible to define" what was a violation and would seriously impede the uninterrupted shipment of cotton to ports for export.[86]

For other observers such as John Watts, it was "Anglo-Saxon energy" that made U.S. slavery dominant. India simply lacked the thorough and extensive energy of white settler colonization that would enable colonial India to fulfill its obligations to metropolitan Britain. Without white management, India's cottons would never meet expectations.[87] The passage of laws alone could not surpass the effectiveness of U.S. slavery in supplying Britain with cotton. Surat cotton came in part to name the failure of India to meet its colonial obligations to Britain.

Crisis Displacement

> In conclusion, it is curious to reflect that the fratricidal war in America should have made itself felt even in the peaceful wilds of Oude, where the Native weaver suffers, in the matter of English thread, with his English fellow-laborer. . . . In the case of the former he has to contend with a diminished demand for Native cotton cloth in addition to the rise in price of the raw material.
> —P. Carnegy, Bengal Chamber of Commerce (1864)

While workers in Lancashire's textile industry complained about Surat cottons, the movement of these cottons to England, along with the re-export of Indian cotton based upon speculation, affected weavers in the North-

Western Provinces in ways that could, from the perspective of the North-Western Provinces, render the Faizabad weaver a "fellow-laborer" with the English factory worker.[88] Weavers in the North-Western Provinces, who had just suffered from famine, experienced and were now directly impacted by crisis-era transformations in cotton production and distribution. Not long after Lancashire's workers received support from India because of economic crisis, weavers in the North-Western Provinces were exposed to the unmediated impact of increased cotton prices.

A broader pattern of crisis displacement techniques had led to English weavers and weavers in the North-Western Provinces being unevenly exposed to capitalist crisis. It was a process whose impact extended far beyond the North-Western Provinces. In the primary cotton-producing district of Berar, a colonial official noted that the increase of cotton in Nagpur was indicative of the large exportation of cotton from the Central Provinces abroad.[89] Within the Bombay Presidency, Samuel Smith observed that "wherever one travels in the interior the same story is heard, that everything is scraped together for export."[90] This had caused cotton spinning in India to nearly come to a halt. Where cotton had previously moved from western to eastern India, the flow of cotton had now been redirected from internal consumption toward export, causing the price of cotton for weavers within India to rise.

The crisis displaced onto the North-Western Provinces offers acute insight into the implications of the global crisis of the 1860s centered in the cotton and textile industry. Cotton consumed by weavers in the North-Western Provinces was often from the Central Provinces.[91] Weavers from the North-Western Provinces were displaced to cities such as Bombay as a "consequence of the cotton famine towards Bombay." At least 300 weavers went on Hajj partially in response to the crisis. Instead, some weavers became taken up as indentured laborers in other British colonies, including Mauritius. As one observer from the Sudder Board of Revenue in the North-Western Provinces noted, "The weavers have betaken themselves to agricultural or other labor, to menial service, emigration to the Mauritius and elsewhere, and even to begging."[92]

On 10 January 1864, the Bengal Chamber of Commerce started an inquiry into the "slackness of demand" for European cotton goods in India. The inquiry concluded that slackness in demand was not the result of increased handloom manufacture.[93] Instead, "the extraordinary rise of price has affected, though unequally, the demand for Native and for European stuffs. The same money only buys half, and often less than half, the quantity of cloth it used to."[94] In the North-Western Provinces, the rise in cotton prices exacerbated the difficult situation of handloom weavers. Weavers could no longer afford to purchase English thread and had been forced to work "from hand to mouth" upon locally spun yarns.[95] This resulted in decreases in the importation of yarns during the previous two years. Further, capital was increasingly diverted from the textile trade toward more profitable cotton speculation. As a colonial official in the North-Western Provinces wrote, "Scarcity of food in the famine year, as a rule, bore with far greater severity on the weaving population than the present dearness in the price of the main staple of their trade has done. It was a noted fact that the larger portion of emaciated hunger-stricken applicants for food at our relief kitchens in 1861, belonging to market-towns were those of the weaving classes."[96] Increase in the price of cotton diminished consumption of both English and Indian textile manufacture.[97] While the Manchester Chamber of Commerce complained of the impact that tariffs had on sales of textiles within India, members were reminded also of the metropolitan manufacturing protectionist basis of these tariffs. As Charles Wood argued, duties on cotton yarn and textile fabrics created a "protective interest" in India, thus "restricting exports" of textiles and yarns to England.[98]

When Manchester factory owners demanded that the Bengal Chamber of Commerce conduct multiple, extensive inquiries into competition from weavers and "native" manufactures in the North-Western Provinces, the inquiry provided directions for the further displacement of handloom manufactures through the expanded sale of Manchester goods. For colonial officials, it was unclear if the cultivation of cotton in India would facilitate or impede this effort. Should improved cotton staples resembling U.S. staples be cultivated on an extensive scale, what beyond tariff policy would give English manufacturers the competitive advantage they currently enjoyed over India through access to cotton produced through slavery in the United States? How could a model based upon cotton cultivated in India, sent to Manchester, and sent back to India in the form of manufactured textile goods compete with a system based upon cotton cultivated in India, manufactured in India, and then sold in India? Divergences over answers to these questions were exacerbated by colonial beliefs in the cheapness of Indian labor, which formed the basis of the belief in cultivating cotton in India in the first place.

For some, the ongoing failure to sell textiles in the North-Western Provinces was indicative of deeper structural problems within the relationship between metropolitan manufacturing and colonial consumption. As an observer for the Bengal Chamber of Commerce noted, despite high cotton prices in India, handloom cloth could be manufactured and sold for less than Manchester goods and local production, which did not have to absorb the cost of exporting cotton as a way to explain the continued weak demand from the North-Western Provinces.[99] In June 1864, the Manchester Chamber of Commerce sent a memorial to Charles Wood requesting that duties on Manchester goods be abolished and that principles of free trade be allowed to reign supreme. The Manchester Chamber of Commerce noted that the price of cotton caused Manchester yarns and goods to remain at a high price, which "materially curtailed the shipments to India."[100] Further, the chamber of commerce argued that the cost of transport of cotton from India to England and from England back to India gave Indian weavers a material advantage that was against the principles of free trade. Instead, the chamber of commerce argued that India was capable of becoming a great exporter of cotton if its imports of textiles could be increased. This was a statement that demanded the making of colonial relations enforced through cotton production, something English capitalists and metropolitan abolitionists had worked to create since at least the 1840s.

Difficulties in selling textiles in colonial markets such as the North-Western Provinces preceded increased costs of production caused by cotton supply shortages during the Civil War. However, the impact of transformations in the availability of cotton and difficulties selling textiles extended beyond the conclusion of the Civil War. In October 1865, concerns emerged over the widespread outbreak of mildew in Manchester goods produced in Lancashire and sent to India.[101] While an inquiry by the Manchester Chamber of Commerce concluded that it could not be determined if textiles produced from Surat cottons were more likely to be damaged by mildew than those produced from other cottons, the possibility suggested the depths of anxiety within Manchester's capitalist class over producing textiles from Surats.[102] Surat cotton was believed to result in a deterioration in the quality and color of yarn and cloth, which in turn resulted in a variety of new bleaching and sizing techniques to improve cloth color, and these new techniques may have contributed to outbreaks of mildew. One English observer connected this directly to the availability of U.S. cotton: "Thus the character of our cotton manufactures have deteriorated during the past ten years; it is now improving again under the fuller supply of American cotton."[103] The Manchester Chamber of Commerce declared that while spot damage existed before the Civil War, its increased magnitude could be attributed to "intense competition and the demand of low priced goods."[104] The capitalist crisis formed in the quality of Manchester goods themselves, in traces of impurity that marked another limit to capital. Manchester's capitalists expected that the return of U.S. cotton meant the end of such impurity.

If mildew and spot damage pointed toward continued difficulties in selling goods in Indian markets, some sought to transform the relationship between production and circulation to better match demands of colonial consumers. During the crisis, it was noted that the price of handloom manufactures increased more than the price of European manufactures but continued to be purchased because of their perceived superiority.[105] Observers reported that it was necessary for Lancashire to manufacture "coarser, thicker, and cheaper" articles to better compete with handloom manufactured textiles.[106]

Following the Civil War, Britain's capitalists increasingly believed that their textile industry must produce commodities that matched the desires of colonial markets by producing these dhotis, lungis, cummerbunds, and other articles specifically to compete with handloom manufactures.[107] The most ambitious project to facilitate this was J. Forbes Watson's *Textile Manufactures and the Costumes of the People of India* (1866), an eighteen-volume set containing 700 samples of Indian textiles.[108] Watson gestured toward a perceived necessity in transforming the process of production and consumption: "We do not make an effort to impose on others *our own tastes and needs*, but we produce what will please the customer and what he wants."[109] The cataloging project sought to enable Manchester goods to meet, match, and make the desires of colonial subjects in India to make India an even greater consumer of Manchester industrialists.[110]

Manufacturers could imitate catalog items and ship the textiles they produced to India.[111] However, other observers such as Calcutta-based Kissen Mohun Mullick offered a different assessment of the productive capacities and impact that Lancashire had and would continue to have upon Indian textile markets. Mullick noted that Britain's capitalists had given Indian handloom production a near "death-blow" by "overwhelming" Indian manufactured cotton twist and piece goods. Mullick continued to note that this caused many to sympathize with the condition of weavers. However, as Mullick continued, "let not those patriots forget that backs once hardly covered with tattered rags that never knew a change, and naked shattered frames which shocked the decent eye and moved the pitiful heart, are now — thanks to Manchester Mills — sheltered under clean suits from head to foot. . . . If our food is dear, our raiment is cheap, and that is no small comfort to us generally."[112]

The colonial contours of the economy could be located in the destroyed economic livelihoods of weavers in Bengal and the North-Western Provinces, where broken bodies in Manchester goods marked metropolitan capitalist expansion. Such visions marked the crucial difference between the position of colonial and metropolitan subjects as mediated by the capitalist marketplace.

Anglo-Saxon Futures

British imperial classificatory techniques, from political economy and agricultural science to the cataloging vision of Watson, were essential to the constitution of and expectations for colonial rule in India. These practices were based upon an expectation that India would become a distinct and unified space, facilitated by infrastructural development while deepening India's export orientation with global capitalism.[113] This complex of rule and knowledge was held together within global capitalism, particularly through formations of colonialism and white supremacy. Colonial knowledge practices were formed through predictions of the future of white supremacy in the United States after slavery, which was essential for the determination of colonial, plantation, and capitalist futures in India. India was subordinated within the global economy in a colonial relationship that depended not so much upon colonial India for the extensive exportation of cotton to Britain but rather as an outlet for Britain's textile manufacturers.

That relationship depended on the future of cotton exports from the American South. In 1866, G. F. Forbes traveled throughout the cotton-producing U.S. South to explore future possibilities of cotton cultivation in the South. Forbes had been extensively involved in efforts to extend and transform cultivation of cotton in India. In 1863, he was appointed the cotton commissioner of the government of Bombay, and he further worked with the Manchester Cotton Company in its failed efforts to export cotton to England.[114] For Forbes, the return of the U.S. South seemed impossible and was visible in the "failure" of the first year of free African American labor. The implications of this failure placed India at the center of the future of global capitalism.

Forbes's assessment of the viability and productive capacity of the post–Civil War South provides insight into the implications of colonial knowledge as a global project at the intersection of political economy and agriculture where precision about formations of white supremacy in the American South were indispensable to knowledge about India. Forbes considered the prospects of the U.S. South to be dismal and identified with white planters against African Americans, lamenting the condition of former slaveholders. For Forbes, emancipation created conditions of labor scarcity, making it impossible for the South to return to its position as sole cotton source for the global textile economy. The first year of African American free labor had failed because African Americans had appropriated their labor power from not only slaveholders but also the market.[115] Fields had become overgrown, an indication of the "difficulty of obtaining labour." Forbes traveled to New Orleans and then up the Mississippi River by steamboat, going through Louisiana, Mississippi, Arkansas, and Tennessee before arriving in Cairo, Illinois. From tours of large plantation estates in Alabama, Louisiana, and Mississippi, Forbes concluded that southern plantations had "sadly fallen away from their former eminence," and the war had destroyed once "noble provinces." This fall was most visible in the destruction of planters' houses and the sparing of slave quarters. Following his tour of the South, Forbes addressed the current and future prospects of African American labor and cotton exports from the South. According to Forbes, the current crop would fail to meet the demands of the global textile industry. Forbes repeated statements from white planters who stated that because following emancipation African Americans were "free to please themselves, they could not get half their former work out of them."[116]

Forbes believed that the very structure of capital accumulation in the South, in the form of land and enslaved people, had been ruined. In his words, the "future prospects" of the South were "dismal" and former slave owners were "utterly ruined and dispirited." Whites had lost everything according to Forbes: "Therefore, when the emancipation was announced, not only was their occupation gone, but they may be said to have lost their all, for, without either the labour or capital to work their land, it became valueless to them." This represented the possible breaking down of the real estate basis of the United States that Du Bois described. For Forbes, it was impossible to imagine the future labor market in the South or the reconstruction of channels of profitability that would make future cotton cultivation possible. Planters were convinced Black labor would not form the future basis of the southern economy and often abandoned raising cotton by formerly enslaved people. As Forbes noted, planters corroborated the "general impression that the 'black man' would never work again as he used to do."[117]

Forbes reflected upon the case of a planter in Louisiana who cultivated 400 acres of land and began to employ all but one of his formerly enslaved laborers. The planter and Forbes were convinced that because emancipated African Americans "had got the impression that they were no longer to 'work like slaves,' they did just as much as they pleased." For Forbes, the "complete failure" of "'freed' slave labour" in the first year of experimentation had broader long-term implications. Racially, white labor would not be able to work in much of the Deep South, and therefore, without African American labor, several districts would cease cotton production and be lost as a source of cotton supply. Forbes concluded, "With such a state of depression and collapse as I witnessed, my impression is that years must pass before large supplies of cotton can be again obtained from those States."[118]

Forbes believed that the South would be unable to return to the large cotton yields that it had exported during the antebellum period. The Cotton Supply Association formed its own conclusions about the implications of the transformations of the South for the cultivation of cotton in India. The Cotton Supply Association stated that it hoped that free labor in the United States would be able to produce cotton while acknowledging that there would be a period of diminished production. At this juncture, the association reported that "India has now arrived at the period when an improved quality must be grown, or the cotton of that country will command attention only when better descriptions cannot be obtained."[119] Multiple sources of cotton supply seemed necessary to stabilize the textile industry, prevent the possibility of disruption, and secure an "uninterrupted and adequate" supply of cotton.[120] A return to dependency upon the United States would be "suicidal."[121]

However, despite such warnings and statements of necessity, by 1870 the United States would begin to return to the position of being the English textile industry's "great source of supply."[122] As the association elsewhere wrote, "The wall of slavery no longer mingles with the whirl of the spindle, and we can now cordially bid Godspeed to all the efforts made to revive and increase the production of American cotton." U.S.-based observers looked toward India and described the "hopeless nature" of attempts to supplant the United States by Indian cotton cultivation.[123] If racist assessments of the U.S. planting and manufacturing classes were pessimistic about free labor, they were also pessimistic about India. De Bow's Review described India as "the land of great promise but of little performance." From the author's perspective, the return of U.S. cotton cultivation would mark the end of India's central position in the cotton supply.[124] In some ways, the meaning of the possible return of the U.S. South can be glimpsed in the crashing markets of colonial cotton suppliers at the conclusion of the Civil War. The value of cotton imported in England from India collapsed from £33,522,104 in 1865–66 to £14,653,509 in 1866–67.[125] While India's exports in cotton increased in 1866, this export was based largely upon old cotton that could not be shipped because of the monetary crisis of 1865.[126] The British imperial dream of a rerouted capitalism through India without the United

States would be, as the subsequent decade would remain, a colonial demand that metropolitan observers believed India failed to adequately meet.

The origins of crisis in the textile industry were bound to social crisis and famine in the North-Western Provinces, as increased cotton prices disproportionately affected weavers in India and the North-Western Provinces. At the same time, the conditions of English workers were imagined in relation to colonial famine. The interlinking of the world across colonial and imperial spaces also made it possible to displace risk from the imperial metropole onto colonial subjects and to burden colonial India with the obligation to produce cotton for metropolitan consumption.

Yet if it is impossible to determine the exact balance between the failed realization of surplus through textiles and increased cotton prices in the textile industry, it is possible to observe that the British imperial vision of India as a market for manufactured goods and a singular producer of cotton remained unrealized. The limits to this vision were part of a history of capital, its destructive tendencies, and existence through rules of racial and colonial domination and dependence. The slow return of cotton cultivation in the U.S. South was itself related to depressed demand for British manufacturing and continued problems in the textile industry's ability to realize profits through textile sales in colonial India. As one Manchester observer noted in 1869, uncertainty about the return of the U.S. South or existing cotton stockpiles prevented capitalists from investing in the promotion of cotton growth. Further, since the end of the Civil War, "the gloomy dulness that has continually hung over the Manchester market, and the utter impossibility of doing business except at a heavy loss . . . has knocked all heart out of capitalists, and prevented them latterly from embarking in the culture of cotton."[127] This described a state of affairs defined by cotton scarcity but determined by the inability to realize surplus value through the production of Manchester goods. Rather than rise and fall or extension, disaster and systemic failure are necessary in a history of capital that recognizes capital's limits and violence.[128]

Later works on Indian agriculture would reflect upon the transformations that did not occur following Black emancipation in the United States. According to Eugene Schrottky's *The Principles of Rational Agriculture* (1876), a small portion of "cotton goods" in India were manufactured within the country, but "by far the larger portion is imported from England, chiefly spun from American cotton."[129] The permanence, or even extension, of relationship following the abolition of slavery was part of a broader failure to realize designs of exploitation colonialism where India would cultivate and export cotton and import textiles manufactured by England.

For those most invested and involved in the project, the limits of the British Empire in realizing an equivalent system for cotton cultivation through a different configuration of colonial space and labor exploitation were already evident. In 1870, at the end of a tumultuous decade of crisis based upon the rattling of the circuits of global capitalism, a statistician for the Manchester Statistical Society articulated a perspective of England's development through the colonization of the Indian economy: "India is not only a cotton plantation: it is also a great cloth market. It is not enough that the Hindoo should send us large quantities of cheap cotton. He should also buy from us large quantities of cloth, at a fair profit to us for making it."[130] Yet in 1870, the colonial demand that India meet its obligation to serve as the beginning and end of a commodity chain that passed through Lancashire's textile industry remained unfulfilled.

8 ::: Settling the Crisis
From Australia to the American South

In *Black Reconstruction*, W. E. B. Du Bois described the "dark and vast sea of human labor" that emerged in the wake of African American emancipation. This sea connected China, India, the Pacific Islands, Africa, the Caribbean, Central America, and the United States. It was conditioned by the rise of a new capitalist imperialism where U.S. slavery had fundamentally transformed the global degradation of labor through racial domination.[1] By centering race and colonialism in the constitution of this sea of human labor, Du Bois reconstructed Karl Marx's insights into how labor works in capital, and his perspective still has much to contribute to more recent writing on shifting sites of production and the channeling of global labor flows.[2]

The course of Black emancipation itself had been enacted in part through the realization of self-determined Black mobility via what Du Bois described as the "mass movement" of enslaved African Americans through a general strike. This was a mass movement in two senses: first, a mass-based Black political struggle against slavery, and second, the actual running away from slavery during the American Civil War, something Du Bois described as a "stampede."[3] Much like a stampede, the course of mid-nineteenth-century labor flows, while unpredictable, had by now gathered sufficient momentum to prevent capital from solely dictating its course.

Across diverse colonial terrain within the British Empire, the prospect of Black emancipation was anticipated and in some ways addressed by what was known as the "coolie question." The "coolie," as Lisa Lowe notes, served as an intermediary form of Asian labor in the context of emancipation.[4] Factory owners, colonial officials, and settlers imagined that coolies would ameliorate economic and colonial disruptions brought about by emancipation, especially by providing plantations with "cheap" labor.[5] In the context of transforming plantation relations, the coolie question was itself a racial discourse in proximity to the "Negro question," following Thomas Carlyle's publication of "Occasional Discourse on the Negro Question" (1849).[6]

Before and after the American Civil War, the question of Asian indentured labor and its implications for U.S. slavery had real implications. In

1857, Leonard Wray arrived in South Carolina from the British colony of Natal to work on the plantations of the statesman, slaveholder, and white supremacist James Henry Hammond. Hammond invited Wray to introduce "imphee" cultivation, a type of sorghum meant to serve southern interests in agricultural diversification and lessen southern economic dependence upon cotton and slave trading.[7] Wray's connection to global plantation economies also made him uniquely positioned in the management of race as an expert in the interpretation of racial difference from coolie and Black to white and in attendant forms of exploitation — slavery, indenture, and wage labor.[8]

Wray had become widely known as a plantation expert following the publication of his manual *The Practical Sugar Planter* — a text circulated and serialized throughout the British Empire and the slaveholding South.[9] According to the southern agricultural journal *De Bow's Review*, *The Practical Sugar Planter* was an "invaluable guide."[10] Wray began his career as a plantation manager on Jamaican slave plantations, which he managed for ten years. Following emancipation within the British Empire, he was one of several planters who moved to British India, where he managed a large North Indian sugar estate at Gorakhpur for three years.[11] He would go on to manage a plantation in the Straits Settlements before traveling to Natal in the 1850s.[12]

At Hammond's Silver Bluff plantation, Wray superintended enslaved African Americans laboring in fields.[13] During dinners, Wray, Hammond, and other prominent white elites discussed the future of plantations and white supremacy. During one conversation, Hammond and Wray were joined by Edmund Ruffin, whose *Farmers' Register* had earlier been foundational to proslavery agricultural and management thought.[14] Conversation turned to labor exploitation, managing race, and Jamaican plantation decline. The discussion was anchored by comparisons between coolie and African American labor.[15] Wray stated his belief in the superiority of Chinese indentured labor considered under the "general, but incorrect, name of 'Coolies.'" Ruffin and Hammond emphasized coolie "mistreatment."[16] For U.S. planters, arguments about the continued presence of Chinese or coolie labor on plantations seemed to offer legitimation of U.S. slaveholding paternalism while demonstrating the centrality of racial coercion for plantations after emancipation.[17]

Wray's observations about slavery on Hammond's plantation informed a subsequent presentation before Britain's Royal Society of Arts in 1858. During the presentation, Wray addressed differences between slavery and British colonial agriculture, imagining racial differences in productive capacities between coolie, "Negro," and white plantation labor. According to Wray, the difference between the "cheap labour" of South Asian coolies and "Negroes" was "enormous."[18] Enslaved African Americans represented the "most skilled description" of labor for cotton cultivation, and Hammond's management brought this labor to a "pitch of perfection." White men could never match Black labor on plantations. For Wray, these differences made it necessary to develop a system of labor management that would be homologous to slavery, different because the English would never "resort to the whip." Wray claimed that planters' management of enslaved labor presented a challenge to make comparable forms of labor exploitation without direct and violent coercion. Throughout the age of African American emancipation, the emphasis often fell upon the former with little regard for the latter.[19] This series of practices assumed a singular form in the emerging settler and plantation context of Australia, where struggles over the racial composition of coerced labor unfolded in relation to the realities of Black emancipation in the United States.

In 1859, the Lancashire textile manufacturer Thomas Bazley, who was also engaged in the Manchester Cotton Company's efforts to transform colonial cotton production in India, gave a speech stating that when emancipation within the British Empire had occurred, no provisions were made for introducing free labor from "other parts of the world." Bazley continued:

> The negroes, when freed from slavery, were enabled to enjoy the comforts of life in great abundance, and were indisposed to work so severely as they had previously done, more especially as their former proprietors declined to recognize the price of labour that they themselves had previously established in the market. ("Hear, hear.") The negroes had the sagacity to see that the price fixed by the masters was something like the market price, and knowing that their masters had received £20,000,000 for emancipation they could not understand why their labour was so much depreciated in value as they found it to be. No mischief could have ensued if free immigration had taken place under certain regulations; but the Chinese, who were excellent laborers, were not permitted to enter the West Indies.[20]

Bazley and other factory owners looked to draw upon new forms of coerced labor such as indenture to thwart the possibility of Black freedom in the context of Black emancipation. Rather than advocating the mass introduction of indentured labor to the United States, British factory owners sought transformations within the British Empire that would instrumentalize and lessen Black emancipation's impact. As one observer quipped, "It seems that the Anglo-Saxon race needs disaster" to transform colonial agrarian relations.[21] Colonial officials, landholding companies, and planting interests within the British Empire repeatedly brought coolie questions and Black emancipation together to craft colonial transformation in relation.

The impact of global capitalist crisis, Black emancipation in the United States, and settler colonialism and indenture also enveloped Queensland, Australia. At the heart of this chapter is an exploration of the tensions within the interests of Queensland settlers and English manufacturers as practices of race, settlement, and white supremacy emerged from the United States and informed territorial conquest in Queensland. Amid the textile industry crisis, white settlers and settling interests examined Queensland and charted a course far removed from that of India's North-Western Provinces, positing the expanded colonization of Queensland as a solution to capitalist crisis. Many white settlers looked especially toward expanded white settlement through the movement of unemployed English textile workers to the colony. Economic disruptions could be navigated through a reordering of colonial and racial relations and the systematic importation of labor—especially white labor—from England, Scotland, and the United States to Queensland.[22]

As will become clear in the pages that follow, ideas and practices of settler white supremacy could come in tension with visions of limitless capitalist growth. Settlers opposed the immigration of Chinese and South Asian labor not on economic but on racial grounds. Factory owners opposed settlers' interest in transforming Queensland into a white man's country based upon unemployed factory labor, preferring instead to contain and restrict the movement of unemployed laborers in order to keep factory wages low. Over the course of this and similar debates, the experience of settler colonialism in the United States, and of settler slavery in particular, became a consistent point of reference in determining expectations for the future of Queensland. Queensland not only was looked toward as a site for potential cotton cultivation but was imagined to be like Louisiana in its capacity to cultivate sugar and rice.[23] Deploying an expectation for the future of Australia based upon the settler colonization of the United States, Robert De Coin wrote, "We believe there are fortunes, large fortunes, to be made in no great length of time, upon well-selected lands adapted for the cultivation of cotton, sugar, and rice in Australia, just as large fortunes were realised by persons who knew how to select lands judiciously in the Southern States of America."[24] Such imaginations were about making different colonial spaces similar for the purposes of expanded colonization.[25] These efforts to reorder Queensland's economy through race and empire failed, though the settler colonial and white supremacist dynamics that dominated this era continued to resonate long after the crisis had passed.

Nineteenth-century Queensland was like the U.S. slaveholding South in one regard: it was a site of extreme violence in the constitution of global capitalism. As Raymond Evans has described, Queensland's frontier was one of the "most violent places on earth during the global spread of Western capitalism in the nineteenth century."[26] In 1859, Queensland comprised roughly 30,000 settlers and possibly more than 100,000 Aboriginal people.[27] Unlike New South Wales and Victoria, where invasion began in the eighteenth century, rapid colonization in Queensland can be traced to the mid-nineteenth century. Settlement in Queensland was predicated on a belief that Aboriginal people would not do the work of empire but would instead be dispossessed, a belief that was informed by white settler interpretations of Aboriginal death in New South Wales and Tasmania and by knowledge about demographic disaster in the Americas.[28] As historians of genocide have noted, in Queensland squatters unleashed unmediated colonial violence uncontrolled by Sydney or London.[29] This violence was passed on from squatters to the Native Police Corps, whose active involvement in the killing of Aboriginal people and in anti-Aboriginal violence was at the heart of the colonization of Queensland during the 1860s.[30] Crucially, as Tracey Banivanua Mar has argued, it was inconsistent with settler colonialism's eliminative drive to openly demand a plantation or agricultural economy based upon Aboriginal labor.[31]

The establishment of Queensland as an independent colony in 1859 and subsequent passage of the Alienation of Crown Lands Act in 1860 provided the legal justification for rapid and expanded territorial conquest through the importation of English, Scottish, and Irish labor. This vision of conquest also relied upon the transformation of Queensland into a site for the growth of sugar, cotton, and tobacco on an extensive scale by European farmers.[32] In this regard, Queensland differed dramatically from the colonies of New South Wales and Victoria, which were not seen as dependent upon forms of mass agricultural production for export as characterized by plantations across the mid-nineteenth-century world.

Different settler factions had differing perspectives—expressed racially—on how the extensive colonization of Queensland should look and work. Some, such as the colony's first immigration official, Henry Jordan, argued that the unique climate of Queensland made it possible for export agricultural commodities such as cotton and sugar to be grown by white settlers. In contrast, whites interested in establishing, owning, and managing plantations along with many English manufacturers invested in keeping as much English labor in the textile manufacturing district as possible maintained that it was necessary to bring laborers from outside of Europe to Queensland. Those interested in establishing plantations looked toward China, the Pacific Islands, and the Indian subcontinent as sites for the reallocation of labor toward Australia. The conditions these laborers were to confront in such schemes were nominally free and notionally subjected. Queensland's settler press, along with its colonial and immigration officials, looked toward the United States, and especially toward U.S. slavery, which especially seemed to provide an important referent in theorizing and implementing a new racial ordering of settler colonial space. The consequences of the debate over the colonization of Queensland were devastating, resulting in an intensification of anti-Aboriginal frontier violence and dispossession and the introduction of indentured laborers from Pacific islands in Melanesia, including New Guinea, Vanuatu, New Caledonia, and the Solomon Islands to the colony beginning in 1863.

Despite their messy antagonisms, both of these arguments were fundamentally about competing visions of white supremacy and were the product of a conjunctural moment that brought Black emancipation in the United States, expanded colonization of Queensland, and global economic crisis together. When Queensland settlers sought to make Queensland a colony of exclusively white settlement, resonance with the white settler republicanism of the United States grew unmistakable. As the white supremacist Walt Whitman once asked, responding to the state of Oregon's proposal of a constitutional ban of people of color from the state entirely, "Is not America for the Whites? And is it not better so?"[33] While in their struggles for freedom Black people in the United States forced a reimagination of the postslavery United States defined by continued presence in the postslavery settler state, Whitman's position on the United States reflected much mainstream republican thought until at least 1863.[34]

Settler republicanism's approach to the presence of people of color—whether in the United States or elsewhere—was violent and antagonistic.[35] Given the sheer tenacity of such views within the United States, it is remarkable that self-emancipating African Americans were able to force their demands upon a white supremacist republic that imagined little place for Black presence. Along similar lines, understanding how the Black and Native presence in the United States informed the colonization of Queensland offers a vantage from which to assess the global constitution of new forms of white supremacy in the midst of U.S. settler slavery's end. These connected histories demand a reconsideration also of the global and trans-imperial constitution of colonial projects and the divide sometimes quickly drawn between the so-called subject empire, exploitation colonies, and white settler colonies.[36] While these categories have provided perspective on colonial differences, they have also foreclosed consideration of the deeper global interrelation between colonial projects, especially those that disrupt conventional categorizations.[37]

The colonization of Queensland and settler slavery in the United States converged in deadly form in the mid-nineteenth century. This convergence was characterized by white racial projects to bring Asian indentured labor to the colony, imagined as simultaneously cheap and degrading to whiteness a belief informed by understandings of U.S. settler slavery. This initial effort was accompanied by a second failed project, extending from 1861 to 1865, to colonize unemployed Lancashire factory workers in Queensland. These projects failed for different reasons. However, following their failure, indentured Pacific Island labor would form the foundation of the colony as agricultural laborers with the settler and planter Robert Towns organizing the arrival of the first Pacific Island laborers in the colony by 1863. The limits of these projects offer insight into the structure and subsequent history of the continuingly entwined histories of British colonization with formations of U.S. colonialism and anti-Black racism.

The Global Appeal of U.S.-Style Settler White Supremacy

In March 1863, following Abraham Lincoln's issuance of the Emancipation Proclamation, Queensland's head of immigration, Henry Jordan, and a white U.S.-based author writing under the name Africanus corresponded through letters to the editor of the *Glasgow Morning Herald* about the connected racial futures of the United States and Queensland. These correspondences put forth competing but interrelated white-supremacist ideas about either projects for Black removal from the United States and colonization in Australia or, against this vision, the making of Queensland into an all-white settler society.

Africanus began his first letter by paraphrasing the biblical verse Matthew 9:37: "The harvest is plentiful, but the workers few." If laborers were sent forth, the colonial transformation of Queensland's economy to meet British demands would be possible. For Africanus, Queensland's labor scarcity was directly connected to Black emancipation in the United States and ongoing projects of Black colonization that sought to remove Black people from the United States. As Africanus wrote, Abraham Lincoln's "great difficulty" revolved around the question of what to do with freedpeople.

According to Africanus, Lincoln had repeatedly suggested that African American "interest demand[ed] that they should leave America."[38]

Africanus was convinced that Black emancipation was irrevocable. He then assessed the feasibility of Black colonization in relation to northern and southern racisms, suggesting that the systematic removal of Black people from the United States to Queensland would be different from the so-called coolie trade because the arrival of formerly enslaved people would necessitate higher wages; "a strong negro man could not live no how on such miserable wages." He further argued that the relocation of Black people from the United States to Queensland would serve the interests of humanity. It would also serve Africanus's aim of whitening the United States through Black removal.

At the time of Africanus's letter, Henry Jordan was in Glasgow working to secure English, Scottish, and Irish emigration to Queensland. In his own letter, Jordan rejected Africanus's plea for the systematic removal of Black people from the United States to the colony. Jordan instead wrote of the need to make Queensland white by rerouting English emigration away from the United States and toward the colony. According to Jordan, Africanus's appeal implied a racial trade between the United States, Britain, and Queensland. Africanus's plan meant "England's colonies in Australia should receive Mr. Lincoln's three or four millions of negroes, whilst our clever cousins in America will, in exchange, generously throw open their arms to receive a like number of our cotton operatives and farm labourers and mechanics." Through colonization, the United States would systematically remove Black people from its borders while simultaneously accepting England's "surplus population." Against this, Jordan insisted upon transforming Queensland into a place of white settlement for English factory workers thrown out of work due to the ongoing crisis in the textile industry.[39]

Jordan concluded that while both Britain and Queensland sympathized with U.S. projects for Black removal, it was impossible for him to have any responsibility for Black people from the United States being brought into competition with white labor in Australia. This would cause "his children [to] get idle, and for them to begin to think that work was not respectable." White settlers in Queensland, Jordan concluded, would become "poor whites." The implication in Jordan's racial imaginary of "poor whites" was that there would be a transformation of productive white freehold farmers into bad whites, who did not work—reflecting a common white belief about what had occurred to nonslaveholding white southerners in the United States. The transformation of white farmers into poor whites was antithetical to Jordan's racial vision of an all-white colony where unemployed people from Europe were transformed into free farming settlers.

The exchange between Jordan and Africanus was part of the much wider global traffic in white supremacist ideas that circulated in the age of Black emancipation in the United States. For Africanus, Black removal from the United States was essential for the remaking of the settler nation into a white republic. For Jordan, European demographic dominance in Queensland was essential to the transformation of the colony into a white man's country. While Jordan's vision of an all-white Queensland would not be realized, the racial and economic logic that underpinned the pursuit of this project reveals how settler colonial white supremacy in Queensland and Black emancipation in the United States were entwined. At the same time, the possibilities of white racial degradation from Black, Asian, and Indigenous presence were bound up together, defying the logic of capital alone by placing a premium on the supremacy of whiteness over and above the demands of capitalist expansion. A similar prioritization of the value of whiteness above all else defined U.S. republicanism.[40]

Projects to settle white people in northern Australia toward the cultivation of cotton had a long history prior to the exchange between Jordan and Africanus in 1863. In 1847, John Dunmore Lang connected northern Australia with the abolition of slavery, arguing that "the rights and interests of humanity" would be served by the cultivation of cotton by "European free labour in Australia."[41] However, in the immediate context of the widespread crisis of capitalism centered in the textile industry, the colonization of Queensland was imagined by colonial officials as a fix to capitalist crisis. British factory owners and aspiring Queensland planters debated how the proper movement and distribution of labor within such a vision could address central causes of the ongoing crisis in factory production— overpopulation, underconsumption, overproduction, and raw material scarcity. Classical political economists had long argued that settler colonies had the capacity to relieve population pressure, create new fields for capital, and generate new markets for British goods.[42] Within all of these possibilities, John Stuart Mill wrote that the "first object" of the settler colonies must be to relieve British surplus populations.[43]

Queensland's Alienation of Crown Lands Act was designed to address this first object. Passed by Queensland's first Parliament, the act offered premiums for the ability to grow U.S. Sea Island cotton.[44] At the same time, the Queensland Parliament passed a series of laws to encourage the arrival of settling immigrants who were "to lay the foundation of the permanent wealth and prosperity of the colony." The purpose of the lands act was to secure white settlers en masse "as speedily as possible, with an industrious and virtuous population."[45]

Along with the passage of these acts, Lang tried to establish the particularity of settlement in Queensland against the Australian colonies of New South Wales or Victoria: "The peculiar character of the labour to be pursued in Queensland, the growth of cotton, the cultivation of sugar cane, and the manufacture of its juices into sugar—will render the presence in that colony of men of superior intelligence, capital, and enterprise, a matter of much more urgent necessity for the development of its resources than in New South Wales or Victoria, in both of which the pursuit of the great mass of the industrial population are pretty similar to those of the mother country."[46] In both New South Wales and Victoria, Chinese participation in mining faced strong opposition, frequently resulting in clashes between white and Chinese miners.[47] In making his case for Queensland as a unique colonial project in Australia, Lang introduced the possibility that what was so often framed as the "coolie question" would play out differently than it had in the other two colonies. Soon enough, white supremacist currents in Queensland would put Lang's thesis to the test.

Black Emancipation, Asian Labor, White Settlers

Within Queensland, among those white settlers who accepted that a migrant labor force would have to be brought to the colony, the primary debate revolved around who these workers would be. Planters such as Erskine Majoribanks advocated for the introduction of "cheap coloured labour." Majoribanks's attention went directly to Black people from the United States. Majoribanks argued that bringing African Americans who had recently been enslaved to the colony would be uniquely profitable because Black people were "accustomed to white superintendence" and would "work all day in the field under a scorching tropical sun."[48] Majoribanks's interest in the work of formerly enslaved people was based upon a white supremacist vision with whites overseeing Black people and extracting profits from this management. While his interest in securing the work of formerly enslaved people from the United States set Majoribanks apart from other white settlers, others were interested in applying the same principles of white management overseeing South Asian, Chinese, or Pacific Island labor.

During the American Civil War, consideration of U.S. slavery enabled Queensland settlers aspiring to be planters to refine their visions of white settler colonization through dependence upon non-Indigenous work, while opponents developed a discourse of opposition to the labor they imagined as coolie to refine arguments in favor of white immigration. This was part of a broader process that carried on past the Civil War when, as Marilyn Lake has contended, identification with white Americans enabled many English and Australians to think about themselves as white men.[49] In *Queensland, Australia: A Highly Eligible Field for Emigration* (1861), John Dunmore Lang, who was actively involved in the promotion of British emigration to Queensland, suggested that the United States suffered from "unspeakable evils" because of the introduction of an "inferior and degraded race, in the form of negro slaves from Africa." He warned that this could be repeated in the event of mass "importation of coolies from India."[50] Criticizing factory owners such as Thomas Bazley for their desire to introduce "a million Chinamen with their wives and children" to Queensland, Lang suggested that they would "produce just the same deteriorating effects upon the free white population here as the presence of the slaves of the Southern States have produced upon the free white population there."[51] The presence of Chinese women and children presented the possibility of white racial degradation, while, in contrast, the presence of white women and children was presented as providing future racial and economic stability.[52] The prospect of Chinese labor in the colony was often met with particular vitriol—a racist response that developed in part as a reaction against earlier Chinese miners' protests in Victoria and New South Wales.[53]

White settlers, colonial bureaucrats, and Manchester capitalists argued on the other hand that a new society founded on the settler plantation defined by coerced migrant work from China, India, New Guinea, or the United States would serve the interests and elevate the position of the white settler regardless of if they owned the plantation.[54] Colonial administrators, including the first governor of Queensland, George Bowen, and the first premier, Robert Herbert, put these arguments forth repeatedly.[55] According to Bowen, "The employment of Chinese or coolies would be to Queensland what machinery has been to England"—an opinion he believed reflected English manufacturers' general opinion.[56] Bowen elsewhere wrote to the English liberal and free trade crusader Richard Cobden to urge that manufacturers invest some of their skill, energy, and capital in the expansion of cotton plantations in Queensland: "There are no restrictions here . . . on the importation of cheap labour from India."[57] Robert Herbert believed that Queensland should be seen as a "tropical colony" and therefore should "seek Indian and/or Chinese labour."[58] Herbert would further support the arrival of South Sea Island labor in the colony, which began in 1863.[59]

For settlers aspiring to be planters and colonial bureaucrats invested in transforming Queensland into a settler colony based upon the plantation, racial investment in the coolie was part of a broader racist vision of the future. This meant that the colonization and transformation of Queensland into a plantation society would make a new category of Queensland capitalist humanity—the planter who lived through the domination of coolie or Black labor founded on the dispossession of Aboriginal land. An observer for the Manchester Cotton Supply Association clinically described the racist comparative approach characteristic of Queensland: "A resident of Sydney, about to experiment on a cotton plantation in Queensland, has engaged a number of negroes, coolies, and Chinese labourers in order to test the several capabilities of the three races."[60] If a plantation race management comparative trial did not occur, the comparative mode of looking defined the aspirations of Queensland settlers who sought to become planters and masters on land they recently stole and were actively working to steal.

While Queensland's plantations would eventually employ Chinese labor displaced from the gold fields of New South Wales and Victoria, the basis of the early Queensland plantation system would become rooted in South Sea Island labor, laborers who would at times be described as "South Sea Island coolies" as a way to understand the position of such laborers within an emerging plantation regime.[61] Such racist descriptions were part of logic defined by the hierarchical organization of the settler colonial economic order for white planter advancement. Yet, the advocacy for the expansion of the plantation system would also be challenged by another white settler interest concerned with making Queensland into a colony that would better white European lives through the transformation of Queensland into a white man's and white-only settler colony.

Settling the White Worker

In the settler press, pseudonymous authors vocally opposed the arrival of so-called coolie labor and urged the permanent settlement of white workers in Queensland instead, often voicing anti-Black racism in the same breath. A "Lancashire Man" wrote to Jordan that all Lancashire workers willing to emigrate should be sent to Queensland to grow cotton: "Let them come in thousands, and soon the manufacturing districts of England will be independent of Jonathan and his niggers for ever."[62] Under the pseudonym "Anglo-Saxon," the writer drew upon the U.S. rhetoric of free soil, stating that all Queensland needed was "free land, free labour and freeholders."[63] This rhetoric drew upon the powerful language of the United States free-soil movement, based upon the construction of racially homogeneous settler states.[64] This free-soil project was a part of a powerful global settler colonial project that connected Australia and the United States. Anglo-Saxon presented the rhetoric of Queensland anti-Black racism in its most vicious form, writing: "Equity to the American slave hardly means iniquity to Queensland, an American nigger is bad enough, but why create Queensland niggers?"[65] For him, as was the case in much of U.S. republicanism, opposition to slavery was defined not by opposition to anti-Black racism but rather vitriolic settler support for the creation of all-white settler ethnostates. This was a vision made through reference to U.S. settler slaveholding society.

According to the perverse, racist logic of many Queensland settlers and their advocates, freehold farming seemed to protect the nobility of white settlers' work against forms of capitalist domination that they saw as possible in slavery contexts.[66] They opposed Asian migrant labor because they saw the presence of Chinese and Indian people in the colony as degrading whiteness, not because indentured labor was exploitative. Queensland settlers invested in white free-soil ideology argued their case through white supremacist investment in settler colonialism. George Wight, a particularly fervent advocate of this position, wrote that it was necessary to give as many white settlers as possible an interest in the soil. This, he believed, would both guarantee long-term colonial development and divert the flow of white immigrants away from the United States and toward Queensland.[67] Wight clearly stated his investment in white labor against coolies, whom he described as a "degraded and opposite race." Constructing such ideas of "opposite" was an argument for a white, racially homogeneous settler colony. Further, minimizing the economic impact slavery had on U.S. economic development, Wight claimed that the country's unparalleled progress could be attributed to the "immigration of poor people, who had no alternative" but to clear land and farm to survive.[68] Wight's goal was to make white farmers a small proprietor class that could serve as the economic basis for Queensland—a belief that others shared.[69]

Defenses of a racially homogeneous colonial society like Wight's were at times tied to arguments, if not always beliefs, that the productivity and efficiency of white cotton farmers would be higher than hired labor in general and higher than South Asian and Chinese indenture in particular.[70] For some, within a calculus of racialized labor productivity, even if white labor would not be more efficient than so-called coolie or South Sea Island labor, it would still be white, and that was enough. This whiteness would ensure the future racial stability of the colony in ways that Indigenous people, Asian, Black, or Indian labor could not. It was further argued that because unemployed English and Scottish textile workers paid taxes to support the British Empire, they were entitled to assisted access to participate in settler colonial projects in Australia.[71]

As this debate continued, for those interested in transforming Queensland into a racially homogeneous settler society, unemployed Lancashire factory workers became especially sought after not only as a labor force but also as an occupying mass. This two-fold interest in unemployed factory workers again reveals linkages between settler colonization, whiteness, and projects to racially shore up capitalist crisis. Henry Parkes, an advocate for immigration to New South Wales, described his hometown of Coventry, where "poor ribbon-weavers are down at starvation point and in Lancashire, it is to be feared, many will. What a perversity in the management of the world that their labour cannot be transferred to where it is so much wanted—Australia!"[72] Advocates for immigration to Queensland pursued their case with fervor that sometimes exceeded even Parkes's emphatic writings.

In 1861, Henry Jordan worked to realize Parkes's vision of white demographic transfer through a project that sought to bring masses of unemployed English factory workers to Queensland. Jordan's efforts combined with short-lived institutions such as the Cotton Districts Emigration Society, formed in 1863 which also sought to facilitate the emigration of factory workers to British colonies and the United States.[73] During a series of lectures in the United Kingdom, Jordan frequently argued for keeping migration within the British Empire rather than enabling the easy passage of English citizens to the United States.[74] Through Jordan's plan, migrants would receive assisted passages, while those who offered to pay for passages would receive land. Jordan himself advocated most strongly for the migration of skilled operatives and overseers, seeking to prevent "the inundation of the colony by paupers, weavers, boys having been convicted of crime and a generally refuse class of persons from the streets."[75] Jordan was further convinced that white labor in Queensland would be able to compete with U.S. cotton cultivation while at the same time providing the white bodies necessary for permanent colonial occupation.[76]

The first immigrants arrived on 16 January 1863 aboard the Black Ball Line, but a campaign to frustrate Jordan's efforts followed soon afterward.[77] According to Jordan, after dispatching the first thousand Lancashire workers to Queensland, Manchester factory owners tried to subvert his efforts, first through open hostilities and then by encouraging handloom weaver emigration, whom Jordan described as the "most useless of the unemployed."[78] While factory owners admitted their preference for the settlement of unemployed factory workers in Queensland rather than in the United States, in general, they opposed emigration through assisted programs. In an editorial later referred to as the "manufacturers' manifesto," Edmund Potter wrote that the factory master could not willingly watch "his" labor supply be removed through assisted migration.[79] Though Potter believed that in the future emigrating artisans farming on "virgin soil" would provide the textile industry with its best customers and work as civilizational pioneers, he also believed that factory workers could not be encouraged to emigrate.[80] Other factory owners, especially Thomas Bazley, advocated for the introduction of Asian labor into Queensland. As another advocate for manufacturers wrote, it was startling to hear of efforts to send factory workers to Queensland in plans supported by the state. The author made these claims while declaring that factory workers were not "starving at home" and could not supply the forms of labor demanded by colonialism.[81]

In addition to factory owners, emerging companies in Queensland dedicated to the introduction of expansive cotton cultivation had often antagonistic attitudes toward proposals for the companies to be based upon white labor. As Jordan noted, the first company to be established in Queensland was convinced that "Asiatic labor was alone suited for the purpose."[82] In contrast, other companies, in part to gain colonial assistance, declared that white "European" labor alone would be pursued.[83]

Jordan's own investments were in white labor and white bodies and especially of unemployed English factory workers. Though he also pursued labor from Scotland, Ireland, and continental Europe, Jordan's focus was especially upon "distressed operatives," unemployed factory laborers from the textile manufacturing districts of Lancashire.[84] This focus caused complaints from both Scotland and Ireland. As one Belfast writer noted, it seemed as if Jordan supported the passage of operatives only from England and that Jordan operated under the principle that "no Irish need apply."[85] In an era defined by Irish immigration to the United States, such moments are a reminder that access to the wages of whiteness was predicated upon settler passage or to profit through what Aileen Moreton-Robinson has described as "white possession."[86]

In addition to direct opposition from factory owners in England, Jordan confronted resistance from committees established for the relief of Lancashire workers — committees that were often enough partially composed of the same factory owners working to frustrate his efforts. Jordan wrote the mayor of Manchester to offer financial assistance for the migration of factory labor to Queensland. Jordan's request was refused because of a belief that "the spinners expected soon to want all of their hands, and could not encourage their being sent away to the colonies."[87] Because of this, Jordan noted the workers who did decide to emigrate to Queensland were in a "pitiable condition" and "entirely destitute" because they had been excluded from receiving any form of relief from relief committees due to their interest in migrating.[88] At the same time, some small new organizations emerged for the purpose of encouraging emigration, including the Manchester Emigrants' Aid Committee and the Lancashire and Queensland Cooperative Emigration Society. However, Jordan was wary that these organizations had ulterior motives for claiming land meant for emigrants.

To counter resistance, Jordan consistently argued that the interest of manufacturers would be best served by encouraging workers to emigrate. He repeatedly stated that unemployed factory workers who emigrated would consume twenty times as many textiles from Great Britain as those who moved to the United States.[89] This argument was meant to convince the many manufacturers who believed that underconsumption and overproduction were the causes of the textile industry crisis and that sending unemployed workers to the colony would facilitate capitalist recovery. In working to encourage emigration, Jordan further met with many factory owners, including Bazley, and also with several liberal statesmen, including John Bright. Based on these meetings, Jordan declared that Lancashire manufacturers were "the most hostile" to emigration and did not appreciate that every person emigrating also became "a customer to the English manufacturer."[90]

Jordan undertook an extensive speaking tour in England and Scotland in 1861 to encourage emigration. In these speeches, he consistently advocated for turning Queensland into a white man's country. In Manchester, Jordan speculated on the profitability of cotton grown by "free European labour," which he estimated would "yield from 75 to 100 per cent on the outlay."[91] In Derby, Jordan imagined the British Empire independent of a foreign cotton supply, growing "not by the seat and groans and tears of three or four millions of slaves, but by the highly remunerative labour of hundreds of thousands of her own free-born sons of the soil."[92] In Leeds, Jordan asked why cotton couldn't be grown by "white labour," arguing that it was a "fallacy that you must have black labour for cotton growing." Jordan further maintained that white labor would be more profitable than enslaved labor and would do "much work toward emancipating the African race from their unhappy bondage."[93] In Liverpool, Jordan made a similar argument, stating that the cultivation of cotton in Queensland by white labor would "deal a death blow to slavery."[94] As he had said in Exeter, it was possible to grow cotton in a British colony by British labour.[95] Though he consistently spoke out against slavery, he did so in pursuit of his own racist vision of making Queensland into a white man's country or racially homogeneous white ethno-state.

Visions of transforming Queensland into a white man's country were connected also to ideas of the family as a cohesive unit that worked to produce colonial stability and permanence. As legislation for emigration declared, white emigrants must principally be married couples, with men under forty and women under thirty-five.[96] Despite these aspirations, ongoing migration to Queensland was characterized by gender asymmetries. During 1861, 5,458 men and 3,491 women moved to Queensland; the subsequent arrival of unemployed Lancashire workers would only heighten the gender disparity with the arrival of more white settler men than women.[97]

Colonial arguments about the comparative racial capacity of white family work for cotton cultivation often went in different directions. One advocate for white settlement stated that equal quantities of cotton would be cultivated in Australia by equal hands at work.[98] Jordan at times claimed English labor would be more productive at cultivating cotton. In other instances, he argued that if one man "being a slave" could cultivate ten acres in Queensland, "one man and a boy" could cultivate the same amount.[99]

Yet the justifications for emigration did not rely solely on racialized productive capacities. Some settlers prioritized colonial white supremacy based upon their commitment to white racial homogeneous settler states. As one author noted, when an "inferior class of labour" was present in a colony, the small farmer was turned into a "miserable being whom his social inferiors despise. It was so in the Southern States of America, where the 'poor whites' were objects of contempt to the negro slaves."[100] Again, these arguments were not so much about how to ensure the export of commodities nor the stabilization of metropolitan capitalism but rather to ensure the future of a white supremacist and racially exclusive settler society based upon interpretations of U.S. settler slavery.

Ultimately, Jordan's efforts to secure white settlers from Britain to work in the colony would result in the arrival of 1,376 "distressed operatives" to Queensland. However, his and others' visions of the transformation of Queensland into a racially homogeneous white man's country would not be realized in the nineteenth century.[101] In 1863, the same year that the first unemployed factory workers arrived, Robert Towns, a settler, planter, and trader who earlier sought to organize projects for the migration labor from Calcutta, sought out South Sea Island laborers. Along with a group of other planters, Towns had been looking toward bringing Asian indentured labor to Queensland since at least 1861. He believed that migrant coolie labor would allow Queensland to compete immediately with sugar from Mauritius, Java, and Manila and ultimately with U.S. cotton.[102] He would play a central role in transforming the relationship between Asian indentured labor, Lancashire workers, and the colonization of Queensland. Towns would further bring the first Pacific Island laborers to the colony in 1863.

Towns explained his efforts to bring over a coolie labor force with reference to both white suffering and Black freedom. Towns argued that it would be "unjust" to force "Anglo-Saxons" to work under a tropical sun.[103] He described that his interest in growing cotton in Queensland was meant to supply "suffering" Lancashire workers with cotton in the place of that provided by U.S. slavery: "I think I deserve the thanks of the community for the introduction of that kind of labor which is suited to our wants, and which may save us from the *inhumanity* of driving to the exposed labor of field work, the less tropically hardy European and children, for I suppose the most thorough advocate of European labor will admit, that in cotton clearing and picking they, as well as the men, must take part in the labor."[104] Towns racially assessed the productive capacity of Pacific Island laborers as "tractable" using such racial assessments as the bases for his plan for forced migration. Towns told his recruiting agent that he preferred children, those between the ages of fourteen and eighteen. He described himself as a "kind master."[105]

While Towns initially proposed bringing Pacific Islanders to Queensland to create vast cotton plantations, this plan would soon fail. Yet, Towns and other planters in the colony would depend upon laborers often kidnapped from Melanesian islands such as New Caledonia and New Guinea to build a new plantation capitalism defined by sugar production. Over 60,000 Pacific Islanders would be taken to Queensland to do the brutal work of sugar production overseen by white settlers. By the 1870s, even Henry Jordan had become involved in sugar cultivation. Yet, given his belief in building a white ethno-state, he operated his estate based upon white labor only. In this, he was an exception to a settler plantation capitalism that was increasingly anchored in dependence upon the coercion of Pacific Island workers.[106]

White Men's Countries and the Anglo-Saxon Roads to Capitalism

In the 1860s, Queensland settlers and bureaucrats put forth a vision of a racially homogeneous white ethno-state and settler colony with a human mass composed of white bodies and white workers reallocated from the shut-down factories of Lancashire. These unemployed workers were to settle cotton farms in Queensland and live new, racially pure, economically productive white lives. This vision was partially defined in antithesis to white racial experiences in the United States. However, that vision dissipated, and settlers increasingly accepted a vision of plantation dominance characterized by white plantation ownership and dependent upon the coercion of South Sea Islanders' work. British colonial commitments to African American freedom or abolition played no role in the ongoing debates about race, empire, and colonization. White settler interest in African American labor in Queensland instead was founded in an investment in the social composition and economic foundations of the colony alone. The two competing settler visions for Queensland's future both entailed colonial conquest and white supremacy and drew upon U.S. settler republicanism and U.S. slavery simultaneously. This debate highlighted the movement of ideas through global capitalism and across settler colonial, franchise colonial, and slavery regimes uniting the slaveholding U.S. South with the settler colonies of the British Empire and colonial India. In the wake of the U.S. Civil War, this circulation would also serve to return these ideas and practices to the United States. In Texas, Thomas Affleck, a slaveholder and white supremacist who once imagined the scientifically managed plantation, would begin a recruitment project to mitigate the disruptions to white-dominated, slavery-produced capitalism. He was inspired by Henry Jordan's efforts to make Queensland into a white man's country.

In his 1868 book, *Greater Britain*, Charles Wentworth Dilke, a Chelsea MP and pro-imperialist, reflected upon travels to both Virginia and Queensland. In Virginia, Dilke asked slaveholders about Black freedom. The slaveholders' responses were presented in the most racist terms and also grounded in a belief that Black people failed to meet the "responsibilities of freedom."[107] Dilke accepted such white supremacist visions as a reason for the necessity of global white supremacy and argued that this justified global white man's dominion. Describing himself as engaged in a political struggle that bound the futures of the English in America and of England and America together, Dilke saw Black emancipation as a historic challenge for white supremacy of "political, ethnological, [and] historic" importance.[108] For Dilke, slavery was bad because of what it did to white people, not because of its anti-Blackness. In identifying so strongly with the cause of the slaveholder, Dilke also facilitated the making of Anglo-Saxon connections between the United States and Britain. As Dilke stated, it was necessary for the United States to create a system where Black people would either "work or starve." This situation could be introduced through the mass importation of labor, Dilke claimed, from China, Bombay, Calcutta, the Pacific Islands, and continental Europe.[109] Dilke saw U.S. white supremacy as inevitably tied to the fate of Anglo-Saxon dominance in the British Empire. Dilke was articulating a future vision of white supremacist capitalism in global perspective.

Dilke further saw the fates of settler colonialism in the United States and Queensland as bound together and mutually intelligible, claiming that in the American Midwest, as in Australia, there was "no future" for Indigenous peoples.[110] He wrote, "It is not for us, who have the past of Tasmania and the present of Queensland to account for, to do more than record the fact that the Americans are not more successful with the red men of Kansas than we with the black men of Australia."[111] These articulations of white supremacist capitalism, new planning documents for a world where slavery was ending, were part of a global project that reacted to the radical struggles for liberation that enslaved people enacted during this era.

Dilke's vision was for a future world characterized less by nations and more by empires and global race struggles.[112] These racist visions of the post-emancipation world index something that Du Bois recognized as painfully emerging in this era, a period where the United States' logic of violent territorial conquest and racialized labor subordination in the service of capitalism continued and expanded rather than disappeared. At the same time, these projects were reactionary in response to the way that formerly enslaved people in the United States had just destroyed the old model of global capitalism made between Britain and the United States that had been propelled by U.S. slavery.

PART IV : : : **Slavery's Pathways**

9 ::: The Toil of Man
Black Emancipation, Chinese Indenture, and the Colonization of Belize

At the 1868 Louisiana State Fair, a large crowd gathered at an exhibition displaying commodities from the central American colony of British Honduras. At one table, spectators looked at exemplary lumber. Another table featured jars of different grades of sugar—"all of Colonial manufacture." The cane was "enormous," a journalist wrote, adding that "planters should *see* it."[1] Just as the size of the cane could not be rendered in language alone, sugar had had an almost unspeakable impact on former U.S. slaveholders. Their lives and livelihoods had been overturned by the American Civil War. For those former slaveholders gathered in New Orleans, to behold such sugar in the aftermath of the war was to imagine the continued possibility of white dominance after Black emancipation in the United States, and beyond.

In April 1868, the *British Honduras Colonist* commented that ships had been continuously arriving at the wharf of Belize for the four or five months previous. Onboard those ships were white southerners, arriving by the hundreds. Many of them were leaving Louisiana, South Carolina, and Texas in the aftermath of the Civil War and resettling in British Honduras.[2] As settlers and planters, these whites imagined producing sugar cane on plantations that they would manage or own.

Authorities in British Honduras welcomed these new arrivals. Already settled whites, colonial officials, and landholding companies imagined these planters colonizing and transforming the colony. Up until that point, the colony's primary export had been mahogany; however, a price decline caused interest in mahogany extraction in the colony to wane. One writer described his vision of former slaveholder transformation, where sugar would depose mahogany as king.[3] Arriving white former slaveholders would convert British Honduras into a colony of "rich fields of the world-famed golden cane." If capital and labor could be obtained, sugar could be produced for export, making good on investments in the colony. The systematic colonization of British Honduras by former U.S. slaveholders was imagined to be capable of revitalizing the colonial economy following stagnation.

The arrival of former U.S. slave owners in British Honduras was the latest phase in a series of British colonial projects to transform the colony's racial and economic foundations and expand plantations through immigration. These projects were defined by efforts to settle and coerce migrant laborers and, at the same time, former U.S. slaveholders during the 1860s. As the lieutenant governor of British Honduras noted in 1863, "We look hopefully, for our future, to the fertility of the Colonial soil stimulated and utilized by human industry, and have passed acts to augment the supply of labour and to encourage the introduction of machinery for agricultural and manufacturing purposes."[4]

The colonial transformation of British Honduras hinged upon the colonization of land and raw material production for exports, particularly sugar. In the classic *Cuban Counterpoint*, Fernando Ortiz noted that sugar created the Cuban latifundia.[5] In British Honduras, the relationship was reversed: already existing large landholding companies dreamed of creating a sugar colony, of exporting sugar to enrich themselves while dispossessing both the Maya and Black Belizeans. After the consolidation of landownership and the formation of large land-owning companies such as the British Honduras Company and Young, Toledo, and Company, efforts to cultivate sugar reemerged on a grander scale. Together, these two companies claimed over 1 million acres of land each (two-fifths of the British colony).[6] The arrival of white former slaveholders followed several other projects to relocate formerly enslaved people from the United States as well as Chinese indentured labor to the colony. Yet these new arrivals served an additional purpose beyond sugar cultivation—the overarching colonial project also sought to repress Maya land struggles against the landholding companies that claimed Belize as their own. Landholding companies had become invested in a racial and colonial project formed between the British Empire and the United States, a project that depended upon the colonial management of race and settlement.

This project took its most concrete form in three interrelated efforts: a concerted attempt to bring formerly enslaved people from the United States to the colony during the American Civil War (1862–63), a turn toward Chinese indentured laborers (1865), and a final project to bring white former slaveholders from Louisiana and South Carolina following the end of the Civil War (1865–ca. 1870). Following the passage of a wide-ranging Immigration Act in 1861, from 1862 through 1863, the British Honduras Company and British diplomatic representatives in Washington, D.C., worked with Abraham Lincoln and his cabinet from 1862 through 1863 in an attempt to arrange Black emigration to British Honduras. Partly as a result of Black refusal to relocate, this project broke down, and company interest shifted toward Chinese indentured laborers. This resulted in the arrival of a single ship, *Light of the Age*, which brought 474 indentured laborers from Xiamen, China, to the colony in 1865, and ended in a violent colonial failure. The companies shifted course once again, settling on the perceived technological, settling, and managerial expertise of white former slaveholders from the United States, seeking their relocation to the colony starting as early as 1865.

With a population of over 25,000 in 1861, British Honduras was small in comparison to India or Jamaica.[7] However, during the eighteenth century British Honduras was among the most profitable colonies within the British Empire as a result of the value of mahogany logwood exports cut by enslaved people. For the British Honduras Company and for colonial legislatures, colonization through plantation development was intended to continue the processes of clearing wilderness through the cutting of mahogany and logwood and the clearing of land that could be turned into plantations or sites of white settlement. In the Northern District, where the British Honduras Company attempted to first enact this transformation, the ongoing Guerra de Castas (or Caste War) on the Yucatán Peninsula coupled with claims of Kekchi and Cruzob Maya sovereignty in the Northern District interrupted the company's land claims. And, through this, the plantation as a form of occupation and Indigenous dispossession seemed to have urgent significance for white settlers.

In reflections upon the relationship between indenture, colonialism, and slavery, Walter Rodney noted that indenture built upon and "approximated" slavery, especially through regimented techniques and command of the production process.[8] In British Honduras, indenture approximated slavery spatially, structurally, and temporally. As British Honduras sought to expand toward plantation development, expectations for the colony formed through interpretation of the histories of slavery and emancipation in the United States.

As this new wave of colonial projects crashed onto the colony, it was also part of a vaster sea of white movements across the British Caribbean to dominate labor after slavery, with immigration becoming a central part of both the logic of colonial occupation and also the redefinition of life and work in the context of enslaved people achieving the end of their enslavement. Across the British Empire, a new, colonial definition of freedom emerged that demanded the subordination of subjects to the continued demands of the plantation economy, one that placed work at the center of this world and saw those Black people who did not work as disposable. At a Kingston meeting in September held in support of increasing the removal of African Americans from the United States to Jamaica, Reverend D. H. Campbell observed, "It had been the wise ordaining of Providence that the fruits and products of the soil could not be obtained without the toil of man; and it is the blight of Providence upon that country which did not possess sufficient people for that purpose."[9] Such a reflection reveals a deeper truth that defined this era: the post-slavery definition of Black freedom was based upon a logic of colonial possession that demanded that the formerly enslaved along with indentured colonial subjects from China and India do the work of empire under white management.

The Pursuit of Black Emancipation in British Honduras

The labor of migrants was essential to the practice of colonization through plantation expansion. After initially seeking to bring indentured South Asian and Chinese labor to British Honduras from 1861 to 1862, the colonial government shifted toward formerly enslaved people in the United States. In U.S. state discourse, formerly enslaved people who had recently escaped plantation slavery or who had been enslaved on plantations conquered by the Union army known as "contrabands" were particularly sought by landholding interests in British Honduras.

The prospect of removing the formerly enslaved from the United States for the transformation of a white ethno-state inspired racist settlers in Queensland. In British Honduras, removal projects converged over two racist definitions of Black freedom produced in a trans-imperial context and according to the British colonial demand for Caribbean export production and U.S. Republican visions of Black removal from the United States. Removal plans had been circulating for decades thanks to the colonization movement, which united white antislavery with racism. The colonization movement's proposals ranged from the encouragement of voluntary self-removal from the United States to forced eliminationist projects that would create a white ethno-state. The American Colonization Society formed in 1817 deported over 13,000 Black people living in the United States to Liberia. Colonization and Black removal ideologies inspired Abraham Lincoln, who believed in racial separation and had long been persuaded by the colonization movement's racism and continued to be so during the American Civil War. As he observed in a 14 August 1862 meeting with five Black delegates, he believed it would be better if Black people, whose presence caused the Civil War, would leave the United States. An observer who witnessed the meeting recorded that Lincoln stated, "It is better for us both, therefore, to be separated."[10]

White racial separatist projects in the United States attracted widespread interest across the British Caribbean in British Guiana, British Honduras, Jamaica, and Trinidad. Beneath colonial bureaucratic discourse about the British Caribbean as a space for Black freedom lay a series of commitments for the continued domination of Black people's lives and work in a series of plans for the indenture of formerly enslaved people in the British Caribbean, bound to contracts of indenture with the future promise of land.[11] British Caribbean colony representatives from British Guiana and British Honduras visited the United States in support of colonization projects. British Guiana's secretary, William Walker, arrived in the United States in September 1862 in an effort to obtain "a supply of the freed negroes from this continent in aid of the cultivation of the staple products of the colony," meeting with the U.S. secretary of the Interior. In addition to Walker's efforts, the manager for the British Honduras Company, John Hodge, would engage in sustained efforts to seek voluntary Black removal from the United States to British Honduras for plantation work.[12]

Hodge himself sought to capitalize on Republican racism and investment in Black relocation through colonization. Hodge described the outbreak of the American Civil War as having "induced the British Honduras Company to abandon their previous intention of hiring coolies in the East Indies and China, for the cultivation of their extensive estates and to rely chiefly upon obtaining the hired labour of those who had been slaves in the country known as emancipated contraband, or freedmen."[13] This led to meetings with Lincoln and his cabinet and travel to contraband camps where he sought to make Black emancipation in the United States work for the British Honduras Company. An alignment between the white Republican interest in Black colonization and the British Honduras colonial demand for plantation labor appeared to be increasingly viable.[14] Yet success still depended on British diplomatic recognition of the Union army and a move away from the British proclamation of neutrality during the American Civil War.

British colonial interest in Black removal to the colony depended upon a demand for Black work rather than a commitment to Black freedom.[15] Hodge stated this point in his most urgent demands for Black labor. He noted that the focus upon Black labor caused the company to be "deprived of the Chinese labourers we expected" and that the hopes of planting cotton and sugar depended upon "obtaining the labourers we can procure in the United States."[16] Together, these comments formed part of a sustained commitment to the redefinition of Black freedom as a freedom that was subordinated to the demands of capitalist production as dominated by former slaveholders, landholders, and colonial bureaucrats.

For the benefit of the British Honduras Company, Hodge seized upon Abraham Lincoln's commitment to racial separation as a way to secure government support for Black removal from the United States—ideally with the Union's financial support. Hodge in some moments presented a vision of Black settlers receiving land of their own and utilized the language of freedom. However, the subsequent experiences of Chinese laborers in British Honduras reveal that this depiction masked the violence of post-slavery sugar plantation production as a murderous project.[17] As Charles Leas, the official U.S. agent in Belize, argued, if formerly enslaved people had relocated to British Honduras, they would have been "subjected to a species of slavery and demoralization far worse than ever existed in our country."[18] Leas's account itself was part of a normalization of U.S. slavery's violence. Yet, it also exposed how beneath the British colonial definition of freedom was subordination to the work of empire's plantations and another violent reality that approximated slavery.

Building the White Republic

In the United States, Black colonization was part of the white Republican commitment to white and Black racial separation.[19] Throughout his presidency, Abraham Lincoln, along with other Republicans, were committed to a vision of a white United States that limited Black presence within its expanding national borders, that concentrated Black people within certain parts of the Union, or that remade the United States into a white ethnostate. These beliefs were themselves influenced not just by the colonization movement but also by Indian removal policy. Richard Blackett has noted that James Watkins, a Black person declared to be a fugitive slave in the United States, believed that Lincoln desired to transform the United States west of the Mississippi into a free white man's country.[20] But, Lincoln also saw the "voluntary" removal of African Americans from the American South as a part of this project.

Republican sympathies toward white racial separatism unfolded in relation to the realities of the American Civil War. Two months after Congress's passage of the Second Confiscation Act of July 1862, which authorized federal forces to free enslaved people from Confederate forces, Lincoln signed a contract with a group of speculators who promised to aid in the colonization of African Americans in Chiriquí, New Grenada (now in Panama).

In a preliminary draft of the Emancipation Proclamation of January 1863, Lincoln suggested that it might be possible to "colonize persons of African descent, with their consent, upon this continent or elsewhere[.]"[21] In April 1863, Lincoln supported the deportation of 453 African Americans to Île-à-Vache, Haiti, a disastrous plan that was aborted after only eleven months.[22] And throughout 1862 and 1863, Lincoln and his cabinet seriously considered John Hodge's proposal for Black colonization in British Honduras.

Hodge arrived in Washington, D.C., on 22 April 1862, accompanied by the British planter J. R. Dickson, who represented British Guiana. With Dickson, Hodge would relentlessly pursue a project to relocate "able-bodied" Black men who he saw as the muscle and sinew of British Honduras's colonial rebirth through the plantation.[23] In a letter to Lord Lyons written on the occasion of his departure from the United States to British Honduras, Hodge described the changing trajectory of his interest in formerly enslaved people who had been declared contraband in the United States. Hodge soon met with Secretary of State William Seward, who stated that there would "be no objection" to "the recruitment of contrabands and others emigrating if they themselves were willing." Hodge would further meet with Secretary of the Interior John Usher and Senator Samuel C. Pomeroy of Kansas, who both supported colonization, with Pomeroy overseeing the Chiriquí colonization project. Pomeroy introduced Hodge to Abraham Lincoln, who sought to ensure that formerly enslaved people removed to British Honduras would "receive same wages as others, and would be entitled to the privileges of natives," agreed that Hodge could move forward with his project without a convention between Britain and the United States. The "privileges of the natives" had violent latitude across U.S. and British Empires. In 1862, Lincoln oversaw the largest mass execution of Native Dakota Sioux.[24] Contemporaneously, Britain enacted eliminationist settler projects and waged blood-soaked wars on "natives" across its empire.

Satisfied following his meeting with the president of the United States, Hodge continued to visit the refugee camps where formerly enslaved people were held near Washington, D.C., and Alexandria, Virginia. Hodge noted that formerly enslaved people would consider relocating "provided their families were allowed to accompany them." Yet because of Hodge's primary interest in the work of able-bodied Black men, he sought financial support to help offset his project of Black removal from the United States because of the cost of relocating women and children. Hodge therefore proposed with the support of Senator Pomeroy that the U.S. should pay for Black passages to British Honduras. Yet Usher ultimately refused to support such payment because of his frustrations over the outfitting of the Confederate Privateer *Alabama* in Britain and its raid on U.S. merchants.[25]

The desire of formerly enslaved people confined in American refugee camps to remain with their families reflected efforts to reunite and stay together. At the same time, following the Second Confiscation Act, which set out a policy for the military enlistment of "able-bodied" men, the contraband camps sheltered a far greater share of women and children.[26] Black women were disproportionately present in these camps, something that presented itself as a problem to Hodge's interest in the work of Black men. For Hodge able-bodied Black men were to form the basis of his plantation settlement project. While children could become adults in time, such a long-term investment was of no interest to Hodge. Black families' desires to remain together thus caused difficulties for Hodge's project.

While visiting refugee camps outside of Washington, D.C., Hodge met with Danforth B. Nichols, superintendent of freedmen, in an attempt to work around the "problem of military enlistment by consideration of dependent families." Hodge imagined ways to use Black families to his end, hoping that the passages of refugees would be supported by the U.S. government. Yet despite Hodge's efforts, Usher would ultimately back away from negotiations because Secretary of War Edwin M. Stanton sought to enlist Black men in these refugee camps into the army.[27]

In response, Hodge worked to convince Stanton of the possibility of mutual benefit for the enlistment of Black men in refugee camps in the Union army and the emigration of freedmen to British Honduras. Hodge met again with Lincoln, who stated that the deportation of freedpeople from the United States was his "honest desire."[28] However, Stanton remained firmly against colonization. Under the pretext of British neutrality, Hodge decided that he could not at present continue to pursue his plan to relocate formerly enslaved people to British Honduras, stating that because he was uncertain whether Britain's government would sanction the emigration, he had been prevented from relocating formerly enslaved people he believed he required and decided to return to British Honduras. The reality that Hodge left unstated was that the enlistment of African American freedmen into the Union army was a social revolution that interrupted his project for a plantation-based colony dependent upon their work and relocation.

Yet, at the heart of the restrictions on Black relocation to British Honduras was Britain's unwillingness to disrupt white Confederate claims on Black people as enslaved.[29] F. F. Elliot of the British Honduras Company offered an overview of the stakes for British neutrality and clarified apprehensions expressed by British colonial officials over enabling Black people designated as "contrabands" to emigrate. How could it be ensured that the emigration of contrabands would not encourage Black escape from slavery? Elliot empathized with Hodge, who had been "debarred" over the late objection made by Lord Lyons from obtaining "the most valuable class of emigrants for agricultural purposes"—freedmen. As Elliot observed, Hodge was instead forced to be confined to the "resident black population of the Northern states, a set of people for the most part whose introduction it is believed, the planters would deprecate as likely to be useless and burdensome."[30] Further, some British colonial officials believed that if the Union were defeated in the Civil War, Black colonization in British Honduras might serve as an embarrassment for the British Empire. The political maneuvers of British politicians and diplomats during this era were defined not by a commitment to Black freedom but by a desire for political stability and a demand for Black labor.[31]

While Hodge asserted that Abraham Lincoln sanctioned the emigration of enslaved people designated as contraband, metropolitan Britain sought to remain neutral during the Civil War without disrupting diplomatic relations with the Confederacy. British diplomats were particularly hesitant to act in any way that might undermine that neutrality, especially through supporting a project to facilitate the relocation of Black people who Confederates claimed as their real estate and property. While Hodge saw in "contrabands" the new laboring basis of British Honduras "because they, and they only can be depended upon for continuous agricultural labor," metropolitan Britain saw its broader strategic interest in neutrality.[32] For the British Honduras Company, formerly enslaved people were to labor continuously subordinated to the demands of the plantation economy. In pursuit of this, the chairman of the British Honduras Company also attempted to intervene, demonstrating the importance of this question by stating that a project also for growing cotton was started in British Honduras and interrupted with "favorable" circumstances except for "the very important one of labour." As the chairman continued, Hodge had "made wonderful progress towards procuring the requisite (black) labourers."[33] Yet metropolitan Britain remained invested in the possibility that their ultimate access to that labor might ultimately be destroyed should the Confederacy win the Civil War. Both positions were invested in the future subordination of Black people to the plantation economy.

Hodge's hubris about the possibility of obtaining African American labor continued in a June letter to Lord Lyons. What once was described as possible now became described as certain: "When last in Washington I could have got several hundred of Contraband and other Emigrants from this neighborhood, and as many colored persons born free belonging to other districts have applied, I trust, notwithstanding the late changes to obtain sufficient to fill a vessel before long."[34] His certainty notwithstanding, Hodge may not have had his finger on the pulse of the social revolution underway.

Alongside the Emancipation Proclamation, a revolution was already in motion, with ramifications for the supporters of colonization, possibly including Lincoln himself. Enthusiasm for colonization projects was increasingly abandoned during 1863, particularly because the enlistment of African American men in the Union army seemed to confer not just the right to remain but also the necessity for the war effort.[35] T. J. Dunning, a London trade unionist leader and important figure within the English working class, offered another perspective that put at the center not Black citizenship through military enlistment but rather Black death: "This feeling against the Negro has abated since they have been enlisted as soldiers in the Federal Army. Two reasons have been given by the American press. First, because it will save the American people from serving in the Army; and secondly, because it will, to that extent, destroy the Negro."[36] This vision of anti-Black violence winning the war and limiting Black presence was also part of a project meant for securing the permanent whiteness of the United States.

To further his project of encouraging Black immigration to the colony, in July 1863 John Hodge brought the Native abolitionist Charles Babcock and future African American politician John Willis Menard to British Honduras. Menard wrote the lieutenant governor of British Honduras, Frederick Seymour, inquiring about the disposition that the colonial government would hold out to "colored people of the United States who would be disposed to remove to this colony as permanent settlers."[37] While Menard stated clearly that his interest was for securing "a permanent home and nationality" for African Americans who came to the colony as settlers, R. Ferguson, who worked for the British Honduras Company and forwarded Menard's letter to Seymour, described Menard as an Illinois farmer who sought to rent or purchase land but who also would bring "others of his fellow countrymen" who would probably have a "supply of labourers with them."[38] This interest characterized the different interests of Black people who sought to relocate to the colony to experiment with freedom and of the colonial officials who sought Black people as laborers. Charles Babcock published a short pamphlet on the possibilities of British Honduras, declaring, "AS PIONEERS, ALL ABLE BODIED, ENERGETIC, INDUSTRIOUS COLORED MEN with their families, and a small capital, emigrating to the colony of British Honduras, *cannot fail of success*."[39] However, despite this enthusiasm, British colonial officials believed that planters were more interested in formerly enslaved people and would most likely view Black arrival from the northern United States as "useless and burdensome."[40]

Babcock was a radical abolitionist, and in Belize he believed that he witnessed a society where race did not matter and where "complexion will make no difference."[41] As a committed colonizationist, Babcock asked, "Is this country preferable to all others yet offered us?" In British Honduras, Babcock met John Roles, a former Louisiana planter, whom he believed to be an abolitionist who advocated for the laborers and was devoted to the "free-labor" cultivation of cotton in Africa, the Caribbean, and Central America. Despite Babcock and Menard's visit to the colony, the differing interests between establishing a nationality and procuring freedmen as plantation labor proved an insurmountable difference for the colony, and Hodge's recruitment project fell apart. According to Seward, "On the other hand it appeared that the great mass of the Slaves preferred even slavery with their homes to freedom without them."[42] While again this minimized the violence of slavery, it also highlighted the refusal of formerly enslaved people to be removed from the United States. No African Americans emigrated to the colony, and the colonial government in Jamaica issued a circular prohibiting African American migration to the colony as interest shifted toward Chinese indentured labor.[43]

Black families refused to remain separated following emancipation. As post-slavery advertisements demonstrate, family members separated through the internal slave trade sought to reunite with one another.[44] On 25 March 1863, a columnist for the abolitionist *Liberator* outlined reasons he believed that Black colonization in British Honduras would not occur: "The change in the policy of the [U.S.] Government, which is now doing what should have been done two years ago, enlisting and taking into the army all colored men that are able to fight, will undoubtedly check emigration for the present. The people are disposed to remain at home, and see what the future may bring forth."[45]

Freedpeople's participation in the project of emancipation limited Republican abilities to pursue colonization projects and also restricted Hodge's efforts to recruit African American laborers to British Honduras.[46] Among other dynamics, the project was foreclosed by the gendered unfolding of Black emancipation. As Thavolia Glymph has demonstrated, Black men's military enlistment also placed Black women in a place differentially exposed to racial violence, which was concentrated in a vision that rendered Black women as surplus and a burden in contraband camps.[47] Hodge disproportionately met with women and children in contraband camps that he visited; the commitment of these women and children in contraband camps to remain together defied the company's logic of profitability.[48] The unfolding of the American Civil War and the decisions made by enslaved people interrupted the course of Black removal from the United States and colonization in British Honduras.

At the same time, there was an increasing realization within the Union army that the course of the Civil War depended upon Black participation, first as laborers for the Union army and subsequently as soldiers. By 1862, for Unionist conservatives, emancipation became seen as a necessary component of the Union's war effort.[49] The Civil War meant a transformation in the conditions in which white racial separatism could survive. Throughout the Civil War, white-supported Black colonization projects such as those promoted by the American Colonization Society were seen as a means to abolish slavery in the United States through Black removal. As the Civil War proceeded, however, colonization and Union victory grew increasingly apart.

When enslaved people escaped to the northern United States, white supremacist sentiments expanded, hindering white efforts to preserve the Union. The increased number of African Americans who were coming to the northern United States forced the question of universal emancipation, even if most white northerners were not ready to face it. There was interest in transferring African Americans in the American South to the North: throughout the spring and summer of 1862 the slaves of rebels were confiscated, and African Americans were authorized to be in the military.[50] Yet, opposition to Black presence in the North was especially intense throughout the same period.[51] Despite this, formerly enslaved people changed the course of the war—in July 1862, the same month as the passage of the Compensation Act, Congress enabled Black military enlistment, and by late summer 1862, Black men and women were already laboring for the Union army.[52] The American Civil War had been transformed into a social revolution and also into a war for Black emancipation, something that went far beyond republican racial views. In the spring and summer of 1863, Black soldiers participated in the battles of Port Hudson, Milliken's Bend, and Fort Wagner.[53] The Union army increasingly saw that its victory was tied to Black emancipation and dependent upon Black enlistment in the army.[54] By 1864, nearly 400,000 African Americans had traveled to Union lines.[55] By the end of the Civil War, over 170,000 African American men had enlisted in the Union army. Enslaved people had transformed the course of the war and transformed it into a war to end slavery. As enslaved people fought for the end of slavery and post-slavery life within the United States, British colonial officials searched for new pathways for the entrenchment of a new settler plantation economy in British Honduras. This interest continued to pass through U.S. slavery.

From Black Colonization to Chinese Indenture

As British Honduras landholders failed to realize a dream of a new plantation colony based upon the labor of formerly enslaved people from the United States, the interest of landholders and colonial bureaucrats returned to demand for the arrival of indentured labor from China. In this demand, they joined British Caribbean colonies, Queensland, the United States, and beyond in the search for coolies to be subordinated to demands of capitalist production, particularly its plantations. This turn toward coolies reflected back upon what was at the heart of the project to bring formerly enslaved people from the United States to the colony, Asian or Black labor managed by white men for the accumulation of colonial wealth and the expansion of colonial rule and Maya dispossession. For both formerly enslaved people and Chinese laborers it was the contract of indenture which was to at once serve as the sign of freedom and free labor while in reality providing the legal force for coercion and subordination to the demands of the plantation.[56] The demands of companies and landholders in British Honduras for Chinese laborers was part of a longer history of predation upon Asian indentured laborers characteristic of British colonies in the post-slavery Caribbean.[57] On 4 July 1865, the immigration office in Belize announced that 474 migrants arrived in Belize from Xiamen (Amoy), China, aboard *Light of the Age*.[58] As the immigration agent of Belize noted upon the arrival of Chinese laborers, "The productive interests of the colony must derive from the introduction of so well selected a body of young docile and generally healthy laborers."[59] Here, the emphasis of the immigration agent was not upon the arrival of new colonial subjects but upon docile bodies that would meet expectations for subordination to an emerging plantation economy. This vision of docile bodies would ultimately result in the death of many of the Chinese people who would suffer from the hands and visions of plantation owners.

The racist investment of colonial officials and landholders in coolies was formed in relation to views of Asian laborers as a global replacement for the plantation labor done formerly by enslaved people. Before turning toward free Black labor from the United States, Hodge wrote that British Honduras's planter class "require Chinese as the Indians from Yucatan have not the necessary intelligence."[60] This vision was what was returned to and, like projects for plantation-making in Australia and the United States, was founded upon the dispossession of Indigenous people from their land rather than their labor. In a conversation with Lincoln about Asian indentured labor, Hodge stated that "coolies" would be turned to only out of necessity should it become impossible to relocate formerly enslaved people to the colony, and once that became impossible, this was where Hodge's interest returned.

White rumors and fears of coolies abounded. White fears of Chinese sexual perversion, same-sex relations, and gender asymmetries in the disproportionate presence of Chinese men meant that "coolies" would be part of colonial society only to the extent that their bodies were vessels containing labor necessary for colonial progress. Beyond this, Chinese laborers were perceived as a racial threat that needed to be contained.

Planters and the colonial state together repeatedly used violence in attempts to dominate and exploit the Chinese migrants who arrived in the colony aboard *Light of the Age*. Yet in spite of the racialized and gendered contempt inherent in these efforts to reduce Chinese life to efficiently managed labor, Chinese laborers fashioned a variety of forms of living and resistance ranging from family protests, to work stoppages, to the mass abandonment of plantations.

Through participation in the coolie trade, burgeoning colonies like British Honduras and destroyed plantation regimes like the American South sought to reconstruct racial regimes firmly based upon the plantation. Asian indentured labor was imagined as the most efficient means to obtain labor at its cheapest rate and extend plantation society. The imagined cheapness of coolie labor was informed by the notion that this labor was limitless and therefore disposable. In the planter imagination, Chinese labor would result in endless white profits.[61] Yet, colonial elites in British Honduras never succeeded in dominating Chinese labor in the ways that they imagined coolies would enable colonial progress. Instead, across the colony, Chinese laborers in British Honduras subverted the smooth functioning of the global coolie trade while making prudent economic decisions in the allotment of money, subverting the interests of their employers and causing a scandal that stretched from the colony to Xiamen. Global family ties, desires to return home, and the responses of families to their children's decisions all presented significant forms of resistance in addition to more direct work stoppages and absconding.

The arrival of Chinese workers in British Honduras in July 1865 was followed shortly by an imperial dispute over wage withholdings arranged by laborers and meant for family members in Xiamen. Tsai La, Ya, Huang Lui, and many others sent letters to their families explaining their condition, asking if their parents had received allotments as promised.[62] Huang Lui instructed his mother to collect money from the emigration office in Xiamen and noted that two dollars was being deducted from his wages.[63] Many Chinese families did not receive the promised allotments, however. In April, Robert Swinhoe, consul at Xiamen, wrote that a large number of "elderly" women had gathered at his office to protest the nonpayment of monthly allotments due to them.[64] Emigration officials claimed, among other things, that Chinese migrants in British Honduras wanted to discontinue withholdings after arriving in the colony. However, in Xiamen, the gathered women stated that it was impossible that their family members who left for British Honduras would "break faith" and "cast them off" without writing letters. The women were convinced the emigration office had invented a story "to swindle them out of their rightful due."[65] Allotment discontinuations caused broad distress among families whose relations reached from China to British Honduras and resulted in protests in Xiamen.[66]

The allotments of Huang Lui, Ya, and Tsai La reveal anxieties inherent in such family separations. Of the immigrant men in British Honduras, 296 left allotments of two dollars and 2 left allotments of one dollar per month. The decision to leave China and travel to British Honduras often rested upon the ability to provide support to families through indentured labor. The colonial government's mishandling of allotments and the inability of migrants and families to confirm what was transpiring with the handling of allotments produced anxiety, financial difficulty, and uncertainty. Theophilus Sampson, who had worked to recruit workers in Xiamen, apologized to Swinhoe for the difficulty caused by family protests but dismissed the women's concerns, stating the gathered protesters "may be elderly women hired to personate such [relations] and excite compassion."[67] In response to Swinhoe's suggestion that letters from family members were necessary, Sampson argued that "they would in all probability declare a document in Chinese, purporting to be signed by illiterate coolies, to be a forgery or an extortion." Sampson finally declared that Chinese laborers were entitled to protection by the colonial government and that it was their wish to discontinue allotments and that this desire must be followed.

The uncertainty for families and immigrants over allotments coupled with the relative lack of concern over assuaging such anxieties was exacerbated by widespread Chinese migrant death on plantations in British Honduras. According to one report, at least twenty immigrants, including Tan Sing Tran, had their allotments canceled after death.[68]

Anti-Chinese Violence for Colonial Development

> The death of the Immigrants is a loss only to the employer and renders it a matter of interest to him to cause every care to be given during sickness. — Immigration Act of 1861

White investment in Chinese migrants as labor resulted in a whole set of racial hatreds once it became apparent that the vision of a smooth function-ing sugar colony based upon their work would not be easily realized. By October 1868, 108 of the 474 Chinese migrants in British Honduras had died. Many died following the outbreak of influenza at one of the largest plantations depending upon Chinese labor, the New River estate.[69] Within two years, colonial discourse shifted from optimism over the possibilities of extracting work from "docile bodies" to deep pessimism that Chinese migrant workers would be effective vessels for the transformation of work.

The same Chinese migrants once seen as capable of clearing Belizean forests and working on plantations now came to be seen as degenerate. A leading medical official responsible for the health of Chinese migrants stated this most clearly, suggesting that the bodily constitution of Chinese men was effective within post-emancipation plantations where the work of settlement and enclosure had been completed and only the less physi-cally destructive tasks of cultivation remained. In Belize, where clearing, settlement, and enclosure still remained, the Chinese were deemed to be racially inadequate. This interpretation emerged in the midst of a rapidly increasing death toll on colonial plantations. Colonial assessments of Chi-nese laboring capacities were accompanied by tropes of decayed morality and depraved sexuality to explain why the bodies of the Chinese in Belize could not be depended upon for colonial improvement.

Chinese migrants were sent to several plantation estates in the colony: Trial Farm (38 employed), Indian Church (57 men and 18 "women and children"), and Tiger Bank (57 men). Aguacate was the largest plantation, where 151 Chinese were sent, including 143 men, 3 women, and 5 children. The experiences of Chinese migrants at Aguacate were characterized by managers' use of extraordinary violence in excess of the demands of pro-duction. According to one medical examiner, the Aguacate Chinese had "the worst" character in the colony. As it turned out, Tarbutt, the planta-tion manager, was filled with "monomaniacal hatred" for these laborers.[70]

Tarbutt remarked that he had initially underestimated the working capacity of Chinese migrants before their arrival. He found that Chinese laborers went "cheerfully to their work indeed the greater part are generally waiting in the fields for the drivers to come and mark out their tasks in the morning."[71] On 30 October 1865, a common day's labor, 120 were working in the fields, 10 were in the hospital, and 10 who were convalescent were at work cutting down brush surrounding both the hospitals and the laborers' homes.[72]

However, Tarbutt's contentment with Chinese migrants transformed during the ensuing year. A report filed by medical examiner Frederick Gahue on 24 July 1866 registered complaints about the capacity of Chinese laborers to form the laboring basis of the plantation while also detailing extreme violence used by Tarbutt against Chinese migrants. Gahue first explained the weakness of Chinese laborers through an anti-Chinese account of opium use and bodily decay:

> Many of the Chinese who were once good labourers, have been utterly ruined by the use of opium—*a habit which many of them have acquired, since their arrival in the colony.* I had to stand by and see hale, muscular men, gradually wasting way under the influence of this poison, without either the manager or myself being able to put a stop to it. The result now is, that many men who, when I first went to Aguacate were good workmen are now, constantly ailing and incorrigibly lazy.[73]

Gahue added to this a second problem that he saw over the racial capacity of Chinese migrants to clear land rather than work on plantations. Chinese migrants, he stated, were inferior to Black and Indigenous labor: "When there is only heavy work to do the Chinese can not be compared to negroes or even Indians and I think this is the reason why the Chinese Immigration has succeed[ed] so well in other parts of the West Indies. There they found estates, ready established on which there was no treefelling to any extent." Gahue concluded by reflecting upon the racial constitution of the Chinese laborers who established plantations. Such work "suited the physical conformation and peculiar temperament of the Chinamen—labor requiring great patience, but not much strength."[74]

After these remarks on the racial capacity of Chinese labor compared with Black and Indigenous labor, Gahue commented on the particular mismanagement of the Aguacate estate: "It is utterly impossible for anyone to manage their people worse than Mr. Tarbutt does his. He has never even read the Immigration act; and is quite unaware of his responsibilities and duties towards the Immigrants. . . . Beginning by hating the Chinese before he saw them, his hatred has been gradually on the increase until, it has now become a monomania."[75] Tarbutt's contempt of Chinese laborers emerged in acts of violence and the refusal of care.

Yet, in an earlier letter to John Hodge, Gahue had reported on the condition of Chinese laborers in a tone that represented his own complicity in their abuse even if he later reported upon Tarbutt's mistreatment of migrants. Addressing workers' diets, he noted that as a result of a general scarcity in the colony, workers were given cornmeal instead of rice. He noted that the cornmeal had "the effect of relaxing the bowels" but was "in point of nutritive qualities . . . much to be preferred to rice."[76]

The doctor further defended the horrible conditions of the Aguacate estate and explained the recent death of three Chinese laborers by suggesting that two died from ulcers caused by "parasitic jiggers," which were a result of "their own laziness and filth." A third died from liver inflammation. These deaths were excusable, in his opinion, because he believed that the three who died did not want to receive medical treatment "and the rest of the Chinese did not wish them to live, as they were such arrant thieves." Despite these deaths, dysentery, and discomfort, Gahue noted that at Aguacate Chinese migrants were "in such good health because they had been over indulged by the late manager."[77]

While Gahue had little difficulty reconciling Chinese death as the result of "laziness and filth," Tarbutt's actions toward Chinese laborers exceeded his own calculating lack of concern. On 4 April 1866, Gahue requested blankets for a laborer denoted only as No. 362. On 19 April, Gahue requested blankets again, noting this time that 362's disease was one "very liable to be aggravated by cold." In response, Tarbutt curtly wrote, "There is no blankets on the estate." Tarbutt's refusal to provide blankets caused the laborer to become chronically ill. Another Chinese immigrant, No. 338, died because of similar neglect, with a debility that Gahue believed required only brandy and a blanket.

As Gahue reflected:

Day after day, I spoke to Mr. Tarbutt about this man, urging him to get the blankets and brandy, but to no effect.
At last, matters came to such a pass, that I requested Mr. Bockley and Mr. Adolphus to ride with me to Santa Cruz and look at the man.
They were both shocked at the man's appearance, and remonstrated with Mr. Tarbutt.[78]

Despite such remonstrations and Gahue's knowledge of the worsening situation, nothing was done, and the man died two days later.

By the end of the year, Tarbutt's estate had become unworkable, and the laborers were relocated to another estate on the Sittee River managed by Antonio Mathe at All Pines. Mathe reflected that the laborers were well housed, well fed, and paid punctually. From this, Mathe declared, the laborers had "become really good labourers for altho they do not as yet get through the task of an able Blackman or Spaniard they are gradually improving in the quantity of work performed and their work is well done." Mathe noted that the complaints of the overseers from the British Honduras Company were "for the most part if not entirely vexatious and made by men determined by prejudice against the Chinamen as we all know was the case with Mr. Tarbutt the faults lay more with the managers than with the men." Mathe himself tried to argue that the reliance upon Chinese labor was not a failure but an experiment that demanded the expanded introduction of Chinese immigrants.[79] However, Chinese laborers would disrupt this project through their own actions against the interests of colonization through plantation development.

Chinese Resistance and the Breakdown of Colonization through Plantation Expansion

Chinese laborers challenged the abuse of planters, overseers, and colonial officials by abandoning the colony completely. By 1868, 155 immigrants had absconded: 100 Chinese laborers abandoned the New River estate in 1866 following the outbreak of severe flu;[80] 30 more fled to Guatemala from the Indian Church estate, where flu had been similarly devastating; and 25 abandoned the San Andres and Trial Farm estates, with some seen at Campache.[81] The laborers who fled from New River joined the Santa Cruz Maya, posing an even greater challenge to the colonial powers.

The Maya formed cross-racial solidarity with the Chinese migrants, which precluded any possibility of returning to the English. As a frustrated British Honduras official reported, "The Chinese, the [Santa Cruz Maya] Chiefs say, are Indians like themselves."[82] In addition, the Santa Cruz whom the Chinese joined stated that it had been ordered that the Chinese be "well treated and taught to work, and to be distributed among Maya officers for that purpose."[83] At the same time, in the midst of the brutal Guerra de Castas, the relationship between the Chinese and the Maya did not amount to simple equality. Bel Cen, a Maya leader, shot a laborer who left his rancho without permission, and three others had already died, though the exact circumstances of this must be interpreted against colonial officials who recorded these events.

The joining of Chinese laborers with the Santa Cruz Maya revealed the weak position the colonial state held in relation to the Cruzob (Santa Cruz

Maya) and the Kekchi (Icaiche), as well as the San Pedro. Resistance to the exploitation of Maya labor was central to the Guerra de Castas.[84] Alienating the Santa Cruz or creating any situation that would disrupt the neutrality of British Honduras threatened to further endanger a fledgling colony that had no real means for protection, even as the Cruzob enabled the Chinese to join them.

Further, colonial progress through agriculture in Belize was intimately bound to the seizing of land, the securing of the colonial border, and the displacement of the Maya. Maya presence was interpreted by planters as deleterious to the possibility of the productive plantation. Xaibe, a Maya festival occurring in May, became one focal point for planter rage over the inability to produce cane.[85] According to a *Sugar Cane* writer, laborers took a week off to participate in the festival. Though planters recognized the celebration as an "odious saturnalia," they felt as if they were forced to accept laborers' participation in order to maintain labor control. The *Sugar Cane* writer continued,

> However much this necessity might have been felt in the infancy of the colony, when the staple of the country was mahogany and logwood, which required no continuous labour save at one season of the year; now that attention is to be turned to agriculture, and especially to the cultivation of the cane and the manufacture of sugar, which, more than any other species of industry, require constant application and uninter-rupted labour; to submit to such a sacrifice at the shrine of Bacchus, and countenance and encourage a usage whose advent occurs at a critical time, in the midst of crop, when the utmost energy and exertion are re-quired to reap the reward of all the planter's previous toil — is a suicidal policy that must subvert his best interests, and entail ruin in the end.[86]

The anonymous author further suggested that Xaibe be substituted with another holiday celebration around Christmastime. Such a suggestion to reorganize time mirrors the holiday practice of the slaveholding South United States, where it was customary for enslaved people to receive a week off during Christmas. Frederick Douglass noted that the holiday, which lasted a week in the American South, was "part and parcel of the gross fraud, wrong, and inhumanity of slavery" because it was a mechanism of social control that presented planters as benevolent while obscuring their brutality.[87] Undergirding the suggestion that Xaibe be revoked in favor of a Christmas celebration was an acknowledgment that such a transforma-tion would enact white control over celebratory leisure time while giving whites the power to revoke the holiday if necessary. Fundamentally, it was an attempt to make time align with plantation production—after all, May was a time of intense activity on sugar plantations, while December was relatively lax.

The inability of the colonial state to confront Maya power in the region became clear in 1867. One report claimed the year would be remembered as "unfortunate" in the colony's history, beginning with a Maya invasion in the colony and the desertion of the entire Western District, with agriculture and woodcutting entirely suspended in the district. The military expenditure caused considerable strain on the colony, and exports declined. The year ended with the Santa Cruz Maya arriving in Corosal and threatening the borders of the colony.[88]

Chinese migrant experiences on the colony's nascent sugar plantations revealed the stakes of an approximation toward slavery characterized by violence without success. Planters proved more successful at killing Chinese migrants than producing cane.[89] At the same time, Chinese laborers challenged and transformed the trajectory of this process, thwarting plantation development and striking a blow to colonization itself. Engaging in work stoppages, strikes, and massive absconding, Chinese laborers precipitated the failure of these efforts. The actions of Chinese immigrants, conditioned by everyday confrontations with overseers, planters, and the colonial state, created new solidarities and affinities that could not have been imagined by the colonial government when soliciting their arrival. Solidarity developed between Chinese laborers who absconded from a particularly violent plantation and the Santa Cruz Maya whom they joined, reworking race in the process. The Santa Cruz Maya to whom Chinese laborers fled saw the Chinese as Indians like themselves and refused to return the laborers to plantations. Against landed interests and the colonial state's vision of sugar plantations securing the border and enriching the colony, the Chinese and Santa Cruz articulated counterpoints to this vision. Despite this, former U.S. slaveholders, having lost their war for the perpetuation of slavery in the United States, turned to settling in British Honduras to manage the project of colonization through plantation development.

The Slaveholders' Colony

From the United States to southern Africa, Australia, and beyond, white settlers enabled the extension of colonial and national projects. In a letter sent to the *British Honduras Colonist*, white Texan settler Z. N. Morrell wrote of his first day in British Honduras: "You would have been reminded of Texas 30 years ago, in examining the maps of the country, and to see emigrants scattering in every direction."[90] Morrell's memory draws attention

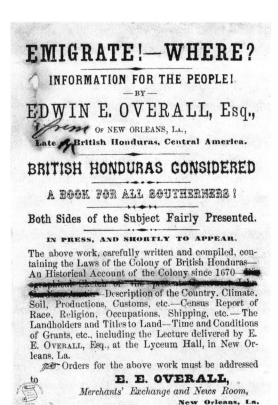

"Emigrate! Where?" advertisement for white southerner emigration to British Honduras. (Courtesy Belize Archives and Records Service)

to the settler expansionist impulse of the American South, recapitulated in British Honduras in approximate form. In the British Caribbean, colonial officials' interest turned toward "the introduction also of a very valuable class of Immigrants of the Anglo-Saxon race from the Southern States" to British Honduras.[91]

In order to secure white planters' safety, white British Hondurans policed an ever-shifting frontier region to prevent attacks by the Maya. These efforts to police the frontier and the arrival of war-hardened planters became increasingly bound together. White southerners seemed necessary not only for managing labor but also for protecting landed property interests against the Santa Cruz Maya. As John Hodge wrote, "The importation of energetic Americans accustomed to arms" would provide an example of "self-reliance in securing safety to life and property within the Colony."[92]

Following the failure to settle land and manage Chinese indentured labor, the technical, managerial, and settling techniques of war-hardened planters such as Samuel McCutchon became seen as integral to the introduction of plantation-based sugar cultivation. By 1870, after McCutchon began to manage sugar production at the Regalia estate for Young, Toledo, and

Company, it was estimated that the plantation was cultivating sugar cane on 250 acres of land.[93] Such increases in production and McCutchon's ability to realize them through the exploitative organization of labor caused the *British Honduras Colonist* to report that sugar cane production in British Honduras would "astonish planters and agriculturalists of other sugar producing countries."[94]

McCutchon was brutal and methodical in organizing and managing plantations in St. Charles Parish, Louisiana. Further, he standardized labor organization and effectively differentiated skilled and unskilled occupations to maximize production.[95] In his 1861 Ormond plantation journals, McCutchon offered descriptive details of the types of labor different enslaved people were to perform and the levels of experience such work positions required. This ordering of labor practices between unskilled and skilled differentiated enslaved people according to age and gender, with women performing different work than men at different levels of intensity in order to maximize productivity. In his journal, McCutchon meticulously noted when enslaved people were sick and regularly calculated their value in inventories. At the same time, McCutchon was attentive to the technological processes of sugar cultivation and observant of global innovations. Employing advanced technology, McCutchon's sugar plantations in south Louisiana came to resemble what W. E. B. Du Bois described as part of capitalism's "worst conceivable form."[96] By 1849, the Ormond plantation had 850 arpents (a little over 700 acres) of sugar plantation land in active cultivation.

Writing for *De Bow's Review*, Charles A. Pilsbury reflected upon the importance of white southern planters in the introduction of new techniques of plantation management in British Honduras, noting that plantations had become "scientific" with the migration of white southerners.[97] Further, the movement of southern planters like McCutchon was seen by white colonists in British Honduras as essential for procuring investments in sugar plantation production: "If the events shall demonstrate that the Southern planters have neither miscalculated the resources of British Honduras nor the effect of their own energy, British capitalists will speedily show the sagacity in recognizing this new channel of profitable employment."[98] Such forms of agricultural collaboration were meant to enable the reconstruction of white racial dominance while also increasing the value of colonial land.

As managers of land and labor with knowledge about sugar cultivation, southern planters like McCutchon were seen as integral to the establishment of plantation regimes. As an organizer of production, McCutchon had demonstrated an ability to mobilize violence against a hierarchically divided labor force in St. Charles Parish. At the Regalia estate, McCutchon showed an interest in the use of scientific methods of machine production for the cultivation of sugar, drawing upon techniques used in other parts of the Caribbean. This increased reliance upon the use of machines was meant to address labor scarcity in the colony. As one plantation observer noted, technological innovations "greatly reduced the amount of hand labour required," making it possible to "dispense with the [N]egro and replace him with European skill."[99]

Yet, in reality, such technological innovations still remained dependent upon a plantation labor force. In 1868, Regalia relied upon a labor force of nearly 100, which included 60 Chinese indentured laborers in addition to labor from the region. The broader patterns of conflict and violence between indentured laborers, planters, and the colonial state can be seen in a series of deaths at Regalia in April 1868.[100]

On 16 April 1868, ten Chinese laborers were sent to clear land on a neighboring estate in return for carpentry services. The laborers' driver returned to complain about a work stoppage, and Regalia's overseer, George Hyde, himself a former slaveholder, was summoned.[101] Upon arrival, Hyde demanded to be shown the leader of the work stoppage. After So Tsing Whan was singled out, Hyde brought him to a nearby estate. According to McCutchon, when Hyde was visiting the estate's sugar house, "the Chinaman walked in the river and was drowned."[102] Laborers brought Whan's body from the river to their quarters at Regalia and refused orders to move Whan's body any further, even after plantation managers and police arrived on the scene.

Chinese migrants identified Hyde as responsible for Whan's death and even stated their desire to kill him. When the following day's inquest returned a verdict of "voluntary drowning," Chinese laborers refused to return to work. To break down the work stoppage, several striking laborers were taken, imprisoned, and forced to two weeks' hard labor on public roads.[103] The cycle of protest and punishment was part of a global wave of extreme plantation violence that accompanied global labor transformations in the era of the American Civil War.

The overlapping racial and colonial projects that brought Black, Chinese, U.S. Confederate slaveholder, Maya, and British colonial histories together in Belize were unable to produce the massive economic shifts that landholding interests envisioned. When W. E. B. Du Bois emphasized the necessity for considering "the stretch in time and space between the deed and the result," he was specifically addressing the complexity of colonial production and metropolitan consumption.[104] Du Bois's emphasis also provides a vantage for considering the continuing transnational impact of U.S. slavery following the American Civil War as it unfolded in 1860s British Honduras.

While McCutchon and other white southerners extended the cultivation of sugar in British Honduras through brutal violence against labor, their efforts ultimately did not transform the economic basis of the colony. *Light of the Age* was the only ship of indentured laborers to arrive in the colony during the period. These colonial projects may have broken down, but U.S. settler slavery's impact extended far beyond in space and time.

10 ::: Keeping Real Estate White

> This rebellion has frequently, and very justly, been styled a
> slaveholders' rebellion. It is likewise a landholders' rebellion, for the
> chief owners of slaves have been the chief owners of land.
> —George W. Julian (1864)

> The real world robbed us of our share.
> —Frantz Fanon, *Black Skin, White Masks*

Following the end of the American Civil War, as white supremacist projects for African American removal largely fell apart and
as settlers and industrialists survived the economic crisis without enacting the types of grand colonial transformation that they
imagined, former slaveholders turned not only to new sites of
empire outside of the continental United States but more generally toward
projects to continue the dispossession of formerly enslaved people within
the continental empire, engaging in new land struggles against Black freedpeople. The white supremacist legal and economic ordering of Black enslavement through white real estate also justified land ownership through
the rule of law and practice of settler empire that enabled and protected the
settler as slaveholder.

Black emancipation abolished the slaveholder as a direct owner of enslaved people, yet this abolition did not dispossess the dominant status of
former slaveholders as landowners. While some slaveholders left the United
States to engage in colonial projects in British Honduras, Brazil, and the
Pacific as part of a wide-ranging Confederate movement, more generally
slaveholders struggled to transform the postslavery United States, depending especially upon their power in landed property. The incomplete nature
of slaveholder dispossession after the American Civil War established the
preconditions that would result in Black dispossession after emancipation.
Building on this foundation, the U.S. Congress and former slaveholders
would work together to justify, reinforce, and perpetuate slaveholders'
landed property claims. Former slaveholders were affirmed by the state as
continued settlers whose landed property claims went unchallenged.

The affirmation of the slaveholders' colonialism enabled a racial separation of labor from the means of production while transforming the white former slaveholder who continued to own land into a southern agrarian capitalist.[1] Real estate through enslavement may have been destroyed, but settler landed possession continued.

As W. E. B. Du Bois argued, abolition-democracy was an "uneasy" alliance that militated against slavery through a broad coalition formed among diverse interests including abolitionists, Republican government, and freedpeople, with slavery at its center. However, as Du Bois also noted, abolition-democracy was a "petty-bourgeois" social formation that ultimately believed in democratic government but "only under the dictatorship of property."[2] To Du Bois, the *primary* concern of freedpeople was "land hunger — this absolutely fundamental and essential thing to any real emancipation of the slaves."[3] The limits of abolition-democracy splintered through debates over the legitimacy of the slaveholders' colonialism and in favor of white real estate. The perpetuation of real estate enabled abolitionists, republicans, and in some cases freedpeople to reconcile with the dictatorship of property that had at its basis both the continued dispossession of Black people and the entrenchment of U.S. continental imperialism.

With the shattering of the coalition that had upheld abolition-democracy, Republicans and the U.S. Congress transformed abolition into a discrete problem within white real estate in the post-emancipation South. The legitimacy of slaveholders' settler empire was affirmed, foretelling the violent dispossession of freedpeople from their labor that was still to come. The Southern Homestead Act in 1866 permitted white homesteading while insisting on Black exclusion from land claims — from a certain perspective, this can be seen as amounting to exclusion from participation as free citizens in the constitutive settler colonialism of the U.S. empire-state.[4] This kind of hierarchical differentiation of subjects has always been and continues to be part of the U.S. settler empire and was compounded by the fact the Southern Homestead Act made land available for homesteading directly through Indigenous dispossessions in the public land states of Alabama, Arkansas, Florida, Louisiana, and Mississippi.

Within a transforming American empire, white republicans, formerly enslaved people, and slaveholders struggled with the contradictions in white real estate. By focusing on the House Committee on Public Lands and congressional efforts for land redistribution following the Civil War, this chapter traces the foreclosure of land redistribution to African Americans not as inevitable but as an assertion of former slaveholders' property claims and a validation of the slaveholders' colonialism.

The postbellum struggle to dispossess Black people and transform the

American South into a "white man's country" becomes especially visible in the efforts of Thomas Affleck, a former slaveholder who was also a central theorist of antebellum plantation management. This chapter will follow Affleck's efforts to redirect European immigration to the South and to effect a racial transformation of the region, remaking the settler economy into one based upon white labor in part inspired by settler colonies across the British Empire.

Freedpeoples' land struggles produced "small" rights and victories rather than the overthrow or substantive transformation of white real estate through land ownership. In settler colonial contexts, citizenship is underwritten by landed possession and occupation. Slaveholders continued to have their real estate rights defended while formerly enslaved people were systematically prevented the rights of citizenship through landed property even as the status of enslaved people as real estate ended. Affleck's racial project to build a white man's country resembling the northern and western United States or the settler colonies of the British Empire substantively failed. Yet these struggles — one for Black emancipation through self-determined land possession and the other to make a racially homogeneous white South — provide insight into how the slaveholder's colonialism continued in the American South following abolition. This affirmation was the foundation of what Du Bois would call the slaveholder's victory following the Civil War.

Black emancipation may have succeeded in exposing the arbitrary foundations of property, but the era of emancipation featured a long campaign to mystify this revelation. This convergence of social institutions ranging from the state, to former slaveholders, to radical white abolitionists worked to affirm white real estate as the basis of U.S. capitalism even as slavery was abolished. With this, in some ways, the slaveholder's victory through settler struggle in the longer Civil War appears foreordained.

Ending White Real Estate?

The proto-nationalist principles of freedpeople, rooted in the demand for Black landownership as the basis for independent Black communities, found new expression during the Civil War.[5] In freedpeoples' land struggles in Port Royal, South Carolina; Ogeechee, Georgia; and Davis Bend, Mississippi, these demands became entangled with Republican and Union army visions of emancipation. While these struggles were successful in bringing about the establishment of free towns such as Burroughs in Georgia and homesteading in rural pockets throughout the South, particularly in Florida, freedpeople's victories for land control proved to be exceptions to the general rule of white real estate. As Du Bois once wrote, the land made available to formerly enslaved people "melted quickly away."[6]

White northerners, Union generals, and radical abolitionists voiced support for and at times even acted to defend Black freehold property. The radical abolitionist Thaddeus Stevens advocated for the confiscation of southern property and its redistribution in forty-acre portions to freedpeople. As Stevens stated, it was impossible for "any practical equality of rights" to exist when a few thousand men monopolized landed property.[7] Yet, while Stevens would argue it was necessary to "strip" white planters of their "bloated estates," radical abolitionists failed to fulfill this vision.[8] This failure was not just the result of being thwarted by the forces of reaction. It was also the product of wavering commitment to the egalitarian principles that white abolitionists professed.

Though such principles may have been insufficient to motivate a defense of Black landholding, Republicans' commitment to Black voting rights was bolstered by considerations of political power. Frederick Douglass consistently emphasized that emancipation from slavery was impossible unless African Americans were enfranchised, viewing enfranchisement as central to Black freedom and American democracy.[9] Fearing a possible union of Democrats and farmers in the American West, Republicans saw future political power tied to Black men's suffrage.[10] Support for Black voting rights supported Republican ambitions. Black property, though, presented no such path for Republican political power.

The American Civil War provided a context for new challenges within the relationship between land and Black life at the core of the real estate principle. During the war, these challenges often emerged through confrontations between once-enslaved African Americans and the Union army. When escaping to Union lines, formerly enslaved African Americans entered a space of juridical uncertainty, neither slave nor free by law. When the Union army conquered Confederate planters' territory, it too underwent transformations. Fugitive slave laws further functioned according to, and were constrained by, logics of territorial conquest.[11] Enslaved peoples' challenges to the real estate principle unfolded within a changing terrain of property in the midst of warfare, where military leaders confiscated land, tools, and instruments of war and debated the position of enslaved people in relation to these acts of confiscation. Enslaved people consistently exploited the incoherence of the real estate logic of U.S. empire by abandoning plantations and moving across Union lines.

In May 1861, three formerly enslaved people fled to Fort Monroe, Virginia. When a Confederate general demanded their return, Union general

Benjamin F. Butler refused, believing that enslaved people would aid in the Confederate war effort and declaring those who ran away "contraband" property.[12] Butler further claimed that the Fugitive Slave Act, which demanded states return to owners those enslaved people who escaped plantations, was not applicable to foreign countries—which was what the Confederate states claimed to be. This issue, when it involved African American men alone, was often framed by the Union army as one of military expediency: Black men could work for the Union army, performing tasks that supported the war effort. However, as Black women and children continued to abandon plantations and arrive at military camps such as Fort Monroe, their presence forced broader challenges to questions of Black freedom.[13]

In response to the presence of African Americans who had either escaped slavery or who were enslaved in places taken by the Union army, the United States passed the First Confiscation Act on 6 August 1861. The act declared that enslaved people who facilitated Confederate war efforts would not be returned to slaveholders. One month later, General John C. Frémont, commander of the Department of the West, declared martial law in Missouri, stating that the slaves of those who aided the Confederacy would be emancipated.[14] Lincoln saw Frémont's claim as going far beyond his intentions with the First Confiscation Act.[15] On 2 November, Lincoln removed Frémont from command. Other Union generals, such as John A. Dix, supported slaveholders' property through the real estate principle and ordered those under his command to refuse African Americans who escaped slaveholders from coming within Union lines. This refusal was intended to show slaveholders that the Union had no investment in Black emancipation.[16]

The Second Confiscation Act, passed a year later on 17 July 1862, confiscated Confederate property to punish rebellion and further shifted the legal definition of African Americans who abandoned plantations and escaped the control of masters. The Second Confiscation Act declared all those who crossed over Union lines "forever free of their servitude." The act further established provisions for the president to pursue Black colonization outside of the United States, a logic that in its own way sought to transform the United States into a white man's country. This hope for colonization seemed to affirm white property and settler claims while abolishing Black slavery simultaneously. Lyman Trumbull, the Illinois congressman who authored both confiscation acts, elaborated upon the logic behind the second act's colonization provisions, stating that they were a result of white northerners' understanding that slavery was the cause of the Civil War but that white constituents also did "not want them [African Americans] set free to come in among us."[17]

Emancipation was imminent, but white politicians and officers projected their own unpreparedness for the change onto freedpeople themselves through tutelage projects. Challenging this logic, the abolitionist Wendell Phillips forcefully stated, "If there is anything patent in the whole history of our thirty years' struggle, it is that the Negro no more needs to be prepared for liberty than the white man."[18] Yet repeatedly, Union officers experimented with the organization of African American labor and landed relations, often with the intention of preparing freedpeople for freedom.[19] After the Battle of Port Royal on 7 November 1861, white planters abandoned South Carolina's Sea Islands, and over 8,000 enslaved people whom these planters had claimed as real estate were no longer enslaved.[20] For northern whites interested in the prospects of African American freedom, Port Royal became a place of "experimentation" to transform enslaved people into wage laborers on commercial plantations. For Black residents of these islands, the absence of planters created conditions of possibility for homesteading and small production, for organizing lives where work was a fundamental but not overwhelming feature.[21] New Englanders traveled to the Sea Islands to oversee experiments with Black education and work to craft a definition of Black labor subordinated to the global economy. At the same time, once-enslaved African Americans in other parts of Confederate territory increasingly left to cross Union lines and find safety in the Sea Islands, with men and women enslaved on other plantations consistently arriving at Beaufort and Hilton Head.[22] In this confluence, the Sea Islands became a site of struggle over the dissolution and affirmation of the real estate principle.

White New Englanders in Port Royal imagined and participated in experiments to design and constrain Black life after emancipation. For Frederick Law Olmsted, the architect, writer, and administrator, the Port Royal experiment was a place for imagining and testing the racial capacity of African Americans to be laboring subjects in a post-slavery world. In 1862, Olmsted worked to gain a position as a guardian overseeing African Americans who had become contraband at Port Royal, drafting and submitting a plan to Lincoln.[23] Olmsted wrote of the freedman, "He does not on this account need an owner, but he does need a guardian, and he knows that he does."[24] As a man interested in the design of parks and places, Olmsted was also interested in the organization and exploitation of Black life after slavery.

While the First and Second Confiscation Acts had seized real estate from Confederate planters, the Direct Tax Act, passed in June 1862 and amended in early 1863, enabled the sale of these confiscated lands and, in law, made possible the transfer of titles from slaveholders to the formerly enslaved.[25] In March 1863, the federal government sold planters' land in the Sea Islands, a policy that made Black landownership at Port Royal possible. In 1863, Edward Philbrick, a Boston manufacturer, purchased 8,000 acres of public land for a Boston textile manufacture owner, while African Americans were able to purchase a total of approximately 2,000 acres through the act.[26] General Rufus B. Saxton wrote to Philbrick that land ownership without purchase was "the indefeasible right of the [N]egro" and that any withholding of land was fraudulent.[27] Still, many white northerners who supported the possibility of Black land ownership demanded this land be made available to African Americans only through purchase, a policy meant to inculcate work discipline and subordinate Black interest to white real estate.[28]

On 16 January 1865, following the conclusion of General William Tecumseh Sherman's March to the Sea, Sherman announced his Special Field Order No. 15—a policy declaring land available for the formerly enslaved from South Carolina to Georgia to Florida. The order declared that land was to be redistributed to freedpeople, who could settle and farm upon the law as free subjects. Sherman's special field order stated that the North would recognize the desire for land among formerly enslaved people.[29]

With the defeat of the Confederacy growing increasingly likely, freedpeople's land struggles seemed to have the greatest chance of success in the Sea Islands.[30] While members of the Freedmen's Bureau sought to rearrange production for expansive cotton cultivation, Black Sea Islanders sought to use garden plots to make sure that they had enough food to eat.[31] As one freedperson made clear, "driving" was no longer acceptable, and true freedom was to be found with owning one's own farm.[32] Emancipation as cultivators' revolt took place not just on the ground but in it, with the flourishing of plants, from corn to sweet potatoes. This also occurred as the rearrangement of relations to the land among freedpeople.[33]

Lincoln's assassination and the elevation of Andrew Johnson to the presidency served to empower freedpeople's antagonists in these land struggles. General Oliver O. Howard was selected by Lincoln and appointed by Johnson to become the Freedmen's Bureau commissioner in May 1865,[34] and in October, Johnson ordered Howard to rearrange the relationships between African Americans and planters.[35] Within days, Howard arrived in South Carolina, meeting with Edisto Island freedmen to deliver the message that land allotted to freedpeople must be returned to planters.[36] This shift in policy faced resistance — General Saxton stepped up the fight, attempting to distribute abandoned and confiscated lands to freedpeople on the Sea Islands. Yet conditions would continue to deteriorate: Saxton would be removed from his post on 9 January 1866, just as South Carolina rice planters grew convinced that a murderous Black insurrection against whites was imminent.[37]

In Georgia, the formerly enslaved challenged the slaveholders' colonialism through demands for self-determined Black landownership. The advance of the Union army and the "general strike" of the enslaved crossing over to Union lines had forced these questions into the open, and with the war at an end, freedpeople demanded answers. The prospects for Black landownership came to the fore during the January 1865 Savannah Colloquy, a meeting between Black religious leaders and Union generals Edwin M. Stanton and William Tecumseh Sherman in Savannah, Georgia. As the Baptist minister Garrison Frazier, who had been enslaved until about 1857, stated in the discussion, "The way we can best take care of ourselves is to have land, and turn it and till it by our own labor." Frazier continued, "I would prefer to live by ourselves, for there is a prejudice against us in the South that will take years to get over."[38] Frazier insisted not only upon land control but also upon the dispossession of the slaveholders from the land that they had colonized.

At Grove Point and Grove Hill in Savannah, lands were subdivided between April and May 1865 with some formerly enslaved people receiving titles for land. The Georgia reservation was an area of land set aside for freedmen along the Georgia coast. At Ogeechee, agents for Rufus Saxton oversaw experiments with life after slavery. However, rather than working on single plots determined by a family, freedpeople cultivated rice together in Ogeechee with what one historian has called a "communal approach to labor."[39] Freedpeople were further organized into militias to defend their land claims.

Johnson's appointment of Oliver O. Howard signaled a stunning reversal — under Howard's leadership the Freedmen's Bureau would focus upon the transformation of freedpeople into laborers rather than landholders. On 26 October 1865, Howard restored land to planters following a speech at Savannah.[40] In spite of these restorations, between November 1866 and January 1867, 108 freedpeople made claims to land following the enactment of the Freedmen's Bureau law in 1866.[41] Meanwhile, freedpeople tried to secure Ogeechee by staging a revolt. Once this revolt was suppressed, African Americans pursued an alternate path to land ownership through the creation of a small African American township called Burroughs at the end of the nineteenth century.[42] In defiance of the varieties of legal and violent suppression deployed against them, they insisted on Black landownership, against all odds.

Mississippi featured contested sites of its own. During the war, the Union army had confiscated six massive plantations at Davis Bend, a peninsula along the Mississippi River. The Davis Bend plantations of Hurricane and Brierfield were sites of triangulated land struggles between freedpeople, former slaveholders, and the Freedmen's Bureau. Located south of Vicksburg, the plantations had become notorious for their unusual management before the Civil War. Owned by Joseph Davis, brother to Jefferson Davis, the plantations enslaved over 350 people. In 1825, Joseph Davis had met the British socialist Robert Owen and imagined organizing his plantations according to principles of paternalistic socialism; he was influenced by these principles in the management of Davis Bend. Even so, the plantations in Davis Bend were entwined with the cruelty that defined U.S. slavery's paternalism. Following emancipation, struggles surrounding landownership at the Davis Bend plantations would ultimately result in the foundation in 1887 of Mound Bayou, a community of freedpeople from the Davis Bend plantations. Soon enough, it too would feature a struggle to control the transformation or destruction of the real estate principle.

Davis Bend fell into freedpeople's hands amid the expropriation of slaveholders, which temporarily turned the world of the plantation South upside down. Joseph Davis had abandoned the Hurricane and Brierfield plantations in 1862, transferring them to Benjamin Montgomery, a man Davis had previously enslaved. Montgomery and Davis struck an agreement: Montgomery would gain his freedom, and in return, the plantations would ultimately be returned to Davis. George Johnson, who was once enslaved at Davis Bend and lived at Mound Bayou, described the exchange to sociologist Charles S. Johnson in 1941:

> Benjamin Montgomery to Joseph Davis: I'm tell you what I want you to do.
> Davis: What is it Ben?
> Montgomery: I want you to deed this land to me. So I'll have it.
> Davis: Ben that won't do no good. . . . Don't you belong to me? The land's mine. You mine. Why, that won't do no good.
> Montgomery: Yes, it will do, master Jeff. It will do.
> Davis: How do you know?
> Montgomery: Master Jeff, can't you free me? My God, free me, man.

George Johnson: Master Jeff held his head down and say, "Ben you right." Davis then deeded the land to Montgomery and freed him.[43]

The notion that Montgomery could argue the case for and then receive not only his freedom but the entire former plantation seems like an impossible history. Nevertheless, the transfer occurred, emancipating Montgomery and securing his land.

After Davis transferred the plantation to Montgomery in 1862, freed-people self-organized agricultural production on the land. When the Union army seized the Davis Bend plantations on 20 December 1863, African American self-organized agricultural production was overtaken in the process. Davis Bend transformed once again—the army contracted freed-people to produce and sell cotton on land leased to northern investors under the rule of martial law, paying freedpeople wages.[44] These wages quickly became reduced from between $10 and $25 per month in 1863 to between $3.50 and $5 in 1864.[45] By October 1864, 3,000 people labored at Davis Bend; the majority were women and children.[46]

Yet the land at Davis Bend would be returned to Benjamin Montgomery following the Civil War. As early as 1865, a practice of leasing between the government and freedpeople emerged with each family provided with a piece of land. Such leases were often under stringent supervision and constant contestation.[47] In addition, some freedpeople worked as laborers for other freedpeople who were able to lease land.[48] Following resolution of the confiscation of properties, on 1 January 1867 this land was officially taken over by Montgomery from Joseph Davis based upon a unique agreement between the two.[49] While this plan enabled landownership for Montgomery, it foreclosed the same possibility for many other freedpeople who had leased land and labored at Davis Bend.[50] In many ways, Montgomery's control of the Davis Bend plantation placed his own landownership against collective control of the land.

Freedpeople's victories in these land struggles were often comparatively small in the context of the larger counter-revolution of whiteness, a process that was racially redistributing lands to whites on the fiction of previous possession.[51] As Sundiata Cha-Jua notes, rural western and southern towns reflected a Black nationalist consciousness "against the grain of American historical development."[52] Freedpeople's successful land struggles in the American South likewise cut against the grain.

Boston Blackwell ran away from a Pine Bluff plantation in October 1863. At the time of his leaving, he was told by his sister that if the overseer saw him, he would be killed. Boston Blackwell replied, "He kill me anyhow."

Another young man came with him, and over the course of their conversations, Blackwell reflected upon the possibilities and meaning of compensation: "That old story 'bout 40 acres and a mule, it make me laugh. Yessum, they sure did tell us that, but I never knowed any pusson which got it. The officers telled us we would all get slave pension. That just exactly what they tell. They sure did tell me I would get a [parcel] of ground to farm. Nothing ever hatched out of that, neither."[53]

A Rule of Property for the American South?

The persistence of white real estate in the slaveholding South following Black emancipation diverged from British colonial relations in a number of ways in mid- to late-eighteenth-century Bengal. Still, in *A Rule of Property for Colonial Bengal*, Ranajit Guha's history of the creation of colonial relations of landed property, the colonial construction of Permanent Settlement in Bengal was revealed to be neither logical nor inevitable; rather, it emerged through an ideological commitment to the "veneration of private property."[54] Guha's account demands reflection on the parallel historical logic that reshaped the American South, arbitrarily venerating slaveholders' colonialism even as the slaveholders' claims upon Black life as real estate were being destroyed. Through veneration and ideological commitment to the idea of white landed property, and through an acceptance of the justness of the colonialism that brought this land into slaveholders' control, the U.S. state affirmed the slaveholders' colonialism at the same time as the abolition of slavery.

Prominent in these efforts was George Washington Julian. An abolitionist, a radical Republican, a member of the U.S. House of Representatives for the state of Indiana, and chairman for the House Committee on Public Lands, Julian joined his fellow radical Republicans in working toward the abolition of slavery during the Civil War. From 1864 on, he became the loudest white advocate for the redistribution of slaveholders' land to freedpeople.

While Julian also advocated for the freeing and arming of African Americans, his rhetoric was disconnected from the struggles of freedpeople on former plantations.[55] Before the Civil War, as an Indiana state senator, Julian had been an abolitionist and opponent of colonization.[56] Julian's record reveals him in some ways as a supporter of abolition-democracy. From 1866 through 1868, Julian advocated for the eight-hour day, putting forth a "Julian" Bill, drawing upon the advice of William Jessup, head of New York's Working Men's Assembly.[57] The proposal for the Julian Bill itself was put forth by Nathaniel P. Banks. In May 1865, five years before the passage of the Fifteenth Amendment, Julian proposed African American suffrage in a congressional caucus but was denounced by others who claimed the public was not prepared.[58] In March 1869, Julian proposed a Sixteenth Amendment Bill, which proposed white women's enfranchisement.

Julian was also a relentless advocate for the interest of the settler as the foundation of U.S. democracy. His positions were not rigorously consistent, however—Julian argued that public lands should not fall into the hands of monopoly interests, especially railroad companies, and suggested that such land could be taken from slaveholders.[59] Julian accepted that public lands were to be settled by patriarchal families, especially white, but insisted that African Americans should also be able to settle and cultivate homesteaded land. Yet Julian's advocacy for freedpeople's inclusion in homesteading would wane following the Civil War and failures of the Southern Homestead Act (1866).

From February through March 1864, Julian advocated for the passage of a homesteading bill to provide veterans with southern land as well as to provide land for those who had labored against the Confederacy—which is to say, freedpeople. The bill proposed that all southern land seized by federal authorities should be made available for homesteading, with eighty acres available to those who served more than two years and forty acres available to all others. The Homestead Act (H.R. 85) was based upon the confiscation and settling of the property of Confederates, and for Julian this meant the seizure and sale of Confederate real estate. According to Julian, the passage of such an act would enable the "reorganization of society in those revolted states."[60] While the bill's language did not state that it would provide land for African Americans, the law was intended to provide freedpeople with the legal right to homestead land previously claimed by former slaveholders.[61]

H.R. 85 stood apart from the set of principles that enabled the passage of the Homestead Act of 1862, an act that had not attacked or transformed white property but rather made public lands (themselves the product of Indigenous dispossession) available to settle. Significantly, H.R. 85 proposed to homestead slaveholders by transferring their confiscated possessions to freedpeople and soldiers, both Black and white.[62] While H.R. 85 did not return or consider the return of land to dispossessed American Indians, the bill also did not accept the legitimacy of the slaveholders' property claims as made through settler slavery.

Debates in Congress over H.R. 85 brought together landed property, white supremacy, and white anxieties over interracial sex, drawing especially upon images of white men's sexual violence against Black women.[63]

Leading voices of opposition to H.R. 85 included Kentucky Unionist Robert Mallory and New York Democrat and copperhead Fernando Wood. Both Mallory and Wood argued that through the very act of being race-neutral in language and policy, the act would not only benefit whites but also and especially African Americans. When the bill stated that "no distinction shall be made on account of color or race," Wood argued to Congress that this was exactly where advocacy and advancement for African Americans could be found. As Wood said of the bill, "Again, it says in substance that 'we will kill or seize the masters, and give their estates to their slaves.' That, in my opinion, is a very grave objection. . . . It is the Black laborer and not the white soldier that excites the philanthropic concern of its framers." Wood further argued that when the bill used the word "laborer" it implied freedpeople because "there are no other laborers [in the South] but black men."[64] This, according to Wood, was the "nigger in its belly." Wood's argument implied that the racial status of land should follow the race of the colonizer, and this would and should not be broken down regardless of the abolition of slavery.[65] This white supremacist language about birth, at a moment of emancipation, was meant to disrupt and prevent Black landownership and repurpose the language that had been definitive of U.S. settler slavery, where the racial status of the child followed that of his or her mother, for the perpetuation of white property.

While Julian opposed Wood and Mallory, all three argued against "equality" through opposition to "miscegenation." For Wood and Mallory, the bill would enable interracial sex. Julian disagreed, claiming that it was the South that most threatened white racial purity. While Mallory and Wood were empathetic to southerners and slavery and Julian strongly opposed, all made arguments in favor of the preservation of white supremacy and white racial purity.

According to Mallory, the homestead policy of distributing former plantation land to African Americans would produce "social equality," enabling not only Black voting and office holding but also interracial sexual relations, all destructive to white racial purity. Julian's reply first addressed the political dimension of emancipated equality, stating that when free homesteads of former slave owners were "tilled by the labor of freemen" and when freedmen had been "converted from chattels into men, with a common right to the soil and stake in society," considerations of Black suffrage would be possible and most effectively advanced by African Americans themselves.[66] Julian then directly addressed racial anxieties over "miscegenation" as put forth by Wood and Mallory, stating that in the South, "slave mothers and slave masters of the South are brought on to the level of equality in its most loathsome forms."[67] Yet Julian furthered Wood and Mallory's arguments about the need for white supremacy when he accepted that racial damage and degeneration would be caused to Anglo-Saxons by interracial sex, maintaining that it occurred in the slaveholding South more often than anywhere else. Julian's reply demonstrates the limits of the advocacy for Black landownership and self-determination among its white proponents.

To defend Black access to homesteading, Julian stated that while Republicans and abolitionists did "sometimes associate" with African Americans, "no such *intimate relations* exist between them and us" like the intimacies that existed between "them and the Democrats of the South." Julian relished descriptions of white southerners' sexual violence, what he called "social equality," to repudiate not the violence of these relations but rather the presence of children from this violence: "Wherever you find an orthodox modern Democrat you will find a mulatto not very far off." The South itself, Julian further argued, advocated for "social equality between negro women and Anglo-Saxon Democrats," and this was the "natural consequence and necessary fruit" of slavery, an institution that was "the mother of treason and of all lesser abominations."[68] For Julian, Black emancipation facilitated the birth of a new form of white racial purity.

Mallory challenged Julian, stating that according to census data in free states "thirty-six per cent of the free colored population of the free states have white blood in their veins, while only one ninth of the slave population shows white blood." Julian argued that this "white blood" migrated from the South with freedpeople who brought with them "perhaps, the blood of the gentleman from Kentucky [Mallory] and other distinguished leaders of his party."[69] The contours of white supremacy that this discourse portended—and the fissures that it exposed—serve as a reminder of the impossibility and narrow-mindedness of the role of white radical abolitionists in failing to constitute abolition-democracy at a crucial political and historical juncture. Not only was sexual violence against Black women euphemized as "social equality" by a key figure within abolition-democracy, but also Republicans such as Julian maintained a sustained commitment to white supremacy even while pursuing Black emancipation, landownership, and voting rights.

H.R. 85 would pass in the House on 12 May 1865 but would be blocked before being brought to the Senate after the attorney general ordered that all slaveholders' property except the enslaved would be returned.[70] Like the failure to pass H.R. 85, this return of land-as-property to planters was neither logical nor inevitable but was rather an affirmation of the sanctity and unassailability of the settlers' property. This affirmation came at the very moment that the arbitrary nature of such property claims was exposed through slavery's abolition. This legislation's failure, even before the war's end, limited the scope of state sponsorship for land redistribution. H.R. 85 was the most sustained congressional effort to redistribute slaveholders' landed property, and its failure signaled the power of the slaveholders' property claims. It was part of a larger failure of abolition-democracy to destroy the slaveholders' colonialism by following the lead of freedpeople in the demand for land redistribution.

The 1866 Southern Homestead Act was originally meant to make public land available in the South for both whites and freedmen. However, in practice the act enabled whites to access land with very little assistance going to African Americans. Julian wrote, "Lands relinquished by any tribe would henceforth fall under the operation of our land laws, instead of being sold in a body to some corporation or individual monopolist. The Southern Homestead law had dedicated to the actual settlement millions of acres of the public domain in the land States of the South, while the Homestead Act of 1862 was splendidly vindicating the wisdom of its policy."[71] As Julian noted, this would have made available land taken by the state through colonialism in the southern public land states of Alabama, Arkansas, Florida, Louisiana, and Mississippi.

H.R. 267 was another homestead bill that was passed in the House after consideration in February 1867 with the purpose of granting approximately 5 million acres of land unused in railroad constructions across Alabama, Mississippi, Louisiana, and Florida. This land would have been available for homesteading by whites and African Americans. However, this bill did not pass in the Senate and died in early 1869.[72] With it also seemed to end the possibility for land redistribution to the formerly enslaved.

Efforts to secure land for freedpeople were part of an acknowledgment by those promoting abolition-democracy that external colonization—as a process of systematic African American removal outside of the borders of the United States—was no longer an option. However, the actual legislature and policies that emerged repeatedly reneged on the possibility of African Americans obtaining any land at all and reaffirmed southern slaveholders' claims to the land. As a result of the Southern Homestead Act and the efforts of the Freedmen's Bureau, approximately 4,000 freedpeople received lands. At the same time, the Freedmen's Bureau itself restored to freedpeople 14,652 acres that had been allotted to them and 400,000 acres that had been never been allotted.[73] Still, in Louisiana, where 330,000 people had been enslaved before the Civil War, fewer than 700 became homesteaders in the state after.

To freedpeople seeking land under the Southern Homestead Act, Florida stood out as a site with particular promise, given that white Floridians' efforts to force Black Floridians to labor had so often been thwarted.[74] Even Frederick Douglass entertained ideas about the formation of an independent African American "colony" in Florida.[75] Yet, ultimately freedpeople made only 4,000 official land claims—perhaps dissuaded by surveyors' fees and other deterrents.[76] When African Americans actually received land in Florida, it was most often swampland or forested.[77] The termination of the Freedmen's Bureau at the end of 1872 ended the possibility for any expansion of further land distribution through the state.[78] Julian's interest and advocacy for land redistribution after African American emancipation disappeared following the Civil War.[79]

Abolishing Settler Colonialism through Empire?

During and after the Civil War, the Republican-led U.S. government oversaw the colonization of the American West. The Civil War and Reconstruction were defined by repeated efforts to abolish and destroy the tribal standing of Five Tribe nations and Native sovereignties across the United States. During the Civil War, the U.S.-Dakota War (1862) in Minnesota resulted in the execution of thirty-eight members of the Dakota community by the state.[80] On 29 November 1864, the militia attack and massacre of a Cheyenne community in the Colorado Territory was carried out by John Chivington, who had earlier waged war on the Confederacy.[81] Further, the Sioux Wars (1865) followed the concluding battles of the American Civil War and were led by Union generals, particularly Philip Sheridan.

Abolitionists debated what state terror against American Indians meant for the project of universal emancipation and for the course of Black emancipation. These debates often touched on the future of American empire and the racial practices of incorporation and differentiation definitive of colonialism. On 11 May 1869, Frederick Douglass noted that while African Americans had secured the right to vote, former planters had "banded together" and determined not to sell land to freedpeople.[82] Douglass argued that it was necessary for abolitionists to facilitate the acquisition of land for freedpeople in order to give them a "fair play" by allowing them to purchase land. Douglass then described the white perpetuation of American Indian genocide through settler colonization to understand the continued possibilities of Black life in the United States. Douglass looked at the arguments of the white Republicans who, like many white southerners, believed that after emancipation, African Americans would be reduced to demographic insignificance. Douglass stated,

> The only reason why the negro has not been killed off, as the Indians have been, is, that he is so close under your arm, that you cannot get at him. If we had set up a separate nationality, gone off on the outer borders of your civilization, right before your bayonets and swords, we should have been pushed off, precisely as the Indians have been pushed off. Our salvation, the salvation of every race in this country, is in becoming an integral part of the American government, becoming incorporated into the American body politic, incorporated into society, having common aims, common objects, and common instrumentalities with which to work with you, side by side.[83]

As Douglass continued, "You might plant on the outer borders of American civilization a race of angels, if you please, and it would be impossible to keep the peace between those angels and this progressive Anglo-Saxon nation." When it is remembered that "progressive" here denotes a fixation on expansion and development, Douglass's idea of the United States as an expanding Anglo-Saxon empire defined the colonial practices at the core of the United States and informed the advice that Douglass recommended abolitionists pursue. Douglass stated that it was through assimilation into the American settler empire that African Americans would thrive in the United States and argued that African Americans were "more like the white man than the Indian, in his tastes and tendencies, and disposition to accept civilization."[84]

But Douglass's argument, as noted by the gathered abolitionists who participated in the debate, also insisted upon the inevitability of Native death. Mrs. Tappan, in contrast, told a story about the appointment of a New Orleans assessor who was regarded as an Indian so that it could be demonstrated that African Americans did not hold any important political position in the South. In addition, Tappan continued to state that it seemed necessary for the American Anti-Slavery Society to form a second society to "prevent the waging of a war of extermination against Indians" and invited Douglass to join. Tappan continued:

> In view of his [Douglass's] discrimination between the Indian and negro, although it may have helped to carry out his line of argument, we must call his attention to a few facts; for if he follows that too closely, he may commit the same sin that the nation has been committing against his

own color. The Indian is an outlaw to-day, and therefore cannot be what a negro is, a citizen. When we shall make him a citizen, and give him the rights and privileges that pertain to the negroes, we shall see whether he will imitate them or not. Instead of that, we send our Sheridans and Shermans to exterminate them. It is not true that they will not imitate.[85]

While Douglass saw death at the hands of settler colonial expansion as inevitable, Tappan saw assimilation as the most likely result. These fates were not in opposition but represented two valences in U.S. settler empire.[86]

The evening's debate was concluded by Wendell Phillips, who addressed the possibility for shifts in white thought. He noted that William Tecumseh Sherman's thought had profoundly changed in relation to African Americans but that this transformation in values did not extend to his views on American Indians.

Phillips described Sherman's belief as transforming from one that the Union could win the war without Black participation and that the North would "keep the negro where he belongs" to an outright advocacy for emancipation. For Phillips this meant that Sherman's perspective could be changed under pressure.

The changes Phillips had in mind followed the model set by the British Empire in its own colonies. He suggested that the United States "take a lesson from England. When she meets a tribe, she does not push it before her, as we do, as Mr. Douglass describes it; she encircles it in the arms of her civil laws." This perspective minimized ongoing violence in the white settler colonies across the British Empire from Canada to New South Wales and against colonial subjects in Natal and India. Undaunted, Phillips proposed that the United States follow the British model that would incorporate American Indians into the American empire and transform those colonized into subjects.

The idea of universal emancipation that Phillips had once advocated now seemed to blur into an imperial vision that insisted that the United States was powerful enough to incorporate "Indian policy," "John Chinaman," the "Irishman," and the "Black man": "No matter where he was born, the American people are strong enough to absorb them all." This idea of a nation "strong enough" to absorb all of its subjects and grant them rights is also a central part of the rule of colonial difference through the incorporation and differentiation of subjects. Even as abolitionists declared the possibility for a universal emancipation through American empire, this empire at its core depended upon the rule of difference.[87]

Phillips would continue to believe in Native incorporation into the

American empire while opposing exclusionary forms of settler colonial warfare. As Angela Murphy notes, Phillips would support Ulysses S. Grant, especially in his pursuit of a peace policy with American Indians throughout the war. Yet, Phillips's colonial logic of incorporation through a campaign of Native assimilation, in general, rarely opposed the expansion of the U.S. empire.[88]

The only former slaveholders who were compelled by the U.S. government to provide freedpeople with land were Native slaveholders from Five Tribes nations (Cherokee, Chickasaw, Choctaw, Creek, and Seminole).[89] The Cherokee Nation had been forcefully dispossessed from the southeastern United States for the expansion of white settler slavery in the 1830s. In Indian Territory (Oklahoma), some members of the Cherokee Nation continued to enslave African Americans. During the Civil War, members of the Cherokee Nation were divided in their support of the Confederacy and the Union. While Cherokee chief John Ross originally supported the Confederacy, this support shifted toward the Union, especially following the Union invasion of Cherokee Territory in 1862. The Confederacy would occupy the Cherokee Nation and instate Stand Watie, a Cherokee Confederate brigadier general, as chief.[90] Following the Treaty of 1866, the Cherokee Nation was compelled to provide freedpeople with land either in the Canadian District, which was southwest of the Arkansas River, or on a tract of land northwest of Grand River.[91] In this regard, land redistribution seemed to be something intended to break apart the power of colonized subjects in a settler colonial regime rather than something meant to produce anything like an abolition-democracy in a post-settler state.

Making the South a White Man's Country

When Black nationalists pursued configurations of nationhood, these arrangements were meant to secure Black autonomy removed from white supremacist violence. Yet leading figures with different views, such as Martin Delany and Henry Highland Garnet, never considered mass Black emigration logistically possible. As Garnet stated in 1858, "Let those who wish to stay, stay here, and let those who have enterprise and wish to go, go and found a nation, of which the colored American can be proud."[92] After emancipation, the majority of freedpeople refused colonization outside of the United States, and land struggles within the country became a primary expression of the nationalism of freedpeople.[93]

As Sterling Stuckey has noted, in the United States, unqualified debates over freedom have most often been debates over "freedom for whites."[94] African American emancipation sparked similar debates for white south-

erners, seeking to revise what white freedom might look like and strategiz-
ing on how to seize the American empire and make it white supremacist. As
freedpeople struggled to gain autonomous land control and transform the
conditions of work in the South, white southerners struggled to remake the
racial order of colonial white supremacy through a variety of approaches
to the reconfiguration of colonized land and labor.[95] After the Civil War,
some former slaveholders used their continued position as landholders to
look toward immigration, focusing especially upon European immigration
as a means to secure racial, political, and economic dominance in the post-
emancipation world.

Opposition to Black freedom in the slaveholding American South was
regionally differentiated. In the Upper South, emancipation and colonization were connected to plans for gradual emancipation, often because of
beliefs that Black and white could not live together without slavery.[96] As
John Hope Franklin observed, the colonization of free African Americans
emerged in relation to slavery, as a belief that slavery as a form of property
was to be protected and that free Black presence destroyed possibilities of
control.[97] In the 1850s, Tennessee, Texas, Louisiana, and Maryland passed
laws to re-enslave African Americans. In 1859, Arkansas passed legislation
to remove free African Americans from the state entirely.[98] Projects of colonization and removal as envisioned by whites were meant to strengthen the
institution of slavery.

Antislavery white interest in colonization among slaveholding states was
uncommon. The antislavery southern white supremacist Hinton Rohan
Helper opposed slavery in the American South through an investment in
transforming the United States into a white man's country through Black
removal rather than colonization.[99] These views sustained his *Impending
Crisis* (1857), which attracted interest from Republicans, including Lincoln. Missouri congressman Francis P. Blair advocated for a model of
colonization based upon the British Empire. According to Blair, a colony
formed through Black removal in Central America would form "our India,
but under happier auspices."[100] However, the post-slavery white nation envisioned by some U.S. slaveholders was not based upon Black colonization but Black disappearance.[101] As the *Southern Intelligencer* reported in
November 1865, the South would be transformed into a white man's country and "under their new condition of freedom, [African Americans would]
be forced to follow the retreating footsteps of the buffalo and the Indian."[102]

Southern slaveholders had often opposed European immigration prior
to the Civil War. This position on European immigration is captured by
James Henry Hammond, who in his 4 March 1858 "Cotton is King" speech

defined the slaveholding South against the rest of the United States: "The great West has been open to your surplus population, and your hordes of semi-barbarian immigrants, who are crowding in year by year." While cities such as Richmond, Charleston, Baton Rouge, and Mobile depended upon foreign-born labor while being fundamentally based upon slavery, Hammond's perspective encapsulated the vision of the southern, large slaveholding class. Before the Civil War, less than 7 percent of free southerners were born out of the United States, while immigrants composed nearly 20 percent of free states' population.[103]

For some white southerners, Black emancipation meant establishing a white racial ethno-state. As bureaus of immigration formed throughout the South for the first time, one commissioner for the Louisiana Bureau of Immigration noted, "It is desirable to build up a homogeneous State."[104] In 1868, the Louisiana Bureau of Immigration's publications included such texts as *Auskunst für Einwanderer nach dem Staate Louisiana* (1868), a pamphlet to encourage German immigration.[105] That same year, as Allison Efford notes, in a bid for acceptance, German Louisianans appealed to white solidarities and white pride through anti-Black racism. The German Democratic Central Committee of the City of New Orleans wrote to Germans in the northern and western United States stating that as (supposedly) intelligent white men it was "humiliating" for Germans to be "placed on the same level" as (allegedly) uneducated African Americans and to be "subordinated to the Negro in every respect."[106] This belief meant that working in the South alongside free Black people was degrading and humiliating to the white race. In response, they had opted to fight racism with more racism.

In the slaveholding South, slaveholders consistently argued for the particular necessity of U.S. slavery for something they called southern civilization. European immigration became essential to a white racial project to secure agricultural and domestic labor. European immigration was also intended by its architects to secure settlers and provide household stability. States across the South, including Arkansas, Texas, Tennessee, and Louisiana, created immigration bureaus immediately following the Civil War. These bureaus often focused exclusively on European immigration. As one observer noted, "It would certainly be contrary to the true interests of South Carolina to yet more multiply the variety of races in her inhabitants."[107]

Southern whites increasingly argued for the superiority of white labor. A South Carolina planter stated that his experience indicated that white labor could cultivate cotton "more economically than Black labor has ever done." The planter continued, stating he managed both types of labor and "would prefer all white" and would also be "pleased to have them settle in my neighborhood."[108] Planters frequently argued that formerly enslaved people would never be "efficient" laborers again. This perspective was often also combined with a racial hatred of Black people and the new reality of Black people who were no longer enslaved living within the same communities.[109]

Such desires, founded in a mythical racial commitment to making society white, were attended by former slaveholders' advocacy and struggles to transform the South into a white man's country.[110] For many white southerners, this did not depend upon Black removal through colonization projects. Instead, the introduction of white labor in the South became part of a broader white supremacist plan to reproduce immigration schemes that had drawn European labor to the northern United States. While white southerners' plans met with little success, even in failure they served a crucial role in perpetuating the slaveholders' colonialism in landholding.

In plans to attract immigrants to the United States, France, Germany, Britain, and Scandinavian countries were seen as most desirable countries. The Louisiana Bureau of Immigration, for example, seemed to support anything other than Chinese labor: "As to the labor question, the hardy workmen from the West, the sturdy Germans and Swedes and colored men now flocking to the Gulf States from Virginia and the Carolinas, seem far more desirable than Chinamen, having neither knowledge of, nor sympathy with, our institutions."[111] It was not just labor that such agencies sought but labor that was white.

Thomas Affleck was a central figure in the short-lived effort to transform the southern states into a white man's country during his life after the Civil War. Before the Civil War, Affleck designed techniques for plantation and race management. Affleck was an organic intellectual for southern slaveholding white supremacy through his advocacy for plantation improvement, expansion, and the scientifically managed plantation. Following the Civil War, he became a fierce and consistent advocate for transforming the American South, and Texas in particular, into a "white man's country" through European immigration. This effort depended specifically upon observations from other regions of white settler colonialism. Affleck looked toward attempts to introduce mass white European immigration to the American West, Queensland, and New Zealand. Affleck's vision for the post-slavery south did not reflect the white supremacist arrangement of agrarian relations that would emerge after emancipation. Yet, Affleck's struggles to transform the South into a white man's country were part of planters' racial struggles to ensure control of the slaveholders' colonialism after emancipation.

Affleck was a southern planter of Scottish birth. He left Dumfries, Scotland, in March 1832, sailing from Liverpool to New York.[112] He first worked in Pittsburgh before settling in Clinton, Indiana.[113] Affleck would become increasingly involved in the plantation economy of the South during the 1840s. After attending the annual fair of the Agricultural, Horticultural, and Botanical Society of Jefferson County, Mississippi, Affleck would decide to join and directly participate in the plantation economy after this first visit.[114] Affleck lived in Mississippi until 1859, when he relocated to Glenblythe, Texas. Following the conclusion of the American Civil War, Affleck traveled to Britain twice, seeking to establish regular and consistent European immigration to the state, looking especially toward Scottish cotters (smallholding farmers). While crossing the Atlantic has been understood as an opportunity for the settler to forget the so-called Old World, Affleck's own Atlantic passages at the end of his life were meant to multiply this Old World in Texas through a new form of anti-Black racism.[115]

In the slaveholding South, Affleck became a leading voice of southern agricultural improvement. He advocated for a regionally independent and diversified plantation economy, joining with other plantation "reformers"—white men who experimented in the cruel refinement of slavery, such as J. D. B. De Bow, Edmund Ruffin, and Noah B. Cloud.[116] Affleck was known for his agricultural writings for the New Orleans *Daily Picayune* and almanacs. Affleck's *Cotton Plantation Record and Account Book* editions were short books produced for the alleged efficient management of cotton and sugar plantations, particularly focused upon overseers' use.[117] First published in 1847, the account books were part of a broader movement of agricultural reform and "improvement" that stretched across the slaveholding South. The books came in two sizes—one smaller for plantations with up to 125 enslaved African Americans and one larger for plantations with greater numbers of people enslaved. The books, along with Affleck's "Overseer's Weekly Report," were intended for the more efficient organization of plantation accounting, bringing white supremacy and plantation management together in a standard, reproducible form. The books reduced long-form description and verbal communication to columns, numbers, and tally marks.[118] The books themselves were inspired by transnational print culture, responding to efforts to address limitations in record keeping in both the British Caribbean and on Louisiana sugar plantations while drawing upon commonly used farmers' account books, which were "in almost universal use in Great Britain."[119]

The account books were used to convey and manage the motion of profit and loss on plantations.[120] Contrary to what some historians have argued, social welfare was conspicuously absent in the design of the account books and, seemingly, even more so in their usage. In 1859, at the Panther Burn plantation in Mississippi, an overseer recorded in one of Affleck's volumes, "Have been so annoyed with sick Negroes did not keep no record of passing events."[121]

After the Civil War, white southerners expressed their ongoing struggle against Black freedom through the language of labor shortage. While in the 1850s planters advocated the reopening of the Atlantic slave trade, following the Civil War former slave owners such as Affleck approached human transfer through efforts to obtain immigrant labor from Scotland, England, and continental Europe and resist Black freedom.[122] This was a struggle not just over land but also over the household within which former planters and freedpeople sought to reorganize productive and gender relations:[123] "I propose to go to Europe only in the spring; and if encouraged . . . by land owners, business men of all classes, the state authorities and all interested, will devote a year or more to the effort, in which I have not a doubt of succeeding to turn such a tide of emigration from all parts of Europe to Texas, as will more than supply the place of the labor lost, and will make our noble state a *white man's country*."[124] In the immediate aftermath of Black emancipation, Affleck saw his interest in European immigration as part of a race war that would transform Texas into a "white man's country." He viewed Europe—England, Scotland, and Germany, in particular—as indispensable to this war and hoped that European immigration would enable the racial resolution of the ordering of agricultural and household labor.

Affleck's interest in the migration of white labor from England, Scotland, and Germany to Texas bridged disparate spaces and was connected to plots for moving white bodies such as those of Henry Jordan. Affleck's model for bringing European labor to Texas drew upon immigration schemes not just to the U.S. North and West but also to Queensland, New Zealand, and Natal. As Affleck stated when in England, "Go where you will, flaunting posters or hand bills will meet the eye in every direction—AUSTRALIA—TASMANIA—QUEENSLAND—NEW ZEALAND—CANADA—CAPE COLONIES—ILLINOIS CENTRAL RAILROAD—IOWA—UTAH—EVERYWHERE—except the Southern States!"[125] Affleck traveled to England and Scotland twice in search of arrangements for bringing labor to Texas. During these visits, Affleck was influenced by the efforts to colonize Queensland and the American West with white labor and believed the South should mount similar efforts. Affleck had a personal copy of *Queensland: Letters from*

Emigrants, with Most Recent Intelligence and seemed to base his own publication of a pamphlet for inducing European immigration to Texas upon Jordan's publications for Queensland.[126] Affleck was invested in a postslavery white racial project based upon Black replacement through European immigration to change Texas into a white man's country. This was part of a broader global project toward the creation of white racial ethno-states.[127]

In Scotland, the *Edinburgh Courant* reported on Affleck's efforts to secure European migration to Texas, noting that Affleck also drew upon observations about Black freedom in the Caribbean:

> The Southern planters have profited by our errors. They know, from the example of the West Indies, that simply to free the negro is to abandon him to the worse slavery of his own brute laziness and passions, and to expose to the risk of ruin any land which has no alternative but to employ him for the brief period which he chooses to work. So they are organizing a measure which will supersede him, and will reduce him to a position compared with which slavery was a paradise.[128]

For Affleck, the immigration of white labor to the United States was part of a demographic struggle for racial control bound to a logic of population competition. It was also bound to a nostalgic personal investment in remaking Texas into a place like Scotland, a nostalgia that emerged through settler colonial models for white racial dominance. These efforts and fantasies also converged in Affleck's personal interest in the employment of his own "countrymen," Scottish cotters in Texas, in plans that he described as "socialish."[129] This belief, better named fascism, was based upon the leveling fraternity between white men in patriarchal societies founded in the settler household.

In December 1865, Affleck left for Britain for the first time after the war to work toward making plans for European immigration. He continued to operate his plantation and contracted African American labor while arranging for a family member to continue to manage the plantation as he prepared to travel to Europe.[130] Affleck focused upon bringing white Europeans to perform both domestic and agricultural labor.

Affleck's visions for immigration were based upon belief in the racial management of the household economy and the gendered and racialized organization of work. These were fused to his earlier definitions of the well-managed plantation as one defined by southern agricultural independence from northern production of items necessary for plantations. In 1845, Affleck stated that his wife made forty-five blankets for enslaved African Americans at his Mississippi plantation, calculating that he had saved at least $120 in the process.[131] His new vision was for an independent white patriarchal household that was not founded upon Black work or presence.

As African American families sought to redefine the gendered and racial relations of work in the post-emancipation South, white families sought to sustain white plantation mistresses' storied removal from laboring in the domestic economy. Affleck saw immigration as essential to this essential "white freedom" and reported upon the cost of importing English chambermaids to Texas.[132] Within the plantation household, white slave-holding women performed tasks that enslaved women had been previously demanded to perform.[133] In one letter signed "Wife and Mother" (that Affleck himself may have written), the writer encountered Black resistance "accompanied by an air which says, 'I am assured that I am just as free and just as good as you are, that you cannot do without me, and should make you feel that I know it.' . . . 'Dismiss her at once' say you, Mr. Editor! And how am I to have my family's cloth's washed." As the "mistress" continued, "My laundry-woman told me only yesterday, when I pointed out a glaring neglect of duty, 'Well, come and show me what I am to do, and I'll do it; but I won't be all the time jawed at.' And this woman has evidently been a well-trained and good servant."[134]

These demands for Black women to work not only at the same pace but also with the same emotional engagement as during slavery suggested the challenge that racialized class struggles posed to white plans and desires. As Affleck wrote elsewhere, "The men and woman have not only treated all authority with more than contempt; but have greatly insulted my wife."[135] In the midst of composing an editorial on 17 May 1866, Affleck paused and noted, "Whilst now writing, a case is forced upon me of insolent bearing on the part of house servants, negroes, in my own household, that is calculated to embitter one's feelings towards the wretched creatures, to a most painful degree. Sooner than endure it a moment longer than I can put good, honest, intelligent white employees in their place, I would sacrifice all I possess."[136] In response to this, it became an objective for Affleck, who worked with the Land, Labor and Immigration Company, to focus upon the recruitment of household workers, because as Affleck suggested, plantation mistresses would appreciate "good, white house servants."[137]

Such recommendations were also intended to relieve "oppressed" white southern women and bring these domestic workers to Houston and Galveston: "How then do the ladies think they can maintain their health and good looks under the labor and skills they are now compelled to resort to for the purpose of having their house work done?"[138] This plea for preserving the "good looks" of white women would inform also the struggle to remake and continue the patriarchal "cult of true [white] womanhood," which would define with devastating consequences the post-Reconstruction nadir, reaching their most violent expression as motivation for white participation in lynchings.

A transformation of relations of gender and race in the household was underway, sparked by Black women's resistance to the old regime of slavery-based household labor relations. As Affleck noted, "It is evident that the lady of the house is forced to submit to a tone and bearing on the part of the [N]egroes that will only be submitted to until better can be done." Affleck continued, "The whole talk is of *immigration* and *white labor*. And no wonder is it that it should be so."[139] This "talk" was directly related to Black women's efforts to transform the household, and Affleck went to considerable length to report upon the cost of importing English chambermaids to Texas.[140]

In addition, Affleck focused upon securing the arrival of immigrant farm laborers.[141] The Texas Land and Labor Company Contract was a share-cropping contract that would provide immigrants with one-third of the cotton crop while also stipulating that employers paid a portion of the passage. Making Texas into a white man's country depended upon transforming agrarian relations, and Affleck stated that he believed that the "not distant end" would be African American deportation.[142] Affleck imagined this in relation to "coolies": "Neither of us approve of, or will do anything toward the introduction of coolies. We can exert no small influence in approving their introduction. . . . We have already more than enough of a low-grade race here now."[143] For Affleck instead, white labor was part of the racial heritage of the United States: "All white Americans are descendants of Europeans; the American nation, in a great measure, owes its existence, wealth and power to immigration from Europe; and although hundred thousands of Europeans have come to the United States, from year to year, it appears not that they have affected our republican form of government."[144] Affleck further noted that English manufacturers were "anxious to turn that tide of immigration South, for by coming here they would be engaged in the production of the great staples, so necessary to sustain England."[145] If this labor went to the northern United States, it was argued that it would take part in manufacturing rather than agricultural production, something that would ultimately be detrimental to England.

Affleck imagined immigration as continuing the exhortation of Patrick Henry in 1779 to "fill up" the country as quickly as possible, and he remained committed to making Texas white until his death.[146] In 1867, Affleck stated that he would not allow any African Americans onto his property. By

1868 he would be dead.[147] And by 1869, it was increasingly accepted that "there is little prospect of any white immigration into Southern States except Texas."[148] Texas would never become the white man's country that Affleck sought to build.

Josephine Ryles wished that her mother, Mary Alexander, was still alive to tell the Works Progress Administration interviewer who visited her what slavery meant.[149] Though Ryles was born into slavery, her mother knew its particularities in ways she did not. Her mother's life experience was punctuated by long, involuntary movement through the internal slave trade and the southwestern expansion of settler slavery, which also caused separation from Ryles's father.[150] Ryles was taken from Nashville, Tennessee, to Mobile, Alabama, and then to Texas. Ryles's mother worked in the plantation household, and her younger brother brought water for enslaved field hands.

With freedom she and her mother left for Galveston, like so many freedpeople who left the rural South for cities.[151] In Galveston, Josephine began working as a domestic servant, an experience that was especially common for free Black women who moved to cities and had been separated from husbands and partners by slavery.[152] While after emancipation Black families often reorganized labor relations through the family to remove Black women's work outside the formal economy, for women such as Alexander, such a reorganization was impossible.

The self-determined movement of Black men and women, the recomposition of families, political rights, the ability to escape the direct violence characteristic of slavery, and the reorganization of labor were all part of what Du Bois characterized as the "upheaval of humanity" that defined emancipation and Reconstruction. Freedpeople reimagined and remade work and life following emancipation, struggling to transform the remuneration of work as being characterized by the amount, capacity, and skill, a combination of forms that would seem to benefit Black workers who surpassed whites. Central to this struggle were freedpeople's efforts to provide for themselves and their families rather than work for masters, especially in anything that approached the conditions of slavery, and movement to cities was central to this struggle.[153] African American refusal to labor within a plantation system characterized by gang labor ultimately informed the emergence of sharecropping.[154] As was frequently argued by the once enslaved, Black people worked harder and better understood the techniques of work and demanded a world where this was properly compensated. An ethical democratic society based upon the dignity of life and work would find African Americans justly remunerated for their labor. But such a society did not exist, nor would it come into existence.

The movement of Alexander and Ryles was central to new realizations of freedom, and the position of Black women, men, and families also defined the nature of this freedom.[155] Many freedpeople sought to make claims to, seize, and redistribute land, something that Republicans, white southerners, and the Freedmen's Bureau resisted together.[156] As Felix Haywood recalled of emancipation, "Nobody took our homes, but right off colored folks started on the move. They seemed to want to get closer to freedom, so they knew what it was—like it was a place or a city."[157] Such a spatial rather than temporal understanding of freedom itself was linked to an impulse toward Black autonomy away from whites.[158]

Yet, finding places of freedom proved elusive; such places had to be made. In cities, whites expected and demanded that Black women would continue to labor within a formal wage-based economy rather than work within their own households.[159] Employment opportunities for Black women and men were increasingly constricted because of color bars. Black women who arrived in cities often were forced by the labor market into working in white homes as domestic servants.[160] Black men found forms of employment once available for free African Americans in cities, such as in barbershops, no longer available. The slaveholder's colonialism seemed to win for white supremacy the longer war.

Conclusion Slavery in the Year 2000

More than 71 million Black people would be enslaved in the United States in the year 2000. Over 300 million white people would live free. Slavery would form the basis for the future wealth of America.[1]

Francis Bonynge, the planter from India who also spent time in China, described this horrible vision of the future in 1852 in his book *The Future Wealth of America*. He also predicted there would be millions more free Black people. His table does not document Indigenous presence at all. He imagined a slavery-based racist empire continuing into the twenty-first century. The vision that Bonynge predicted for the present century is different but not untethered from the terrible present conjunctural crisis in capitalism. But this present—amid ecological catastrophe, capitalist breakdown, state-sanctioned racial killing, new global land grabs, and pandemic—is very much a product of the world of slavery, capital, and empire that was built, dismantled, and remade in the mid-nineteenth century.

Even the communist vision of an alternative seems in some ways hopeless. In 1846, Karl Marx noted that the National Reform movement's efforts to apportion 160 acres of land to settlers from Europe would "by its own inner logic inevitably press on to communism."[2] Even if this were so, it would be communism through the European settler colonization of North America—the breaking down of Native land and its reapportioning to white immigrant settlers. Still, Marx seriously considered immigrating to Texas.

Nearly twenty years later, well after the publication of *The Communist Manifesto* and right before the completion of *Capital*, Marx could recognize Black emancipation's significance in catalyzing the working-class movement against capitalism. Yet, this recognition still failed to center Black land struggles as pressing toward a logic of communism or breaking apart capitalism. Friedrich Engels's own understanding of Black emancipation struggles was based upon anti-Black racism. Using the language of white supremacy, he wrote to Marx that freedpeople would "turn into small squatters as in Jamaica."[3] Engels mocked and disparaged through white

TABLE A.   POPULATION OF THE UNITED STATES.

	Whites.	Slaves.	Free Colored.	Total.
1830,	10,526,246	2,008,043	320,596	
1840,	14,189,108	2,487,213	386,245	
1850,	19,668,736	3,179,589	419,173	23,267,498
1860,	26,552,793	3,910,894	482,049	30,945,736
1870,	34,518,630	4,810,399	554,356	39,883,385
1880,	43,148,287	5,916,790	637,508	49,702,585
1890,	53,935,358	7,277,651	733,134	61,946,143
1900,	67,419,197	9,051,510	843,104	77,313,811
1910,	84,273,996	11,133,351	969,579	96,376,928
1920,	105,342,495	13,694,029	1,115,015	120,151,539
1930,	131,678,119	16,843,655	1,282,267	149,804,041
1940,	164,597,646	20,717,695	1,474,607	186,789,948
1950,	205,747,060	25,482,764	1,695,798	232,925,622
1960,	257,183,825	31,343,799	1,950,167	290,487,781
1970,	321,479,781	38,553,872	2,242,692	362,276,345
1980,	401,849,726	47,421,262	2,079,095	451,850,064
1990,	502,312,157	58,328,252	2,965,959	563,606,368
2000,	627,890,296	71,743,749	2,410,852	703,044,897

Whites are estimated to increase up to 1860, at the rate of 35 per cent.; up to 1870, 30 per cent.; from 1870, 25 per cent.; Slaves, from 1850, 23 per cent.   Free Colored, from 1850, 15 per cent.

Had the Slave been calculated at 28 per cent., which is near their average rate of increase, it would make them, in the year 2000, 128,126,630, more than 1 to every 5 whites.

Table by Francis Bonynge envisioning U.S. population growth. (Francis Bonynge, *The Future Wealth of America* [New York: Published by the author, 1852])

supremacist language Black land-based liberation struggles in the United States.

For Marx, Black freedom struggles clarified the contradictions between labor and capital in and beyond the United States. In a letter thanking the Cuban slave owner Francois Lafargue for sending a bottle of wine, he wrote further, "The workers in the North have at last fully understood that white labour will never be emancipated so long as black labour is still stigmatized." This sentiment would also be incorporated within the first volume of *Capital*.[4] The end of slavery meant the intensification of class struggle to Marx, an interpretation that subordinated the meaning of Black freedom to the project of universal working-class emancipation.

Earlier, in the *Grundrisse*, Marx had described emancipation in Jamaica in slightly different terms. Marx noted that enslaved people had "ceased to be slaves," not to become wage laborers but instead "self-sustaining peasants working for their own consumption."[5] Yet, the significance of such transformations was lost on Marx. They did not escape W. E. B. Du Bois's notice, however.[6]

Black liberation struggles were somewhere other than what Marx understood, closer to Frantz Fanon's observations about the emergence of oppositional histories within settler colonial capital that are "not in the service of a higher unity."[7] Du Bois reflected that it was not the emancipation of labor alone but Black freedom coupled with providing 1 million free families with forty-acre freeholds that could have provided a basis for "real democracy." This, in turn, may "easily have transformed the modern world."[8] Du Bois posited future unities across diverse spaces of capital and empire, contingent not just upon the emancipation of labor but also on transformed relationships with the land, the destruction of white supremacy, and decolonization. This relationship was forged in the context of colonial and imperial histories marked by the breakdown and redistribution of Native land. Yet, this was an account for the possible emergence of a history of emancipation rather than a historical or theoretical account of what actually occurred.

Instead, U.S. settler slavery made an unbreakable linkage between race and extreme violence within colonial and capitalist relations, a linkage that extended past Black emancipation.

In the North-Western Provinces, the *Coolie-nama*, or "book of coolies" emerged as part of this reshaping colonial world. Written in Hindi by M. Kempson, a colonial official in the North-Western Provinces in 1866, the *Coolie-nama* was distributed throughout the region with the self-avowed purpose to counteract the "misinformation" given by "evil people" who sought to prevent individuals from gaining the full benefits of becoming coolies and traveling to settler colonies.[9] It presented information necessary to move coolies across the British Empire from Natal to Mauritius to Trinidad.

Beyond its self-avowed purpose, the *Coolie-nama* was the product and vision of a logic of colonial repopulation and global demographic shifts. The *Coolie-nama* described South African Zulus and Indigenous Guianese as *jungli log*, or wild and uncivilized, inadequate for the tasks of plantation labor and the agricultural demands of the British Empire. Instead, the *Coolie-nama* explained that coolies would move to British Guiana, Trinidad, and Natal to perform a variety of forms of labor, from growing cotton to cultivating tobacco. The condition of the coolie was free from exploitation in the *Coolie-nama*, even as coolies were meant to perform critical agricultural labor. The text presents the possibility of moving labor from an overpopulated North India to agriculturally more productive colonies imagined as underpopulated and there enjoying a better life.[10] Despite pressures of social disruption, the *Coolie-nama* was also a response to opposition to relocation.[11] The number of laborers sent from Calcutta decreased markedly every year following the 1860–61 famine year, and the year before the publication of the *Coolie-nama* only 6,145 laborers were sent from Calcutta.

The vision of the *Coolie-nama*, of coolies moving across the British Empire providing cheap labor free from exploitation while facilitating Indigenous dispossession, was part of a broader cynical white imagination of the coercion of labor after the abolition of slavery.[12] Du Bois recognized what Marx did not fully see, this world as it painfully emerged during his era. It was a world where the United States' logic of violent territorial conquest and racialized labor subordination in the service of capital continued and expanded rather than disappeared.

In the upheavals that disrupted mid-nineteenth-century capitalism, challenged the British Empire, and ended racial slavery in the United States, another world was struggled for and partially realized. The song "The Trouble of the World" captured both the trouble of this world of death and slavery and also the possibility of this trouble coming to the end.[13] The lyrics "I wish I was in Jubilee" in the song wished for freedom from the world of slavery and death, from the trouble of the world.

That wish subverted in so many ways the dreams of white men such as Bonynge, who imagined slavery extending into the twenty-first century. But still, what is the present in relation to the struggle of enslaved people to be in jubilee?

Acknowledgments

The University of North Carolina Press has provided great support, and I would like to thank everyone who worked to produce this book, including Jay Mazzocchi, Catherine Hodorowicz, Dylan White, and Kim Bryant. I am especially grateful to editor Brandon Proia for his support, encouragement, and friendship. Julie Bush offered indispensable copyediting support. Thank you also to Margaretta Yarborough for proofreading and to Mark Mastromarino for compiling the index. The two anonymous readers of this book provided important commentary that informed the completion of this book.

Antoinette Burton, Sundiata Cha-Jua, Moon-Kie Jung, Manu Karuka, and David Roediger guided this project in its earliest stage. I was right when I approached Antoinette and said that I thought I might need to talk with her. Dave has helped me navigate many storms since we met in a Milwaukee blizzard. In Champaign, James Barrett, Teresa Barnes, Utathya Chattopadhyaya, Clarence Lang, James Kilgore, Sharony Green, Cassandra Osei, Miloš Jovanović, Archana Prakash, John Marquez, and T. J. Tallie all offered important advice, mentorship, friendship, and guidance.

The Center for the Study of Slavery and Justice at Brown University has provided significant support, especially through the Ruth J. Simmons Postdoctoral Fellowship. Maiyah Gamble-Rivers, Shana Weinberg, Diane Straker, and Catherine Van Amburgh have all made the center the dynamic place that it is. Postdoctoral fellows Nic John Ramos, Crystal Eddins, and Roselyne Gérazime have been the greatest of friends. CSSJ fellows including Bedour Alagraa, Felicia Bevel, Ricarda Hammer, Johanna Obenda, Daniel Platt, Anni Pullagura, and Heather Sanford have also made the CSSJ the intellectually dynamic center it is known to be. Without Anthony Bogues, this project would not have been completed. I am grateful for his support and intellectual vision. I completed this project at Drexel University and would like to thank the history department at Drexel for their incredible support. At the CSSJ, Michael Ralph and Prasannan Parthasarathi participated in a manuscript review workshop that was essential to the process of manuscript revision.

The Center for the Study of Race and Ethnicity in America has been the best neighbor at Brown. Tricia Rose, Stéphanie Larrieux, and Caitlin Scott have all provided crucial support. I am further grateful to Brian Meeks and Brown University's Africana studies department. The Weatherhead Initiative on Global History at Harvard University has provided a dynamic space for engaged consideration of the history of global capitalism. I am further grateful to my colleagues at Firelight Films who have taught me much about how to tell history. It has been a joy to learn from Naz Habtezghi, Hazel Gurland-Pooler, Jarobi Moorhead, and Kevina Tidwell. Marcia Smith is a source of inspiration, and Stanley Nelson's vision is legendary.

Many individuals have read or commented on parts of this project and provided other critical support. I would particularly like to thank Mary Alpuche, Aaron Benanav, Debjani Bhattacharyya, Anthony Bogues, Guilia Carabelli, Titas Chakraborty, Meghna Chaudhuri, John Clegg, Brian Connolly, João Costa Vargas, Felicia De-

naud, Daniel Denvir, Andreas Eckert, Zophia Edwards, Elizabeth Esch, Roquinaldo
Ferreira, Matthew Guterl, Paget Henry, Moon-Kie Jung, Patsy Lewis, Sophie Loy-
Wilson, Kris Manjapra, Jörg Nagler, Mae Ngai, Seth Rockman, Matt Schutzer, Joan
Scott, Anandaroop Sen, Naoko Shibusawa, Françoise Vergès, Rupa Viswanath, Rosie
Warren, and Andrew Zimmerman. I am further grateful to Patrick Bellegarde-Smith,
Caroline Bressey, Michael Gordon, Catherine Hall, Jennifer Morgan, Marcus Rediker,
Tanika Sarkar, Alan Singer, and Carol Stabile for their inspiration.

This book depended upon the support of archivists and librarians at the Agricultural and Horticultural Society of India, Brown University, Duke University, John Ry-
lands Library, the Lancashire Archives, the Louisiana and Lower Mississippi Valley
Collections at Louisiana State University, Manchester Central Library, the Mississippi
State Archives, the National Archives of Belize, the National Archives of India, the
National Archives of the United Kingdom, the National Library of India, Nehru Memo-
rial Museum and Library, Queensland State Archives, the South Carolina Historical
Society, the State Archives of West Bengal, the State Library of New South Wales, the
University of Illinois at Urbana-Champaign, and the Wisconsin State Historical So-
ciety. The American Institute of Indian Studies, the New Orleans Center for the Gulf
South, and the University of Illinois at Urbana-Champaign all also provided crucial
research support.

Without Mekhola Gomes, I would have quit this project long ago and recently. She
has been constant in support and precise in criticism. I am grateful for this and so much
more. My parents, Kathy and Glenn Sell, and Valerie Sell and Dustin Underwood, are
the best. Edith Sell inspired me to finish this book.

I have no idea what the future holds, but it is worth fighting to live differently, to end
the present world devastatingly built in part through the histories of this book.

Notes

Abbreviations

AHSI   Agricultural and Horticultural Society of India, Kolkata
BARS   Belize Archives and Records Services, Belmopan
BL   British Library, India Office, London
HCPP   *Return of Papers in the Possession of the East India Company Showing Measures taken since 1836 to Promote the Cultivation of Cotton House of Commons Parliamentary Papers*, vol. 42, 1847
JRL   John Rylands Library, University of Manchester Library
MALS   Manchester Archives and Local Studies
MECW   Karl Marx and Frederick Engels, *Marx and Engels Collected Works*, 50 vols. (London: Lawrence and Wishart, 1975–2004)
NAI   National Archives of India, Delhi
NAUK   National Archives of the United Kingdom, London
SLQ   State Library of Queensland, Brisbane

Introduction

1. Draper, *Price of Emancipation*; Chatterjee, "Abolition by Denial"; Lightfoot, *Troubling Freedom*; Major, *Slavery, Abolitionism, and Empire in India*.

2. C. Hall et al., *Legacies of British Slave-Ownership*; Manjapra, "Plantation Dispossessions."

3. C. Hall, *Civilising Subjects*, 105–6; Turner, "The Jamaica Slave Rebellion of 1831."

4. Horrox and Hall, *The Spectre of Marxism*.

5. C. Anderson, "After Emancipation: Empires and Imperial Formations," in Hall, Draper, and McClelland, *Emancipation and the Remaking of the British Imperial World*, 113–30; Banivanua Mar, *Violence and Colonial Dialogue*; Guterl, "After Slavery"; Kale, *Fragments of Empire*.

6. Guyatt, *Bind Us Apart*.

7. M-K. Jung, "Racial Constitution."

8. Kerr-Ritchie, *Rebellious Passages*, 33.

9. In 1830, the United States was 1.75 million square miles; following the annexation of Texas, it was nearly 3 million. *1830 Census: Population of the United States*; *1860 Census: Population of the United States*. For continental imperialism in the United States, see Karuka, *Empire's Tracks*, 168–85.

10. Draper, "Helping to Make Britain Great: The Commercial Legacies of Slave-Ownership in Britain," in *Legacies of British Slave-Ownership*, 78–126.

11. Gallagher and Robinson, "Imperialism of Free Trade."

12. Legassick and Ross, "From Slave Economy to Settler Capitalism," 314. For a critical history of colonialism, indigeneity, and anti-Black racism in southern Africa, see Tallie, *Queering Colonial Natal*.

13. For an indispensable account of colonial agrarian conquest in India focused on

Punjab, see Bhattacharya, *The Great Agrarian Conquest*. Sharma, *Empire's Garden*; Behal and Mohapatra, "Tea and Money versus Human Life," 142–72; Kumar, *Indigo Plantations and Science in Colonial India*; Ali, *A Local History of Global Capital*.

14. Inikori, *Africans and the Industrial Revolution in England*, 193.

15. J. Brown, *Slave Life in Georgia*, 13 and 171; Collins, *Scinde and the Punjaub*.

16. Beckert, *Empire of Cotton*; Riello, *Cotton: The Fabric that Made the Modern World*; Clapham, *An Economic History of Modern Britain*, vol. 2, 27; Pomeranz, *The Great Divergence*; Parthasarathi, "The Great Divergence," 278.

17. Bailey, "The Other Side of Slavery," 40; Ballagh, *South in the Building of a Nation*, 166.

18. S. Remond, "The Negroes in the United States of America," in Robbins and Gates, *Portable Nineteenth-Century African American Women Writers*, 89.

19. "How to Make India take the Place of America as Our Cotton Field."

20. Lowe, *Immigrant Acts*, 27–28; Roediger and Esch, *The Production of Difference*.

21. Fox-Genovese and Genovese, *Slavery in White and Black*, 97–152.

22. C. Hall, "Going A-Trolloping: Imperial Man Travels the Empire," in *Gender and Imperialism*, ed. Clare Midgley, 180–99; Logan, "A British East India Company Agent in the United States, 1839–1840," 267–76. English factory owners such as Henry Ashworth also travelled to the U.S. South, making such comparisons. Henry Ashworth, *A Tour in the United States, Cuba and Canada*, e.g. 101. Other British travelers who published about plantation relations in the American South include Hall, *Travels in North America in the Years 1827 and 1828*; Mitchell, *Ten Years in the United States*; Roles, *Inside Views of Slavery on Southern Plantations*; and Majoribanks, *Queensland*, 7.

23. Roediger, *Colored White*, 108; Rugemer, *The Problem of Emancipation*, 258–76; Karp, "King Cotton, Emperor Slavery: Antebellum Slaveholders and the World Economy," in Gleeson and Lewis, *The Civil War as Global Conflict*, 47.

24. Pollard, *Black Diamonds Gathered in the Darkey Homes of the South*, 9.

25. Ruffin, *Diary of Edmund Ruffin*, vol. 1, ed. William Kauffman Scarborough, 97, 99; Sanyal, *Reminiscences and Anecdotes*, vol. 1 (Calcutta, 1894), 39, qtd. in Blair Kling, *The Blue Mutiny*, 110.

26. Polanyi, *The Great Transformation*, 3–20; Hobsbawm, *The Age of Extremes*.

27. Holden, "Generation, Resistance, and Survival"; Kling, *Blue Mutiny*; Burton, *Trouble with Empire*; Gopal, *Insurgent Empire*.

28. Du Bois, *The World and Africa*, 12.

29. Henderson, "Charles Pelham Villiers," 35.

30. Sargent, *England, the United States, and the Southern Confederacy*, 157.

31. "Economic Manuscripts of 1861–1864," in *Marx-Engels Collected Works*, vols. 31–35.

32. Luxemburg, *Accumulation of Capital*; Midnight Notes, *The New Enclosures*; Coulthard, *Red Skin, White Masks*.

33. Marx, *Capital*, 763–64.

34. For example, see Marx, "The British Cotton Trade," *New-York Daily Tribune*, 14 October 1861. As Moishe Postone writes, "although capitalism is, of course, a class society, class domination is not the ultimate ground of social domination in that society, according to Marx, but itself becomes a function of a superordinate 'abstract' form of

domination." Postone, *Time, Labor, and Social Domination*, 126. The historical account of slavery in Marx's writing situates slavery as part of historical capitalism, but representations of slavery in *Capital* are often not primarily concerned with the realities of slavery.

35. Marx, *Capital*, vol. 1, 519.

36. See, for example, "Negroes Wanted," *The North-Carolinian*, 1 February 1851. "Cash! . . . ," *Slave Advertisement*, Library of Congress, LC-USZ62-62799. On use of term likely for description of enslaved people, see Block, *Colonial Complexions*, 50–51; Smallwood, "What Slavery Tells Us about Marx."

37. Sh. Sweeney, "Black Women in Slavery and Freedom"; Johnson, "The Pedestal and Veil"; Robinson, *Black Marxism*.

38. Robinson, *Black Marxism*.

39. A. Kumar, "Marx and Engels on India," 493–504.

40. Marx, "The British Rule in India," *New-York Daily Tribune*, June 25, 1853; Habib, "Karl Marx and India"; Naved, "The Colonial Encounter in Marxist Terms"; D. Chakrabarty, "Marx after Marxism."

41. According to Rebecca Karl, "The AMP died an appropriate death in the 1930s and should remain dead." Karl, *The Magic of Concepts*, 42; Banaji, *Theory as History*, 17–23. In contrast, Gayatri Spivak suggests that the AMP marked the outside of the feudalism/capitalism circuit and was paradoxically not identifiable with Asia despite its name nor was it a mode of production. Spivak, *Critique of Postcolonial Reason*, 72–86.

42. Marx, *Capital*, 479. Marx himself would continue to revise this assessment in his late notebooks. Anderson, *Marx at the Margins*.

43. Coulthard, *Red Skin, White Masks*, 7.

44. Emmanuel, "White-Settler Colonialism and the Myth of Investment Imperialism."

45. Marx, *Capital*, 940; Humphrys, "The Birth of Australia."

46. Kale, *Fragments of Empire*.

47. Robinson, *Black Marxism*; Byrd, Goldstein, Melamed, Reddy, "Predatory Value."

48. Wynter, "Beyond the Categories of the Master Conception."

49. James, *The Black Jacobins*.

50. For early accounts of the centrality of slavery in the making of capitalism, see W. Williams, *Africa and the Rise of Capitalism*, 39–40, passim. As Joseph Inikori notes, the history of capitalism has often been bound to the history of the industrial revolution with two general contending interpretive tendencies. One tendency emphasizes the role of foreign trade and plantation slavery in the Americas establishing the foundations for the industrial revolution. A second tendency emphasizes internal transformations within England. Inikori, "Capitalism and Slavery, Fifty Years After," 51–80; Drescher, "British Capitalism and British Slavery"; Robinson, "Capitalism, Slavery and Bourgeois Historiography."

51. For an overview, see Rockman, "What Makes the History of Capitalism Newsworthy?," 439–66; Beckert and Rockman, *Slavery's Capitalism*. For critiques, see Johnson, "Brute Ideology"; Hudson, "Racist Dawn of Capitalism"; Enstad, "The 'Sonorous Summons' of the New History of Capitalism, Or, What Are We Talking about

When We Talk about Economy," 83–95; Kramer, "Embedding Capital"; Clegg, "Capitalism and Slavery"; Stanley, "Histories of Capitalism and Sex Difference"; Jakes and Shokr, "Finding Value in *Empire of Cotton*."

52. Liu, *Tea War*; Kumar, *Indigo Plantations and Science in Colonial India*; Sharma, *Empire's Garden*; Beckert, *Empire of Cotton*; Ali, *A Local History of Global Capital*; Hahn, *Making Tobacco Bright*.

53. Banivanua Mar, *Violence and Colonial Dialogue*; Kale, *Fragments of Empire*; Lowe, *Intimacies of Four Continents*; Johnson, *River of Dark Dreams*; Manjapra, "Plantation Dispossessions"; Zimmerman, *Alabama in Africa*; Morgan, "Accounting for the 'Most Excruciating Torment'"; Lowe, *The Intimacies of Four Continents*.

54. Liu, "Production, Circulation, and Accumulation," 767–88; Jakes and Shokr, "Finding Value in *Empire of Cotton*"; S. Hall, "Race, Articulation, and Societies Structured in Dominance."

Chapter 1

1. E. C. Briscoe to Ziba B. Oakes, 8 March 1857, Ziba B. Oakes Papers, 1852–1857, Boston Public Library, available online at https://www.digitalcommonwealth.org/collections/commonwealth:ht24xg09z; Drago, introduction to *Broke by the War*; Tadman, *Speculators and Slaves*, 36–40.

2. Rothman, *Slave Country*; Johnson, *River of Dark Dreams*; Schermerhorn, *Business of Slavery*.

3. For examples of Oakes's interest in land speculation, see F. C. Barber to Ziba B. Oakes, 17 January 1855, and E. A. Gibbes to Ziba B. Oakes, 29 January 1857, Oakes Papers. For other slave traders involved in land speculation, see Stephenson, *Isaac Franklin*; and Yagyu, "Slave Traders," 90–91.

4. Johnson, "Introduction"; Johnson, *Soul by Soul*, 19–44.

5. Du Bois, *Black Reconstruction*, 7.

6. For accounts of the limits of Du Bois's concept of work in *Black Reconstruction*, see Hartman, "Belly of the World"; and M-K. Jung, "Enslaved." For the importance of enslavement beyond work to settler colonial regimes, see King, "Labor's Aphasia."

7. W. E. B. Du Bois to Harcourt, Brace and Company, 31 January 1935, W. E. B. Du Bois Papers, 1803–1999, Special Collections and University Archives, University of Massachusetts Amherst, available online at https://credo.library.umass.edu/view/pageturn/mums312-b074-i230/#page/1/mode/1up. Du Bois had a deep understanding of post-slavery real estate. Du Bois, *Philadelphia Negro*.

8. Morris, *Southern Slavery and the Law*, 61–80; Copeland, "Nomenclature of Enslaved Africans."

9. As Thomas D. Morris writes, real property laws were variously applied to enslaved people in more than one-third of jurisdictions in the slave South. Morris, *Southern Slavery and the Law*, 64.

10. Du Bois does not neglect the legal definition of slavery as chattel even while he consistently emphasizes its real estate character in *Black Reconstruction*. As a legal category, K-Sue Park has noted a breakdown in the boundaries between real and personal or chattel property within the history of colonial America and the early United States. See Park, "Money, Mortgages, and the Conquest of America."

11. Du Bois, *Black Reconstruction*, 700; Roediger, *Wages of Whiteness*; Glymph, "Du

Bois's *Black Reconstruction*"; Spivak, "General Strike." See also Hartman, "Belly of the World."

12. Wynter, "Beyond the Categories," 81.

13. Connolly, *World More Concrete*, 6.

14. Real estate as a concept in *Black Reconstruction* could be seen as an interrogation of what C. L. R. James called the "new forms created in the context of slavery." James, "Atlantic Slave Trade and Slavery," 133. For an expansion upon this idea, see Bogues, "We Who Were Slaves"; and Schermerhorn, *Business of Slavery*, 77.

15. Deloria, *Behind the Trail of Broken Treaties*, 113. See also Karuka, *Empire's Tracks*, 179.

16. Rogin, *Fathers and Children*, 75-110.

17. Inikori, *Africans and the Industrial Revolution in England*, 193.

18. Rana, *Two Faces of American Freedom*.

19. M-K. Jung, "Racial Constitution."

20. K. Morgan, "Mercantilism and the British Empire."

21. Moreton-Robinson, *White Possessive*, 138; Banner, "Why *Terra Nullius*?"

22. R. Guha, *Rule of Property*; Gidwani, "'Waste' and the Permanent Settlement in Bengal."

23. Rabin, *Britain and Its Internal Others*; Wiecek, "Somerset."

24. Copy of Proceedings, 7 February 1772, King's Bench, London, p. 44, Granville Sharp Collection, 1768-1803, New York Historical Society, available online at http://digitalcollections.nyhistory.org/islandora/object/islandora%3A153558.

25. Newman, *Dark Inheritance*; Rabin, "'In a Country of Liberty?'"; Wiecek, "Somerset."

26. M-K. Jung, "Racial Constitution."

27. Waldstreicher, *Slavery's Constitution*; Lynd, "Abolitionist Critique."

28. Einhorn, *American Taxation*, 121.

29. Dunbar-Ortiz, *Indigenous Peoples' History*, 124.

30. Finkelman, "Slavery and the Northwest Ordinance"; Heerman, *Alchemy of Slavery*; Wolfe, "*Corpus Nullius*," 130.

31. Melish, *Disowning Slavery*.

32. *Constitution of the United States of America*. See further, David, "Fugitive Slave Law of 1793."

33. Baker, *Prigg v. Pennsylvania*, 140-51; Blackett, *Captive's Quest for Freedom*.

34. These figures are from the 1810 and 1860 censuses.

35. J. Morgan, "Accounting for 'The Most Excruciating Torment,'" 185-86; E. Williams, "British West Indian Slave Trade"; compare Eltis, "Traffic in Slaves."

36. Tadman, "Demographic Cost of Sugar," 1537.

37. V. Brown, *Reaper's Garden*, 52-53.

38. J. Morgan, *Laboring Women*, 55-56.

39. J. Morgan, "*Partus sequitur ventrem*."

40. Deutsch, "Constitutional Controversy."

41. Austin, *Baring Brothers*, 17-18.

42. Thomas Jefferson to Allan B. Magruder, 11 February 1804, and Thomas Jefferson to John Breckinridge, 25 November 1803, in McClure, *Papers of Thomas Jefferson*, 37, 458.

43. John Hammond, "'They Are Very Much Interested,'" 360. By the time of the

Missouri Crisis (1819–20), Jefferson believed in the diffusion of slavery across a larger geographic space, which would ultimately result in the end of slavery. Dierksheide, "'Great Improvement,'" 169.

44. John Hammond, "'They Are Very Much Interested,'" 360; Thomas Jefferson to John Breckinridge, 25 November 1803, in McClure, *Papers of Thomas Jefferson*, 40; Scanlon, "Sudden Conceit"; Herschthal, "Slaves, Spaniards, and Subversion"; Lachance, "Politics of Fear."

45. Dunbar-Ortiz, *Indigenous Peoples' History*, 96; Johnson, *River of Dark Dreams*, 45; John Hammond, "'They Are Very Much Interested'"; Beckert, *Empire of Cotton*.

46. Parthasarathi, *Why Europe Grew Rich*, 12.

47. John Hammond, "'They Are Very Much Interested,'" 358.

48. Veracini, *Settler Colonialism*, 66.

49. Veracini, 66.

50. Copeland, "Nomenclature of Enslaved Africans"; Best, *Fugitive's Properties*, 8. For death in the transfer of real property, see Blackmar, "Inheriting Property and Debt."

51. McKittrick, "Plantation Futures."

52. B. Connolly, *Domestic Intimacies*, 190–94.

53. Truth, *Narrative of Sojourner Truth*, 13; Harris, "Finding Sojourner's Truth." Ball, *Slavery in the United States*, 16.

54. See, for example, Bill of Sale for a Slave Sold by Mrs. Marie Jean Villier of St. Landry Parish, Louisiana, to Louis DeBlanc of St. Martin Parish, Louisiana, MSS. 434, Louisiana and Lower Mississippi Valley Collections, Louisiana State University Libraries.

55. Spillers, "Mama's Baby, Papa's Maybe."

56. For slaveholder interest in the sale of enslaved people to cover debt following the death of a slaveholder, see H. Johnson to William Johnson, 30 December 1844, William Johnson Papers, box 1, folder 11, p. 30, Mississippi Department of Archives and History, Jackson.

57. Jones-Rogers, "[S]he Could . . . Spare One Ample Breast.'"

58. Kilbourne, *Debt, Investment, Slaves*.

59. Berry, *Price for Their Pound of Flesh*, 2.

60. Jacobs, *Incidents in the Life of a Slave Girl*, 16.

61. H. Brown, *Narrative of Henry Box Brown*, 34.

62. Millward, "'Relics of Slavery,'" 26; Onuf, "Every Generation Is an 'Independent Nation'"; S. Green, *Remember Me to Miss Louisa*.

63. Schweninger, *Families in Crisis in the Old South*.

64. E.g., "Last Will and Testament of Henry Clay," University of Kentucky, available online at https://www.uky.edu/Libraries/KLP/bib/klp1991-1.html.

65. Kaplan, "Manifest Domesticity."

66. Rogin, *Fathers and Children*.

67. Andrew Jackson, Will, 7 June 1843, Andrew Jackson Papers, 1775–1874, Library of Congress, available online at http://hdl.loc.gov/loc.mss/maj.01109_0095_0099.

68. Peterson, *Indians in the Family*, 141.

69. On slavery's serial dispossessions, see A. Byrd, *Captives and Voyagers*; and Du Bois, *Black Reconstruction*, 20.

70. J. F. E. Hardy (Grantor) to Isaac McDunn (Grantee), "Bill of Sale Slave Mary

and Child (Sarah)," Book 24, p. 586, dated 1 April 1852, Register of Deeds, Buncombe County, North Carolina, available online at https://registerofdeeds.buncombecounty .org/External/LandRecords/protected/DocumentDetails.aspx?BaseFileNumb=ppU %2bPzlfKes%3d&ImageID=OpBcSYj795s%3d .

71. Isaac McDunn (Grantor) to John W. Ballew (Grantee), "Bill of Sale Slaves May & Child (Sally)," Book 25, p. 485, dated 2 March 1855, Register of Deeds, Buncombe County, North Carolina, available online at https://registerofdeeds.buncombecounty .org/External/LandRecords/protected/DocumentDetails.aspx?BaseFileNumb=U36 DU1ICDOM%3d&ImageID=05RnfPbxjaw%3d.

72. Jacobs, *Incidents in the Life of a Slave Girl*, 24; B. Connolly, *Domestic Intimacies*, 192.

73. Finger, "Termination and the Eastern Band of Cherokees"; Garrison, *Legal Ideology of Removal*.

Chapter 2

1. In March 1845, the U.S. Congress passed a resolution for the annexation of Texas.

2. Frederick Douglass, "The Annexation of Texas: An Address Delivered in Cork, Ireland on 3 November 1845," in P. Foner, *Life and Writings of Frederick Douglass*, 71.

3. Frederick Douglass to William A. White, 30 July 1846, in P. Foner, 148. See also William Lloyd Garrison to Levi Woodbury, 14 March 1845, in Merrill, *Letters of William Lloyd Garrison*, 290-94.

4. R. Campbell, *Empire for Slavery*.

5. "The *Volks-Tribune*'s Political Economy and Its Attitude towards Young America," *MECW*, 6:35-51; Blackburn, *Marx and Lincoln*, 2; Bronstein, *Land Reform*.

6. Marx, *Capital*, 395; Ghorashi, "Marx on Free Trade."

7. Hobsbawm, *Age of Revolution*, 34.

8. Morrison, "Before Hegemony," 399-400; North, *Economic Growth of the United States*; Semmel, *Rise of Free Trade Imperialism*; Chalmers, *Estimate of the Comparative Wealth*.

9. Carrington, "American Revolution"; Carrington, *British West Indies*.

10. Crowley, "Neo-mercantilism and the *Wealth of Nations*," 347; Sheffield, *Observations on the Commerce of the American States*.

11. Trade patterns were not fundamentally transformed by the American Revolution. Yokota, *Unbecoming British*, 63.

12. Yokota, 64; Sloan, *Principle and Interest*; Breen, *Marketplace of Revolution*; Matson, *Economy of Early America*; Buck, *Development of the Organisation of Anglo-American Trade*. On the nullification crisis, see Ericson, "Nullification Crisis." For an overview of slaveholder struggles over tariff policy, see Freehling, *Prelude to Civil War*, 89-207.

13. Eacott, *Selling Empire*.

14. Thomas Jefferson to John Adams, 19 November 1785, in Boyd, *Papers of Thomas Jefferson*, 43.

15. Hyam, *Britain's Imperial Century*, 64. See also Ramusack and Burton, "Feminism, Imperialism and Race"; and Roeckell, "Bonds over Bondage."

16. W. Jones, *Aberdeen and the Americas*, 25. The Walker Tariff reversed a U.S. tariff passed in August 1842 that established a 120 percent tariff against British cotton

textiles. On southern support for the tariff, see Belko, *Triumph of the Antebellum Free Trade Movement*, 157–58.

17. R. J. Walker to I. L. Scott and others, 28 June 1847, Transcription of Robert J. Walker's Letter Book, to 1848, Robert J. Walker Papers, ULS Archives and Special Collections, University of Pittsburgh.

18. Wynter, "Novel and History." As a stage in the history of capitalism, monopoly capitalism is most commonly periodized between the late nineteenth century through approximately the post–World War II era with an imperial-oriented violence exerted through the economy.

19. Macfie and Sons to Robert Peel, 17 April 1846, Robert Peel Papers, Add. MS. 40590, BL; Memorial of Sugar Refiners to Robert Peel, 2 May 1846, Peel Papers, Add. MS. 40591, 88.

20. James Mill put forth an idea with broad influence, that free trade stood in opposition to "unnatural" accumulation of landed property by Jamaican slaveholders. For slavery-produced sugar in free-trade Britain, see Huzzey, "Free Trade."

21. C. Hall, *Civilising Subjects*.

22. E. Williams, *Capitalism and Slavery*, 153. See also C. Taylor, *Empire of Neglect*.

23. Legassick and Ross, "From Slave Economy to Settler Capitalism," 286.

24. Richard Cobden to Joseph Sturge, 26 February 1841, in Howe, *Letters of Richard Cobden*, 216; Pickering and Tyrell, *People's Bread*, 110.

25. Joseph Sturge to Robert J. Peel, 12 May 1846, Add. MS. 4059, 363, Peel Papers, BL. As Sturge wrote, "The comparatively high price and short supply of sugar and the probable deficiency of the coming crop of sugar in the west indies appears to give the public a strong claim for this measure now and it should never be forgotten that the 20 million, which were given to the planters at the time the emancipation act was passed[,] leaves them perhaps less claim to any further protection than other interests."

26. George Wilson to John C. Calhoun December 5, 1844, in *Papers of John C. Calhoun*, 20: 485.

27. "Free Trade," *The Liberator*, 22 August 1845; John C. Calhoun to George Wilson, 24 March 1845, in *Papers of John C. Calhoun*, 17:642, 21:444–45.

28. Calhoun to Wilson, 24 March 1845.

29. Charles Augustus Davis to John Calhoun, 3 June 1846, in *Papers of John C. Calhoun*, 23:162; An American, "Commerce of British India."

30. The American Chamber of Commerce of Liverpool to Robert Peel, January 1845[?], 103, Peel Papers, BL.

31. Abbott Lawrence to John C. Calhoun, 30 April 1845, in *The Papers of John C. Calhoun*, vol. 21, 517. For U.S. slaveholder fears of future competition with India, see A Kentuckian [Duff Green], "War with America: An Examination of the Instigations and Probable Effects," *Great Western Magazine and Anglo-American Journal*, April 1842, 70–71; and "The East India Question," *Southern Planter*, February 1842, 1, 2.

32. For post-emancipation implications of this territorial relation, see Beckert, "American Danger."

33. Sturgis, *John Bright and the Empire*, 7.

34. Sturgis, 16.

35. Sturgis, 19.

36. Sturgis, 9.

37. Kling, *Blue Mutiny*, 46.

38. Jenny Proctor, Federal Writers' Project: Slave Narrative Project, vol. 16, Texas, Part 3, Lewis-Ryles, 1936, www.loc.gov/item/mesn163/.

39. In his *Philosophy of Manufactures*, Andrew Ure would note that the United States principally depended upon gunny cloth from India, while Kentucky hemp would also be used for bagging cotton. Ure, *Philosophy of Manufactures*, 627-31; Yazoo, "Cotton Bagging, Blankets, Clothing, &C," *Southern Planter*, January 1842, 21. The term "gunny" has a Sanskrit etymology from "goni," meaning "sack." "Gunny Bags against Kentucky Bagging," *Farmers' Register*, October 1841, 600; William W. Worsley to Henry Clay, 31 December 1840, *The Papers of Henry Clay*, 470; Olmsted, *A Journey through Texas*, 57; Ure, *Philosophy of Manufactures*, 627; "East India Hemp," *Louisville Journal*. Reprinted in United States Department of Agriculture, *Annual Report of the Commissioner of Patents, for the Year 1848*, 574-77.

40. Clark-Pujara, *Dark Work*.

41. Yazoo, "Cotton Bagging, Blankets, Clothing, & C.," 21.

Chapter 3

1. F. C. Brown to P. Grant, Esq., Collector of Malabar, Anjarakandy, 14 March 1862, in F. Brown, *Supply of Cotton from India*, 31 in Henry Ashworth Papers, Lancashire Archives, Preston.

2. Scholars have debated the causes and character of this crisis at length. For one significant account, see Luxemburg, "History of Crises," 402-4.

3. Edelson, *Plantation Enterprise*; Sharrer, "Indigo Bonanza"; Coon, "Eliza Lucas Pinckney."

4. For the early history of indigo in colonial North America, see F. Knight, *Working the Diaspora*, 87-95; and P. Wood, *Black Majority*. For indigo and slavery in the British Caribbean, see Shepherd, *Slavery without Sugar*.

5. Nash, "South Carolina Indigo," 387.

6. R. Guha, "Neel-Darpan"; Sartori, *Bengal in Global Concept History*. For an overview of indigo in India, see Nadri, *Political Economy of Indigo*, 221 (prices).

7. P. Kumar, *Indigo Plantations*; Freedgood, *Ideas in Things*.

8. Major, *Slavery, Abolitionism, and Empire*, 327.

9. *Report of the British India Society First Annual Meeting*, 26. Eric Williams would instead describe the colonial expansion of slavery in terms of a passing of the baton between plantation regions. E. Williams, *Capitalism and Slavery*, 7. For the ambiguous uses of "free" in relation to labor, see Banaji, "Fictions of Free Labor"; Johnson, *River of Dark Dreams*, 153-54; and Wright, "Review of *River of Dark Dreams*," 878.

10. Anti-Slavery Society, *Free Trade and Free Labour, The Surest Means of Abolishing the Slave Trade and Slavery*.

11. Zastoupil, *John Stuart Mill*, 14; Logan, "British East India Company Agent"; Tuteja, "American Planters"; Tuteja, "Agricultural Technology in Gujarat"; T. Banerjee, "American Cotton Experiments"; Leacock and Mandelbaum, "Nineteenth-Century Development Project"; Royle, *On the Culture and Commerce of Cotton in India*.

12. William Elliott, "Reflections on the State of Our Agriculture, Especially on the Advantage of Cultivating Indigo, & c.," *Southern Agriculturist* (February 1828): 64; McCurry, *Masters of Small Worlds*, 7-8; L. Jones, "William Elliott."

13. T. Spalding, "On the Culture of Sugar and Indigo," *Southern Agriculturist* 1 (November 1828): 483–85. For further on U.S. slavery and indigo production in India, see T. Spalding, "Observations and Extracts on the Manufacturing of Indigo in Bengal," 3 (May 1830): 247–50; George M. Gibbes, "On the Method of Manufacturing Indigo on the Coast of Coromandel, in India, and Senegal, under the Auspices of the French Government," *Southern Agriculturist* 1 (1828) 110–15.

14. Kling, *Partner in Empire.*

15. George Thompson, *Lectures on British India* (1840), 153.

16. Tripathi, *Trade and Finance*; Chowdhury, *Growth of Commercial Agriculture.*

17. For the causes of the slave trade ban, see Brady, "Slave Trade and Sectionalism."

18. Anti-Slavery Society, *Free Trade and Free Labour, The Surest Means of Abolishing the Slave Trade and Slavery* (London: 1840?), 1.

19. Yang, *Limited Raj*, 133–35.

20. Bose, *Peasant Labour*, 47, 74–76; P. Kumar, "Plantation Science."

21. M. Jones, *Birthright Citizens.*

22. Amin, *Sugarcane and Sugar*; Bosma, *Sugar Plantation*; Huzzey, "Free Trade," 359–73.

23. "Impolicy of Slavery," 345.

24. Memorial of the Directors of the Manchester Chamber of Commerce, January 1861, Proceedings of the Manchester Chamber of Commerce, MALS; Fergusson, *Letters to Lord Stanley*, 25. On contract law and indigo, see Roy, "Indigo and Law."

25. Bonynge, *Future Wealth of America*, 132. For Bonynge's influence on tea cultivation, see Fullilove, *Profit of the Earth.*

26. Chaplin, "Creating a Cotton South"; Rothman, *Slave Country*, 113.

27. Partridge, "On the Manufacturing of Indigo," 242.

28. On value and slavery, see Berry, *Price for Their Pound of Flesh.*

29. Ideas about indigo's destructiveness to the body can be found in journals such as the *American Cotton Planter*. "The injury he complained of is produced during the beating process; for so rapid is the absorption of oxygen gas from the atmosphere, during the operation, that those who stand over it must be breathing an air with its vital principle so diminished as to render it unfit to sustain animal life." "Madder and Indigo," *American Cotton Planter*, 299–300.

30. "The Cultivation and Preparation of Indigo," *De Bow's Review* (1855): 51; Charles W. Capers, "Observations on Indigo, Poppy, Grass, and Buckwheat," *Southern Agriculturist*, July 1832, 349; A South-Carolinian, *Refutation of the Calumnies*, 51–52.

31. Wailes, *Report on the Agriculture and Geology of Mississippi*, 135–38.

32. Baptist, *Half Has Never Been Told.*

33. "On Malaria," *Farmers' Register* 2 (June 1834): 21.

34. On Haitian slavery, the Haitian Revolution, and indigo, see Dubois, *Avengers of the New World*; and Garrigus, "Blue and Brown."

35. "East India Cotton," *Southern Quarterly Review* (April 1842): 446–92.

36. Ferrer, *Freedom's Mirror.*

37. "Note by the Editor on the Cultivation of Indigo," *Southern Agriculturist*, April 1829, 163–64.

38. Donald B. Jones, "Observations on the Choice of Indigo Seed," *Southern Agriculturist* 3 (1830): 566–67. At the same time, U.S. observers also looked at the shift

in indigo and remarked, "Since our planters have beat all the efforts of the East India Company to rival them in the cultivation of cotton, it appears to us that their honor is somewhat at stake to regain their lost reputation in the cultivation of indigo." "Cultivation of American Indigo," *Scientific American* 12, 1 (1856): 8.

39. Herbert, *War of No Pity*, 68; W. H. Russell, "Sahib and the Nigger," *The Times* (London), 20 October 1858; C. Hall, "Economy of Intellectual Prestige"; Semmel, *Governor Eyre Controversy*.

40. On nineteenth-century whiteness in the United States, see A. Saxton, *Rise and Fall of the White Republic*; Roediger, *Wages of Whiteness*; D. Bell, *Idea of Greater Britain*; and Dilke, *Greater Britain*.

41. A. Rao and B. G. Rao, *The Blue Devil. Nil Darpan* (Calcutta, 1860), 15; Banerjee, "Who, or What, is Victorian?," 213–23; Kling, *Blue Mutiny*.

42. Grant, *Minute by the Lieutenant-Governor of Bengal*, 12; Sartori, *Liberalism in Empire*, 98–107.

43. Ball, *Slavery in the United States*, 18.

44. Ball, *Slavery in the United States*, 131. Blassingame, *Slave Testimony*, xxiii; Baptist, *Half Has Never Been Told*, 168.

45. H. Knight, *Letters from the South and West*, 115.

46. McKittrick, "Plantation Futures."

Chapter 4

1. Samuel Tayler to Elizabeth Frances Blyth, 2 September 1838, in Easterby, *South Carolina Rice Plantation*, 339; Baptist, "Toxic Debt"; Lepler, *Many Panics of 1837*.

2. Tayler had been sold to Mobile for $1,900. He believed he could be repurchased for between $1,000 and $1,100.

3. Samuel Tayler to Elizabeth Frances Blyth, 2 September 1838.

4. A. Byrd, *Captives and Voyagers*; Hartman, "Belly of the World."

5. In 1859, the largest single sale of enslaved people in the United States occurred when 436 enslaved people were sold by the rice and cotton planter Pierce Butler. A. Bailey, *Weeping Time*; Du Bois, *Black Reconstruction*, 45.

6. "Gang of 25 Sea Island Cotton and Rice Negroes," auction notice, Schomburg Center for Research in Black Culture, New York Public Library, https://digital collections.nypl.org/items/510d47df-a25f-a3d9-e040-e00a18064a99.

7. Fullilove, *Profit of the Earth*, 77.

8. Francis Bonynge, "Cultivation of Tea, Indigo, & C.," *De Bow's Review* (1851): 514.

9. Adas, *Burma Delta*; Coclanis, "Distant Thunder"; Cheng, *Rice Industry of Burma*.

10. Charles Dickens, "Rice," *Household Words* 33 (1856): 6–14.

11. A Lady, *New London Cookery*.

12. Public Health, *Sixth Report of the Medical Officer*, 241.

13. W. Brown, *Sketches of Places and People Abroad*, 101.

14. "Speech of George Thompson," in *British India: The Duty and Interest of Great Britain*, 5.

15. Midgley, *Feminism and Empire*, 41–64.

16. Beckert, *Empire of Cotton*, 113–14.

17. *Substances Used as Food*, 107–9.

18. Edward T. Heriot to Cousin, April 1854, Edward T. Heriot Papers, Rubenstein Library, Duke University.

19. Berry, *"Swing the Sickle,"* 32–34.

20. Clifton, "Charles Manigault's Essay," 106; "Notice of the Agricultural Society of South Carolina, on the Profits of the New Trade of Rough Rice," 16 October 1827, Minutes of the Agricultural Society of South Carolina, South Carolina Historical Society, Charleston.

21. B. Wood, *Women's Work*; Dusinberre, *Them Dark Days*.

22. P. Morgan, "Work and Culture."

23. A. Bailey, *Weeping Time*, 123.

24. J. Bryan, "On the Culture of Rice," *Southern Agriculturist* 5 (October 1832): 530.

25. Q.E.D., "Answer to Queries of an Observer on the Culture of Rice," *Southern Agriculturist* 5 (December 1832): 630–31.

26. Johnson, *River of Dark Dreams*.

27. Olmsted, *Journey in the Seaboard Slave States*, 471–75. For inland rice cultivation techniques, see Hugh Rose, "Answers: Queries on the Culture of Rice," *Southern Agriculturist*, April 1828, 167–70.

28. Ben Horry, Federal Writers' Project: Slave Narrative Project, vol. 14, South Carolina, Part 2, Eddington-Hunter (1938), Library of Congress, https://www.loc.gov /item/mesn142/.

29. James Calhart James, Federal Writers' Project: Slave Narrative Project, vol. 8, Maryland, Brooks-Williams (1936), 35, Library of Congress, https://www.loc.gov/item /mesn080/; Kemble, *Journal of a Residence*, 134.

30. Charles Munnerlyn, "Answers: Queries on the Culture of Rice," *Southern Agriculturist* 1 (May 1828): 220–21; James H. Claiborne, "Answers: Queries on the Culture of Rice," *Southern Agriculturist* 1 (July 1828): 311.

31. "Plantation Journal, 1844," in *Life and Labor on Argyle Island*, 8–9; House, *Planter Management and Capitalism*, 60.

32. Experiments with cultivation techniques from India, China, Egypt, and Spain also occurred within South Carolina. See, for example, Minutes of the South Carolina Agriculture Society, 1825–60, 1 October 1825, South Carolina Historical Society, Charleston.

33. Clifton, "Charles Manigault's Essay"; Clifton, "Jehossee Island"; Clifton, "Rice Driver," 331.

34. Brewster, *Summer Migrations and Resorts*.

35. Clifton, "Rice Driver," 335.

36. B. McBride, "Directions for Cultivating the Various Crops Grown at Hickory Hill," *Southern Agriculturist* 3 (May 1830): 288.

37. Stuckey, *Slave Culture*, 304.

38. U. Phillips, *Life and Labor in the Old South*, 115–17; Schwalm, *A Hard Fight for We*, 27; Olmsted, *Journey in the Seaboard Slave States*, 475; House, *Planter Management*, 60.

39. E. Elliot, "History and Cultivation of Rice," *De Bow's Review* 11 (1851): 306.

40. Maggie Black, Federal Writers' Project: Slave Narrative Project, vol. 14, South

Carolina, Part 1, Abrams-Durant (1936), 59, Library of Congress, https://www.loc.gov/resource/mesn.141/.

41. Chaplin, *Anxious Pursuit*, 227–74.

42. Starobin, *Industrial Slavery in the Old South*, 20–21; Lander, "Manufacturing in South Carolina," 61.

43. Thomas Naylor to William Lucas, 9 October 1823, Jonathan Lucas Papers, South Carolina Historical Society.

44. Elizabeth Blyth Papers, Rubenstein Library, Duke University.

45. "Patents Lately Enrolled," *Edinburgh Magazine*, 1 March 1819, 275.

46. "Industry of the Southern and Western States," *De Bow's Review* 6, nos. 4–5 (1848): 288; "Steam Rice Mills," *Washington Quarterly Magazine of Arts, Science and Literature* 1, no. 2 (1824): 133.

47. "The New Trade in Rough Rice," *Southern Agriculturist* 1 (October 1828): 460.

48. Egerton, *He Shall Go Out Free*.

49. Franklin and Schweninger, *Runaway Slaves*.

50. R. W. R., "Utility of Machinery," *Southern Agriculturist* 2, no. 9 (September 1846): 466.

51. B. Hall, *Travels in North America*, vol. 3, 165.

52. "Polk's Special Message, 23 March 1846," in *Tariff from the White House, Extracts from the Messages*, 64.

53. Bonynge, "Cultivation of Tea, Indigo, & C.," 513.

54. City Rustic, "On the Pounding of Rice," *Southern Agriculturist* 1 (August 1828): 351.

55. Kemble, *Journal of a Residence*, 151.

56. Dusinberre, *Them Dark Days*, 50–51.

57. Elliot, "History and Cultivation of Rice"; Gray, *History of Agriculture*, 731.

58. Fanon, *Wretched of the Earth*, 7.

59. Q.E.D., "Answer to Queries of an Observer on the Culture of Rice," 634.

60. Pinckney, *Address Delivered in Charleston*, 9, 14–15; Asaka, *Tropical Freedom*, 47, 49.

61. Gilmore, *Golden Gulag*, 28.

62. "Objects of This Journal," *British Indian Advocate* 1 (1 January 1841): 2.

63. Wynter, "Novel and History," 101.

64. Robb, *Peasants, Political Economy, and Law*, 80.

65. N. Bhattacharya, *The Great Agrarian Conquest*.

66. R. Knight, "On the Cultivation of Carolina Paddy," General, August 1873, 9–14, State Archives of West Bengal, Kolkata; Ali, *Local History of Global Capital*.

67. Amin, *Sugarcane and Sugar*; Bosma, *Sugar Plantation*; E. Williams, *Capitalism and Slavery*; Huzzey, "Free Trade."

68. Draper, *Price of Emancipation*; Manjapra, "Plantation Dispossessions."

69. Viswanath, *Pariah Problem*, 5.

70. J. Sharma, "British Science."

71. Behal and Mohapatra, "'Tea and Money.'"

72. Robb, *Peasants, Political Economy, and Law*, 80.

73. P. Kumar, *Indigo Plantations*; D. Arnold, "Agriculture and 'Improvement.'"

74. The AHSI was based in Bengal and dedicated to agricultural improvement

throughout India, especially through the introduction of new staples and cultivation techniques.

75. Radhakanta Deb, "On the Cultivation of Cotton and Tobacco in Central India," *Transactions of the Agricultural and Horticultural Society of India* 2 (1836) [1830]: 70–73. Deb made these observations within the context of cotton and tobacco cultivation. For his views on rice, see Radhakanta Deb, "On the Culture of Paddy in Twenty Different Districts," *Transactions of the Agricultural and Horticultural Society of India* 2 (1836): 193–95; Subhas Bhattacharya, "Indigo Planters"; and Sengupta, *Conservative Hindu.*

76. Radhakanta Deb, "On the Culture of Paddy in Twenty Different Districts," *Transactions of the Agricultural and Horticultural Society of India* 2 (1836): 193–95. "Report from the Society of Arts on Nipal Rice, Thibet Wool, Safflower, &C.," *Transactions of the Agricultural and Horticultural Society of India* 3 (1839): 120. On Bengal cultivation efforts, see *Report of the Agricultural and Horticultural Society of India*, 8, 12.

77. Minutes, 18 October 1831, Minutes of the South Carolina Agricultural Society, 1825–60.

78. Cecil Beadon to James Hume, 11 November 1846, Minutes of the Agricultural and Horticultural Society of India, 1843–46, AHSI.

79. Beadon to Hume, 11 November 1846.

80. Experimental Sowing of Carolina Paddy, 30 September 1874, No. 2886, Financial Department, Agriculture, Produce and Cultivation, State Archives of West Bengal.

81. "Successful Introduction of American Rice into the District of Purneah," *Transactions of the Agricultural and Horticultural Society of India*, 8 July 1840, Library of the Agricultural and Horticultural Society of India (Kolkata). On success and failure in capitalism, see Birla, "Failure via Schumpeter."

82. Logan, "British East India Company Agent"; Florio, "Poverty to Slavery"; Olmstead, "Antebellum U.S. Cotton Production."

83. Woodman, *King Cotton and His Retainers*, 15.

84. T. Bayles to James Cosmo Melvill, 1 June 1840, *HCPP*, no. 15, p. 19.

85. Bayles to Melvill, p. 28.

86. James Morris to J. V. Hughes [22 December 1841], *HCPP*, no. 2, p. 329.

87. Urzee (Petition) from Rangasamy Naick, 13 September 1842, Rice Cultivation in Coimbatore, IOR/F/4/2025/91369, BL. Available online at http://www.bl.uk/manuscripts/FullDisplay.aspx?ref=Ior/f/4/2025/91369.

88. Videe Sen, *Mahazurnamah* (Memorandum), 21 September 1842, Coimbatore Rice. BL. Available online at http://www.bl.uk/manuscripts/FullDisplay.aspx?ref=Ior/f/4/2025/91369.

89. James Morris to Brother, December 1842, James M. Morris Papers, Caroliniana Library, University of South Carolina, Columbia.

90. E.C. Lovell, Revue Office, 9 March 1843. Rice Cultivation in Coimbatore, IOR/F/4/2025/91369, BL. Available online at http://www.bl.uk/manuscripts/FullDisplay.aspx?ref=Ior/f/4/2025/91369.

91. Cotton, *List of European Tombs in the Bellary District with Inscriptions*, 41.

92. Another project was explored at a jail at Ranchi.

93. Carolina Paddy, Bengal, General, P.N. 171-73, September 1869, State Archives of West Bengal, Kolkata.

94. James, "The Atlantic Slave Trade and Slavery," 151.

95. Hartman, "Belly of the World."

96. E. Elliot, "History and Cultivation of the Rice," 307.

97. Fields-Black, *Deep Roots*.

Chapter 5

1. Robinson, "Capitalism, Marxism, and the Black Radical Tradition." In addition to Robinson, important interventions in thinking through this relationship include Lowe, *Intimacies of Four Continents*, 135-71; Prakash, "Colonialism, Capitalism and the Discourse of Freedom"; I. Chatterjee, "Abolition by Denial"; and J. Byrd, *Transit of Empire*, esp. xxiv-xxv.

2. Banaji, "Fictions of Free Labour: Contact, Coercion, and So-Called Unfree Labour," in *Theory and History*, 134.

3. This was, as Goenpul scholar Aileen Moreton-Robinson has noted, "driven by the logic of capital." Moreton-Robinson, *White Possessive*, 51; Moore, *Emergence of the Cotton Kingdom*; Woodman, *King Cotton and His Retainers*, 3-187.

4. Quoted in I. Collins, *Scinde and the Punjaub*, 10.

5. Du Bois, *Negro*, 115; Marx, *Capital*, 925; J. Byrd, "Return to the South," esp. 619-20; Johnson, "Pedestal and the Veil."

6. R. Ray, "Introduction," *Entrepreneurship and Industry in India*, 19.

7. Habib, "Colonization of the Indian Economy"; I. Ray, *Bengal Industries*, 52-87; Mitra, *Cotton Weavers of Bengal*, 4, 33; Ghosal, *Economic Transition*, 30.

8. S. Sharma, "1837-38 Famine in U.P."; Bayly, *Rulers, Townsmen, and Bazaars*, 295-98.

9. Kling, *Partner in Empire*, 167-77; Mehrotra, "Landholders' Society"; Mehrotra, "British India Society."

10. *Report of the British India Society First Annual Meeting*, 6.

11. *Report of the British India Society First Annual Meeting*, 24. William Lloyd Garrison dreamed of a time when the "free" cotton of India would be manufactured by British industry "to the overthrow of slavery and the slave-trade throughout the world!" William Lloyd Garrison to Joseph Pease, 30 September 1840, Selected Letters of William Lloyd Garrison, Boston Public Library Anti-slavery Collection, available online at https://archive.org/details/lettertoesteemedoogarr8.

12. Thompson, according to his daughter Amelia Chesson, had become "impressed with the conviction" that growing cotton in India and the abolition of slavery in the United States were "identical." As Thompson wrote, "every smoking chimney and noisy machine and huge brick edifice and piled up cotton wagon and pale faced factory child called upon me to go forward with all boldness and earnestness in the cause of the Slave in America which is the cause of India and the enterprises must be wedded and proceed indissolubly together till they together triumph." Extract from Amelia Chesson's Notebooks, 20 September 1839, Raymond English Antislavery Collection, 3/5, JRL.

13. Wendell Phillips, "Letter to George Thompson," *Speeches, Lectures, and Letters*, 10.

14. Zimmerman, *Alabama in Africa*, 40.

15. Prakash, "Colonialism, Capitalism and the Discourse of Freedom," 11; James Oakes, "The Peculiar Fate of the Bourgeois Critique of Slavery," in Winthrop D. Jordan, *Slavery and the American South*, 46. For Marx, free labor generally referred to two distinct economic conditions, one of wage laborers seeking employment and another of property-owning small producers. E. Foner, *Free Soil*, x–xi; Banaji, "Fictions of Free Labour."

16. J. Byrd, *Transit of Empire*, xxv.

17. Rana P. Behal and Prabhu Mohapatra, "Rise and Fall of the Indenture System in the Assam Tea Plantations, 1840–1908," in Daniel, Bernstein, and Brass, *Plantations, Proletarians, and Peasants*, 142. William Adam delineated forms of so-called slavery in British India at the first British and Foreign Anti-Slavery Society Convention in 1840. Adam, "Slavery in India."

18. "Cultivation of Cotton in British India," *Farmers' Register*, October 1840, 582; "Minute of H. T. Prinsep," Cotton (India), *HCPP*, no. 15, p. 19; P. Kumar, *Indigo Plantations*, 79–81.

19. *Second Annual Report of the Aborigines Protection Society*, 17; Laidlaw, "'Justice to India.'"

20. Stokes, "Agrarian Society," 528.

21. Hazareesingh, "Cotton, Climate, and Colonialism," 3–8; Logan, "British East India Company Agent"; Tuteja, "American Planters"; Tuteja, "Agricultural Technology in Gujarat"; T. Banerjee, "American Cotton Experiments"; Leacock and Mandelbaum, "Nineteenth-Century Development Project"; Aukland, "Minute on Cotton Cultivation," *HCPP*, no. 4, p. 8.

22. Olmstead and Rhodes, "Biological Innovation." Compare Baptist, *Half Has Never Been Told*, 111–44. Throughout the 1830s, the AHSI imported and distributed American cotton seed throughout colonial India in efforts that repeatedly failed. See Minutes and Proceedings of the Agricultural and Horticultural Society of India, 1835 to 1866, AHSI. See also Monthly Proceedings of the Agricultural and Horticultural Society of India, 15 January 1858, NAI; and Summary of Proceedings Showing the Result of the Introduction of Foreign Cotton Seed, Revenue and Agricultural Department Proceedings, 22 June 1840, no. 25, NAI.

23. Clarkson, "Speech of Thomas Clarkson." See also Thomas Clarkson to Joseph Pease, 13 June 1843, in Thomas Clarkson Papers, Doc. 79, St. John's Library, Cambridge University; and "Cultivation of Cotton in British India," *Correspondence of the Journal of Commerce*, 31 August 1840. This was not the first effort to build off of cotton cultivation in the United States. In 1813, the East India Company sent Bernard Metcalfe, from a plantation economy in Georgia with expertise in cotton ginning, to India. In Malwan, in 1817, there was an experiment with the cultivation of Bourbon cotton. In 1827 and 1828, Basil Hall traveled throughout the southern United States, reporting on plantation production and sending his observations to the East India Company along with cotton seed and gins. See Alex Elphinstone, "Letters from Mr. Elphinstone Relative to His Experiments in the Cultivation of Cotton at Rutagherry," *Annual Report of the Transactions of the Bombay Chamber of Commerce*; Robert Wight, "Remarks on the Cultivation of Cotton; Principally with Reference to the Finer Foreign Varieties,"

Madras Journal of Literature and Science 6 (1837): 79–110; *American Farmer* 42, no. 9 (1828): 329–30; and B. Hall, *Travels in North America*.

24. Olmstead, "Antebellum U.S. Cotton Production," 20; Florio, "Poverty to Slavery."

25. Du Bois, *World and Africa*, 17–44.

26. Oakes, *Ruling Race*, 174–75.

27. Douglass, *Narrative of the Life of Frederick Douglass*, 12.

28. For the shifting boundaries of the North-Western Provinces, see Jain, *Hindu Society*, 4–12.

29. For overviews of agrarian relations in the North-Western Provinces during this period, see Metcalf, *Land, Landlords, and the British Raj*, 47–163; and Bayly, "Age of Hiatus."

30. J. G. Bruce to H. Torrens, *HCPP*, no. 61, p. 103.

31. "Revenue Department to Governor-General of India in Council," 2 July 1840, *HCPP*, no. 20, p. 24.

32. Quoted in Medlicott, *Cotton Hand-Book*, 302.

33. See also Zimmerman, *Alabama in Africa*.

34. On Natchez's central role, see Libby, *Slavery and Frontier Mississippi*.

35. Thomas Bayles to James Cosmo Melvill, *HCPP*, no. 21, p. 25.

36. John McCullough, "The Cultivation of Cotton in India," *Charleston Mercury*, 22 September 1857.

37. "Ginning of East India Cotton," *Hazard's United States Commercial and Statistical Register* 3, no. 9 (August 1840): 134.

38. 9 September 1840, Proceedings of the Agricultural Society of India, 1839 to 1840, AHSI.

39. Mann, "Ecological Change in North India"; S. Sharma, "1837–38 Famine in U.P."; S. Sharma, *Famine, Philanthropy, and the Colonial State*; Bayly, *Rulers, Townsmen, and Bazaars*, 295–98.

40. Medlicott, *Cotton Hand-book*, 320; T. J. Finnie, "Views and Considerations on Farming in India," *Journal of the Agricultural and Horticultural Society of India* 1, no. 2 (1842): 120; "Extracts from Finnie's Journal, February 1842," *HCPP*, no. 115, p. 157.

41. Finnie, "Views and Considerations on Farming in India," 120.

42. Hartman, *Scenes of Subjection*, 21.

43. "Extracts from Private Journals," *HCPP*, no. 115, p. 155.

44. Stampp, *Peculiar Institution*, 100. If he meant the opposite, his observations went against the logic of the plantation South, where masters and overseers remarked upon the need for direct surveillance of enslaved African Americans—something that the overseer was essential for.

45. "Extracts from Private Journals" (April through October 1841), *HCPP*, no. 65, p. 109.

46. Roediger and Esch, *Production of Difference*, 19–63.

47. Stokes, "Agrarian Society."

48. "Extracts from Finnie's Private Journal for April," *HCPP*, no. 117, p. 162.

49. "Extracts from Finnie's Private Journal for April," 162.

50. "Extracts from Finnie's Private Journal for August," *HCPP*, no. 122, p. 179.

51. Raikes, *Notes on the Northwestern Provinces*, 49.

52. "Extracts from Finnie's Private Journal for September," *HCPP*, no. 131, p. 190.

53. "Extracts from Finnie's Private Journal for July," *HCPP*, no. 121, p. 176.

54. "Extracts from Finnie's Private Journal for June," *HCPP*, no. 120, p. 168.

55. Fanon, *Wretched of the Earth*, 7; "Extracts from Finnie's Private Journal for June," 168.

56. "Extracts from Finnie's Private Journal for June," 168.

57. "Extracts from Finnie's Private Journal for June," 168.

58. "Extracts from Finnie's Private Journal for June," 168.

59. "Extracts from Finnie's Private Journal for July," *HCPP*, no. 121, p. 176.

60. "Extracts from Finnie's Private Journal for July," 176.

61. "Extracts from Finnie's Private Journal for July," 176.

62. "Extracts from Finnie's Private Journal for July," 177.

63. "Extracts from Finnie's Private Journal for July," 176.

64. *East India* (Improvements in Administration). *Return*. February 1858, p. 32. Birla, "Failure via Schumpeter."

65. Said, "Travelling Theory," in *World, the Text, and the Critic*, 244.

66. Marx, *Capital*, 931–40. Footnote 4 quotes from Marx's own earlier observation "A negro is a negro. In certain relations he becomes a slave."

67. Marx, *Capital*, 931–40. Coulthard, *Red Skin*, 10.

68. For more complex histories of Swan River Colony, see Hetherington, "Aboriginal Children."

69. Marx, *Capital*, 940.

70. Medlicott, *Cotton Hand-book*, 340.

71. Wolfe, "Settler Colonialism," 394.

72. Samuel Cartwright, "The Slave Trade and the Union," *Memphis Daily Appeal*, 23 September 1854.

73. T. J. Finnie [Brahminee Bull], "Dr. Cartright [*sic*] and Slavery in the East Indias," *Memphis Daily Appeal*, 10 October 1854.

Chapter 6

1. Cotton Supply Association, "Address: To the Cotton Workers of Great Britain: Sparks Among the Cotton," PKWR0(4) (Manchester: John J. Sale, 1859–60?), JRL.

2. Henry Ashworth, "Cotton: Its Cultivation, Manufacture and Uses," *Journal of the Society of Arts*, 12 March 1858, 262. See also I. Collins, *Scinde and the Punjaub*, 5. As I. G. Collins observed, "A deficient crop, a slave insurrection, or a diplomatic blunder, occurring thousands of miles from our shores . . . may suddenly, but fatally, put an end to our manufacturing supremacy, and lay the proud fabric of our commercial greatness level with the dust, never to rise again!" W. Brookes, "Cotton and Queensland."

3. Dadabhai Naoroji, "The Supply of Cotton," *Cotton Supply Reporter*, 1 February 1864, 394.

4. J. B. Smith, one manufacturer who did attempt to secure Indian cotton supplies, complained of the "apathy" of cotton manufacturers before the outbreak of the U.S. Civil War. See J. B. Smith, 25 January 1862, Stockport Letters 1852–74, MS. 923.2 S. 341, MALS.

5. I. Collins, *Scinde and the Punjaub*, 10; J. Brown, *Slave Life in Georgia*, 13.

6. The significance of this interlinkage is captured in the letters of a Manchester merchant who reported regularly on demand for textiles in India and the influence of prices of cotton from the United States. See Samuel Studdard Papers, DDSP 73/4/3, Lancashire Archives, Preston. For an example of the general correlation of the price of cotton and the price of textiles, see graph for "Prices of Cotton, Cotton Yarn, and Power Loom Cloth, in Each Month from 1842 to 1848," Henry Ashworth Papers, DDAS 2/3, Lancashire Archives. I use "goods" and "Manchester goods" throughout this chapter to refer to any Manchester-produced cotton goods imported into India and synonymously with piece goods. See "Piece Goods," *Hobson and Jobson*. However, some usage has referred to piece goods as cut or stitched articles and loom garments as uncut and unstitched articles. For the significance of the realization of surplus, see Harvey, *Limits to Capital*, 75–97.

7. As Henryk Grossman noted, "The question of where the surplus value is realised is quite irrelevant. All that matters is the magnitude of the surplus value." Grossman, *Law of the Accumulation and Breakdown of the Capitalist System*, 125–26.

8. Farnie, "Cotton Famine," 154–55; Farnie, *English Cotton Industry*, 138. A series of scholars and contemporary observers have converged over the crisis in the textile industry as a product of overaccumulation: R. Arnold, *History of the Cotton Famine*, 81–83, 89; Henderson, *Lancashire Cotton Famine*; Farnie, *English Cotton Industry*; Toole, "Workers and Slaves," 166–67; Harnetty, *Imperialism and Free Trade*. At first, Marx suggested that the slowdown in production in Lancashire was "motivated" by the blockade. See Karl Marx, "A London Workers' Meeting," *MECW*, 19:153. However, following the 30 January 1862 meeting of the Manchester Chamber of Commerce, Marx revised his opinion to argue that the crisis in the cotton industry was the result of neither the blockade of southern ports nor the American protectionist Morrill Tariff but instead the "steadily continuing overproduction" since 1858, which corresponded with a "glutting of the Asian markets." First published in *Die Presse*, 8 February 1862; *MECW*, 19:160–62. For a perspective that argues Marx believed the shortage of raw materials was the cause of the crisis, see Perleman, *Marx's Crises Theory*, 42–54.

9. Jaconets from Bombay, DDAS 2/4; Potter Brothers to H&E Ashworth, 1 April 1845. DDAS 2/4. Henry Ashworth Papers. Lancashire Archives.

10. Baird Smith, *Report on the Commercial Condition of the North-Western Provinces*, 3. "Appendix M: Presentation of Testimonial to Colonel R. Baird Smith," 24 September 1861, in *Reports of the Committee of the Bengal Chamber of Commerce from 1 May to 31 October 1861*, lxxv.

11. Habib, "Colonization of the Indian Economy."

12. For an overview of the role of the bazaar, see R. Ray, "Asian Capital."

13. Tsing, "Supply Chains," 148–49.

14. Clapham, *Economic History of Modern Britain*, 2:313. See also 1:255–56.

15. Tsing, *Friction*, 4. For clarification, accumulation on an expanded scale here is different from the model of extraction, that is, the core-periphery relationship defined by the core's consumption of the periphery's produce. As suggested above, the circuit of Manchester goods was more complicated in the relationship that it introduced between the slaveholding South, manufacturers, and colonial markets such as the North-Western Provinces. This chapter builds upon old and new scholarship on disaster within capitalism and empire; see Bordiga, "Murder of the Dead."

16. To Owen, Owens and Sons, from Merchant, Hamburg, 10 May 1842, OWN 3/2/8/2, Owen, Owens and Sons Papers, JRL.

17. To Owen, Owens and Sons, from Merchant, Cape Town, 24 March 1843, OWN 3/2/8/4 and OWN 3/2/8/5, JRL.

18. 13 November 1865 and 3 January 1866, Proceedings of the Manchester Chamber of Commerce, 1858–67, MALS.

19. From Merchant, Calcutta, to Owens, Owen and Sons, 6 October 1842, OWN 3/2/5/4/37, JRL. For persistent concerns over holidays within the Bengal commercial community, see *Reports of the Committee of the Bengal Chamber of Commerce from 1 May to 31 October 1861*, 6–8; "Appendix B: Hindoo Holidays," *Reports of the Committee of the Bengal Chamber of Commerce*, 14 May 1861, V–XIV, BL; and Karl Marx, *A Contribution to the Critique of Political Economy*, Part 1, in *MECW*, 29:325.

20. Beckert, *Empire of Cotton*, 245. See also Beckert, "Emancipation and Empire."

21. Beckert, *Empire of Cotton*, 245.

22. See, for example, Stoler and Cooper, "Between Metropole and Colony," 1.

23. S. Bhattacharya, *Financial Foundations of the British Raj*, 251; Pares, "Economic Factors in the History of the Empire," 135.

24. Logan, "India's Loss." On failures of cotton cultivation within Kwa-Zulu Natal, see Matthew Schnurr's observation: "Almost all ended in failure as a result of some combination of unsound planning, a misreading of the landscape, poor implementation and African resistance." Schnurr, "Cotton as Calamitous Commodity," 116.

25. Zimmerman, *Alabama in Africa*, 28.

26. Baird Smith, *Report on Commercial Condition*, 3; "Appendix M: Presentation of Testimonial to Colonel R. Baird Smith," 24 September 1861, in *Reports of the Committee of the Bengal Chamber of Commerce from 1 May to 31 October 1861*, lxxv. Henryk Grossman went so far as to suggest that the destruction of capital through the cost of counterinsurgency during the Indian Rebellion created "breathing space for the accumulation of capital." Grossman, *Law of the Accumulation and Breakdown of Capitalism*, chap. 3.

27. Report of the Committee, Submitted at the General Meeting of 2 February 1859, in *Reports of the Committee of the Bengal Chamber of Commerce from 1 June to 31 December 1858*, 38–39, BL.

28. Farnie, "Cotton Famine," 154–55.

29. Report of the Committee, Submitted at the General Meeting of 2 February 1859, in *Reports of the Committee of the Bengal Chamber of Commerce from 1 June to 31 December 1858*, 39, BL. Decreased demand in China further contributed to the crisis in demand. See Marx, "The British Cotton Trade," *New-York Daily Tribune*, 14 October 1861; and Levi, "On the Cotton Trade and Manufacture," 41.

30. "Manchester Chamber of Commerce," *The Times*, 31 January 1860.

31. Ellison, *Cotton Trade of Great Britain*, 94; Henderson, "Cotton Famine on the Continent."

32. Batten, *Information Regarding the Slackness of Demand, Selections from the Records of Government, NWP*, vol. 1, 120. MF no. 1775. See also Bagchi, "De-industrialization in India in the Nineteenth Century: Some Theoretical Implications," in *Colonialism and Indian Economy*, 67–69.

33. Henderson, "Cotton Famine in Lancashire," 40; N. Hall, "Liverpool Cotton

Market and the American Civil War"; N. Hall, "Liverpool Cotton Market and Cotton Re-exports," 259, 266.

34. On cotton from the interior to Bengal, see G. H. M. Batten to R. Simpson, [29 October 1863], *Selections from the Records of Government, NWP*, vol. 1, 178, MF no. 1775. On cotton from Agra to Bombay, see *Circulars for Report on Slackness of Demand* in *Selections from the Records of Government, NWP*, vol. 1, 196, MF no. 1775.

35. Rivett-Carnac, *Report on Operations in the Cotton Department for the Year 1867*, 63–65. For a list of complaints against Surat cottons, see A Practical Man, "To the Editor: Indian versus American Cotton," *The Economist*, 13 April 1861, 399. Compare "Indian versus American Cotton," *Bengal Hurkaru*, 25 March 1862.

36. "Now since the cotton of Berar is not materially distinguishable in quality from that of Surat, it must be exported at a price much like that of the latter, and consequently its price in the interior must be as much lower than that of cotton grown near the coast, as to counteract the cost of its 300 miles of land carriage." Chapman, *Cotton and Commerce of India*, 51. Compare Satya, *Cotton and Famine in Berar*, 170: " 'Oomra' (name of Berar cotton) had a great name and reputation in the markets of London, Liverpool, and Manchester."

37. Charnock, *Verba Nominalia*, 294; Zerah Colburn, "On the Ginning of Cotton," *Journal of the Society of Arts* (10 March 1865); "The Cotton Supply of Great Britain," *New York Times*, 31 January 1865.

38. "The Cost of Indian Cotton," *Spectator*, 12 October 1861, reprinted in *Friend of India*, 28 November 1861. See also "Cotton Is Bread!," *Cotton Supply Reporter* 16 July 1860, 178–79; and "What's to Be Done?," *Cotton Supply Reporter*, 15 October 1862, 1041. George McHenry noted in 1863, " 'A Silk purse cannot be made out of a sow's ear'; no more can India ever be capable of superseding the Southern States of America in quality of cotton, to say nothing of price . . . [among] advantages possessed by the States for the culture of their principal staple (among which is their excellent system of slavery, which if discontinued would ruin them, and England too)," McHenry, *The Cotton Trade*, 53. McHenry's proslavery argument, of course, proved incorrect. In 1862, Napoleon III said to John Slidell, "As to the culture of cotton in India supplanting yours I consider the idea entirely chimerical. If you do not give it to us we cannot find it elsewhere." Quoted in Pomeray, "French Substitutes," 560. Wilson, *John Slidell*, 86.

39. Clapham, *Economic History of Modern Britain*, vol. 2, 222.

40. S. Bhattacharya, *"Laissez Faire* in India," 11–13.

41. The company also worked to produce cotton in Australia, where it also failed. In 1866, its possessions in Australia were auctioned away.

42. John Bright to J. B. Smith, 24 December 1863, in Letters from John Bright to J. B. Smith, J.B. Smith Papers, MALS. See also Balston, *Cultivation of Cotton*, 15: "Even now a fall of 8d. per lb. in American cotton, would close the export trade from the Indus and the Ganges, so inferior is the quality produced." Bright would endorse Reconstruction legislation.

43. Crosthwaite, *Notes on the North-Western Provinces*, 40. For a similar perspective during the Lancashire cotton famine, see "How to Make India take the Place of America as Our Cotton Field." See also observations from Samuel Lang for the Bengal Chamber of Commerce: "Much has already been done both by the Government and the merchants of India to meet this emergency, as much probably as can be done with

safety until more evidence is forthcoming that the capitalists of Lancashire and elsewhere are willing to take their part in the risk and expense attending the speculation."
"Appendix B: The Honourable Samuel Lang," *Half-yearly Report of the Committee of
the Bengal Chamber of Commerce*, dated 5 December 1861, V, BL.

44. "Information Regarding the Cultivation of Cotton in the North Western Provinces," from Secretary of Sudder Board of Revenue, to Secretary to Government,
North-Western Provinces (no. 470), dated Allahabad, 24 June 1862, in *Selections from
the Records of Government, NWP*, 68, 66-93, MF no. 1775. See also Scott, *Seeing Like
a State*, 262. On the influence of price, see *Half-yearly Report of the Committee of the
Bengal Chamber of Commerce*, 1 May to 31 October 1862, CLXVII. Colonial officials
consistently lamented that small-hold cultivators would not respond to price alone, a
perspective that encouraged imaginations of violence. Peter Harnetty concluded that
cotton producers in mid-nineteenth-century India responded directly according to the
stimulus provided by cotton prices. Peter Harnetty, "Cotton Exports and Indian Agriculture," *Economic History Review* 24, no. 3 (1971): 414-21.

45. On local consumption of cotton within the North-Western Provinces, see
G. H. M. Batten, Secretary Sudder Board of Revenue, to George Couper, Secretary
of Government, NWP [18 October 1864], *Selections from the Records of Government,
NWP*, 162.

46. S. Smith, *My Life-Work*, 60.

47. *Ninth Annual Report of the Executive Committee of the Cotton Supply Association*
(Manchester: Guardian Steam-Printing Offices, 1866), 1, JRL.

48. Bayly, *Birth of the Modern World*, 161; Owen, *Cotton and the Egyptian Economy*,
89-140, 122-24.

49. Zimmerman, "Cotton Booms," *Journal of the Gilded Age and Progressive Era*,
456-57.

50. Wheeler, *Madras versus America*, 237, 235-38; Cassels, *Cotton*, 346, cited in
Logan, "India's Loss," 44; M. Hammond, "Southern Farmer," 468; S. Smith, *My Life-
Work*, 59-60; Raghavaiyangar, *Memorandum of the Progress of the Madras Presidency*,
59. On New Orleans as the foundation of the Manchester trade, see Letter from J. B.
Smith, 6 May 1863, in Stockport Letters 1852-74, J. B. Smith Papers, MALS.

51. For raw materials as a factor in production cost, see Heinrich, *Introduction to
the Three Volumes of Karl Marx's "Capital,"* 105. In Marx's critique of political economy
there are two senses for the term "raw material." The first, *rohstaff*, contains the sense
of a natural product untouched by human labor; the second, *rohmaterial*, describes
materials that are the product of human labor but have not yet entered into a final commodity form. Cotton is a raw material in the latter sense. See Marx, *Grundrisse*, 521.

52. James, "American People."

53. "Appendix M: Presentation of Testimonial to Colonel R. Baird Smith," 24 September 1861, in *Reports of the Committee of the Bengal Chamber of Commerce from 1 May
to 31 October 1861*, lxxv.

54. Chunder, *Travels of a Hindoo*, 347-48.

55. Baird Smith, *Report on the Commercial Condition*, 6.

56. Baird Smith, 6.

57. Singh, *Starvation and Colonialism*, 29-30. "The famine of 1860-1 affected
only the Districts between the Jumna and the Sutlej, and was the result partly of the

Mutiny, and partly of deficient rainfall in the two preceding years, followed by a failure of the monsoon in 1860." *Imperial Gazetteer of India*, vol. 20 (Oxford: Clarendon Press, 1908), 329; Loveday, *History and Economics of Indian Famines*, 45; Dutt, *Famines and Land Assessments in India*, 7. Hari Shanker Srivastava noted that the dislocation of agriculture was a cause. See Srivastava, *History of Indian Famines*, 31; Crooke, *North-western Provinces*, 171–72; H. G. Keeve, Esquire Magistrate of Mozuffernuggur to F. Williams Commissioner of Meerut, 14 November 1860, Home, Public, 29 December 1860, 46–48A, NAI; and Dickinson, *Famine in the North-West Provinces of India*.

58. B. M. Bhatia has argued that the rebellion had a further impact because of the burning of stores of grain, destroyed during the rebellion. Bhatia, *Famines in India*, 59. While the destruction of grain was reported at the time, not all thought this was possible. See A. C., "Statistics of the Famine," *Friend of India*, 28 March 1861.

59. Chunder, *Travels of a Hindoo*, 361–62.

60. Chunder, 368.

61. George Couper to William Grey, Measures Considered Necessary for the Relief of the Population of Some of the Districts of the N.W. Provinces in Consequence of the Partial Failure of the Harvest, Home, Public, 22 October 1860, 102–3 [11 October 1860], NAI.

62. Report on the Works Executed in 1860–61 and 61–62 from the Several Grants Made for the Relief of the Starving Population of the North Western Provinces during the Late Famine, I.SUP 17/8, BL.

63. Girdlestone, *Report on Past Famines*, 80–81; Baird Smith, *Report of Colonel Baird Smith*, 2.

64. Editorial, *Bombay Times*, 3 July 1861.

65. Baird Smith, *Famine Report*, 27; R. C. Dutt, *Famines and Land Assessment in India*, 8. As Mike Davis has noted, famine deaths in the colonial period were often grossly underestimated. Davis, *Late Victorian Holocausts*, 113. S. Smith, *Cotton Trade of India*.

66. Baird Smith, *Famine Report*, 27.

67. Baird Smith, 28.

68. Baird Smith, 27.

69. Mangru, "From Bengal to British Guiana," 86–87. This emigration would continue to be contributed to by the economic distress in the North-Western Provinces. As G. H. M. Batten of the Sudder Board of Revenue observed, "The weavers have betaken themselves to agricultural or other labor, to menial service, emigration to the Mauritius and elsewhere, and even to begging," in *Selections from the Records of Government, NWP*, vol. 1, 189, MF no. 1775.

70. *Report of the Revised Land Revenue Settlement of the Rohtak District*, 46–47; Stokes, *Peasant and the Raj*, 67.

71. George Couper, "Memorandum from the Government of the North-Western Provinces" Home, Public, 28 September 1860, 62–65A, NAI. This also occurred during the 1837–38 famine.

72. *Report of the Revised Land Revenue Settlement of the Rohtak District*, 46–47.

73. The name *Sattrah* derived its name from the Vikram Samvat calendar within which the Gregorian year 1860 was equivalent to 1917. *Report of the Revised Land Revenue Settlement of the Rohtak District*, 46–47. I am grateful to Babu Lal Sharma for con-

versations about the meaning of these. The translations are modifications of those in the Rohtak District Report.

74. Compare Harnetty, "Cotton Exports and Indian Agriculture," 423. Harnetty argues that work on communications found an alternative and "probably" more profitable means of livelihood for weavers.

75. Habib, "Colonization of the Indian Economy," 29-30, 36-38; Banerjei, *Monograph on the Cotton Fabrics of Bengal*, 2-4; Ghosal, *Economic Transition*, 20-33.

76. Baird Smith, *Report on the Commercial Condition*, 17. Likewise, in Ghazipur district, the Manchester trade had demonstrated an impact that caused approximately 52 percent to be clothed in Manchester goods.

77. Firoz Shah, "The Azamgarh Proclamation," *Delhi Gazette*, 29 September 1857. In his important explanation of the causes of revolt, Sayyid Ahmad Khan noted the importation of English textiles as having a major impact, especially upon weavers: "No one even thinks nowadays of buying country-made thread or matches, and the country cloth weavers have been ruined. When by the Divine Will, Hindustan became an appanage of the Crown of Great Britain, it was the duty of Government to enquire into and lessen as much as possible the sufferings of its subjects. By not doing so many who would otherwise have been staunch friends of the British, joined the rebels." Khan, *Causes of the Indian Revolt*, 36. See also R. Mukherjee, "Azamgarh Proclamation." On the displacement of Indian manufacture, see S. Smith, *Cotton Trade of India*, 3.

78. Baird Smith, *Report on the Commercial Condition*, 16. See also "The Cotton Goods Trade in the North West," *Friend of India*, 6 June 1861.

79. Baird Smith, *Report on the Commercial Condition*, 3.

80. Baird Smith, 11.

81. *Imperial Gazetteer of India*, vol. 5, 264; Farnie, "Cotton Famine," 154-55; Srivastava, *History of Indian Famines*, 60.

82. Metcalf, *Ideologies of the Raj*, 29.

83. Scott, *Seeing Like a State*.

84. Baird Smith, *Report on the Commercial Condition*, 15.

85. Bayly, *Indian Society*, 198.

86. Meena, "Famine in Late 19th Century India"; Polanyi, *Great Transformation*, 168; Davis, *Late Victorian Holocausts*, 9-10.

87. S. Bhattacharya, "*Laissez Faire* in India," 3; Dutt, *Famines and Land Assessments in India*, xii; Baird Smith, Report, Part II, 45-46. After receiving Baird Smith's report, Canning was most interested in the question of a Permanent Settlement of the Land Revenue. Home Department to George Couper, Home, Public, 7 October 1861, 20-26 (A), NAI.

88. Stokes, *English Utilitarians*, 131; Stokes, *Peasant and the Raj*, 76. Reality, Stokes argues, diverged from this theoretical power.

89. Baird Smith, *Report on Famines*, Part II, 83. Baird Smith specifically cited the Nerbudda. See Sven Beckert, *Empire of Cotton*, 252-53.

90. Stokes, *Peasant and the Raj*, 91; Baird Smith, *Report on Famines*, Part II, 83.

91. Davis, *Late Victorian Holocausts*, 142; Sweeney, "Indian Railways and Famine"; Stokes, *Peasant and the Raj*, 10; Satya, "British Imperial Railways," 75-76.

92. S. Bhattacharya, "*Laissez Faire* in India," 7-8.

93. Balston, *Cultivation of Cotton*, 12.

94. Naoroji, "Commerce of India," 77.

95. Bakhtin, "The Problem of Speech Genres," in *Speech Genres and Other Late Essays*, 87–88.

96. Christopher Herbert, *War of No Pity*; W. H. Russell, "Sahib and the Nigger," *The Times*, 20 October 1858; C. Hall, "Economy of Intellectual Prestige"; Semmel, *Governor Eyre Controversy*; Metcalf, *Aftermath of Revolt*, chap. 8.

97. Blackburn, *Marx and Lincoln*, 40; C. Hall, "Economy of Intellectual Prestige," 14; "Address of the International Working Men's Association to Abraham Lincoln, President of the United States, Authored by Marx between 22 and 29 November 1864," *The Bee-Hive*, 7 November 1865, available online at https://www.marxists.org/archive/marx/iwma/documents/1864/lincoln-letter.htm.

98. C. Hall, "Rethinking Imperial Histories," 3–29.

99. "Henry Ashworth and Murray Gladstone to William Ewart Gladstone," in 24 April 1862, Proceedings of the Manchester Chamber of Commerce, 1858–1867, MALS.

100. *Reports of the Inspectors of Factories for the Half Year Ending 31 October 1861*, 14.

101. Mill, *Principles of Political Economy*, 339.

102. In her unfinished *Introduction to Political Economy*, Rosa Luxemburg made a startling claim about the Lancashire textile crisis (1860–65): "The only ones who suffered from the crisis were the workers. For the industrialists this crisis meant big business. The workers had to bear all the costs of the crisis." Luxemburg, "History of Crises," in *The Complete Works of Rosa Luxemburg*, vol. 1, 402–4.

103. Toole, "Workers and Slaves," 167.

104. Toole, 173.

105. Toole, 172. For fears, see Letter from Son to J. Kay Shuttleworth, JKS/1/1/587, 25 March 1863, J. Kay Shuttleworth Papers, JRL.

106. Boston, *British Chartists in America*, 57–64; Toole, "Workers and Slaves."

107. *Report of the American International Relief Committee for the Suffering Operatives of Great Britain*; Gow, *Civil War in America*, 26.

108. Erickson, "Encouragement of Emigration," 256.

109. Gow, *Civil War in America*, 24. D. J. Oddy maintains that the cotton famine became "a famine in a truer sense" by the end of 1862 when it assumed the form of a nutritional famine "even though levels of food intake, at least among the families recorded by Dr. Edward Smith, were surprisingly high." Oddy, "Urban Famine," 86, 84.

110. Lincoln, "Letter to the Working-Men of Manchester."

111. Schmidt, *Influence of Wheat and Cotton*.

112. For an overview of previous famine relief projects, see S. Sharma, *Famine, Philanthropy, and the Colonial State*.

113. Baird Smith, *Report*, 30.

114. "The Famine," *Friend of India*, 24 January 1861; Ambirajan, "Political Economy," 21. This broke from the policy of previous North Indian states. C. Campbell, "Bombay Scarcity Relief Policies," 80.

115. Davis, *Late Victorian Holocausts*, 287; George Couper, Secretary to the Government of the North Western Provinces to F. Williams, Measures for Alleviating the Distressed Condition of the Population of the Mozaffarghar District, Home, Public, 29 December 1860, 46-8A [4 December 1860], NAI.

116. Report on the Works Executed in 1860-61 and 61-62 from the Several Grants

Made for the Relief of the Starving Population of the North Western Provinces during the Late Famine, 12, I.SUP 17/8, BL.

117. J. B. Smith, letter, 3 September 1862, in Stockport Letters 1852-74, MALS.

118. Henderson, *Lancashire Cotton Famine*, 89-90; Selleck, *James Kay-Shuttleworth*, 335-36.

119. Oddy, "Urban Famine," 74; Boyer, "Poor Relief."

120. Baille, *What I Saw in Lancashire*, 15.

121. *Report on the Administration of the North-Western Provinces for the Year 1860-61*, 102, BL; George Couper, Secretary to the Government of the Northwest Provinces to E. C. Bayley, Secretary to the Government of India, No. of Orphans to be Provided Out of the Famine Fund in the NWP and Punjab, Home, Public A, 2 February, 1-5 [16 October 1863], NAI.

122. Couper to Bayley, 16 October 1863.

123. Couper to Bayley, 16 October 1863.

124. According to Baird Smith, Strachey designed the plan for relief in Moradabad and it was practically carried out by Sayyid Ahmed Khan. Baird Smith, *Report on Famine*, 15.

125. *Report on the Administration of the North-Western Provinces for the Year 1860-61*, 105.

126. Crooke, *North-western Provinces*, 171-72.

127. *Report on the Administration of the North-Western Provinces for the Year 1860-61*, 102.

128. Baird Smith, *Report on Famine*, 13-14.

129. *Report on the Administration of the North-Western Provinces for the Year 1860-61*, 98; George Couper, Secretary to the Government of the North Western Provinces to F. Williams, dated 4 December 1860, Home, Public, 29 December 1860, 46-8A, Measures for Alleviating the Distressed Condition of the Population of the Mozaffarghar District, NAI.

130. Girdlestone, *Report on Past Famines*, xix-xxii.

131. Sabyasachi Bhattacharya, "*Laissez Faire* in India," 2; Mill, *Principles of Political Economy*.

132. Loveday, *History and Economics of Indian Famines*, 47.

133. From Off. Secy. to the Govt. of India with the Governor General to Secretary to the Government of North West Provinces, dated 18 December 1860, Home, Public, 29 December 1860, 46-8A, Measures for Alleviating the Distressed Condition of the Population of the Mozaffarghar District, NAI.

134. "Famine Relief Asylums at Delhi," *Mofussilite*, 23 February 1861.

135. "From the *Times* 10 April," *Bombay Times*, 8 May 1861.

136. 18 May 1861, To Secretary to Government of the Punjab, Home, Public, 1 June 1861, 8A, NAI. Relief Operations in the North-West Provinces, from the Indian Famine Committee of Edinburgh to the Secretary to the Government of India, Home, Public B, Proceedings, 20 May 1861, 120-21, NAI.

137. Telegram from the Financial Commissioner, Lahore, to the Secretary to the Government of India, 19 May 1861, and Telegram from the Secretary to the Government of India to the Financial Commissioner, Lahore, dated 21 May 1861, NAI.

138. William Cubitt, Home, Public, 21 June 1861, 88, 87–90, dated 18 May 1861. In a subsequent letter Cubitt requested that this statement be kept in confidence. Home, Public, 21 June 1861, no. 90, NAI.

139. In response, Canning noted that the donations from the "English public have removed all ground for anxiety." Canning to Cubitt, Home, Public, 18 May 1861, nos. 37–38, NAI.

140. S. R. Graves to Governor General Canning, "Regarding the Remittance to India," [9 April 1861], Home, Public, 18 May 1861, 39–42A, NAI.

141. Baird Smith, *Report on Famine*, 108.

142. Baird Smith, 108. This figure included Rs 6,15,989 spent on relief work; charitable contributions expended were Rs 4,65,374. In addition to this, Rs 2,87,000 was added to the figure on advances on seed and cattle.

143. Singh, *Starvation and Colonialism*, 41–42.

144. The total value of grain given was Rs 2,87,000. Baird Smith, Report on Famine, 106.

145. Baird Smith, *Report on Famine*, 108.

146. Honorary Secretary, Punjab Famine Relief Fund, to Secretary to Government of Punjab, dated 15 October 1861, Home, Public A, 4 December 1861, 5, NAI.

147. From R. H. Davies, Secretary to the Government of Punjab and Its Dependencies Home, Public A, 4 December 1861, 4, NAI.

148. W. Grey, Secretary to the Government of India to R. H. Davies, Secretary to the Government of Punjab, dated 4 December 1861, Home, Public A, 4 December 1861, 9, NAI.

149. Couper to Bayley, 2 February.

150. R. Arnold, *History of the Cotton Famine*, 36.

151. "Distress in Lancashire," *New York Times*, 26 November 1862.

152. Engels, "In the Case of Brentano versus Marx Regarding Alleged Falsifications of Quotation," in *MECW*, 27:129.

153. William A. Rose to Governor General of India dated 2 January 1863, Home, Public, 10 February 1863, 27A, NAI; "Distress in Lancashire: Appropriation of the Indian Famine Surplus Fund," *Observer*, 4 January 1863.

154. Translation of a Khureeta from His Highness the Maha Rao Raja of Ulwar to the Political Agent, Ulwar, dated 16 October 1862, Foreign, Political A, December 1862, 8–10, NAI. Despite such donations, historians commemorating the relief of Manchester would argue that India "did not send over a single rupee towards the relief of the distressed operatives." See McCall, *Cotton Famine*, 13.

155. McCall, *Cotton Famine*, ccxi.

156. Walton, *Lancashire*, 285; Oddy, "Urban Famine."

157. An Englishman, *Popular Cookery*, 20.

158. Noble, "Fluctuations in the Death Rate."

159. Noble, 17.

Chapter 7

1. Brice, *Indian Cotton Supply*, 5; Henry Ashworth Papers, DDAS/3, Lancashire Archives, Preston. "Where Is Cotton to Come from to Keep the Mills at Work?," *Cot-*

ton Supply Reporter, 15 May 1861. Such invocations of the transformation of the U.S. South continued in the 1870s. See Frederick Campbell, "On India as a Field for Private Enterprise," *Journal of the Society of Arts*, 15 March 1872, 337.

2. For an overview of the Manchester Cotton Company's work, see Harnetty, "India and British Commercial Enterprise."

3. "The Manchester Cotton Company," *The Times* (London), 19 August 1862.

4. "Mr. George Thompson on the Cotton Supply," *Cotton Supply Reporter*, 1 February 1862; Ali, *Local History of Global Capital*.

5. Beckert, *Empire of Cotton*, 254; *Times of India*, 3 October 1862; A. Guha, "Growth of Acreage of Cotton in India 1851-1901." Guha argues that temporary scarcity caused by the U.S. Civil War placed a price impetus for Indian cultivators to put more land under cotton cultivation. Despite a crash, the same level of exports and cotton acreage as had been achieved in 1860 were maintained. "Cotton Crop in the Central Provinces of India," *Manchester Courier and Lancashire General Advertiser*, 26 January 1869. The relationship between price increases and the impact of cotton cultivation on the ground in India during the American Civil War has been a source of debate. The figures referenced to settle this debate are themselves inaccurate. It has been claimed that the increase in cultivation was possibly as much as 50 percent; the actual amount could have been significantly less. Statistics about expanded cotton cultivation were tied to transforming representational practices within land revenue figures. As one contemporary observer in the Central Provinces wrote, "In the great cotton-growing tract of these provinces, the Wurdah district, where the Hingunghat cotton is grown, an increase of upwards of 18,000 acres is shown. The districts of the Chutteesgurh division also show an increase but this, he thinks, is chiefly attributable to more accurate statistics consequent on the advance of the land revenue settlement in these districts, rather than to any considerable extension of the cultivation." "Cotton Crop in the Central Provinces of India," *Manchester Courier and Lancashire General Advertiser*, 26 January 1869.

6. Estimates on the future cotton supply: "It is unnecessary to remark that the entire aspect of the question would be changed in a moment by any certain prospect of peace in America." "The Future Supply of Cotton," *Berbice Gazette and British Guiana Advertiser*, 9 July 1864.

7. On crisis displacement techniques, see Bond, "Volatile, Uneven, and Combined Capitalism," 127.

8. Lees, *Tea Cultivation*, 93-94. Lees further reflected upon this in *The Land and Labour of India*, v:

> Circumstances however have altered materially since then. When my Review was written (1862), the operatives of the manufacturing districts of England were suffering from the severities of the famine which followed the stoppage of the cotton supplies which ensued on the breaking out of the American war. A cry had been raised in England with the view of inducing Her Majesty's Government to compel the natives of India to grow sufficient cotton to keep the looms of Manchester and Lancashire in full work, and thus save the trade of the cotton spinners from ruin, and the operatives from starvation. But no guarantee was offered that the cotton would be bought when grown, nor any forethought or regard shown for the lamentable consequences that would have overtaken the people of India, if millions of

acres of land having been sown with cotton, the American war should have ceased before the crop was reaped.

I had hoped that some more solid benefit to India than enriching the cotton dealers of Bombay would have resulted from the circumstances of England in 1862; but unfortunately those who pressed their views in the direction above-mentioned on Lord Halifax (then Sir Charles Wood), while thousands of their countrymen were suffering from want around them, had not any more practical measures to propose for the regeneration of the agricultural interests of this country, and for the relief of the poor starving operatives at their doors, than discussions on the abstract principles of political economy.

9. Henderson, "Cotton Famine in Lancashire," 41.

10. For logistic space, see Cowen, *Deadly Life of Logistics*.

11. Patrick Smollett qtd. in "The Cotton Supply," *House of Commons Debate*, vol. 167, 19 June 1862.

12. *Third Annual Report of the Executive Committee of the Cotton Supply Association* (Manchester: John J. Sale, 1860), 31, JRL; "Proceedings" in *Second Annual Report of the Executive Committee of the Cotton Supply Association* (Manchester: Cave and Sever, 1859), 39, JRL.

13. "Supply of Indian Cotton to England," 28 February 1861, Accounts and Papers of the House of Commons (1863), vol. 44, 15–16. Compare Sven Beckert, *Empire of Cotton*, 250.

14. Tripathi, "Opportunism of Free Trade," 257. Information was compiled for distribution, yet the efficacy of such volumes remains in question. See Wheeler, *Handbook to the Cotton Cultivation in the Madras Presidency*; and Medlicott, *Cotton Hand-Book*. Information on the North-Western Provinces is contained within Medlicott.

15. Thomas Bazley, *Cotton Supply Reporter*, 15 January 1859.

16. *Report on the Administration of the North-Western Provinces for the Year 1860–61*, 85.

17. Du Bois, *Black Reconstruction*, 5.

18. Marrs, *Railroads in the Old South*, 112; Silver, *Manchester Men*, 128.

19. J. A. Mann, "On the Cotton Trade of India," *Journal of the Royal Asiatic Society of Great Britain* 17 (January 1860): 361.

20. "Where Is Cotton to Come from to Keep the Mills at Work?," *Cotton Supply Reporter*, 15 May 1861. Such invocations of the transformation of the U.S. South continued in the 1870s. See Frederick Campbell, "On India as a Field for Private Enterprise," *Journal of the Society of Arts*, 15 March 1872, 337. For later invocations of Anglo-Saxonism, see Kramer, "Empires, Exceptions, and Anglo-Saxons"; and Kaplan, "Manifest Domesticity," 594.

21. "Proceedings," in *Second Annual Report of the Executive Committee of the Cotton Supply Association*, 32, JRL. On colonial settlement and the English bodily constitution, see D. Arnold, *Tropics and the Traveling Gaze*.

22. J. Watts, *Facts of the Cotton Famine*, 437.

23. "Money-Market and City Intelligence," *The Times*, 18 July 1861; Owen, *Cotton and the Egyptian Economy*, 97–98.

24. "Manchester Cotton Company," *Times*, 29 August 1861.

25. "Manchester Cotton Company."

26. "Report of the Manchester Cotton Company," *Times*, 19 August 1862.

27. "Report of the Manchester Cotton Company."

28. Harnetty, "India and British Commercial Enterprise," 399; J. C. Marshman, "Notes on the Cultivation of Cotton in the District of Dharwar; Past Present, and Future."

29. No. 10 Public Works Despatch from the Secretary of State to the Government of Madras, dated 6 October 1858, in *East India* (Sedashegar Harbour). J. N. Fleming, "Manchester Cotton Company: The Chamber of Commerce," *Times of India*, 31 October 1861. "The Manchester Cotton Company," *Times*, 19 August 1862.

30. Enclosure no. 11, "Cotton Company" (Limited). Members included prominent manufacturers Thomas Bazley, John Cheetham, and Edmund Ashworth. *East India* (Sedashegar Harbour).

31. "Manchester Cotton Company (Limited)," *London Gazette*, 23 September 1864. In Australia, by 19 February 1866, the company's materials were sold at public auction.

32. G. F. Forbes, "To the Chairman and Members of the Bombay Chamber of Commerce," *Times of India*, 28 October 1861.

33. Loftus, "Time, History and the Making of the Industrial Middle Class," 29–51; S. Smith, *My Life-Work*, 26.

34. S. Smith, *My Life-Work*, 26–27.

35. S. Smith, 26–27.

36. S. Smith, 45.

37. Chandavarkar, *The Origins of Industrial Capitalism in India*, 22–23.

38. S. Smith, *My Life-Work*, 45–55.

39. S. Smith, 55.

40. S. Smith, 14.

41. "Information Regarding the Cultivation of Cotton in the North Western Provinces" from Secretary of Sudder Board of Revenue, to Secretary to Government, North Western Provinces (no. 470), dated Allahabad, 24 June 1862, in *Selections from the Records of Government, NWP*, 68, 66–93, MF no. 1775; Scott, *Seeing Like a State*, 262.

42. S. Smith, *Cotton Trade of India*, 2.

43. On the impact of famine on cotton cultivation, see *Cotton Supply Reporter*, 1 August 1858; Satya, *Cotton and Famine in Berar*; and Beckert, *Empire of Cotton*, 327. Compare Peter Harnetty, "Cotton Exports and Indian Agriculture," *Economic History Review* 24, no. 3 (1971): 414–21.

44. Beckert, *Empire of Cotton*, 253, 288–91. Rivett-Carnac, *Report on Operations in the Cotton Department for the Year 1867*, 40.

45. Rivett-Carnac, *Many Memories*, 167; Rivett-Carnac, *Report on Operations in the Cotton Department for the Year 1867*, 45. Rivett-Carnac notes that his first objective is improvement of the indigenous plant and second is to experiment with foreign cultivation.

46. P. Saunders to William Grey, dated 1 September 1861, in Medlicott, *Cotton Hand-book for Bengal*, 173.

47. Medlicott, *Cotton Hand-book*, 70.

48. Medlicott, 70, 223–24.

49. S. Smith, *Cotton Trade of India*, 28.

50. Baptist, *Half Has Never Been Told*, 142.

51. Wes Brady, Federal Writers' Project: Slave Narrative Project Texas Narratives, vol. 16, Part 1, Adams-Duhon, 134. Available online at http://hdl.loc.gov/loc.mss/mesn.161.

52. Johnson, *River of Dark Dreams*, 249–50; Pargas, *Slavery and Forced Migration*, 139–40; Saxton, *Cotton Planter's Manual* (1857), 135–36.

53. J. Saxton, *Cotton Planter's Manual*, 265.

54. Johnson, "Pedestal and the Veil," 304.

55. Tsing, "Sorting Out Commodities," 23.

56. "How to Make India Take the Place of America as Our Cotton Field"; S. Smith, "Letter XII: Can India Take the Place of America?," *The Cotton Trade of India*, 58. In his autobiography, Smith further reflected,

> I concluded that there was no basis for the belief that large stocks of cotton existed in the interior of the country, and that there was little chance of Indian cotton becoming a substitute for American, as it was far inferior in staple, and could not be radically changed; yet that the high price would draw a greatly increased supply so long as it lasted, for there was literally a stream of gold pouring at that time into Western India. These views were substantially confirmed by the result, for after the American War was over, and ample supplies came back from America at nearly the old price, the Indian supply fell back, or nearly so, to its old dimensions, and our spinners and manufacturers returned to the use of American cotton. (S. Smith, *My Life-Work*, 59–60).

57. Harnetty, "India and British Commercial Enterprise," 413–14.

58. Hazareesingh, "Cotton, Climate, and Colonialism," 12.

59. Rivett-Carnac, *Report on Operations in the Cotton Department for the Year 1867*, 68.

60. Lyall, "The Old Pindaree" in *Verses Written in India*. Poem dated on the Nerbadda, 1866.

61. Rivett-Carnac, *Many Memories*, 132.

62. Marx, *The Poverty of Philosophy*, in *MECW*, vol. 6, 168.

63. Daniel Defoe, "Untitled," *Review*, 10 January 1713, 89.

64. Logan, "India's Loss," 40.

65. *Reports of the Inspectors of Factories for the Year Ending October 1863*, 41–43; Marx, *Capital*, vol. 3, in *MECW*, 37:132–33.

66. R. Arnold, *History of the Cotton Famine*, 474; Communist Party History Group, "Our History," 3–4.

67. Jesse Leach, "Surat Cotton, as It Bodily Affects Operatives in Cotton Mills," *The Lancet* 82 (5 December 1863): 125.

68. Leach, 126.

69. Leach, 125.

70. *Reports of the Inspectors of Factories for the Half year Ending 31 October 1863*, 62.

71. Leach, "Surat Cotton, as It Bodily Affects Operatives in Cotton Mills," 125.

72. "The Calamities of Lancashire . . . ," *Spectator*, 7 May 1864.

73. *Reports of the Inspectors of Factories for the Half year Ending 31 October 1863*, 12–13.

74. *Reports of the Inspectors of Factories for the Half year Ending 31 October 1863*, 61.

75. *Reports of the Inspectors of Factories for the Half year Ending 31 October 1863*, 44.

76. *Reports of the Inspectors of Factories for the Half year Ending 31 October 1863*, 61.

77. Waugh, *Home Life*, 271; Logan; "India's Loss," 41.

78. "Surat Warps," *Notes and Queries*, 3 June 1865, 432.

79. Owen Ashmore, "The Diary of James Garnett of Low Moor, Clitheroe, 1858–1865," 122.

80. R. Arnold, *History of the Cotton Famine*, 167.

81. R. Arnold, 469.

82. Logan, "India's Loss," 42. For a perspective on adulteration's extent, see S. Smith, *Cotton Trade of India*, 29, 35.

83. From the Deputy Commissioner, Oomraotee District to the Commissioner, Hyderabad Assigned Districts, Foreign, General, August 1867, No. 66(A) [30 March 1867], NAI.

84. Manchester Chamber of Commerce, "Ordinary Meeting of the Board," 23 February 1870, 417, *Proceedings of the Manchester Chamber of Commerce*, MCL. The Bombay Cotton Act further only applied to the cotton of the Bombay Presidency while "the shipments of cotton from Madras commonly called 'Western' cotton leave much to be desired in regard to packing and the deliberate intermixture of seed after ginning in the bales." Manchester Chamber of Commerce, "Meeting of Sub-Committee on the 'Bombay Cotton Frauds Act,'" 4 March 1870, 425, Proceedings of the Manchester Chamber of Commerce, MALS.

85. Manchester Chamber of Commerce, "Ordinary Meeting of the Board," 23 February 1870, 423–26. Proceedings of the Manchester Chamber of Commerce. MALS.

86. Manchester Chamber of Commerce, "Ordinary Meeting of the Board," Proceedings of the Manchester Chamber of Commerce, 424.

87. J. Watts, *Facts of the Cotton Famine*, 447.

88. P. Carnegy, Deputy Commissioner, Fyzabad in Oudh, "Appendix D: Official Papers Regarding Native Cotton Manufactures," 24 January 1864, in *Report of the Committee of the Bengal Chamber of Commerce*, 1 November 1863 to 30 April 1864 (1864), xlviii, BL.

89. "Result of Enquiries into the Actual Out-Turn of Cotton Cultivation in the Central Provinces," Foreign, Rev. A., September 1863, 26–29, NAI.

90. S. Smith, *Cotton Trade of India*, 6, 50.

91. Rivett-Carnac, *Report on Operations in the Cotton Department for the Year 1867*, 21.

92. *Circulars for Report on Slackness in Demand*, 189.

93. *Circulars for Report on Slackness in Demand*, 188.

94. *Circulars for Report on Slackness in Demand*, 189.

95. Quoted in Bojapuri, "Indian Cottons and the Cotton Famine," 41–42; *Circulars for Slackness in Demand*, 192.

96. *Circulars for Report on Slackness in Demand*, 210.

97. *Circulars for Report on Slackness in Demand*, 210.

98. "Meeting of the Board of Directors, Wednesday 15 January 1862," in Proceedings of the Manchester Chamber of Commerce, 1858–67, GB127.M8/2/6, MALS. See also "Memorial to the Right Honorable Sir Charles Wood"; "Resolution," 20 August

1860; "Meeting of the Board of Directors," 12 February 1862; "Meeting of the Board of Directors," 12 March 1862; and "Adjoined Meeting," 13 March 1862, in Proceedings of the Manchester Chamber of Commerce.

99. "Appendix N (2) Out-Turn of Cotton in the Central Provinces for the Season 1862," Bengal Chamber of Commerce to E. C. Bayley dated 13 October 1863, in *Report of the Committee of the Bengal Chamber of Commerce* 1 May to 31 October 1863 (Calcutta: Sanders, Cones and Co., 1863), lxxvii–lxxviii, BL.

100. Proceedings of the Manchester Chamber of Commerce, 15 June 1864, MALS.

101. Proceedings of the Manchester Chamber of Commerce, 26 October 1865, 13 November 1865, MALS.

102. "Report of the Committee of the Manchester Chamber of Commerce Appointed to Consider the Subject of Mildew in Cotton Goods," in Proceedings of the Manchester Chamber of Commerce, 3 January 1866, MALS.

103. William B. Forwood, "The Influence of Price upon the Cultivation and Consumption of Cotton during the Ten Years 1860–70," *Journal of the Statistical Society of London* 33, no. 3 (1870): 375; A Practical Man, "To the Editor: Indian versus American Cotton," *The Economist*, 13 April 1861, 399.

104. "Report of the Committee upon Mildew" [dated 21 April 1873] in Minutes of the Manchester Chamber of Commerce, 30 April 1873, 794, MALS.

105. Sudder Board of Revenue to Government of the Northwest Provinces, *Report Regarding the Slackness of Demand for European Cotton Goods*, 16 March 1864, quoted in Watson, *Textile Manufactures*, 26–27n1; Full Report in *Selections from the Records of Government, NWP*, vol. 1.; Borpujari, "Indian Cottons and the Cotton Famine."

106. Borpujari, "Indian Cottons and the Cotton Famine," 192. In the Calcutta trade, the increased significance of shirtings over cambrics and jaconets seemed to emerge after 1840: "Jaconnets [*sic*] have for some time past attracted very little attention, owing in our opinion to the very cheap rates at which shirtings have been sold, the increase in the consumption of the latter fabrics have this year been immense, and appear to be prefered [*sic*] by all classes of natives, in this country they find them much more durable, than either Cambrics or Jaconnets, and therefore interfering much with their sale." From Calcutta Merchant to Owen, Owens, and Sons, 14 August 1841, Owen, Owens and Sons Papers, OWN3/2/5/3/43, JRL; Dr. J. Forbes Watson's Work on Textile Manufacturers and Costumes of the People of India, Home, Public, December 1866, 209–14 (B), NAI. See also W. Pearce to Henry Ashworth, 1 April 1845, Henry Ashworth Papers, DDAS/2, Order Book, Lancashire Archives.

107. *Circulars for Report on Slackness in Demand*, 218.

108. Watson's project was inextricably bound to efforts to grow cotton in India; he corresponded with the AHSI and published *On the Growth of Cotton in India* (1859). Watson was further involved in the publication of the ethnographic and racially classificatory *People of India* (1868).

109. Watson, *Textile Manufactures*, vol. 1, 2.

110. Watson, vol. 1, 2.

111. Memorandum on the Distribution in Britain and India of the Collections of Specimens of the Textile Manufactures of India, Home, Public, December 1866, 209–14 (B), NAI.

112. Mullick, *Brief History of the Bengal Commerce*, 14.

113. Prakash, *Another Reason*, 4. See also Cohn, *Colonialism and Its Forms of Knowledge*.

114. Krishnan, "Empire's Metropolis," 11–19; Rungta, *Rise of Business Corporations in India*; Tripathi, *Oxford History of Indian Business*; Tripathi and Makrand, *Business Houses*; Subramanian, *Three Merchants of Bombay*; Das, *Banking and Industrial Finance*.

115. G. F. Forbes, *Report on Cotton in the Southern States*, Royal Geographical Society of London, Z-94.

116. G. F. Forbes, *Report on Cotton in the Southern States*, Royal Geographical Society of London, Z-94.

117. G. F. Forbes, *Report on Cotton in the Southern States*, Royal Geographical Society of London, Z-94.

118. G. F. Forbes, *Report on Cotton in the Southern States*, Royal Geographical Society of London, Z-94. Such moments repeated earlier concerns voiced not only in white southern newspapers but also the Indian press such as the *Bengal Hurkaru* that reported that the changing condition of African Americans made it impossible to imagine that African American labor would produce cotton in comparable amounts or at comparable prices. "Indian versus American Cotton," *Bengal Hurkaru*, 25 March 1862.

119. Cotton Supply Association, *Eighth Annual Report of the Executive Committee of the Cotton Supply Association* (Manchester: Guardian Steam Printing Offices, 1865), 10 JRL.

120. Cotton Supply Association, *Ninth Annual Report of the Executive Committee of the Cotton Supply Association* (Manchester: Guardian Steam-Printing Offices, 1866), 11, JRL.

121. Cotton Supply Association, *The Eighth Annual Report of the Executive Committee*, 7, JRL.

122. I. Watts, *Cotton Supply Association*, 103. This reflection was made in immediate relation to Australia. While the Manchester Cotton Supply Association narrated itself as crucial to protecting the interests of Manchester industry through its active exertions to develop the cotton supply of India, its actual successes were much fewer in number than it implied. This marked the period of 1857 to 1870 as another era when the hope for establishing India as a permanent and singular source for the export of cotton to English industry was a failure.

123. Loring and Atkinson, *Cotton Culture*, 168; "Memorial to the Indian Government by the Cotton Supply Association in 1870," in Watts, *Cotton Supply Association*, 144.

124. Edward Atkinson, "The Cotton Resources of the South, Present and Future," *De Bow's Review* (August 1866): 142, 143–44; Loring and Atkinson, *Cotton Culture*, 167. See also Testimony of Samuel Batchelder, 32; Testimony of Edward Atkinson, 7; and Testimony of Samuel Frothingham Jr., 15, in Appendix to Special Report No. 3, *Selections from the Testimony taken by the United States Commission, in Respect to Cotton as a Source of National Revenue* (printed 14 March 1866).

125. Ranade, *Sir Bartle Frere*, 66.

126. Ranade, 66.

127. Hoyle, *Inquiry into the Causes*, 9.

128. Burton, *Trouble with Empire.*

129. Schrottky, *Principles of Rational Agriculture*, 263. On Schrottky, see P. Kumar, *Indigo Plantations*, 116-19.

130. J. C. Ollerenshaw, "Our Export Trade in Cotton Goods to India," *Manchester Statistical Society*, 109. This was a principle of free trade imperialism that had roots much earlier in critiques of the East India Company's role by advocates of free trade. Stokes, *English Utilitarians*, 38.

Chapter 8

1. Du Bois, *Black Reconstruction*, 15-16; Lowe, *Intimacies of Four Continents*; Jung, "*Black Reconstruction* and Empire"; Greene, "The Wages of Empire: Capitalism, Expansionism, and Working-Class Formation."

2. Harvey, *Seventeen Contradictions*, 115-16; Mandel, *Late Capitalism*, 170-71.

3. Du Bois, *Black Reconstruction*, 57-62.

4. Lowe, *Intimacies of Four Continents*, 24-25.

5. Metcalf, *Imperial Connections*, 136. On racial reading of Asian labor as cheap, see Day, *Alien Capital*, 7-8. For overview of labor in the context of Black emancipation, see Jaynes, *Branches without Roots*, 3-74; and E. Foner, "Reconstruction and the Crisis of Free Labor," in *Politics and Ideology*, 119-57. As Moon-Ho Jung notes, "coolies" were a "conglomeration of racial imaginings" rather than a specific people, and I use the term coolie in this sense. Jung, *Coolies and Cane*, 109.

6. Carlyle, "Occasional Discourse on the Negro Question" (republished as *Occasional Discourse on the Nigger Question* [London: T. Bosworth, 1853]); C. Hall, "Economy of Intellectual Prestige."

7. Faust, *James Henry Hammond and the Old South*, 122-23; Olcott, "Sugar from the Sorgho," *Southern Cultivator* 15, 5 (May 1857): 142. Wray first spoke in New York before working to introduce sorghum on the plantations of Hammond, of Cassius Clay in Louisville, Kentucky, and of a third planter in Georgia. "Sugar from the African Sorghum," *Charleston Mercury*, 14 April 1857; "The New Sugar Cane," *Charleston Mercury*, 16 June 1857.

8. On the management of racial difference see: Lowe, *Immigrant Acts*, 27-28; Roediger and Esch, *The Production of Difference.*

9. Wray, *The Practical Sugar Planter.*

10. Leonard Wray, "Culture and Manufacture of Sugar," *De Bow's Review* 12, 6 (June 1852): 646.

11. Amin, *Sugarcane and Sugar in Gorakhpur*, 28.

12. *Proceedings of the Select Committee on Sugar and Coffee Planting*, 14 February 1848, 45, 58-62, 72-74.

13. James Henry Hammond Papers, 1 May 1857, Reel 1, 606-7. *Records of Ante-Bellum Southern Plantations* (RA-BSP). Series A, Part 1, Selections from the South Caroliniana Library, University of South Carolina.

14. Mathew, "Edmund Ruffin and the Demise of the *Farmers' Register.*"

15. Ruffin, *Diaries*, vol. 1, 74.

16. Wray, *The Practical Sugar Planter*, 83-84. Edmund Ruffin, *Diaries*, 103-6. The three would also meet at a gathering of the U.S. Agricultural Society in Washington, D.C. on 15 January 1858. Ruffin, *Diaries*, 147-48.

17. James Henry Hammond, *Speech: Delivered at Barnwell C.H., South Carolina* (29 October 1858), 47. Jung, *Coolies and Cane*, 20, 28–30. Karp, *This Vast Southern Empire*.

18. Wray, "Culture and Preparation of Cotton," 83.

19. Jaynes, *Branches without Roots*, 58.

20. Thomas Bazley, "From the Bradford Observer," *Cotton Supply Reporter*, 1 January 1859.

21. Brice, *Indian Cotton Supply*, 5.

22. Harvey, *Limits to Capital*, 431–38. See also Arrighi, "Spatial and Other 'Fixes.'"

23. De Coin, *History and Cultivation*, 235.

24. De Coin, 236–37.

25. Lowe, "Insufficient Difference."

26. Evans, "Plenty Shoot 'Em," 167–68.

27. Reynolds and May, "Queensland," 171.

28. Reynolds and May, 176.

29. D. Moses, "Antipodean Genocide?," 99.

30. D. Moses, 102; Evans, "Plenty Shoot 'Em," 156–58. See also Evans, *History of Queensland*; and Evans, "Plenty Shoot 'Em," 165. The Native Police Corps was especially active in North, Central, and Western Queensland.

31. Banivanua Mar, *Violence and Colonial Dialogue*, 76. For connections between settler colonialism in the United States and Australia, see Aileen Moreton-Robinson, *White Possessive*; and Wolfe, *Traces of History*, 1–84.

32. On the colonial construction of climate and the tropics within the British Empire, see D. Arnold, *Tropics and the Traveling Gaze*. On climate in the American South, see Oakes, "The Peculiar Fate of the Bourgeois Critique of Slavery," in *Slavery and the American South*, 44–45.

33. *Constitution of Oregon*, 7; McLagan, *Peculiar Paradise*; Walt Whitman, "Prohibition of Colored Persons," *Brooklyn Daily Times*, 6 May 1858.

34. On republicanism, see E. Foner, *Free Soil*, xxii. On the long history of racial separation in the United States, see Guyatt, *Bind Us Apart*.

35. Rana, *Two Faces of American Freedom*; M-K. Jung, *Beneath the Surface of White Supremacy*.

36. Early taxonomies inserting this division can be found in Fieldhouse, *Economics and Empire*.

37. Veracini, *Settler Colonialism*. Indigenous studies scholarship has often not accepted this binary. See Moreton-Robinson, *White Possessive*; and Lake and Reynolds, *Drawing the Global Colour Line*.

38. Africanus, "An American Opinion on Queensland as a Cotton Producing Country," *Glasgow Morning Journal*, 30 March 1863. This is the source for the next few paragraphs as well.

39. Henry Jordan, "An American Opinion on Queensland as a Cotton Producing Country," republished from *Glasgow Morning Journal* in *The Western Times* (Exeter, England), 21 April 1863.

40. On the United States, see A. Saxton, *Rise and Fall of the White Republic*.

41. J. D. Lang, *Cooksland in North-Eastern Australia*, 223, 172.

42. Ballantyne, "Remaking the Empire from Newgate," 32–33.

43. J. S. Mill to F. Sinnett, [Melbourne], 22 October 1857, in *Letters of John Stuart Mill* 188–89.

44. *Acts and Regulations Relating to the Waste Lands in the Colony of Queensland*, 17–18.

45. John Dunmore Lang to Colonial Secretary of Queensland, Immigration to Be Effected under the Crown Lands Alienation Act, 28 November 1860, COL/A10, 1137549, Queensland State Archives, Brisbane.

46. Lang to Colonial Secretary of Queensland.

47. Ngai, "Chinese Miners."

48. Majoribanks, *Queensland*, 7.

49. Lake, "White Man under Siege," 48.

50. Lang, *Queensland*, 231 (from a speech delivered in 1860).

51. "The Coolie Question," *Moreton Bay Courier*, 16 April 1861. Henry Jordan made this argument with particular reference to a suggestion that freedpeople be brought to Queensland: "An American Opinion on Queensland as a Cotton Producing Country Republished from *Glasgow Morning Journal*," *Western Times* (Exeter, England), 21 April 1863.

52. Veracini, *Settler Colonialism*, vii.

53. R. G. W. Herbert to J. Broadhurst, 11 April 1861, Extra Colonial Letterbooks (61/90), COL/P1, Queensland State Archives; Kyi, "'Most Determined.'"

54. On "suitability" of coolies, see Moles, "Indian Coolie Labour Issue," 1347; Charles Nicholson and Others to His Excellency Sir George F. Bowen Governor of the Colony of Queensland, "Memorial on the Subject of Asiatic Labor," in *Asiatic Labor* (Queensland: Legislative Assembly, dated 30 July 1861), SLQ; Banivanua Mar, *Violence and Colonial Dialogue*, 76. On white labor in the United States, see Samuel A. Cartwright, "How to Save the Republic, and the Position of the South in the Union," *De Bow's Review* 11 (August 1851): 185.

55. Moles, "Indian Coolie Labour Issue," 1348.

56. On Bazley's interest in Queensland cotton, see Thomas Bazley to Henry Parkes, 2 October 1861, in *Parkes Correspondences*, vol. 6, 395–96, State Library of New South Wales, Sydney.

57. Bowen, *Thirty Years of Colonial Government*, 20.

58. Knox, *Queensland Years*, 28.

59. Knox, 29.

60. *Fifth Annual Report of the Executive Committee of the Cotton Supply Association* (Manchester: John J. Sale, 1862), 20, JRL.

61. Hope, *In Quest of Coolies*, 3, 110.

62. "The First Cotton Harvest in Queensland," *York Herald*, 22 November 1862.

63. Anglo-Saxon, "The Manchester Panic," *Moreton Bay Courier*, 13 April 1861.

64. On the U.S. free-soil movement as a project to build a racially homogeneous white society, see Frederickson, *The Black Image in the White Mind*, 130–62.

65. Anglo-Saxon, "The Manchester Panic."

66. This was also the case in the United States.

67. Wight, *Queensland*, 101.

68. Brookes, "Cotton and Queensland."

69. Wight, *Queensland*, 101.

70. Wight, 101–3. This opinion was also repeated: "Lancashire and Queensland Co-operative Emigration Society," *Daily News* (London), 24 January 1863.

71. *Correspondence on the Cotton Famine*, 3–4.

72. Parkes, *Australian Views of England*, 19.

73. *Reports of the Inspectors of Factories for the Half Year Ending 30 April 1863*, 53.

74. "Lectures on Queensland," *Isle of Wight Times*, 22 February 1865.

75. Annual Emigration Report, 1861–62, 432, Henry Jordan Papers, SLQ; "The Distress in Lancashire," *Manchester Courier and Lancashire General Advertiser*, 6 December 1862.

76. "Queensland," *Chamber's Encyclopaedia*, vol. 8 (1868). This entry was written by Jordan. See *Report of Queensland Emigration under the Land Order System for the Two Years Terminating 30 April 1865*, 173, Henry Jordan Papers.

77. *Manchester Courier and Lancashire General Advertiser*, 31 January 1863; Johnston, "Selling of Queensland," 380.

78. Henry Jordan, Second Annual Report of the Queensland Emigration Commission, for 1862–63, Henry Jordan Papers.

79. Edmund Potter, "The Cotton Districts and Emigration," *The Times* (London), 24 March 1863; Marx, *Capital*, 720.

80. Potter, "The Cotton Districts and Emigration."

81. R. Arnold, *History of the Cotton Famine*, 368.

82. Henry Jordan, *First Annual Emigration Report*, 1861–62, 438, Henry Jordan Papers.

83. H. Jordan, *First Annual Emigration Report*.

84. H. Jordan, 458.

85. "The Distress among the Hand-Loom Weavers," *Belfast News-Letter*, 27 January 1863.

86. Moreton-Robinson, *White Possessive*.

87. H. Jordan, Second Annual Report of the Queensland Emigration Commission, for 1862–63, 462.

88. H. Jordan, 466.

89. H. Jordan, 471.

90. H. Jordan, 458.

91. *Manchester Courier and Lancashire General Advertiser*, 22 June 1861.

92. "Emigration to Queensland and the Cotton Supply," *Derby Mercury*, 14 August 1861.

93. "Queensland as the Cotton Field of England," *Leeds Mercury*, 24 September 1861.

94. "Lecture on Queensland," *Daily Post* (Liverpool), 3 December 1861.

95. "Queensland: The Cotton Supply, and Emigration," *Western Times*, 22 February 1862.

96. "Queensland Emigration Office, Directions to Be Observed by Persons Wanting Free Passage to Queensland," COL/12, Queensland State Archives.

97. H. Jordan, *Second Annual Emigration Report*, 477.

98. De Coin, *History and Cultivation*, 227.

99. *Report from the Select Committee on the Resignation and Return of Mr. Jordan, Emigration Commissioner in England, Together with the Proceedings of the Committee*

and Minutes of Evidence (Queensland, Legislative Assembly, 19 July 1864), 40, box 16167 O/S, Henry Jordan Papers.

100. *Brisbane Courier*, 13 December 1864.

101. The pursuit of the White Australia Policy certainly drew upon visions such as Jordan's. Griffiths, "Making of White Australia."

102. Charles Nicholson and Others to George F. Bowen, "Memorial on the Subject of Asiatic Labor," in *Asiatic Labor* (Queensland: Legislative Assembly, dated 30 July 1861), SLQ.

103. Louisiana planters used similar rhetoric: M-H. Jung, *Coolies and Cane*, 29-40.

104. *South Sea Islanders* (Importation of), 26 August 1863, in *Asiatic Labor* (dated 30 July 1861), SLQ. Towns complained that English labor brought to the colony had not worked hard enough and demanded too high wages.

105. Robert Towns to Ross Lewin, 29 May 1863, Letters by Robert Towns, 1862-1873, Robert Towns & Co. Papers, CYReel2648, 191-96, State Library of New South Wales, Sydney.

106. William Fryar, "The Slave Trade in Polynesia," *Sugar Cane* 5 (1 February 1873): 102; Graves, *Cane and Labour*, 35-38.

107. Dilke, *Greater Britain*, 28.

108. Dilke, 15.

109. Dilke, 27-35.

110. Dilke, 85.

111. Dilke, 86-87.

112. Dilke, 572.

Chapter 9

1. *British Honduras Colonist*, 29 February 1868.

2. On slaveholder recruitment see Simmons, *Confederate Settlement*, 30-31.

3. On mahogany, see Bulmer-Thomas and Bulmer-Thomas, *Economic History of Belize*, 97.

4. *British Honduras Colonist*, 11 April 1868.

5. F. Ortiz, *Cuban Counterpoint*.

6. Bulmer-Thomas and Bulmer-Thomas, *Economic History of Belize*, 97.

7. According to the 1861 census, the population consisted of 13,789 males and 11,846 females and was racially delineated as follows: English and mixed, 3,967; African and mixed, 4,666; Indian and mixed, 9,015; Spanish and mixed, 5,523; Carib and mixed, 1,952; other countries, 512. John Gardiner Austin to John Eyre, 10 August 1865, 92r102, BARS.

8. Rodney, *History of the Guyanese Working People*, 39.

9. "American Immigration," *Jamaican Guardian*, 18 and 19 September 1862.

10. Masur, "African American Delegation to Abraham Lincoln." "The President himself is inclined to the opinion that the most desirable thing for both races was to separate them, and to reserve North America Exclusively for the whites." Lord Lyons to Earl Russell, 26 December 1862 FO/5, NAUK. See also Horne, *Negro Comrades of the Crown*, 206.

11. Francis Hincks (Demerara) to Duke of Newcastle, 22 August 1862, FO/5, NAUK.

12. William Walker to Lord Russell, 29 September 1862, FO/5, NAUK.

13. John Hodge to Lord Lyons, 9 July 1863, 85r320, BARS; Hodge to Heriot, 1 July 1863, 85r300-01, BARS. As early as June 1851, the secretary of state of British Honduras suggested that the colony should seek the emigration of the "black and coloured population" within the United States. "Chronology" in Burdon, *Archives of British Honduras*, 3:13; "151, 5 June 1851, R37 Governor, Jamaica to Superintendent, Forwarding a Circular Dispatch," in Burdon, *Archives of British Honduras*, 3:146. Trinidad previously sought African Americans through the passage of ordinances to encourage migration. In 1840, Nathaniel Peck and Thomas Price traveled to Trinidad and British Guiana to survey the prospects for Black migration to the colony with some success in recruiting migrants. In 1851, Trinidad further passed legislation to encourage migration.

14. Slavery had been officially abolished in British Honduras on 1 August 1838. However, emancipation within British Honduras differed from much of the West Indies in that the plantation as an economic unit based upon the production of commodities for metropolitan consumption did not exist there. Instead, enslaved Black people who labored in the colony worked as woodcutters. However, this woodcutting labor was not intended to clear land for plantations. For an overview of this period see Shoman and Bolland, *Land in Belize*, 58–101.

15. The British diplomat Lord Richard Lyons stated this clearly: "It is from the Southern Ports, that the President [Lincoln] most wishes to send Negroes, and it is from those ports that the most useful class, the 'field hands,' would be most easily sent." Lord Lyons to Earl Russell, 23 January 1863, PRO 30/22/37, NAUK.

16. "Letter from the British Honduras Company," John Hodge to Sir F. Rogers, 18 November 1862, 884/2, NAUK.

17. Compare Page and Magness, *Colonization after Emancipation*, 51.

18. Shoman and Bolland, *Land in Belize*, 86; Clegern, *British Honduras*, 36; Leas to F. Seward, 12 August 1864, 12 September 1864, Alex Henderson to Leas, 8 September 1864, and Leas to Henderson, 10 September 1864, Despatches from the United States Consuls in Belize, FM T-334, roll 3.

19. Wesley, "Lincoln's Plan," 8. For an overview of colonization, see Mills, "Exporting the Racial Republic." On the intersection between Black nationalism and colonization, see Blackett, "Martin R. Delany"; Mattox, "Mayor of San Juan del Norte?"; Guyatt, "Impossible Idea?"; and Guyatt, "America's Conservatory."

20. Blackett, "Lincoln and Colonization," 22.

21. "Preliminary Emancipation Proclamation," in *Collected Works of Abraham Lincoln*, vol. 5, 368–70. Guyatt, "A Topic Best Avoided."

22. Lockett, "Abraham Lincoln and Colonization"; Vorenberg, "Abraham Lincoln."

23. James Mitchell to Abraham Lincoln, 11 June 1863, FO/5, NAUK.

24. Chomsky, "The United States–Dakota War Trials."

25. John Hodge to Lord Lyons, 9 July 1863, 85r320, BARS. Hodge to Heriot, 1 July 1863, 85R300-01, BARS.

26. Taylor, *Embattled Freedom*, 84.

27. Hodge to Heriot, 1 July 1863, 85R300-01, BARS.

28. John Hodge to Lord Lyons, 9 July 1863, BARS. See further, Magness and Page, *Colonization after Emancipation*, 37.

29. Lord Lyons to W. H. Seward, 17 June 1863, 85r292–93, BARS. Lyons also wrote

to the governor of Jamaica informing him of Hodge's progress. See Lyons to Governor of Jamaica, 18 June 1863, 85r294–97, BARS.

30. F. F. Elliot to A. Layard, 31 July 1863, 85r306–07, BARS.

31. For the phrase, see Baron, "Demand for Black Labor."

32. Hodge to Heriot, 1 July 1863, 85r300–01, BARS.

33. J. R. Robertson to F. Rogers, 15 July 1863, 85r298, BARS.

34. John Hodge to Lord Lyons, 13 June 1863, 85r290, BARS.

35. Fredrickson, *Big Enough to Be Inconsistent*, 113–14.

36. Quoted in Harrison, "British Labor and American Slavery," 294. See also Downs, *Sick from Freedom*.

37. John W. Menard to F. Seymour, 3 August 1863, 83r416, BARS.

38. R. Ferguson to F. Seymour, 5 August 1863, 83r415, BARS.

39. Babcock, *British Honduras*, 16.

40. F. F. Elliot to A Layard 31 July 1863, 85r306–07, BARS.

41. "Emigration to Honduras," *The Liberator*, 25 March 1864. The *Liberator* article concluded noting that emancipated African Americans would determine their own fate in the United States, having been recently enabled to officially fight in the Union army. "West India Correspondence," *Anti-slavery Reporter and Aborigines' Friend*, 1 January 1864. See also Magness, "British Honduras Colony."

42. Lyons to Russell, 26 December 1862, FO 5/934, NAUK.

43. The British Honduras Company in concert with the colonial administration was not the only interest to pursue colonization. Aaron Columbus Burr, too, sought to establish a Lincoln Colony for Black colonization in Belize. As Janet Coryell has noted, Burr's efforts to establish this colony combined humanitarian actions with self-interest. Coryell, "'Lincoln Colony.'"

44. See online database *Last Seen: Finding Family after Slavery*, Informationwanted.org. See, for example, "Isaac Williams Offers $200 Reward to Anyone Who Can Find His Grandson," *South Carolina Leader*, 9 December 1865, https://informationwanted.org/items/show/3559.

45. "Emigration to Honduras"; Fredrickson, *Big Enough to Be Inconsistent*, 114.

46. E. Forbes, "African-American Resistance to Colonization"; Bennett, "Was Abe Lincoln a White Supremacist?"; Berlin, "Who Freed the Slaves? Emancipation and Its Meaning in American Life"; Fields, "Who Freed the Slaves?"; and MacPherson, "Who Freed the Slaves?," all in Ward, *Civil War*; Roediger, *Seizing Freedom*.

47. Thavolia Glymph, "'This Species of Property': Female Slave Contrabands in the Civil War," in Campbell and Rice, *Woman's War*, 55–71; Glymph, "Du Bois's *Black Reconstruction*."

48. Stuart to Earl Russell, 18 October 1862, FO/5, NAUK.

49. Fredrickson, *Big Enough to Be Inconsistent*, 98.

50. Voegeli, "Rejected Alternative," 768; Hoffman, "From Slavery to Self-Reliance."

51. Voegeli, "Rejected Alternative," 769, 773.

52. Fields, "Who Freed the Slaves?," in *Freedom: A Documentary History*, vol. 1, 181; Berlin et al., "The Destruction of Slavery," in *Freedom: A Documentary History*, vol. 1, 394.

53. Berlin et al., "The Destruction of Slavery," 398.

54. Fields, "Who Freed the Slaves?," 181.

55. S. Hahn, *Political Worlds*, 61.

56. Lowe, *Intimacies of Four Continents*, 24.

57. Look Lai, *Indentured Labor, Caribbean Sugar*.

58. *Light of the Age* left carrying 445 men, 14 women, 16 boys, 2 girls, and 3 infants. Six men died during the passage. Frederick Oham to the Emigration Commissioner, 9 July 1865, 89r112, BARS.

59. Immigration Agent to Governor Austin, 4 July 1865, 89r102-3, BARS.

60. John Hodge to F. Rogers, 23 August 1862, 80r233, BARS.

61. On racial reading of Asian labor as "cheap," see Day, *Alien Capital*, 7-8.

62. Chinese immigrants who arrived in British Honduras were generally described in official records according to passenger numbers. "'Tsai La (217)' to His Mother," 89r466; "'Ya (434)' to His Parents," 89r467; "'Huang Lui (78)' to His Mother," 89r468-9, BARS.

63. "'Huang Lui (78)' to His Mother."

64. Robert Swinhoe to T. D. Boyd (Chief Emigration Agent, Amoy), 18 April 1866, 94r79, BARS.

65. Swinhoe to Boyd.

66. "Allotments Stopped or Unclaimed," 89r261-62, BARS.

67. Theophilus Sampson to Robert Swinhoe, 28 May 1866, 94r37-70, BARS.

68. "Allotments Stopped or Unclaimed."

69. James R. Longden to J. P. Grant, 23 October 1868, 98r295, BARS.

70. Gahue to Austin, 24 July 1866, 89r403, BARS.

71. Report on the Condition of Chinese Laborers (Fragment) 1865, 89r196, BARS.

72. Report on the Condition of Chinese Laborers (Fragment).

73. Report on the Condition of Chinese Laborers (Fragment). Gahue to Austin, 24 July 1866, 89r404, BARS.

74. Gahue to Austin, 24 July 1866, 89r405; Report on the Condition of Chinese Laborers (Fragment).

75. Gahue to Austin, 24 July 1866, 89r407, BARS.

76. Dr. Gahue to Mr. Hodge, 5 January 1866, 89r256, BARS.

77. Dr. Gahue to Mr. Hodge, 5 January 1866, 89r256, BARS.

78. Gahue to J. Gardiner Austin, 30 July 1866, 89r411-12, BARS.

79. Antonio Mathe to L. G. Austin, 10 November 1866, 89r509, BARS.

80. Gahue suggested that the absconding Chinese abandoned plantations because, after allotments, they lacked any income to support themselves. Gahue to Austin, 24 July 1866, 89r407-8, BARS.

81. J. R. Longden to J. P. Grant, 23 October 1868, 98r295, BARS.

82. Edwin Adolphus to Thomas Graham, 4 October 1866, 89r494, BARS; St. John Robinson, "The Chinese of Central America: Diverse Beginnings, Common Achievements," in Lai and Chee-Beng, *Chinese in Latin America and the Caribbean*, 107-8; Ropp, "Chinese in Belize"; Shing, "Central America and the Chinese"; D. H. Lewis, "Chinese of Belize."

83. Adolphus to Graham, 89r494, BARS.

84. Cal, "Anglo Maya Contact in Northern Belize," 30, 223.

85. On Xaibe, see McNairn, "Baiting the British Bull"; and Muntsch, "Xaibe."

86. "Rough Notes Taken on a Flying Visit to the Northern District of British Honduras," *Sugar Cane* 1 (1 January 1870): 29–30.

87. Douglass, *Narrative of the Life of Frederick Douglass*, 65.

88. "Reports on the Blue Book for the Year 1867," in Burdon, *Archives of British Honduras*, vol. 3, 19 June 1868.

89. M-H. Jung, *Coolies and Cane*, 5.

90. *British Honduras Colonist*, 11 April 1868. Morrell relocated from Mississippi to Texas in the 1830s.

91. J. G. Austin to Governor Eyre, 6 April 1865, 92r39, BARS.

92. John Hodge to Lieutenant Governor J. Gardiner, Austin, 3 May 1866, CO 123/121, NAUK.

93. Great Britain, Parliament, House of Commons, *Accounts and Papers of the House of Commons* (Ordered to be printed, 1870), 28.

94. *British Honduras Colonist*, 14 March 1868.

95. Follett, *Sugar Masters*, 51, 98, 112.

96. Du Bois, *The Negro*, 115.

97. Charles A. Pilsbury, "Southern Immigration—Brazil and British Honduras," *De Bow's Review* 4, no. 6 (December 1867): 537–45.

98. *British Honduras Colonist*, 22 February 1868.

99. *British Honduras Colonist*, 14 March 1868.

100. Samuel McCutchon Papers, 315–16. *Records of Antebellum Southern Plantations from the Revolution through the Civil War*, University Publications of America. Samuel McCutchon Papers. Microfilm. Series I, Pt. 1, Selections from Louisiana State University: Reels 5–6.

101. "George Hyde," Legacies of British Slave-ownership database, https://www.ucl.ac.uk/lbs/person/view/11629.

102. McCutchon Papers, 315–16.

103. McCutchon Papers, 315–16.

104. Du Bois, *The World and Africa*, 42.

Chapter 10

1. Du Bois, *Black Reconstruction*, 237. Du Bois also noted that the South existed as an oligarchy "similar to" but not the same as European imperialism.

2. Du Bois, 595.

3. Du Bois, 601.

4. For the United States as empire-state, see Left Quarter Collective, "White Supremacist Constitution of the U.S. Empire-State." Black abolitionists drew connections between schemes for their removal from the United States and American Indian dispossessions during the 1830s. See, for example, James M. Whitfield to Samuel E. Cornish and James McCune Smith: "The treatment of the American Indians and the bad faith exercised towards them, are enough to convince every reflecting mind of the folly of proposing separate settlements for colored men, in the United States." *Colored American*, 18 May 1839, Black Abolitionist Papers, reel 3, 0062.

5. Cha-Jua, *America's First Black Town*, 3.

6. Du Bois, "Freedmen's Bureau," 358.

7. "6 September 1865," in Palmer, *Selected Papers of Thaddeus Stevens*.

8. "10 March 1866," in Palmer, *Selected Papers of Thaddeus Stevens*, 108; E. Foner, "Thaddeus Stevens, Confiscation, and Reconstruction," in *Politics and Ideology*, 162.

9. Frederick Douglass, "The Need for Continuing Anti-Slavery Work" (9 May 1865), in P. Foner, *Life and Writings of Frederick Douglass*, vol. 4, 167.

10. P. Foner, "Introduction," in *Life and Writings of Frederick Douglass*, vol. 4, 16–17.

11. Karuka, "Fugitive Decolonization."

12. Manning, "Working for Citizenship in Civil War Contraband Camps," 178.

13. "General Butler and the Contraband of War," *New York Times*, 2 June 1861.

14. David Herbert Donald, *Lincoln*, 314.

15. Donald, 315.

16. Dix, *Memoirs of John Adams Dix*, 40; Syrett, *Civil War Confiscation Acts*, 12.

17. *Congressional Globe*, 37th Congress, 2nd Sess., 944.

18. P. Foner, *Life and Writings of Frederick Douglass*, vol. 4, 544n1.

19. Oubre, *Forty Acres and a Mule*, 11.

20. Ochiai, "Port Royal Experiment Revisited," 94.

21. Ochiai, 96.

22. *Negroes at Port Royal*, 6.

23. L. Roper, "Frederick Law Olmsted," 279.

24. Quoted in L. Roper, 279.

25. Ochiai, "Port Royal Experiment Revisited," 97–98. See also Randall, *Constitutional Problems under Lincoln*.

26. Stampp and Litwack, "The Ballot and Land for the Freedmen, 1861–1865," in *Reconstruction*; Ochiai, "Port Royal Experiment Revisited," 98.

27. Rufus Saxton to Edward S. Philbrick, 15 June 1864. Rufus B. and S. Willard Saxton Papers, Manuscripts and Archives, Yale University Library. Available online at https://ldhi.library.cofc.edu/exhibits/show/after_slavery_educator/unit_three_documents/document_four.

28. "William C. Ganett, January 1863," in Pearson, *Letters from Port Royal*, 148; Pease, "Three Years among the Freedmen," 104–5.

29. Ciambala, "Freedmen's Bureau," 598.

30. Rose, *Rehearsal for Reconstruction*, 200.

31. Hoffman, "From Slavery to Self-Reliance," 14; Ochiai, "Port Royal Experiment Revisited"; Ochiai, *Harvesting Freedom*.

32. Hoffman, "From Slavery to Self-Reliance," 17.

33. Rose, *Rehearsal for Reconstruction*.

34. Oubre, *Forty Acres and a Mule*, xiii.

35. Ciambala, "Freedmen's Bureau," 608.

36. Simkins and Woody, *South Carolina during Reconstruction*, 230.

37. Fierce, "Black Struggle for Land during Reconstruction," 14–15; Schwalm, *Hard Fight for We*, 187.

38. Cox, "Promise of Land for the Freedmen," 429. For a full account see Appendix F, "Colloquy with Colored Ministers," 12 January 1865, in Townsend, *Anecdotes of the Civil War in the United States*.

39. Ciambala, "Freedmen's Bureau," 603.

40. K. Bell, "'Ogeechee Troubles,'" 379; Cimbala, "Freedmen's Bureau"; Rapport, "Freedmen's Bureau."

41. K. Bell, "'Ogeechee Troubles,'" 383–84.

42. Bell, 397.

43. Charles S. Johnson WPA Interview with George Johnson, Mound Bayou, Mississippi, September 1941, available online at the Library of Congress, Voices from the Days of Slavery, https://www.loc.gov/podcasts/slavenarratives/transcripts/slavery_johnson.pdf. I have reformatted this dialogue for clarity.

44. Glymph, "Second Middle Passage," 86–87, 93.

45. Hermann, *Pursuit of a Dream*, 47–49.

46. Glymph, "Second Middle Passage," 94.

47. Glymph, 120.

48. Glymph, 191.

49. Glymph, 225.

50. Glymph, 226–34.

51. Glymph, *Out of the House of Bondage*, 209–10; Roediger, *Seizing Freedom*, 46.

52. Cha-Jua, *America's First Black Town*, 217.

53. "Interview with Boston Blackwell," in *Slave Narratives: A Folk History of Slavery in the United States from Interviews with Former Slaves*, Vol. 2, Arkansas Narratives, Part 1, 114–17.

54. R. Guha, *Rule of Property*, 17.

55. Lanza, *Agrarianism and Reconstruction Politics*, 14.

56. Riddleberger, *George Washington Julian*, 33–34.

57. Roediger and Foner, *On Our Own Time*, 110.

58. Montgomery, *Beyond Equality*, 82; Julian, *Political Recollections*, 263–64.

59. Riddleberger, *George Washington Julian*, 170.

60. Julian, *Speeches on Political Questions*, 217–18; Riddleberger, *George Washington Julian*, 191.

61. Riddleberger, *George Washington Julian*, 189.

62. *Congressional Globe*, 38th Cong., 1st sess., 2249.

63. Collins, *Black Feminist Thought*, 158.

64. *Congressional Globe*, 38th Cong., 1st sess., 2233; Roark, "George W. Julian: Radical Land Reformer," 36; Hoffnagle, "Southern Homestead Act," 614.

65. For birth, Black women, and the use of gestational language to describe the basis of capital, see Hartman, "Belly of the World."

66. *Congressional Globe*, 38th Cong., 1st sess., 12 May 1866, 2250.

67. Quoted in Riddleberger, *George Washington Julian*, 194.

68. *Congressional Globe*, 38th Cong., 1st sess., 1864, 2251.

69. *Congressional Globe*, 2251.

70. Pope, "Southern Homesteads for Negroes," 202. On 29 May 1865, President Andrew Johnson issued his "Proclamation of Amnesty and Reconstruction," which called for the "restoration of all rights of property, except as to slaves" for those Confederates and slaveholders who rebelled.

71. Julian, *Political Recollections*, 329.

72. Lanza, *Agrarianism and Reconstruction Politics*, 99–104.

73. Randall, *Constitutional Problems under Lincoln*, 341.

74. P. Ortiz, *Emancipation Betrayed*, 17–22. Frances Ellen Watkins Harper reported that nearly 9,000 African Americans owned land in 1870; however, other estimates were considerably beneath this. If this higher estimate is true, this would make slightly under 10 percent of African American landowners in 1870 and under 5 percent of the total population of Florida Black landowners. Ortiz, 19.

75. W. Moses, *Creative Conflict*, 108.

76. Hoffnagle, "Southern Homestead Act," 618, 622.

77. Pope, "Southern Homesteads for Negroes," 205.

78. Hoffnagle, "Southern Homestead Act," 625.

79. Riddleberger, "George W. Julian."

80. Chomsky, "United States–Dakota War Trials."

81. Fowler, "Arapaho and Cheyenne Perspectives."

82. "Thirty Sixth Anniversary of the American Anti-Slavery Society," *National Anti-Slavery Standard*, 11 May 1869.

83. "Thirty Sixth Anniversary of the American Anti-Slavery Society."

84. "Thirty Sixth Anniversary of the American Anti-Slavery Society."

85. "Thirty Sixth Anniversary of the American Anti-Slavery Society."

86. Left Quarter Collective, "White Supremacist Constitution of the U.S. Empire-State."

87. P. Chatterjee, *Nation and Its Fragments*.

88. Angela Murphy, "Wendell Phillips and the American Indian," in Aisirithe and Yacovone, *Wendell Phillips*, 239–71.

89. T. Smith, "Nations Colliding," 317; M. Bailey, *Reconstruction in Indian Territory*, 60–72.

90. Brad Agnew, "Our Doom as a Nation Is Sealed," in Clampitt, *Civil War and Reconstruction in Indian Territory*, 73–74.

91. "Article 4, Treaty with the Cherokee, 1866," in Kappler, *Indian Affairs*, vol. 2, 943. Agnew, "Our Doom as a Nation Is Sealed," 79.

92. Ullman, *Beginnings of Black Nationalism*, 213.

93. Franklin, *From Slavery to Freedom*, 240.

94. Stuckey, *Ideological Origins*, 3.

95. Kolchin, *First Freedom*, 9.

96. Ford, *Deliver Us from Evil*, 297.

97. Franklin, *From Slavery to Freedom*, 237.

98. Franklin, 221.

99. D. Brown, "Attacking Slavery from Within," 559. While Brown, Hinton's biographer, claims it is inaccurate to make anti-Black racism a prime or minor motivating factor, this is a highly tendentious claim. One can see racism in *Land of Gold* (1855), including anti-Black racism.

100. Quoted in Nicholas Guyatt, " 'Future Empire of Our Freedmen,' " in Arenson and Graybill, *Civil War Wests*, 98–99.

101. Kolchin, *First Freedom*, 9.

102. Couch, "Crisis in Color: Racial Separation in Texas during Reconstruction," in *Dance of Freedom*, 125.

103. James Henry Hammond, "Speech of Hon. James H. Hammond, of South Carolina, on the Admission of Kansas, under the Lecompton Constitution Delivered in the Senate of the United States, March 4, 1858" (Lemuel Towers: Washington, D.C., 1858). Berlin and Gutman, "Natives and Immigrants," 1176.

104. *Report of the Commissioners of Emigration to the General Assembly of Louisiana*, 4.

105. Kathman, *Information for Immigrants into the State of Louisiana*; "Department of Immigration and Labor," *De Bow's Review* (November 1867): 468–79.

106. "Mit Verstand und Intelligenz begabt, mit Kapital und Arbeitskraft augerüstet," *Columbus Westbote*, 29 October 1868, quoted in Efford, "New Citizens," 171.

107. "European Immigration," *De Bow's Review* (July–August 1867): 102.

108. Loring and Atkinson, *Cotton Culture*, 87.

109. Loring and Atkinson, 88; G. Forbes, *Report on Cotton in the Southern States*.

110. Loring and Atkinson, *Cotton Culture*, 112.

111. *Report of the Commissioners of Emigration to the General Assembly of Louisiana*, 5.

112. R. Williams, "Mississippi Career," 6–7, 113–42.

113. Williams, 10–13.

114. Williams, 28.

115. Henry David Thoreau, "Walking," *The Atlantic*, June 1862, available online at http://www.theatlantic.com/magazine/archive/1862/06/walking/304674/.

116. Weymouth Jordan, "Noah B. Cloud's Activities on Behalf of Southern Agriculture"; Genovese, *Political Economy of Slavery*, 124–53.

117. R. Williams, "Mississippi Career," 45.

118. Johnson, *River of Dark Dreams*, 244–45.

119. Affleck, *Southern Rural Almanac, and Plantation and Garden Calendar, for 1851* (1851), 25.

120. Caitlin Rosenthal, "Slavery's Scientific Management: Masters and Managers," in Beckert and Rockman, *Slavery's Capitalism*, 62–86.

121. "24 & 25 June 1859," Panther Burn Record and Account Book, Mississippi Department of Archives and History, Jackson.

122. On reopening of African slave trade, see Takaki, "Movement to Reopen"; and Du Bois, *Suppression of the African Slave Trade to the United States of America*, 168–93.

123. Schwalm, *A Hard Fight for We*, 188.

124. Thomas Affleck to C. Dehorse, 18 September 1865, MSS. 3, 1263 Letterbook (1865–1868), box 21, v. 14, Thomas Affleck Papers, Louisiana and Lower Mississippi Valley Collections, Louisiana State University Libraries.

125. Letter from Mr. Affleck, 9 May 1866, box 31, 55, Item 18, Affleck Papers.

126. 1865 *Queensland* (printed pamphlets), box 31, 45, Affleck Papers.

127. Affleck to unknown recipient, September 1865, 13, MSS. 3, 1263 Letterbook (1865–1868), box 21, v. 14, Affleck Papers.

128. Affleck to unknown recipient, 1 February 1867, box 31, 62, item 29, Affleck Papers. As one supporter of Affleck's plan noted, unless white immigrants were introduced it was possible that white planters would experience the same "calamities as those in Jamaica." Galveston *Tri-Weekly News*, 18 December 1865. Cole, "Texas

Career," 250. Affleck also was to make arrangements to supply the British with beef and mutton.

129. Thomas Affleck to C. Dehorse, 18 September 1865; Thomas Affleck letter, July 1867, Scrapbook, 1866–67, item 37, Affleck Papers.

130. Cole, "Texas Career," 247.

131. Thomas Affleck, "Agriculture and Rural Economy of the South," *Cultivator* (Albany, N.Y.) 2, no. 1 (1845): 30.

132. "Circular: Immigration and Labor," 21 May 1866, Appendix B, folder 54, Affleck Papers.

133. Glymph, *Out of the House of Bondage*, 139; Hunter, *To 'Joy My Freedom*.

134. A Wife and Mother, ca. June 1866, box 31, folder 54 Scrapbook, item 4, Affleck Papers.

135. Affleck to B. J. Arnold, 2 November 1865, Letterbook, box 21, v. 14, p. 19.

136. "Editorial," Scrapbook Immigration, box 31, folder 55 item 16, Affleck Papers.

137. "House Servants to Order," Scrapbook Immigration box 31, folder 54, ca. 1866, Affleck Papers.

138. "House Servants to Order."

139. "Traveler," "To Country, the Crops, Labor, Immigration, & Co.," *Galveston News*, 3 July 1866, box 31, Affleck Papers.

140. "Circular: Immigration and Labor," 21 May 1866, Affleck Papers.

141. "Texas Land, Labor and Immigration Company," box 31, v. 16, Scrapbook Immigration, Affleck Papers.

142. Affleck to Hayman, 22 November 1865, box 21, v. 14, Affleck Papers.

143. Affleck to Hayman.

144. "Circular," February 1866, box 31, folder 55, Scrapbook, Affleck Papers.

145. May 1866, Scrapbook Immigration box 31, folder 55, Affleck Papers.

146. Rana, *Two Faces of American Freedom*.

147. Thomas Affleck to Henry Lafone, 26 June 1867, box 21, v. 14, Affleck Papers.

148. "From some recently published reports . . . ," *Australasian* (Melbourne), 18 September 1869.

149. The WPA Federal Writers' Project extended from 1936 to 1938 and comprised over 2,000 interviews with former slaves across seventeen states. Rawick, *From Sundown to Sunup*, xiii–xxi.

150. R. Campbell, *Empire for Slavery*.

151. Hunter, *To 'Joy My Freedom*, 21; J. Jones, *Labor of Love*, 51.

152. Josephine Ryles, in *Slave Narratives: A Folk History of Slavery in the United States from Interviews with Former Slaves*, vol. 16, Texas Narratives, Part 3, 278–79.

153. J. Jones, *Labor of Love*, 46.

154. Jonathan Wiener, "Class Structure," 976.

155. Glymph, *Out of the House of Bondage*, 137–66.

156. Schwalm, *Hard Fight for We*, 156; Glymph, "Second Middle Passage."

157. Felix Haywood, Federal Writers' Project: Slave Narrative Project, vol. 16, Texas, Part 2, Easter-King, 133. Available online at https://www.loc.gov/item/mesn162/.

158. Litwack, *Been in the Storm So Long*, 292–335; Kolchin, *First Freedom*, 3–29.

159. J. Jones, *Labor of Love*, 45.

160. Hunter, *To 'Joy My Freedom*, 21.

Conclusion

1. Bonynge, *Future Wealth of America*, vii.

2. "The *Volks-Tribune*'s Political Economy and Its Attitude towards Young America," in *MECW*, 6:35–51; Blackburn, *Marx and Lincoln*, 2; Bronstein, *Land Reform*.

3. Engels to Marx, 15 July 1865, *MECW*, 42:167.

4. Karl Marx to Francois Lafargue, 12 November 1866, *MECW*, 42:334.

5. Marx, *Grundrisse*, 325–26.

6. Du Bois, "Karl Marx and the Negro"; Du Bois, "Marxism and the Negro Problem."

7. Fanon, *Wretched of the Earth*, 4.

8. Du Bois, *Black Reconstruction*, 602.

9. D. G. Pitcher, "Report on the System of Recruiting Labourers for the Colonies, 1882," in Mangru, *Kanpur to Kolkata*, 43–44.

10. Kempson, *Coolie-nama*.

11. Mangru, "From Bengal to British Guiana," 68–70.

12. Jaynes, *Branches without Roots*.

13. William Francis Allen, Charles Pickard Ware, and Lucy McKim Garrison, *Slave Songs of the United States* (1867), 8.

Bibliography

Archives
Agricultural and Horticultural Society of India, Kolkata
        Minutes of the Agricultural and Horticultural Society of India
        Proceedings of the Agricultural and Horticultural Society of India
Belize Archives and Records Services, Belmopan
Boston Public Library
        Ziba B. Oakes Papers
British Library, India Office, London
Caroliniana Library, University of South Carolina, Columbia
        James M. Morris Papers
Confederate Archive and Relic Room, Columbia, S.C.
        Colin J. McRae Papers
Dolph Briscoe Center for American History, University of Texas at Austin
John Rylands Library, University of Manchester Library
        Amelia Chesson Papers
        Annual Reports of the Executive Committee of the Cotton Supply Association
        George Thompson Papers
        J. Kay Shuttleworth Papers
        Owen, Owens and Sons Papers
        Raymond English Antislavery Collection
Lancashire Archives, Preston
        Henry Ashworth Papers
        Samuel Studdard Papers
Louisiana and Lower Mississippi Valley Collections, Louisiana State University
    Libraries
        Samuel McCutchon Papers
        Thomas Affleck Papers
Manchester Archives and Local Studies
        J. B. Smith Papers
        Manchester Chamber of Commerce Minutes
        Proceedings of the Manchester Chamber of Commerce
Manchester Central Library
Mississippi Department of Archives and History, Jackson
        William Johnson Papers
National Archives of India, New Delhi
National Archives of the United Kingdom, London
National Library of India, Kolkata
Nehru Memorial Library and Museum, Delhi
New York Historical Society
        Granville Sharp Collection

Queensland State Archives, Brisbane
Royal Geographical Society of London
    G. F. Forbes, *Report on Cotton in the Southern States*
Rubenstein Library, Duke University
    Edward T. Heriot Papers
    Elizabeth Blyth Papers
South Carolina Historical Society, Charleston
    Jonathan Lucas Papers
    Minutes of the South Carolina Agriculture Society, 1825–60
State Archives of West Bengal, Kolkata
State Library of New South Wales, Sydney
    Robert Towns & Co. Papers
State Library of Queensland, Brisbane
    Henry Jordan Papers
St. John's Library, Cambridge University
    Thomas Clarkson Papers
Wisconsin State Historical Society, Madison
    James Rood Doolittle Papers

Microfilm Collections
Black Abolitionist Papers
Despatches from the United States Consuls in Belize
Records of Ante-bellum Southern Plantations

Online Archival Collections
Boston Public Library Anti-slavery Collection
    Selected Letters of William Lloyd Garrison
University of Kentucky
    "Last Will and Testament of Henry Clay"
Legacies of British Slave-ownership database
Library of Congress
    Andrew Jackson Papers
    Federal Writers' Project: Slave Narrative Project
    Voices from the Days of Slavery
Register of Deeds, Buncombe County, North Carolina
Rufus B. and S. Willard Saxton Papers, Manuscripts and Archives, Yale University
    Library
Schomburg Center for Research in Black Culture, New York Public Library
Special Collections and University Archives, University of Massachusetts Amherst
    W. E. B. Du Bois Papers
ULS Archives and Special Collections, University of Pittsburgh
    Robert J. Walker Papers

Magazines, Newspapers, and Periodicals

American Cotton Planter

Anti-slavery Reporter and Aborigines'
    Friend

Asiatic Journal

The Atlantic

Australasian

The Bee-Hive

Belfast News-Letter

Bengal Hurkaru

Berbice Gazette and British Guiana
    Advertiser

Besley's Devonshire Chronicle and
    Exeter News

Bombay Times

Brisbane Courier

British Honduras Colonist

British Indian Advocate

Brooklyn Daily Times

Charleston Mercury

Cleveland Herald

Correspondence of the Journal of
    Commerce

Cotton Supply Reporter

Cultivator (Albany, N.Y.)

Daily National Intelligencer

Daily News (London)

Daily Post (Liverpool)

De Bow's Review

Delhi Gazette

Derby Mercury

The Economist

Edinburgh Magazine

Farmers' Register

Friend of India

Glasgow Morning Journal

Great Western Magazine and Anglo-
    American Journal

Hazard's United States Commercial and
    Statistical Register

Household Words

Isle of Wight Times

Jamaican Guardian

Journal of the Agricultural and
    Horticultural Society of India

Journal of the East India Association

Journal of the Society of Arts

Leeds Mercury

The Liberator

The Lion

London Gazette

Madras Journal of Literature and
    Science

Manchester Courier and Lancashire
    General Advertiser

Memphis Daily Appeal

Mofussilite

Moreton Bay Courier

National Anti-slavery Standard

New-York Daily Tribune

New York Times

The North-Carolinian

Notes and Queries

Observer

Proceedings of the Bengal Chamber of
    Commerce

The Republican

Scientific American

Southern Agriculturist

Southern Planter

Southern Quarterly Review

Spectator

Sugar Cane

The Times (London)

Times of India

Transactions of the Agricultural and
    Horticultural Society of India

Transactions of the Manchester Statistical
    Society

Washington Quarterly Magazine of Arts,
    Science and Literature

Western Times (Exeter, England)

York Herald

Primary Published Sources

Acts and Regulations Relating to the Waste Lands in the Colony of Queensland.
    Brisbane: T. P. Pugh's Printing Office, 1861.

Adam, William. "Slavery in India: A Paper Presented to the General Anti-slavery Convention." 1840.

Affleck, Thomas. *Southern Rural Almanac, and Plantation and Garden Calendar, for 1851*. New Orleans: Office of the Picayune, 1851.

Allen, William Francis, Charles Pickard Ware, and Lucy McKim Garrison. *Slave Songs of the United States*. New York: A. Simpson & Co., 1867.

An American. "The Commerce of British India, Viewed in Its Probable Influence on the Slave Products of the United States." 1841.

Annual Report of the Transactions of the Bombay Chamber of Commerce, 1841–42. Bombay: Courier Press, 1842.

Anti-Slavery Society. *Free Trade and Free Labour, the Surest Means of Abolishing the Slave Trade and Slavery*. London, 1840.

Arnold, R. Arthur. *History of the Cotton Famine: From the Fall of Sumter to the Passing of the Public Works Act*. London: Saunders, Otley, and Co., 1864.

Ashmore, Owen, ed. "The Diary of James Garnett of Low Moor, Clitheroe, 1858–1865, Part 2: The American Civil War and the Cotton Famine." *Transactions of the Historic Society of Lancashire and Chesire* 123 (1972): 105–43.

Ashworth, Henry. *A Tour in the United States, Cuba, and Canada*. Manchester: J. Heywood, 1861.

Babcock, Charles. *British Honduras: Central America, a Plain Statement to Colored People of the U.S. Who Contemplate Emigration*. Salem, Mass.: Published by the author, 1863.

Baille, Rev. John. *What I Saw in Lancashire*. London: James Nisbet, 1862.

Baird Smith, Richard. *Report on the Commercial Condition of the North West Provinces of India*. (East India) *Parliamentary Papers* 29 (1862).

Ball, Charles. *Slavery in the United States: A Narrative of the Life and Adventures of Charles Ball*. New York: John S. Taylor, 1837.

Balston, W. *The Cultivation of Cotton in India: A Letter to H. D. Seymour, Esq., M.P.* London: W. Pl. Metchim and Co., 1863.

Bentinck, William. "Minute of the Governor-General." 30 May 1829, 274–80. In *East India Company's Affairs Report and General Index*.

Bonynge, Francis. *The Future Wealth of America*. New York: Published by the author, 1852.

Bowen, G. F. *Thirty Years of Colonial Government, from the Papers of G. F. Bowen*. Vol. 1. London, 1889.

Boyd, Julian P., ed. Thomas Jefferson to John Adams, 19 November 1785. *The Papers of Thomas Jefferson*. Vol. 9. *November 1785–June 1786*. Princeton: Princeton University Press, 1954.

Brice, A. C. *Indian Cotton Supply, the Only Effectual and Permanent Measure for Relief to Lancashire*. Cornhill: Smith, Elder, and Co., 1863.

British India: Speeches Delivered by Major-General Brigg and George Thompson at the Annual Meeting of the Glasgow Society. Edinburgh: Oliphant, Jun. and Co., 1839.

British India: The Duty and Interest of Great Britain, to Consider the Condition and Claims of Her Possessions in the East. London: Johnston and Barrett, 1839.

Brookes, W. "Cotton and Queensland." Paper read before the Queensland Philosophical Society, 3 July 1860.

Brown, Elizabeth W. *The Whole World Kin: A Pioneer Experience among Remote Tribes and Other Labors of Nathan Brown*. Philadelphia: Hubbard Brothers, 1890.

Brown, F. C. *The Supply of Cotton from India*. Letters of F. C. Brown. London: P. S. King, 1863.

Brown, Henry Box. *Narrative of Henry Box Brown*. Boston: Brown and Stearns, 1849.

Brown, John. *A Memoir of Robert Blincoe, an Orphan Boy*. Manchester: J. Doherty, 1832.

Brown, John. *Slave Life in Georgia: A Narrative of the Life, Sufferings, and Escape of John Brown, a Fugitive Slave, Now in England*. Edited by Louis Alexis Chamerovzow. London: 1855.

Burdon, John Alder, ed. *Archives of British Honduras*. 3 vols. London: Sifton Praed, 1931–35.

Brown, William Wells. *Sketches of Places and People Abroad*. Boston: John P. Jewett and Co., 1855.

Calhoun, John C. *The Papers of John C. Calhoun*. Vols. 1–27. Columbia: University of South Carolina Press, 1959–2003.

Carlyle, Thomas. "Occasional Discourse on the Negro Question." *Fraser's Magazine for Town and Country*, February 1849.

Cassels, Walter R. *Cotton: An Account of Its Culture in the Bombay Presidency*. Bombay, 1862.

Chalmers, George. *An Estimate of the Comparative Wealth of Great Britain, during the Present and Four Preceding Reigns: And of the Losses of Her Trade from Every War since the Revolution*. London, 1786.

Chambers's Encyclopaedia. Vol. 8. London: W. and R. Chambers, 1868.

Chapman, John. *Cotton and Commerce of India*. London: John Chapman, 1851.

Charnock, Richard Stephen. *Verba Nominalia; or, Words Derived from Proper Names*. London: Trubner and Co., 1866.

Chunder, Bholanauth. *Travels of a Hindoo to Various Parts of Bengal and Upper India*. Vol. 1. London: N. Trubner and Co., 1869.

Clarke, C. B. "The Cultivation of Rice in Bengal." *Bulletin of Miscellaneous Information* 24 (1888): 253–80.

Clarkson, Thomas. "Speech of Thomas Clarkson." London, 1840.

Clay, Henry. *The Papers of Henry Clay*. Vol. 9. Edited by Robert Seager II and Melba Porter Hay. Lexington: University Press of Kentucky, 1988.

Cobden, Richard. *The Letters of Richard Cobden, 1815–1847*, Volume 1. Edited by Anthony Howe. Oxford: Oxford University Press, 2007.

Collins, I. G. *Scinde and the Punjaub, the Gems of India, in Respect to Their Vast and Unparalleled Capabilities of Supplanting the Slave States of America, in the Cotton Markets of the World: Or, an Appeal to the English Nation on Behalf of Its Great Cotton Interest, Threatened with Inadequate Supplies of Raw Materials*. Manchester: A. Ireland and Co., 1858.

The Congressional Globe, 37th Cong., 2nd Sess. 2 December 1861 to 17 July 1862. Washington, D.C.: John C. Rives, 1861–62.

The Congressional Globe, 38th Cong., 1st Sess. 7 December 1863 to 4 July 1864. Washington, D.C.: John C. Rives, 1863–64.

The Constitution of Oregon, Framed by the Constitutional Convention Which Met at Salem on Monday August 17 1857. Portland: S. J. McCormick, 1857.

Correspondence on the Cotton Famine, Showing How It Affects the Present Position and Future Prospects of the Common Interests. Manchester: Thomas Sowler and Sons, 1865.

Cotton, J. J. *List of European Tombs in the Bellary District with Inscriptions Thereon.* Collectorate Press: Bellary, 1894.

"The Cotton Famine and the Lancashire Operatives: A Poem by a Factory Girl." Preston: W. and J. Dobson, 1862.

"The Cotton Supply." *House of Commons Debates*, vol. 167, 19 June 1862, cc754-93. Available online at: https://api.parliament.uk/historic-hansard/commons/1862 /jun/19/papers-moved-for.

Cotton Supply Association. "Address: To the Cotton Workers of Great Britain: Sparks among the Cotton." Manchester: John J. Sale, 1859-60[?].

Crooke, William. *The North-western Provinces of India, Their History, Ethnology, and Administration.* London: Methuen and Co., 1897.

Crosthwaite, Charles. *Notes on the North-Western Provinces of India.* London: W. H. Allen, 1869.

Deb, Radhakanta. "On the Culture of Paddy in Twenty Different Districts." *Transactions of the Agricultural and Horticultural Society of India* 2 (1836): 193-95.

De Coin, Robert. *History and Cultivation of Cotton and Tobacco.* London: Chapman and Hall, 1864.

Defoe, Daniel. "Untitled." *Review*, 10 January 1713, 89.

Delany, Martin. *The Condition, Elevation, Emigration, and Destiny of the Colored People of the United States.* N.p., 1852.

Dickinson, John. *The Famine in the North-West Provinces of India: How We Might Have Prevented It, and May Prevent Another.* London: P. S. King, 1861.

Dilke, Charles Wentworth. *Greater Britain: A Record of Travel in English-Speaking Countries during 1866 and 1867.* London: Macmillan, 1868.

Dix, Morgan. *Memoirs of John Adams Dix.* New York: Harper, 1883.

Douglass, Frederick. *Narrative of the Life of Frederick Douglass, an American Slave.* Boston: Anti-slavery Office, 1849.

Easterby, J. H., ed. *The South Carolina Rice Plantation as Revealed in the Papers of Robert F. W. Allston.* Chicago: University of Chicago Press, 1945.

East India (Improvements in Administration). *Return.* 9 February 1858.

East India (Sedashegar Harbour). *Return* in Accounts and Papers, vol. 43. London: House of Commons, 1863.

Ellison, Thomas. *The Cotton Trade of Great Britain.* London: Effingham Wilson, 1886.

An Englishman. *Popular Cookery: Being a Reprint of a Pamphlet Entitled, "Cookery for the Lancashire Operatives," Gratuitously Circulated during the Cotton Famine in 1863.* Manchester: A. Ireland and Co., 1871.

Erickson, Charlotte. "The Encouragement of Emigration by British Trade Unions, 1850-1900." *Population Studies* 3 (1949): 248-73.

Failing, A. D. *Uncle Tom in England; or, A Proof That Black's White: An Echo to the American Uncle Tom.* London: Houlston and Stoneman; J. Bennett, 1852.

Fergusson, W. F. *Letters to Lord Stanley on the Dearth of Cotton, and the Capability of India to Supply the Quantity Required.* London: A. H. Baily and Co., 1863.

Forbes, G. F. *Report on Cotton in the Southern States.* London: Royal Geographical Society, 1866.

A Former Resident of Dacca. *A Descriptive and Historical Account of the Cotton Manufacture of Dacca, in Bengal.* London: John Mortimer, 1851.

Forwood, William B. "The Influence of Price upon the Cultivation and Consumption of Cotton during the Ten Years 1860–70." *Journal of the Statistical Society of London* 33, no. 3 (1870): 366–83.

Ghose, Jogendra Chunder, ed. *The English Works of Raja Rammohun Roy.* Vol. 2. Calcutta: Srikanta Roy, 1901.

Girdlestone, C. E. R. *Report on Past Famines in the North-Western Provinces.* Allahabad: Government Press, 1868.

Gow, Dan. *Civil War in America: A Lecture Delivered in Aid of the Lancashire Relief Fund on November 24, 1862.* Manchester: Abel Heywood, 1862.

Grant, John Peter. *Minute by the Lieutenant-Governor of Bengal on the Report of the Indigo Commission.* Calcutta: Bengal Secretariat Office, 1861.

Half-yearly Report of the Committee of the Bengal Chamber of Commerce, 1854–69.

Hall, Basil. *Travels in North America in the Years 1827 and 1828.* 3 vols. Edinburgh: Cadell and Company, 1829.

Hammond, James. *Anniversary Oration of the State Agricultural Society of South Carolina.* Columbia: A. S. Johnston, 1841.

Hammond, James Henry. *Speech: Delivered at Barnwell C.H., South Carolina*, 29 October 1858, 323–57. In *Selections from the Letters and Speeches of the Hon. James H. Hammond.* New York: John F. Trow and Co., 1866.

Hildreth, Richard. *Archy Moore, the White Slave; or, Memoirs of a Fugitive.* New York and Auburn: Miller, Orton and Mulligan, 1856.

Hobson-Jobson: A Glossary of Anglo-Indian Colloquial Words and Phrases and of Kindred Terms. Edited by Henry Yule and A. C. Burnell. London: John Murray, 1903.

Hope, James L. A. *In Quest of Coolies.* London: Henry S. King and Co., 1872.

House, Albert V., ed. *Planter Management and Capitalism in Ante-bellum Georgia: The Journal of Hugh Fraser Grant Ricegrower.* New York: Columbia University Press, 1954.

"How to Make India Take the Place of America as Our Cotton Field." N.d., 1862–63[?].

Hoyle, William. *An Inquiry into the Causes of the Present Long-Continued Depression in the Cotton Trade.* Manchester: J. Heywood, 1869.

Imperial Gazetteer of India. Vol. 20. Oxford: Clarendon Press, 1908.

"Impolicy of Slavery—East Indian Monopoly, and West Indian Privileges." *Oriental Herald and Colonial Review* 16 (1828): 345.

Jacobs, Harriet Ann. *Incidents in the Life of a Slave Girl.* Boston, 1861.

Julian, George W. *Political Recollections, 1840 to 1872.* Chicago, 1884.

———. *Speeches on Political Questions.* New York: Hurd and Houghton, 1872.

Kappler, Charles J., ed. *Indian Affairs: Laws and Treaties.* Vol. 2. Washington: Government Printing Office, 1904.

Kathman, J. C. *Information for Immigrants into the State of Louisiana*. New Orleans: Republican Office, 1868.

Kemble, Frances Anne. *Journal of a Residence on a Georgian Plantation in 1838–1839*. New York: Harper and Brothers, 1863.

Kempson, M. *Coolie-nama*. Allahabad, India: Government Publishers, 1866.

Khan, Sayyid Ahmed. *The Causes of the Indian Revolt*. Oxford: Oxford University Press, 2000 [1858].

Kilbourne, Richard Holcombe. *Debt, Investment, Slaves: Credit Relations in East Feliciana Parish, Louisiana, 1825–1885*. Tuscaloosa: The University of Alabama Press, 2014.

Knight, Henry. *Letters from the South and West*. Boston: Richardson and Lord, 1824.

A Lady [Maria Eliza Ketelby Rundell and Esther Copley]. *The New London Cookery*. 9th ed. London: Joseph Smith, ca. 1840.

Lang, J. D. *Cooksland in North-Eastern Australia; The Future Cotton-Field of Great Britain: Its Characteristics and Capabilities for European Colonization*. London: Longman, Brown, Green, and Longmans, 1847.

———. *Queensland, Australia: A Highly Eligible Field for Emigration and the Future Cotton-Field of Great Britain*. London: Edward Stanford, 1861.

Leach, Jesse. "Surat Cotton, as It Bodily Affects Operatives in Cotton Mills." *The Lancet* 82 (December 1865): 648–49.

Lees, W. Nassau. *The Land and Labour of India*. London: Williams and Norgate, 1867.

———. *Tea Cultivation, Cotton and Other Agricultural Experiments in India: A Review*. London: W. H. Allen, 1863.

Levi, Leone. "On the Cotton Trade and Manufacture as Affected by the Civil War in America." *Journal of the Statistical Society of London* 26, no. 1 (1863): 26–48.

Lincoln, Abraham. "Letter to the Working-Men of Manchester, England." 19 January 1863. *The Complete Works of Abraham Lincoln*. Vol. 8. New York: The Tandy-Thomas Company, 1905.

Liotard, L. *Memorandum Regarding the Introduction of Carolina Rice into India*. Calcutta: Home and Revenue Department, 1880.

Loring, F. W., and Charles F. Atkinson. *Cotton Culture and the South Considered with Reference to Emigration*. Boston: A. Williams and Co., 1869.

Lyall, Alfred. *Verses Written in India*. London: Kegan, Paul, Trench and Co., 1889.

Majoribanks, Erskine. *Queensland: A Wide Field for the Safe and Profitable Investment of British Capital, More Particularly in the Growth of Cotton*. Edinburgh: Princes Street, 1865.

Mann, J. A. "On the Cotton Trade of India." *Journal of the Royal Asiatic Society of Great Britain* 17 (1860): 346–87.

Marshman, J. C. "Notes on the Cultivation of Cotton in the District of Dharwar; Past Present, and Future." *Journal of the Royal Asiatic Society* 19 (1862): 351–60.

McCall, Hugh. *The Cotton Famine of 1862–63*. Belfast and London: William Mullan and Son, 1881.

McCulloch, John Ramsay. *A Dictionary, Practical, Theoretical and Historical, of Commerce and Commercial Navigation*. London: Longman, Green, 1859.

McHenry, George. *The Cotton Trade: Its Bearing Upon the Prosperity of Great Britain and Commerce of the American Republics.* London: Saunders, Otley, and Co., 1863.

Medlicott, J. G. *Cotton Hand-Book for Bengal.* Calcutta: Savielle and Cranenburg, 1862.

Midnight Notes. *The New Enclosures.* Jamaica Plain, Mass.: Midnight Notes, 1990.

Mill, John Stuart. *The Letters of John Stuart Mill.* Vol. 1. Edited by Hugh S. R. Elliot. London: Longmans, Green, and Co., 1910.

———. *Principles of Political Economy.* Vol. 2. London: Longmans, Green, Reader, and Dyer, 1871.

Mitchell, D. W. *Ten Years in the United States; Being an Englishman's View of Men and Things in the North and South.* London: Smith, Elder, 1862.

Mullick, Kissen Mohun. *Brief History of the Bengal Commerce.* Vol. 2. Calcutta, 1871–72.

Naoroji, Dadabhai. "The Commerce of India." Paper delivered at the Meeting of the Society of Arts. *Journal of the East India Association* 5, no. 2 (15 February 1871): 69–92.

The Negroes at Port Royal: Report of E. L. Pierce, Government Agent, to the Hon. Salmon P. Chase. Boston: R. F. Wallcut, 1862.

Noble, Daniel. "Fluctuations in the Death Rate." Read 23 October 1863. *Transactions of the Manchester Statistical Society*, Session 1863–64, 1–18. Manchester: Manchester Statistical Society.

Northup, Solomon. *Twelve Years a Slave.* Auburn: Derby and Miller, 1853.

Olcott, H. S. "Sugar from the Sorgho." *Southern Cultivator* 15, no. 5 (May 1857): 142–43.

Olmsted, Frederick Law. *The Cotton Kingdom.* Vols. 1 and 2. New York: Mason Brothers, 1862.

———. *A Journey in the Seaboard Slave States.* Vol. 1. New York: Dix and Edwards, 1856.

———. *A Journey through Texas.* New York: Dix, Edwards and Co., 1857.

Palmer, Beverly Wilson, ed. *Selected Papers of Thaddeus Stevens.* Vol. 2. Pittsburgh: University of Pittsburgh Press, 1998.

Parkes, Henry. *Australian Views of England: Eleven Letters Written in the Years 1861 and 1862.* London and Cambridge: Macmillan and Co., 1869.

Partridge, William. "On the Manufacturing of Indigo in This Country." *American Journal of Science and Arts* 18, no. 2 (1830): 242–43.

Pearson, Elizabeth Ware. *Letters from Port Royal Written at the Time of the Civil War.* Boston: W. B. Clarke, 1906.

Pennington, James W. C. *The Fugitive Blacksmith.* London: Charles Gilpin, 1849.

Phillips, Wendell. *Speeches, Lectures and Letters.* Boston: Lee and Shepard, 1894.

Pinckney, Charles. *An Address Delivered in Charleston before the Agricultural Society of South Carolina at Its Anniversary Meeting.* Charleston: A. E. Miller, 1829.

Pollard, Edward Alfred. *Black Diamonds Gathered in the Darkey Homes of the South.* New York: Pudney and Russell, 1859.

Proceedings of the Select Committee on Sugar and Coffee Planting. London: House of Commons, 1848.

Public Health, *Sixth Report of the Medical Officer of the Privy Council*. With Appendix. London: Parliament House of Commons, 1863.

Raghavaiyangar, Srinivasa. *Memorandum of the Progress of the Madras Presidency during the Last Forty Years of British Administration*. Madras: Government Press, 1893.

Raikes, Charles. *Notes on the Northwestern Provinces of India*. London: Chapman and Hall, 1852.

Report from the Select Committee of the House of Lords Appointed to Inquire into the Present State of the Affairs of the East India Company and into the Trade between Great Britain, the East Indies and China. House of Commons, 1830.

Report of the Agricultural and Horticultural Society of India. Calcutta: Bishop's College Press, 1842.

Report of the American International Relief Committee for the Suffering Operatives of Great Britain, 1862–63. New York: C. A. Alvord, 1864.

Report of the British India Society First Annual Meeting. London, 1840.

Report of the Commissioners of Emigration to the General Assembly of Louisiana. New Orleans: A. L. Lee, 1870.

Report of the Revised Land Revenue Settlement of the Rohtak District of the Hissar Division in the Punjab. Lahore: W. Ball, 1880.

Reports of the Committee of the Bengal Chamber of Commerce from 1 May to 31 October 1861. Calcutta: Sanders, Cones, and Co., 1861.

Reports of the Inspectors of Factories for the Half Year Ending 31 October 1861. London: George E. Eyre and William Spottiswoode, 1862.

Reports of the Inspectors of Factories for the Half Year Ending 30 April 1863. London: George E. Eyre and William Spottiswoode, 1863.

Reports of the Inspectors of Factories for the Half Year Ending 31 October 1863. London: George E. Eyre and William Spottiswoode, 1863.

Return of Papers in the Possession of the East India Company Showing Measures Taken since 1836 to Promote the Cultivation of Cotton. House of Commons Parliamentary Papers. Vol. 42. 1847.

Rivett-Carnac, J. H. *Many Memories of Life in India at Home and Abroad*. London: W. Blackwood, 1910.

―――. *Report on Operations in the Cotton Department for the Year 1867*.

Roles, John. *Inside Views of Slavery on Southern Plantations*. New York: John A. Gray and Green, Printers, 1864.

Roper, Moses. *Narrative of the Adventures of Moses Roper, from American Slavery*. London: Darton, Harvey, and Darton, 1837.

Royle, J. Forbes. *Illustrations of the Botany and Other Branches of the Natural History of the Himalayan Mountains, and of the Flora of Cashmere*. Vol. 1. London: W. H. Allen and Co., 1839.

―――. "Memorandum as to the Introduction of Useful Plants into India." *Transactions of the Agricultural and Horticultural Society of India* 3 (1837): 37–42.

―――. *On the Culture and Commerce of Cotton in India*. London: Smith, Elder, and Co., 1851.

Ruffin, Edmund. *Diary of Edmund Ruffin: October 1856–April 1861*. Vol. 1. Edited by William Kauffman Scarborough. Baton Rouge: Louisiana University Press, 1972.

Sanyal, Ram Gopal. *Reminiscences and Anecdotes of Great Men of India*. Vol. 1. Calcutta: Ram Gopal Sanyal,1894.

Sargent, F. W. *England, the United States, and the Southern Confederacy*. London: S. Low, Son & Co. 1863.

Saxton, J. A. *The Cotton Planter's Manual*. New York: C. M. Saxton and Co., 1857.

Schmidt, Louis Bernard. *The Influence of Wheat and Cotton on Anglo-American Relations during the Civil War*. Reprinted from the July 1918 *Journal of History and Politics*. Iowa City: State Historical Society of Iowa, 1919.

Schrottky, Eugene. *The Principles of Rational Agriculture Applied to India and Its Staple Products*. Bombay: Times of India Office, 1876.

The Second Annual Report of the Aborigines Protection Society. London, 1839.

Selections from the Records of Government, NWP. Vol. 1. Allahabad, 1864. *Selections from the Testimony taken by the United States Commission, in Respect to Cotton as a Source of National Revenue*. 39th Cong., 1st Sess. Washington, D.C.: House of Representatives, 1866.

Sheffield, John. *Observations on the Commerce of the American States with Europe and the West Indies*. Philadelphia: Robert Bell, 1783.

Slave Narratives: A Folk History of Slavery in the United States from Interviews with Former Slaves. Washington, D.C.: Works Progress Administration, 1941.

Smith, Samuel. *The Cotton Trade of India Being a Series of Letters Written from Bombay in the Spring of 1863*. London: Effingham Wilson, Royal Exchange, 1863.

————. *My Life-Work*. London: Hodder and Stoughton, 1902.

A South-Carolinian. *A Refutation of the Calumnies Circulated against the Southern and Western States Respecting the Institution and Existence of Slavery*. Charleston, 1822.

Substances Used as Food, as Exemplified in the Great Exhibition. London: Society for Promoting Christian Knowledge, 1854.

Tariff from the White House, Extracts from the Messages. Washington, D.C.: Gray and Clarkson, 1888.

Taylor, William Cooke. *The Hand Book of Silk, Cotton, and Woollen Manufactures*. London: Richard Bentley, 1843.

Thompson, George. *Lectures on British India*. Pawtucket, R.I.: William and Robert Adam, 1840.

Towns, Robert. *South Sea Island Immigration for Cotton Culture: A Letter to the Hon. the Colonial Secretary of Queensland*. Sydney: Reading and Wellbank, [1863].

Townsend, E. D. *Anecdotes of the Civil War in the United States*. New York: D. Appleton and Company, 1884.

Truth, Sojourner. *Narrative of Sojourner Truth*. Edited by Olive Gilbert. Battle Creek, Mich.: Review and Herald Office, 1884.

United States Department of Agriculture. *Annual Report of the Commissioner of Patents, for the Year 1848*. Washington: Wendell and Van Benthuysen, 1849.

Ure, Andrew. *The Philosophy of Manufactures: Or, Exploration of the Scientific, Moral, and Commercial Economy of the Factory System of Great Britain*. London: Charles Knight, 1835.

Wailes, B. L. C. *Report on the Agriculture and Geology of Mississippi*. N.p., 1854.

Watson, J. Forbes. *The Textile Manufactures and the Costumes of the People of India*. 18 vols. London: G. E. Eyre and W. Spottiswoode, 1866.

Watts, Isaac. *The Cotton Supply Association: Its Origin and Progress*. Manchester: Tubbs and Brook, 1871.

Watts, John. *Facts of the Cotton Famine*. London: Simpkin, Marshall, and Co., 1866.

Waugh, Edwin. *Home Life of the Lancashire Factory Folk*. Manchester: John Heywood, 1867.

Wheeler, J. Talboys. *Madras versus America: A Handbook of Cotton Cultivation*. New York: Virtue and Yorston, 1866.

Wight, George. *Hand-book to the Cotton Cultivation in the Madras Presidency*. Madras: J. Higginbotham, 1862.

———. *Queensland: The Field for British Labour and Enterprise, and the Source of England's Cotton Supply*. London: G. Street, 1863.

Wray, Leonard. *The Practical Sugar Planter; A Complete Account of the Cultivation and Manufacture of the Sugar-Cane*. London: Smith, Elder and Co., 1848.

Secondary Published Sources

Adas, Michael. *The Burma Delta: Economic Development and Social Change on an Asian Rice Frontier, 1852–1941*. Madison: University of Wisconsin Press, 1974.

Ahmed, A. F. Salahuddin. *Social Ideas and Social Change in Bengal, 1818–1835*. Leiden: Brill, 1965.

Aisirithe, A. J., and Donald Yacovone, eds. *Wendell Phillips, Social Justice, and the Power of the Past*. Baton Rouge: Louisiana State University Press, 2016.

Albritton, Robert, Bob Jessop, and Richard Westra, eds. *Political Economy and Global Capitalism: The 21st Century, Present and Future*. London: Anthem Press, 2010.

Ali, Tariq O. *A Local History of Global Capital: Jute and Peasant Life in the Bengal Delta*. Princeton: Princeton University Press, 2018.

Ambirajan, Srinivasa. "Political Economy and Indian Famines." *South Asia* 1, no. 1 (1971): 20–28.

Amin, Shahid. *Sugarcane and Sugar in Gorakhpur: An Inquiry into Peasant Production and Capitalist Enterprise in Colonial India*. Oxford: Oxford University Press, 1984.

Anderson, Kevin. *Marx at the Margins: On Nationalism, Ethnicity, and Non-Western Societies*. Chicago: University of Chicago Press, 2016.

Arenson, Adam, and Andrew R. Graybill, eds. *Civil War Wests: Testing the Limits of the United States*. Oakland: University of California Press, 2015.

Arneil, Barbara. "The Wild Indian's Venison: Locke's Theory of Property and English Colonialism in America." *Political Studies* 44 (1996): 60–74.

Arnold, David. "Agriculture and 'Improvement' in Early Colonial India: A Prehistory of Development." *Journal of Agrarian Change* 5, no. 4 (2005): 505–25.

———. *The Tropics and the Traveling Gaze: India, Landscape, and Science, 1800–56*. Seattle: University of Washington Press, 2006.

Arrighi, Giovanni. "Spatial and Other 'Fixes' of Historical Capitalism." *Journal of World-Systems Research* 10, no. 2 (2004): 527–39.

Arrighi, Giovanni, Terence K. Hopkins, and Immanuel Wallerstein. "The Liberation of Class Struggle?" *Review* 10, no. 3 (1987): 403–24.

Asaka, Ikuko. "'Our Brethren in the West Indies': Self-Emancipated People in Canada and the Antebellum Politics of Diaspora and Empire." *Journal of African American History* 97, no. 3 (2012): 219–39.

———. *Tropical Freedom: Climate, Settler Colonialism, and Black Exclusion in the Age of Emancipation.* Durham: Duke University Press, 2017.

Austin, Peter E. *Baring Brothers and the Birth of Modern Finance.* London: Routledge, 2016.

Bagchi, Amiya. *Colonialism and Indian Economy.* New Delhi: Oxford University Press, 2010.

Bailey, Anne C. *The Weeping Time: Memory and the Largest Slave Auction in American History.* Cambridge: Cambridge University Press, 2017.

Bailey, M. Thomas. *Reconstruction in Indian Territory: A Story of Avarice, Discrimination, and Opportunism.* Post Washington, N.Y.: Kennikat Press, 1972.

Bailey, Ronald. "The Other Side of Slavery: Black Labor, Cotton, and Textile Industrialization in Great Britain and the United States." *Agricultural History* 68, no. 2 (1994): 35–50.

Baker, H. Robert. *Prigg v. Pennsylvania: Slavery, the Supreme Court, and the Ambivalent Constitution.* Lawrence: University Press of Kansas, 2012.

Bakhtin, Mikhail. *Speech Genres and Other Late Essays.* Edited by Carly Emerson and Michael Holquist. Austin: University of Texas Press, 1986.

Ballagh, James Curtis, ed. *South in the Building of a Nation.* Vol. 5. Richmond: Southern Historical Publication Society, 1909.

Ballantyne, Tony. "Remaking the Empire from Newgate: Wakefield's *A Letter from Sydney.*" In *Ten Books that Shaped the British Empire,* edited by Antoinette Burton and Isabel Hofmeyr, 239–49. Durham: Duke University Press, 2014.

Banaji, Jairus. *Theory and History: Essays on Modes of Production and Exploitation.* Leiden: Brill, 2010.

Banerjee, Sukanya. "Who, or What, Is Victorian? Ecology, Indigo, and the Transimperial." *Victorian Studies* 58, no. 2 (2016): 213–23.

Banerjee, Tarasankar. "American Cotton Experiments in India and the American Civil War." *Journal of Indian Studies* 37 (1969): 425–32.

Banerjei, N. N. *Monograph on the Cotton Fabrics of Bengal.* Calcutta: Bengal Secretariat Press, 1898.

Banivanua Mar, Tracey. *Violence and Colonial Dialogue.* Honolulu: University of Hawai'i Press, 2007.

Banner, Stuart. "Why *Terra Nullius*? Anthropology and Property Law in Early Australia." *Law and History Review* 23, no. 1 (2005): 95–131.

Baptist, Edward. *The Half Has Never Been Told: Slavery and the Making of American Capitalism.* New York: Basic Books, 2014.

———. "Toxic Debt, Liar Loans, and Securitized Human Beings: The Panic of 1837 and the Fate of Slavery." *Common-Place* 10, no. 3 (2010). http://www.common-place-archives.org/vol-10/no-03/baptist/.

Baron, Harold M. "The Demand for Black Labor: Historical Notes on the Political Economy of Racism." *Radical America* 5 (1971): 1–46.

Basler, Roy, ed. *The Collected Works of Abraham Lincoln.* Vol. 5. New Brunswick: Rutgers University Press, 1953.

Bayly, C. A. "The Age of Hiatus: The North Indian Economy and Society, 1830–1850." In *Trade and Finance in Colonial India, 1750–1860*, edited by Asiya Siddiqi, 218–49. Delhi: Oxford University Press, 1995.

———. *The Birth of the Modern World, 1780–1914: Global Connections and Comparisons*. Malden, Mass.: Blackwell, 2004.

———. *Indian Society and the Making of British India*. Cambridge: Cambridge University Press, 1987.

———. *Rulers, Townsmen, and Bazaars: North Indian Society in the Age of British Expansion, 1770–1870*. Cambridge: Cambridge University Press, 1983.

Bearce, George Donham. *British Attitudes toward India, 1784–1858*. Oxford: Oxford University Press, 1961.

Beckert, Sven. "American Danger: United States Empire, Eurafrica, and the Territorialization of Industrial Capitalism, 1870–1950." *American Historical Review* 112, no. 4 (2017): 1139–40.

———. "Emancipation and Empire: Reconstructing the Worldwide Web of Cotton Production in the Age of the American Civil War." *American Historical Review* 109, no. 5 (2004): 1405–38.

———. *Empire of Cotton*. New York: Knopf, 2014.

Beckert, Sven, and Seth Rockman. *Slavery's Capitalism: A New History of American Economic Development*. Philadelphia: University of Pennsylvania Press, 2016.

Behal, Rana P., and Prabhu Mohapatra. "'Tea and Money Versus Human Life': The Rise and Fall of the Indenture System in the Assam Tea Plantations, 1840–1908." *Journal of Peasant Studies* 19, nos. 3–4 (1992): 142–72.

Belko, Stephen W. *The Triumph of the Antebellum Free Trade Movement*. Gainesville: University Press of Florida, 2012.

Bell, Duncan. *The Idea of Greater Britain: Empire and the Future of World Order, 1860–1900*. Princeton: Princeton University Press, 2007.

Bell, Karen. "'The Ogeechee Troubles': Federal Land Restoration and the 'Lived Realities' of Temporary Proprietors, 1865–68." *Georgia Historical Quarterly* 85, no. 3 (2001): 375–97.

Bennett, Lerone. "Was Abe Lincoln a White Supremacist?" *Ebony* 23, no. 4 (1968): 35–40, 42.

Berlin, Ira, and Herbert G. Gutman. "Natives and Immigrants, Free Men and Slaves: Urban Workingmen in the Antebellum American South." *American Historical Review* 88, no. 5 (1983): 1175–1200.

Berlin, Ira, Barbara J. Fields, Thavolia Glymph, Joseph P. Reidy, and Leslie S. Rowland. *Freedom: A Documentary History of Emancipation, 1861–1867*. Vol. 1, *The Destruction of Slavery*. New York: Cambridge University Press, 1985.

Berry, Daina Ramey. *The Price for Their Pound of Flesh: The Value of the Enslaved, from Womb to Grave, in the Building of a Nation*. Boston: Beacon Press, 2017.

———. *"Swing the Sickle for the Harvest Is Ripe": Gender and Slavery in Antebellum Georgia*. Urbana: University of Illinois Press, 2007.

Best, Stephen M. *The Fugitive's Properties: Law and the Poetics of Possession*. Chicago: University of Chicago Press, 2004.

Bhatia, B. M. *Famines in India: Study in Some Aspects of the Economic History of India, 1860–1945*. Bombay: Asia Publishing House, 1963.

Bhattacharyya, Debjani. *Empire and Ecology in the Bengal Delta: The Making of Calcutta*. Cambridge: Cambridge University Press, 2018.

Bhattacharya, Neeladri. *The Great Agrarian Conquest: The Colonial Reshaping of a Rural World*. Ranikhet, India: Permanent Black, 2018.

Bhattacharya, Sabyasachi. *The Financial Foundations of the British Raj: Ideas and Interests in the Reconstruction of Indian Public Finance, 1858–72*. Hyderabad, India: Orient Longman, 2005.

———. "Laissez Faire in India." *Indian Economic and Social History Review* 2, no. 1 (1965): 1–22.

Bhattacharya, Subhas. "Indigo Planters, Ram Mohan Roy and the 1833 Charter Act." *Social Scientist* 4, no. 3 (1975): 56–65.

Bhattacharya, Tithi. *The Sentinels of Culture: Class, Education, and the Colonial Intellectual in Bengal (1848–85)*. Oxford: Oxford University Press, 2005.

Birla, Ritu. "Failure via Schumpeter: Market Globality, Empire, and the End(s) of Capitalism." *Social Research* 83, no. 3 (2016): 645–71.

———. *Stages of Capital: Law, Culture, and Market Governance in Late Colonial India*. Durham: Duke University Press, 2008.

Blackburn, Robin. *Marx and Lincoln: An Unfinished Revolution*. London: Verso, 2011.

Blackett, Richard. *Beating against the Barriers: Biographical Essays in Nineteenth-Century Afro-American History*. Baton Rouge: Louisiana State University Press, 1986.

———. *Building an Antislavery Wall: Black Americans in the Atlantic Abolitionist Movement, 1830–1860*. Ithaca: Cornell University Press, 1983.

———. *The Captive's Quest for Freedom: Fugitive Slaves, the 1850 Fugitive Slave Law, and the Politics of Slavery*. New York: Cambridge University Press, 2018.

———. "Lincoln and Colonization." *OAH Magazine of History*, October 2007, 19–22.

———. "Martin R. Delany and Robert Campbell: Black Americans in Search of an African Colony." *Journal of Negro History* 62, no. 1 (1977): 1–25.

Blackmar, Elizabeth. "Inheriting Property and Debt: From Family Security to Corporate Accumulation." In *Capitalism Takes Command: The Social Transformation of Nineteenth-Century America*, edited by Michael Zakim and Gary J. Kornblith, 93–117. Chicago: University of Chicago Press, 2012.

Blassingame, John. *Slave Testimony: Two Centuries of Letters, Speeches, Interviews, and Autobiographies*. Baton Rouge: Louisiana State University Press, 1977.

Block, Sharon. *Colonial Complexions: Race and Bodies in Eighteenth-Century America*. Philadelphia: University of Pennsylvania Press, 2018.

Bogues, Anthony. "We Who Were Slaves." *Souls* 20, no. 4 (2019): 368–74.

Bond, Patrick. "Volatile, Uneven, and Combined Capitalism." In *Political Economy and Global Capitalism: The 21st Century, Present and Future*, edited by Robert Albritton, Bob Jessop, and Richard Westra, 127–58. London: Anthem Press, 2010.

Bordiga, Amadeo. "Doctrine of the Body Possessed by the Devil." *Battaglia Communista* 21 (1951). https://www.marxists.org/archive/bordiga/works/1951/doctrine.htm.

———. "Murder of the Dead." *Battaglia Communista* 24 (1951). https://www.marxists.org/archive/bordiga/works/1951/murder.htm.

Borpujari, Jitendra G. "Indian Cottons and the Cotton Famine, 1860–65." *Indian Economic and Social History Review* 10, no. 1 (1973): 37–49.

Bose, Sugata. *Peasant Labour and Colonial Capital*. Cambridge: Cambridge University Press, 2008.

Bosma, Ulbe. *The Sugar Plantation in India and Indonesia — Industrial Production, 1770–2010*. Cambridge: Cambridge University Press, 2013.

Boston, Ray. *British Chartists in America, 1839–1900*. Manchester: Rowman and Littlefield, 1971.

Boyer, G. R. "Poor Relief, Informal Assistance, and Short Time during the Lancashire Cotton Famine." *Explorations in Economic History* 34, no. 1 (1997): 56–76.

Brady, Patrick. "The Slave Trade and Sectionalism in South Carolina, 1787–1808." *Journal of Southern History* 38, no. 4 (1972): 601–20.

Bray, Francesca, Peter A. Coclanis, Dagmar Schaefer, and Edda Fields-Black, eds. *Rice: Global Networks and New Histories*. Cambridge: Cambridge University Press, 2015.

Breen, Timothy. *The Marketplace of Revolution: How Consumer Politics Shaped American Independence*. New York: Oxford University Press, 2004.

Brewster, Lawrence Fay. *Summer Migrations and Resorts of South Carolina Low-Country Planters*. New York: AMS Press, 1947.

Bronstein, Jamie L. *Land Reform and Working-Class Experience in Britain and the United States, 1800–1862*. Stanford: Stanford University Press, 1999.

Brown, David. "Attacking Slavery from Within: The Making of 'The Impending Crisis of the South.'" *Journal of Southern History* 70, no. 3 (2004): 541–76.

Brown, Vincent. *The Reaper's Garden: Death and Power in the World of Atlantic Slavery*. Cambridge, Mass.: Harvard University Press, 2008.

Buck, Norman S. *The Development of the Organisation of Anglo-American Trade, 1800–1850*. New Haven: Yale University Press, 1925.

Bulmer-Thomas, Barbara, and Victor Bulmer-Thomas. *The Economic History of Belize: From the Seventeenth Century to Post-Independence*. Benque Viejo del Carmen, Belize: Cubola Books, 2012.

Burton, Antoinette. "Tongues Untied: Lord Salisbury's 'Black Man' and the Boundaries of Imperial Democracy." *Comparative Studies in Society and History* 42, no. 3 (2000): 632–61.

———. *The Trouble with Empire: Challenges to Modern British Imperialism*. Oxford: Oxford University Press, 2015.

———. "Who Needs the Nation? Interrogating 'British' History." *Journal of Historical Sociology* 10, no. 3 (1997): 227–48.

Burton, Antoinette, and Isabel Hofmeyr, eds. *Ten Books That Shaped the British Empire*. Durham: Duke University Press, 2014.

Byrd, Alexander X. *Captives and Voyagers: Black Migrants across the Eighteenth-Century British Atlantic World*. Baton Rouge: Louisiana State University Press, 2008.

Byrd, Jodi. "Follow the Typical Signs: Settler Sovereignty and Its Discontents." *Settler Colonial Studies* 4, no. 2 (2013): 151–54.

———. "A Return to the South." *American Quarterly* 66, no. 3 (2014): 609–20.

———. *Transit of Empire: Indigenous Critiques of Colonialism*. Minneapolis: University of Minnesota Press, 2011.

Byrd, Jodi, Alyosha Goldstein, Jodi Melamed, and Chandan Reddy. "Predatory Value: Economies of Dispossession and Disturbed Relationalities." *Social Text 36*, no. 2 (2018): 1–18.

Cal, Angel Eduardo. "Anglo Maya Contact in Northern Belize: A Study of British Policy toward the Maya during the Caste War of Yucatán, 1847-72." Master's thesis, University of Calgary, 1985.

Campbell, Charles P. "Bombay Scarcity Relief Policies in the Age of Reform, 1820–40." Ph.D. diss., University of Canterbury, 2009.

Campbell, Edward D. C., and Kym Rice, eds. *A Woman's War: Southern Women, Civil War, and the Confederate Legacy*. Charlottesville: University of Virginia Press, 1996.

Campbell, Gwyn, ed. *Abolition and Its Aftermath in Indian Ocean Africa and Asia*. New York: Routledge, 2005.

Campbell, Randolph B. *An Empire for Slavery: The Peculiar Institution in Texas, 1821–1865*. Baton Rouge: Louisiana State University Press, 1989.

Carney, Judith. *Black Rice: The African Origins of Rice Cultivation in the Americas*. Cambridge, Mass.: Harvard University Press, 2009.

Carrington, Selwyn H. H. "The American Revolution and the British West Indies' Economy." *Journal of Interdisciplinary History* 17, no. 4 (1987): 823–50.

———. *The British West Indies during the American Revolution*. Providence, R.I.: Foris Publications, 1988.

Cateau, Heather, and S. H. H. Carrington. *Capitalism and Slavery Fifty Years Later: Eric Eustace Williams—A Reassessment of the Man and His Work*. New York: Peter Lang, 2000.

Cha-Jua, Sundiata Keita. *America's First Black Town, Brooklyn, Illinois, 1830–1915*. Urbana: University of Illinois Press, 2000.

Chakrabarty, Dipesh. "Marx after Marxism: Subaltern Histories and the Question of Difference." *Polygraph* 6-7 (1993): 10–16.

———. *Provincializing Europe: Postcolonial Thought and Historical Difference*. Princeton: Princeton University Press, 2008.

Chaplin, Joyce. *An Anxious Pursuit: Agricultural Innovation and Modernity in the Lower South, 1730–1815*. Chapel Hill: University of North Carolina Press, 1993.

———. "Creating a Cotton South in Georgia and South Carolina." *Journal of Southern History* 57, no. 2 (1991): 171–200.

Chatterjee, Indrani. "Abolition by Denial: The South Asian Example." In *Abolition and Its Aftermath in Indian Ocean Africa and Asia*, edited by Gwyn Campbell, 150–62. New York: Routledge, 2005.

Chatterjee, Partha. *The Nation and Its Fragments: Colonial and Postcolonial Histories*. Princeton: Princeton University Press, 2007.

Chattopadhyay, Gautam, ed. *Bengal: Early Nineteenth Century Documents*. Calcutta: Research India Publications, 1978.

Cheng, Siok-Hwa. *The Rice Industry of Burma, 1852–1940*. Kuala Lumpur, Malaysia: University of Malay Press, 1968.

Chomsky, Carol. "The United States–Dakota War Trials: A Study in Military Injustice." *Stanford Law Review* 43, no. 1 (1990): 13–98.

Chowdhury, Benoy *Growth of Commercial Agriculture in Bengal (1757–1900)*. Calcutta: R. K. Maitra, 1964.

Ciambala, Paul A. "The Freedmen's Bureau, the Freedmen, and Sherman's Grant in Reconstruction Georgia, 1865–1867." *Journal of Southern History* 55, no. 4 (1989): 597–632.

Clampitt, Bradley R., ed. *The Civil War and Reconstruction in Indian Territory*. Lincoln: University of Nebraska Press, 2015.

Clapham, J. H. *An Economic History of Modern Britain*. Vols. 1 and 2. Cambridge: Cambridge University Press, 1930–32.

Clark-Pujara, Christy. *Dark Work: The Business of Slavery in Rhode Island*. New York: New York University Press, 2016.

Clegern, Wayne M. *British Honduras: Colonial Dead End, 1859–1900*. Baton Rouge: Louisiana University Press, 1967.

Clegg, John. "Capitalism and Slavery." *Critical Historical Studies* 2, no. 2 (2015): 281–303.

Clifton, James M. "Charles Manigault's Essay on the Economics of Milling Rice [1852]." *Agricultural History* 52, no. 1 (1978): 104–10.

———. "Jehossee Island: The Antebellum South's Largest Rice Plantation." *Agricultural History* 59, no. 1 (1985): 56–65.

———. *Life and Labor on Argyle Island: Letters and Documents of a Savannah Rice Plantation, 1833–1867*. Savannah: The Beehive Press, 1978.

———. "The Rice Driver: His Role in Slave Management." *South Carolina Historical Magazine* 82 (1981): 331–53.

Coclanis, Peter A. "Distant Thunder: The Creation of a World Market in Rice and the Transformations It Wrought." *American Historical Review* 98, no. 4 (1993): 1050–78.

Cohn, Bernard. *Colonialism and Its Forms of Knowledge: The British in India*. Princeton: Princeton University Press, 1996.

Cole, Fred C. "The Texas Career of Thomas Affleck." Ph.D. diss., Louisiana State University, 1942.

Collins, Patricia Hill. *Black Feminist Thought*. New York: Routledge, 2000.

Communist Party History Group. "Our History: The Lancashire Cotton Famine." No. 24. London: Communist Party History Group, 1961.

Connolly, Brian. *Domestic Intimacies: Incest and the Liberal Subject in Nineteenth-Century America*. Philadelphia: University of Pennsylvania Press, 2014.

Connolly, Nathan. *A World More Concrete: Real Estate and the Remaking of Jim Crow South Florida*. Chicago: University of Chicago Press, 2014.

Coon, David L. "Eliza Lucas Pinckney and the Reintroduction of Indigo Culture in South Carolina." *Journal of Southern History* 42, no. 1 (1976): 61–76.

Cooper, Frederick, and Ann Laura Stoler, eds. *Tensions of Empire: Colonial Cultures in a Bourgeois World*. Berkeley: University of California Press, 1997.

Copeland, R. W. "The Nomenclature of Enslaved Africans as Real Property or Chattels Personal: Legal Fiction, Judicial Interpretation, Legislative Designation, or Was a Slave a Slave by Any Other Name." *Journal of Black Studies* 40, no. 5 (2010): 946-59.

Coryell, Janet L. "'The Lincoln Colony': Aaron Columbus Burr's Proposed Colonization of British Honduras." *Civil War History* 43, no. 1 (1997): 5-16.

Coulthard, Glen. *Red Skin, White Masks: Rejecting the Colonial Politics of Recognition*. Minneapolis: University of Minnesota Press, 2014.

Cowen, Deborah. *The Deadly Life of Logistics*. Minneapolis: University of Minnesota Press, 2014.

Cox, Lawanda. "The Promise of Land for the Freedmen." *Mississippi Valley Historical Review* 45, no. 3 (1958): 413-40.

Cox, Oliver Cromwell. *Capitalism as a System*. New York: Monthly Review Press, 1964.

Crouch, Barry. *The Dance of Freedom: Texas African Americans during Reconstruction*. Austin: University of Texas Press, 2007.

Crowley, John E. "Neo-mercantilism and *The Wealth of Nations*: British Commercial Policy after the American Revolution." *Historical Journal* 33, no. 2 (1990): 339-60.

Daniel, E. Valentine, Henry Bernstein, and Tom Brass, eds. *Plantations, Proletarians, and Peasants in Colonial Asia*. London: Frank Cass, 1992.

Das, Nabagopal. *Banking and Industrial Finance in India*. Calcutta: Modern Publisher's Syndicate, 1936.

David, C. W. A. "The Fugitive Slave Law of 1793 and Its Antecedents." *Journal of Negro History* 9, no. 1 (1924): 18-25.

Davis, Mike. *Late Victorian Holocausts: El Niño Famines and the Making of the Third World*. New York: Verso, 2001.

Day, Iyko. *Alien Capital: Asian Racialization and the Logic of Settler Colonial Capitalism*. Durham: Duke University Press, 2016.

Deloria, Vine, Jr. *Behind the Trail of Broken Treaties: An Indian Declaration of Independence*. New York: Delacorte Press, 1974.

Deutsch, Eberhard P. "The Constitutional Controversy over the Louisiana Purchase." *American Bar Association Journal* 53, no. 1 (1967): 50-57.

Dierksheide, Christa. "'The Great Improvement and Civilization of that Race'": Jefferson and the 'Amelioration' of Slavery, 1770-1826." *Early American Studies* 6, no. 1 (Spring 2008): 165-97.

Donald, David Herbert. *Lincoln*. New York: Simon and Schuster, 1995.

Donald, Diana. "Pangs Watched in Perpetuity: Sir Edwin Landseer's Pictures of Dying Deer and the Ethos of Victorian Sportsmanship." In *Killing Animals*, edited by the Animal Studies Group, 50-68. Urbana: University of Illinois Press, 2006.

Downs, Jim. *Sick from Freedom: African-American Illness and Suffering during the Civil War and Reconstruction*. New York: Oxford University Press, 2012.

Doyle, Don, Jörg Nagler, and Marcus Gräser, eds. *The Transnational Significance of the American Civil War*. New York: Palgrave, 2016.

Drago, Edmund L. Introduction to *Broke by the War: Letters of a Slave Trader*, edited by Edmund L. Drago, 1-33. Columbia: University of South Carolina Press, 1991.

Draper, Nicholas. *The Price of Emancipation: Slave-Ownership, Compensation, and British Society at the End of Slavery*. Cambridge: Cambridge University Press, 2009.

Drescher, Seymour. "British Capitalism and British Slavery." *History and Theory* 26, no. 2 (1987): 179–96.

———. *The Mighty Experiment: Free Labor vs. Slavery in British Emancipation*. New York: Oxford University Press, 2002.

Dubois, Laurent. *Avengers of the New World: The Story of the Haitian Revolution*. Cambridge, Mass.: Harvard University Press, 2004.

Du Bois, W. E. B. "An Appeal to the World: A Statement of Denial of Human Rights to Minorities in the Case of Citizens of Negro Descent in the United States of America and an Appeal to the United Nations for Redress." New York: NAACP, 1947.

———. *Black Reconstruction in America, 1860–1880*. New York: Harcourt, Brace and Company, 1935. Reprint, New York: The Free Press, 1998.

———. *Dusk of Dawn: An Essay toward an Autobiography of a Race Concept*. New York: Schocken Books, 1940.

———. "The Freedmen's Bureau." *Atlantic Monthly*, March 1901, 354–65.

———. *The Gift of Black Folk*. Boston: Stratford, 1924.

———. "Karl Marx and the Negro." *The Crisis*, March 1933, 55–56.

———. "Marxism and the Negro Problem." *The Crisis*, May 1933, 103–4, 118.

———. *The Negro*. New York: Henry Holt, 1915.

———. *The Philadelphia Negro*. 1899. Reprint, New York: Oxford University Press, 2007.

———. *The Souls of Black Folk*. Chicago: A. C. McClurg, 1903. Reprint, New York: Blue Heron Press, 1953.

———. *The Suppression of the African Slave Trade to the United States of America, 1638–1870*. New York: Longmans, Green and Co., 1896. Reprint, New York: Social Science Press, 1954.

———. *The World and Africa*. New York: International Publishers, 1965.

Dunbar-Ortiz, Roxanne. *An Indigenous Peoples' History of the United States*. Boston: Beacon Press, 2014.

Dusinberre, William. *Them Dark Days: Slavery in the American Rice Swamps*. New York: Oxford University Press, 1996.

Dutt, R. C. *Famines and Land Assessments in India*. London: Kegan Paul, Trench, Trübner, 1900.

Eacott, Jonathan. *Selling Empire: India in the Making of Britain and America, 1600–1830*. Chapel Hill: University of North Carolina Press, 2017.

East, Dennis. "The New York and Mississippi Land Company and the Panic of 1837." *Journal of Mississippi History* 33, no. 4 (1971): 299–331.

Edelson, S. Max. *Plantation Enterprise in Colonial South Carolina*. Cambridge, Mass.: Harvard University Press, 2011.

Edwards, Steve. "Factory and Fantasy in Andrew Ure." *Journal of Design History* 14, no. 1 (2001): 17–33.

Efford, Alison. "New Citizens: German Immigrants, African Americans, and the

Reconstruction of Citizenship, 1865-1877." Ph.D. diss., Ohio State University, 2008.

Egerton, Douglas R. *He Shall Go Out Free: The Lives of Denmark Vesey*. Lanham, Md.: Rowman and Littlefield, 2004.

Einhorn, Robin L. *American Taxation, American Slavery*. Chicago: University of Chicago Press, 2008.

Eltis, David. "The Traffic in Slaves between the British West Indian Colonies, 1807-1833." *Economic History Review* 25, no. 1 (1972): 55-64.

Eltis, David, Philip Morgan, and David Richardson. "Agency and Diaspora in Atlantic History: Reassessing the African Contribution to Rice Cultivation in the Americas." *American Historical Review* 12, no. 5 (2007): 1329-58.

————. "Black, Brown, or White? Color-Coding American Commercial Rice Cultivation with Slave Labor." *American Historical Review* 115, no. 1 (2010): 164-71.

Emmanuel, Arghiri. "White-Settler Colonialism and the Myth of Investment Imperialism." *New Left Review* 73 (May June 1972): 35-57.

Engels, Friedrich. *The Condition of the Working-Class in England*. New York: Charles Scribner's Sons, 1892.

Enstad, Nan. "The 'Sonorous Summons' of the New History of Capitalism, or, What Are We Talking about When We Talk about Economy?" *Modern American History* 2, no. 1 (2019): 83-95.

Ericson, David F. "The Nullification Crisis, American Republicanism, and the Force Bill Debate." *Journal of Southern History* 61, no. 2 (1995): 249-70.

Evans, Raymond. *A History of Queensland*. Cambridge: Cambridge University Press, 2007.

————. "Plenty Shoot 'Em: The Destruction of Aboriginal Societies along the Queensland Frontier." In *Genocide and Settler Society: Frontier Violence and Stolen Indigenous Children in Australia*, edited by D. Moses, 150-73. New York: Berghahn Books, 2004.

Fanon, Frantz. *Black Skin, White Masks*. 1952. Reprint, London: Pluto Press, 2008.

————. *The Wretched of the Earth*. New York: Grove Weidenfeld, 1963.

Farnie, D. A. "The Cotton Famine in Great Britain." In *Great Britain and Her World, 1750-1914: Essays in Honour of W. O. Henderson*, edited by Barrie M. Ratcliffe, 153-78. Manchester: Manchester University Press, 1975.

————. *The English Cotton Industry and the World Market, 1815-1896*. Oxford: Clarendon Press 1979.

Farrar, W. V. "Andrew Ure, F.R.S., and the Philosophy of Manufactures." *Notes and Records of the Royal Society of London* 27, no. 2 (1973): 299-324.

Faust, Drew Gilpin. *James Henry Hammond and the Old South: A Design for Mastery*. Baton Rouge: LSU Press, 1985.

Ferreira, Roquinaldo. *Cross-Cultural Exchange in the Atlantic World: Angola and Brazil during the Era of the Slave Trade*. Cambridge: Cambridge University Press, 2014.

Ferrer, Ada. *Freedom's Mirror: Cuba and Haiti in the Age of Revolution*. Cambridge: Cambridge University Press, 2014.

Fieldhouse, D. K. *Economics and Empire, 1830–1914*. Ithaca: Cornell University Press, 1973.

Fields-Black, Edda L. *Deep Roots: Rice Farmers in West Africa and the African Diaspora*. Bloomington: Indiana University Press, 2008.

Fierce, Milfred C. "Black Struggle for Land during Reconstruction." *Black Scholar* 5, no. 5 (1974): 13–18.

Finger, John R. "Termination and the Eastern Band of Cherokees." *American Indian Quarterly* 15, no. 1 (Spring 1991): 153–70.

Finkelman, Paul. "Slavery and the Northwest Ordinance: A Study in Ambiguity." *Journal of the Early Republic* 6, no. 4 (1986): 343–70.

Flood, Gavin, ed. *The Blackwell Companion to Hinduism*. Malden, Mass.: Blackwell, 2003.

Florio, Christopher. "From Poverty to Slavery: Abolitionists, Overseers, and the Global Struggle for Labor in India." *Journal of American History* 102, no. 4 (2016): 1005–24.

Fogel, Robert, and Stanley Engerman. *Time on the Cross: The Economics of American Negro Slavery*. New York: Little, Brown, 1974.

Follett, Richard. *The Sugar Masters: Planters and Slaves in Louisiana's Cane World, 1820–1860*. Baton Rouge: Louisiana State University Press, 2005.

Foner, Eric. *Free Soil, Free Labor, Free Men: The Ideology of the Republican Party before the Civil War*. Oxford: Oxford University Press, 1995.

———. *Politics and Ideology in the Age of the Civil War*. Oxford: Oxford University Press, 1980.

———. *Reconstruction: America's Unfinished Revolution, 1863–1877*. New York: Harper & Row, 1988.

Foner, Philip S., ed. *Life and Writings of Frederick Douglass*. Vols. 1–5. New York: International Publishers, 1950–1975.

Forbes, Ella. "African-American Resistance to Colonization." *Journal of Black Studies* 21, no. 2 (1990): 210–23.

Ford, Lacy K. *Deliver Us from Evil: The Slavery Question in the Old South*. Oxford: Oxford University Press, 2009.

Fowler, Loretta. "Arapaho and Cheyenne Perspectives: From the 1851 Treaty to the Sand Creek Massacre." *American Indian Quarterly* 39, no. 4 (2015): 364–90.

Franklin, John Hope. *From Slavery to Freedom: A History of Negro Americans*. 3rd ed. New York: Vintage, 1967.

Franklin, John Hope, and Loren Schweninger. *Runaway Slaves: Rebels on the Plantation*. Oxford: Oxford University Press, 1999.

Fredrickson, George. *Big Enough to Be Inconsistent*. Cambridge: Harvard University Press, 2009.

———. *Black Image in the White Mind: Debate on Afro-American Character and Destiny, 1817–1914*. New York: Harper and Row, 1971.

Freedgood, Elaine. *Ideas in Things: Fugitive Meaning in the Victorian Novel*. Chicago: University of Chicago Press, 2010.

Freehling, William W. *Prelude to Civil War: The Nullification Controversy in South Carolina, 1816–1836*. New York: Harper and Row Publishers, 1965.

Frykenberg, Robert. "Constructions of Hinduism at the Nexus of History and Religion." *Journal of Interdisciplinary History* 23, no. 3 (1993): 523–50.

Fullilove, Courtney. *The Profit of the Earth: The Global Seeds of American Agriculture*. Chicago: University of Chicago Press, 2017.

Gallagher, John, and Ronald Robinson. "The Imperialism of Free Trade." *Economic History Review* 5, no. 1 (1953): 1–15.

Garrigus, John. "Blue and Brown: Contraband Indigo and the Rise of a Free Colored Planter Class in French Saint-Domingue." *The Americas* 50 (October 1993): 233–63.

Garrison, Tim Alan. *The Legal Ideology of Removal: The Southern Judiciary and the Sovereignty of Native American Nations*. Athens: University of Georgia Press, 2002.

Genovese, Eugene D. *The Political Economy of Slavery*. 1961. Reprint, New York: Vintage, 1965.

———. *Roll, Jordan, Roll: The World the Slaves Made*. New York: Pantheon Books, 1974.

Ghorashi, Reza. "Marx on Free Trade." *Science and Society* 59, no. 1 (1995): 38–51.

Ghosal, H. R. *Economic Transition in the Bengal Presidency, 1793–1833*. Calcutta: Firma K. L. Mukhopadhyay, 1966.

Gibson, J. R. *European Settlement and Development in North America*. Toronto: University of Toronto Press, 1978.

Gidwani, Vinay. "'Waste' and the Permanent Settlement in Bengal." *Economic and Political Weekly*, 25 January 1992, PE-39–46.

Gilmore, Ruth Wilson. *Golden Gulag: Prisons, Surplus, Crisis, and Opposition in Globalizing California*. Berkeley: University of California Press, 2007.

Gilroy, Paul. *The Black Atlantic: Modernity and Double Consciousness*. London: Verso, 2007.

Gleeson, David T., and Simon Lewis, eds. *The Civil War as Global Conflict: Transnational Meanings of the American Civil War*. Columbia: University of South Carolina Press, 2014.

Glymph, Thavolia. "Du Bois's *Black Reconstruction* and Slave Women's War for Freedom." *South Atlantic Quarterly* 112, no. 3 (2013): 489–505.

———. *Out of the House of Bondage: The Transformation of the Plantation Household*. Cambridge: Cambridge University Press, 2008.

———. "The Second Middle Passage: The Transition from Slavery to Freedom at Davis Bend, Mississippi." Ph.D. diss., Purdue University, 1994.

Gómez, Laura E. *Manifest Destinies: The Making of the Mexican American Race*. New York: New York University Press, 2007.

Gomez, Michael. *Exchanging Our Country Marks: The Transformation of African Identities in the Colonial and Antebellum South*. Chapel Hill: University of North Carolina Press, 1998.

Gopal, Priyamvada. *Insurgent Empire: Anticolonial Resistance and British Dissent*. New York: Verso, 2020.

Goswami, Manu. "Autonomy and Comparability: Notes on the Anticolonial and the Postcolonial." *Boundary 2* 32, no. 2 (2005): 201–25.

Graves, Adrian. *Cane and Labour: The Political Economy of the Queensland Sugar Industry*. Edinburgh: Edinburgh University Press, 1993.

Gray, Lewis Cecil. *History of Agriculture*. Vol. 2. Washington: Carnegie Institution of Washington, 1933.

Green, Sharony. *Remember Me to Miss Louisa: Hidden Black-White Intimacies in Antebellum America*. DeKalb: Northern Illinois University Press, 2015.

Green, Toby. *Fistful of Shells: West Africa from the Rise of the Slave Trade to the Age of Revolution*. London: Penguin Books, 2019.

Greene, Julie. "The Wages of Empire: Capitalism, Expansionism, and Working-Class Formation." In *Making the Empire Work: Labor and United States Imperialism*, edited by Daniel E. Bender and Jana K. Lipman, 35–58. New York: New York University Press, 2015.

Griffiths, Philip Gavin. "The Making of White Australia: Ruling Class Agendas, 1876–1888." Ph.D. diss., Australia National University, 2006.

Grossman, Henryk. *Law of the Accumulation and Breakdown of Capitalism*. 1929. https://www.marxists.org/archive/grossman/1929/breakdown/cho2.htm.

Guha, Amalendu. "Growth of Acreage of Cotton in India 1851–1901: A Quantitative Account." *Artha Vijnana* 15, no. 1 (1973): 1–56.

Guha, Ranajit. *Dominance without Hegemony: History and Power in Colonial India*. Cambridge, Mass.: Harvard University Press, 1997.

———. "Neel-Darpan: The Image of a Peasant Revolt in a Liberal Mirror." *Journal of Peasant Studies* 2, no. 1 (1974): 1–46.

———. *A Rule of Property for Colonial Bengal: An Essay on the Idea of Permanent Settlement*. Paris: Mouton, 1963.

Guterl, Matthew Pratt. "After Slavery: Asian Labor, the American South, and the Age of Emancipation." *Journal of World History* 14, no. 2 (2003): 209–41.

———. *American Mediterranean*. Cambridge: Harvard University Press, 2013.

Guyatt, Nicholas. "America's Conservatory: Race, Reconstruction and the Santo Domingo Controversy." *Journal of American History* 97 (2011): 974–1000.

———. *Bind Us Apart*. New York: Basic Books, 2016.

———. "An Impossible Idea? The Curious Career of Internal Colonization." *Journal of the Civil War Era* 4, no. 2 (2014): 234–63.

———. "A Topic Best Avoided." *London Review of Books*. 33, no. 23 (2011). Available online at: https://www.lrb.co.uk/the-paper/v33/n23/nicholas-guyatt/a-topic-best-avoided.

Habib, Irfan. "Colonization of the Indian Economy, 1757–1900." *Social Scientist* 3, no. 8 (1975): 23–53.

———. "Karl Marx and India." *Marxist* 33 (July–September 2017): 1–5.

———, ed. *Karl Marx on India*. New Delhi: Tulika Books, 2006.

Hahn, Barbara. *Making Tobacco Bright*. Baltimore: Johns Hopkins University Press, 2011.

Hahn, Steven. *The Political Worlds of Slavery and Freedom*. Cambridge, Mass.: Harvard University Press, 2009.

Hall, Catherine. *Civilising Subjects: Metropole and Colony in the English Imagination, 1830–1867*. Cambridge: Malden, 2009.

————. "The Economy of Intellectual Prestige: Thomas Carlyle, John Stuart Mill, and the Case of Governor Eyre." *Cultural Critique* 12 (Spring 1989): 167–96.

————. "Rethinking Imperial Histories: The Reform Act of 1867." *New Left Review* 208 (1994): 3–29.

Hall, Catherine, Nicholas Draper, and Keith McClelland, eds. *Emancipation and the Remaking of the British Imperial World.* Manchester: Manchester University Press, 2014.

Hall, Catherine, Nicholas Draper, Keith McClelland, Katie Donington, and Rachel Lang, eds. *Legacies of British Slave-Ownership.* Cambridge: Cambridge University Press, 2014.

Hall, Nigel. "The Liverpool Cotton Market and Cotton Re-exports, c. 1815–1914." *Northern History* 43, no. 2 (2006): 257–71.

————. "The Liverpool Cotton Market and the American Civil War." *Northern History* 34, no. 1 (1988): 149–69.

Hall, Stuart. *Cultural Studies 1983: A Theoretical History.* Durham: Duke University Press, 2016.

————. "The Neoliberal Revolution: Thatcher, Blair, Cameron—The Long March of Neoliberalism Continues." *Soundings* 48 (2011): 9–27.

————. "Race, Articulation and Societies Structured in Dominance." In *Sociological Theories: Race and Colonialism*, edited by United Nations Educational Scientific and Cultural Organisation, 305–43. Paris: UNESCO, 1980.

Hall, Stuart, and Doreen Massey. "Interpreting the Crisis." *Soundings* 44 (Spring 2010): 59–60.

Hammond, John Craig. "'They Are Very Much Interested in Obtaining an Unlimited Slavery': Rethinking the Expansion of Slavery in the Louisiana Purchase Territories, 1803–05." *Journal of Early American History* 23, no. 3 (2003): 353–80.

Hammond, M. B. "The Southern Farmer and the Cotton Question." *Political Science Quarterly* 12, no. 3 (1897): 450–75.

Harnetty, Peter. "Cotton Exports and Indian Agriculture." *Economic History Review* 24, no. 3 (1971): 414–21.

————. *Imperialism and Free Trade: Lancashire and India in the Mid-Nineteenth Century.* Vancouver: University of British Columbia Press, 1972.

————. "India and British Commercial Enterprise: The Case of the Manchester Cotton Company, 1860–64." *Indian Economic and Social History Review* 3, no. 4 (1966): 396–420.

Harris, Cheryl I. "Finding Sojourner's Truth: Race, Gender, and the Institution of Property." *Cardozo Law Review* 18 (November 1998): 319–410.

————. "Whiteness as Property." *Harvard Law Review* 106, no. 8 (107): 1707–91.

Harrison, Royden. "British Labor and American Slavery." *Science and Society* 25, no. 4 (1961): 291–314.

Hartman, Saidiya. "The Belly of the World: A Note on Black Women's Labors." *Souls* 18, no. 1 (2016): 166–73.

————. *Scenes of Subjection: Terror, Slavery and Self-Making in Nineteenth-Century America.* New York: Oxford University Press, 1997.

Harvey, David. *The Limits to Capital.* 1982. Reprint, New York: Verso, 2006.

————. *Seventeen Contradictions and the End of Capitalism*. Oxford: Oxford University Press, 2014.

Hazareesingh, Sandip. "Cotton, Climate, and Colonialism in Dharwar, Western India, 1840–1880." *Journal of Historical Geography* 38 (2012): 1–17.

Heerman, M. Scott. *The Alchemy of Slavery: Human Bondage and Emancipation in the Illinois Country, 1730–1865*. Philadelphia: University of Pennsylvania Press, 2018.

Heinrich, Michael. *An Introduction to the Three Volumes of Karl Marx's "Capital."* New York: Monthly Review Press, 2012.

————. "Invaders from Marx: On the Uses of Marxian Theory, and the Difficulties of a Contemporary Reading." https://libcom.org/library/invaders-marx-on -uses-marxian-theory-difficulties-a-contemporary-reading-michael-heinric. First published in German in *Jungle World*, 21 September 2005.

Henderson, W. O. "Charles Pelham Villiers." *History* 37, no. 129 (1952): 25–39.

————. "The Cotton Famine in Lancashire." *Transactions of the Historic Society of Lancashire for the Year 1932* 84 (1933): 37–62.

————. "The Cotton Famine on the Continent, 1861–65." *Economic History Review* 14 (April 1933): 195–207.

————. *The Lancashire Cotton Famine 1861–65*. New York: A. M. Kelley, 1969.

Herbert, Christopher. *War of No Pity: The Indian Mutiny and Victorian Trauma*. Princeton: Princeton University Press, 2008.

Hermann, Janet. *The Pursuit of a Dream*. Oxford: Oxford University Press, 1981.

Herschthal, Eric. "Slaves, Spaniards, and Subversion in Early Louisiana: The Persistent Fears of Black Revolt and Spanish Collusion in Territorial Louisiana, 1803–1812." *Journal of the Early Republic* 36, no. 2 (2016): 283–311.

Hetherington, Penelope. "Aboriginal Children as a Potential Labour Force in Swan River Colony, 1829–50." *Australian Studies* 16, no. 33 (1992): 41–55.

Hobsbawm, Eric. *The Age of Capital, 1848–1875*. New York: Scribner, 1975.

————. *The Age of Revolution: Europe, 1789–1848*. 1962. Reprint, New York: Vintage Books, 1996.

————. *Industry and Empire: The Making of Modern English Society*. New York: Pantheon Books, 1968.

Hoerder, Dirk, ed. *American Labor and Immigration History, 1877–1920s*. Urbana: University of Illinois Press, 1983.

Hoffman, Edwin D. "From Slavery to Self-Reliance: The Record of Achievement of the Freedmen of the Sea Island Region." *Journal of Negro History* 41, no. 1 (1965): 8–42.

Hoffnagle, Warren. "The Southern Homestead Act: Its Origins and Operation." *The Historian* 32, no. 4 (1970): 612–29.

Holden, Vanessa. "Generation, Resistance, and Survival: African-American Children and the Southampton Rebellion of 1831." *Slavery and Abolition* 38, no. 4 (2017): 673–96.

Horne, Gerald. *The Deepest South: The United States, Brazil, and the African Slave Trade*. New York: New York University Press, 2007.

————. *Negro Comrades of the Crown: African Americans and the British Empire Fight the U.S. before Emancipation*. New York: New York University Press, 2012.

————. *The White Pacific: U.S. Imperialism and Slavery in the South Seas after the Civil War*. Honolulu: University of Hawaii Press, 2007.

Horrox, Alan, and Stuart Hall. *Karl Marx: The Spectre of Marxism*. Written by Stuart Hall. London: Thames Television, 1983.

Hudson, Peter James. "The Racist Dawn of Capitalism." *Boston Review*, 14 March 2016. Available online at http://bostonreview.net/books-ideas/peter-james-hudson -slavery-capitalism.

Humphrys, Elizabeth. "The Birth of Australia: Non-Capitalist Social Relations in a Capitalist Mode of Production." *Journal of Australian Political Economy* 70 (Summer 2012): 110–29.

Hunter, Tera W. *To 'Joy My Freedom: Southern Black Women's Lives and Labors after the Civil War*. Cambridge, Mass.: Harvard University Press, 1999.

Huzzey, Richard. *Freedom Burning: Anti-slavery and Empire in Victorian Britain*. Ithaca: Cornell University Press, 2012.

————. "Free Trade, Free Labour, and Slave Sugar in Victorian Britain." *Historical Journal* 53, no. 2 (2010): 359–79.

Hyam, Ronald. *Britain's Imperial Century, 1815–1914: A Study of Empire and Expansion*. New York: Palgrave, 2005.

Inikori, Joseph. *Africans and the Industrial Revolution in England: A Study in International Trade and Economic Development*. Cambridge: Cambridge University Press, 2002.

————. "Capitalism and Slavery, Fifty Years After: Eric Williams and the Changing Explanations of the Industrial Revolution." In *Capitalism and Slavery Fifty Years Later: Eric Eustace Williams—A Reassessment of the Man and His Work*, edited by Heather Cateau and S. H. H. Carrington, 51–80. New York: Peter Lang, 2000.

————. "Market Structure and the Profits of the British African Trade in the Late Eighteenth Century." *Journal of Economic History* 41, no. 4 (1981): 745–76.

Jain, P. C. *Hindu Society of North-Western Province, 1801–1856*. New Delhi: Puja Publishers, 1986.

Jakes, Aaron, and Ahmad Shokr. "Finding Value in *Empire of Cotton*." *Critical Historical Studies* 4, no. 1 (2017): 107–36.

James, C. L. R. [J. R. Johnson]. "The American People in 'One World': An Essay in Dialectical Materialism" *New International* 10, no. 7 (July 1944): 225–30. Available online at https://www.marxists.org/archive/james-clr/works/1944/07 /one-world.htm.

————. "The Atlantic Slave Trade and Slavery: Some Interpretations of Their Significance in the Development of the United States and the Western World." In *Amistad I*, edited by John A. Williams and Charles F. Harris, 119–64. New York: Vintage Books, 1970.

————. *The Black Jacobins: Toussaint L'Ouverture and the San Domingo Revolution*. 1938. Reprint, New York: Penguin Books, 2001.

————. "Revolution and the Negro." *New International* 5 (December 1939): 339–43. Available online at https://www.marxists.org/archive/james-clr/works/1939/12 /negro-revolution.htm.

Jaynes, Gerald. *Branches without Roots: Genesis of the Black Working Class in the American South*. Oxford: Oxford University Press, 1986.

Jenks, Leland Hamilton. *The Migration of British Capital to 1875*. New York: Knopf, 1927.

Johnson, Walter. "Brute Ideology." *Dissent*, Fall 2014. https://www.dissentmagazine .org/article/brute-ideology.

———. "Introduction: The Future Store." In *The Chattel Principle: Internal Slave Trades in the Americas*, edited by Walter Johnson, 1–31. New Haven: Yale University Press, 2005.

———. "The Pedestal and the Veil: Rethinking the Capitalism/Slavery Question." *Journal of the Early Republic* 24, no. 2 (2004): 299–308.

———. *River of Dark Dreams: Slavery and Empire in the Cotton Kingdom*. Cambridge, Mass.: Harvard University Press, 2013.

———. *Soul by Soul: Life inside the Antebellum Slave Market*. Cambridge, Mass.: Harvard University Press, 1999.

Johnston, W. Ross. "The Selling of Queensland: Henry Jordan and Welsh Emigration." *Journal of the Royal Historical Society of Queensland* 14, no. 9 (1991): 379–92.

Jones, Jacqueline. *Labor of Love, Labor of Sorrow: Black Women, Work, and the Family, from Slavery to the Present*. New York: Vintage Books, 1985.

Jones, Lewis Pinckney. "William Elliott, South Carolina Nonconformist." *Journal of Southern History* 17, no. 3 (1951): 361–81.

Jones, Martha S. *Birthright Citizens: A History of Race and Rights in Antebellum America*. Cambridge: Cambridge University Press, 2018.

Jones, Wilbur Devereux. *Aberdeen and the Americas*. Athens: University of Georgia Press, 1958.

Jones-Rogers, Stephanie. " '[S]he Could . . . Spare One Ample Breast for the Profit of Her Owner': White Mothers and Enslaved Wet Nurses' Invisible Labor in American Slave Markets." *Slavery and Abolition* 38, no. 2 (2017): 337–55.

Jordan, Weymouth T. "Noah B. Cloud's Activities on Behalf of Southern Agriculture." *Agricultural History* 25, no. 2 (1951): 53–58.

Jordan, Winthrop D., ed. *Slavery and the American South*. Jackson: University of Mississippi Press, 2003.

Joyner, Charles. *Remember Me: Slave Life in Coastal Georgia*. Athens: University of Georgia Press, 2011.

Jung, Moon-Ho. "*Black Reconstruction* and Empire." *South Atlantic Quarterly* 112, no. 3 (2013): 465–71.

———. *Coolies and Cane: Race, Labor, and Sugar in the Age of Emancipation*. Baltimore: Johns Hopkins University Press, 2006.

Jung, Moon-Kie. *Beneath the Surface of White Supremacy: Denaturalizing U.S. Racisms Past and Present*. Stanford: Stanford University Press, 2015.

———. "The Enslaved, the Worker, and Du Bois's *Black Reconstruction*: Toward an Underdiscipline of Antisociology." *Sociology of Race and Ethnicity* 5, no. 2 (2019): 157–68.

———. "The Racial Constitution of the U.S. Empire-State." In *Beneath the Surface of White Supremacy: Denaturalizing U.S. Racisms Past and Present*, 55–82. Stanford: Stanford University Press, 2015.

Kale, Madhavi. *Fragments of Empire: Capital, Slavery, and Indian Indentured*

Labor in the British Caribbean. Philadelphia: University of Pennsylvania Press, 1998.

Kaplan, Amy. "Manifest Domesticity." *American Literature* 70, no. 3 (1998): 581–606.

Karl, Rebecca. *The Magic of Concepts: History and the Economic in Twentieth-Century China*. Durham: Duke University Press, 2017.

Karp, Matthew. *This Vast Southern Empire: Slaveholders at the Helm of American Foreign Policy*. Cambridge: Harvard University Press, 2018.

Karuka, Manu. *Empire's Tracks: Indigenous Nations, Chinese Workers, and the Transcontinental Railroad*. Oakland: University of California Press, 2019.

———. "Fugitive Decolonization." *Theory and Event* 19, no. 4 (2016) muse.jhu.edu /article/633284..

———. "The Wealth of Natives: Toward a Critique of Settler Colonial Political Economy." *Settler Colonial Studies* 3, nos. 3–4 (2013): 295–310.

Keane, Angela. "Richard Carlile's Working Women: Selling Books, Politics, Sex, and *The Republican*." *Literature and History* 15, no. 2 (2006): 20–33.

Kelley, Robin D. G. *Freedom Dreams: The Black Radical Imagination*. Boston: Beacon Press, 2008.

———. *Race Rebels: Culture, Politics, and the Black Working Class*. New York: Free Press, 1996.

Kerr-Ritchie, Jeffrey R. *Rebellious Passages: The Creole Revolt and America's Coastal Slave Trade*. Cambridge: Cambridge University Press, 2019.

King, Tiffany. "Labor's Aphasia: Toward Antiblackness as Constitutive to Settler Colonialism." *Decolonization: Indigeneity, Education and Society*, June 10, 2014. decolonization.wordpress.com/2014/06/10/labors-aphasia-toward-antiblackness -as-constitutive-to-settler-colonialism/.

Kling, Blair. *The Blue Mutiny: Indigo Disturbances in Bengal, 1859–62*. Philadelphia: University of Pennsylvania Press, 1966.

———. *Partner in Empire: Dwarkanath Tagore and the Age of Enterprise in Eastern India*. Berkeley: University of California Press, 1976.

Knight, Frederick C. *Working the Diaspora: The Impact of African Labor*. New York: New York University Press, 2010.

Knox, Bruce. *The Queensland Years of Robert Herbert, Premier*. St. Lucia: University of Queensland Press, 1977.

Koditschek, Theodore. "Capitalism, Race, and Evolution in Imperial Britain, 1850–1900." In *Race Struggles*, edited by Theodore Koditschek, Sundiata Keita Cha-Jua, and Helen A. Neville, 48–79. Urbana: University of Illinois Press, 2009.

Kolchin, Peter. *First Freedom: The Responses of Alabama's Blacks to Emancipation and Reconstruction*. Westport, Conn.: Greenwood Press, 1972.

Kramer, Paul A. "Embedding Capital: Political-Economic History, the United States, and the World." *Journal of the Gilded Age and Progressive Era* 15 (2016): 331–62.

———. "Empires, Exceptions, and Anglo-Saxons: Race and Rule between the British and United States Empires, 1880–1910." *Journal of American History* 88, no. 4 (2002): 1315–53.

Krishnan, Shekar. "Empire's Metropolis: Money, Time, and Space in Colonial Bombay, 1870–1930." Ph.D. diss., MIT, 2014.

Kull, Andrew. "The Enforceability after Emancipation of Debts Contracted for the Purchase of Slaves." *Chicago-Kent Law Review* 70, no. 2 (1994): 493–538.

Kumar, Ashutosh. "Marx and Engels on India." *Indian Journal of Political Science* 53, 4 (1992): 493–504.

Kumar, Mohinder. "Karl Marx, Andrew Ure, and the Question of Managerial Control." *Social Scientist* 12, no. 9 (1984): 63–69.

Kumar, Prakash. *Indigo Plantations and Science in Colonial India.* Cambridge: Cambridge University Press, 2012.

———. "Plantation Science: Improving Natural Indigo in Colonial India, 1860–1913." *British Journal for the History of Science* 40, no. 4 (2007): 537–65.

Kvach, John F. *De Bow's Review: The Antebellum Vision of a New South.* Lexington: University of Kentucky Press, 2013.

Kyi, Anna. " 'The Most Determined, Sustained Diggers' Resistance Campaign': Chinese Protests against the Victorian Government's Anti-Chinese Legislation, 1855–1862." *Provenance* 8 (2009). http://prov.vic.gov.au/publications/provenance /provenance2009/diggers-resistance-campaign.

Lachance, Paul. "The Politics of Fear: French Louisianians and the Slave Trade, 1786–1809." *Plantation Society in the Americas* 1, no. 2 (1979): 162–97.

Laidlaw, Zoë. " 'Justice to India—Prosperity to England—Freedom to the Slave!' Humanitarian and Moral Reform Campaigns on India, Aborigines and American Slavery." *Journal of the Royal Asiatic Society* 22, no. 2 (2012): 299–324.

Lake, Marilyn. "The White Man under Siege: New Histories of Race in the Nineteenth Century and the Advent of White Australia." *History Workshop Journal* 58 (2004): 41–62.

Lake, Marilyn, and Henry Reynolds. *Drawing the Global Colour Line: White Men's Countries and the International Challenge of Racial Equality.* Cambridge: Cambridge University Press, 2008.

Lander, Ernest M. "Manufacturing in South Carolina, 1815–60." *Business History Review* 28, no. 1 (1954): 59–66.

Lanza, Michael L. *Agrarianism and Reconstruction Politics.* Baton Rouge: Louisiana State University Press, 1990.

Leacock, Seth, and David G. Mandelbaum. "A Nineteenth Century Development Project in India: The Cotton Improvement Program." *Economic Development and Cultural Change* 3, no. 4 (1955): 334–51.

Lebowitz, Michael A. *Beyond Capital: Marx's Political Economy of the Working Class.* New York: Palgrave Macmillan, 2003.

Left Quarter Collective. "White Supremacist Constitution of the U.S. Empire-State: A Short Conceptual Look at the Long First Century." *Political Power and Social Theory* 20 (2009): 167–200.

Legassick, Martin, and Robert Ross. "From Slave Economy to Settler Capitalism: The Cape Colony and Its Extensions, 1800–54." In *The Cambridge History of South Africa*, vol. 1, edited by Carolyn Hamilton, Bernard K. Mbenga, and Robert Ross, 253–318. Cambridge: Cambridge University Press, 2010.

Lepler, Jessica M. "1837: Anatomy of a Panic." Ph.D. diss., Brandeis University, 2008.

————. *The Many Panics of 1837: People, Politics, and the Creation of a Transatlantic Financial Crisis.* Cambridge: Cambridge University Press, 2013.

Lewis, David H. "The Chinese of Belize: A Geographical Interpretation." Master's thesis, University of Wisconsin–Milwaukee, 1989.

Lewis, David Levering. *W. E. B. Du Bois: The Fight for Equality and the American Century, 1919–1963.* New York: Henry Holt, 2000.

Libby, David J. *Slavery and Frontier Mississippi.* Jackson: University of Mississippi Press, 2004.

Lightfoot, Natasha. *Troubling Freedom: Antigua and the Aftermath of British Emancipation.* Durham: Duke University Press, 2015.

Linebaugh, Peter, and Marcus Rediker. *The Many Headed Hydra: Sailors, Slaves, Commoners, and the Hidden History of the Revolutionary Atlantic.* Boston: Beacon Press, 2000.

Littlefield, Daniel C. *Rice and Slaves: Ethnicity and the Slave Trade in Colonial South Carolina.* Baton Rouge: Louisiana State University Press, 1981.

Litwack, Leon. *Been in the Storm So Long.* New York: Knopf, 1981.

Liu, Andrew B. "Production, Circulation, and Accumulation: The Historiographies of Capitalism in China and South Asia." *Journal of Asian Studies* 78, no. 4 (2019): 767–88.

————. *Tea War: A History of Capitalism in China and India.* New Haven: Yale University Press, 2020.

Locke, John. *Two Treatises of Government.* Edited by Peter Laslett. Cambridge: Cambridge University Press, 1988.

Lockett, James D. "Abraham Lincoln and Colonization: An Episode That Ends in Tragedy at L'Ile à Vache, Haiti, 1863–1864." *Journal of Black Studies* 21, no. 4 (1991): 428–44.

Loftus, Donna. "Time, History and the Making of the Industrial Middle Class: The Story of Samuel Smith." *Social History* 42, no. 1 (2017): 29–51.

Logan, Frenise A. "A British East India Company Agent in the United States, 1839–1840." *Agricultural History* 48, no. 2 (1974): 267–76.

————. "India's Loss of the British Cotton Market after 1865." *Journal of Southern History* 31, no. 1 (1965): 40–50.

Look Lai, Walton. *Indentured Labor, Caribbean Sugar: Chinese and Indian Migrants to the British West Indies, 1838–1918.* Baltimore: Johns Hopkins University Press, 2003.

Look Lai, Walton, and Tan Chee-Beng, eds. *The Chinese in Latin America and the Caribbean.* Leiden: Brill, 2010.

Loveday, Alexander. *The History and Economics of Indian Famines.* London: G. Bell and Sons, 1914.

Lowe, Lisa. *Immigrant Acts: On Asian American Cultural Politics.* Durham: Duke University Press, 1996.

————. "Insufficient Difference." *Ethnicities* 5, no. 3 (2005): 409–14.

————. *The Intimacies of Four Continents.* Durham: Duke University Press, 2015.

Luxemburg, Rosa. "History of Crises." In *Complete Works of Rosa Luxemburg.* Vol. 1. New York: Verso Press, 2013.

Lynd, Staughton. "The Abolitionist Critique of the United States Constitution." In *Class Conflict, Slavery, and the United States Constitution*, 153–83. New York: Bobbs-Merrill, 1967.

Magness, Phillip W. "The British Honduras Colony: Black Emigrationist Support for Colonization in the Lincoln Presidency." *Slavery and Abolition* 34, no. 1 (2013): 39–60.

Major, Andrea. *Slavery, Abolitionism, and Empire in India, 1772–1843*. Liverpool: Liverpool University Press, 2012.

Mandel, Ernest. *Late Capitalism*. London: New Left Review, 1975.

Mangru, Basdeo. "From Bengal to British Guiana: The Emigration of Indian Indentured Labour, 1854–1885." Ph.D. thesis, University of London, 1981.

———, ed. *Kanpur to Kolkata: Labour Recruitment for the Sugar Colonies*. Hertford, UK: Hansib Publications Limited, 2015.

Manjapra, Kris. "Necrospeculation: Postemancipation Finance and Black Redress." *Social Text* 37, no. 2 (2019): 29–65.

———. "Plantation Dispossessions: The Global Travel of Agricultural Racial Capitalism." In *American Capitalism: New Histories*, edited by Sven Beckert and Christine Desan, 361–88. New York: Columbia University Press, 2018.

Mann, Michael. "Ecological Change in North India: Deforestation and Agrarian Distress in the Ganga-Jamna Doab, 1800–1850." *Environment and History* 1, no. 2 (1995): 201–20.

Manning, Chandra. "Working for Citizenship in Civil War Contraband Camps." *Journal of the Civil War* 4, no. 2 (2014): 172–204.

Marable, Manning. *How Capitalism Underdeveloped Black America*. Boston: South End Press, 1983.

Marrs, Aaron. *Railroads in the Old South: Pursuing Progress in a Slave Society*. Baltimore: Johns Hopkins University Press, 2009.

Marx, Karl. *Capital*. Vol. 1. New York: Vintage Books, 1977.

———. *Grundrisse: Foundations of the Critique of Political Economy*. New York: Penguin Books, 1993.

Marx, Karl, and Frederick Engels. *Marx and Engels Collected Works*. 50 vols. London: Lawrence and Wishart, 1975–2004.

Masur, Kate. "The African American Delegation to Abraham Lincoln: A Reappraisal." *Civil War History* 56, no. 2 (2010): 117–44.

Mathew, W. M. "Edmund Ruffin and the Demise of the *Farmers' Register*." *The Virginia Magazine* 94, 1 (1986): 3–24.

Matson, Cathy. *The Economy of Early America: Historical Perspectives and New Directions*. University Park: Pennsylvania State University Press, 2006.

Mattox, Jake. "The Mayor of San Juan del Norte? Nicaragua, Martin Delany, and the 'Cotton Americans.'" *American Literature* 81, no. 3 (2009): 527–54.

McCalman, Iain. "Anti-slavery and Ultra-radicalism in Early Nineteenth-Century England: The Case of Robert Wedderburn." *Slavery and Abolition* 7, no. 2 (1986): 99–117.

McClure, James P., ed. *The Papers of Thomas Jefferson*. Vol. 42, *16 November 1803–10 March 1804*. Princeton: Princeton University Press, 2016.

McCurry, Stephanie. *Masters of Small Worlds: Yeoman Households, Gender Relations.* New York: Oxford University Press, 1977.

McGrath, Ann, ed. *Contested Ground: Australian Aborigines under the British Crown.* St. Leonards, NSW: Allen and Unwin, 1995.

McIntyre, Michael. "Race, Surplus Population and the Marxist Theory of Imperialism." *Antipode* 43, no. 5 (2011): 1439–1515.

McKittrick, Katherine. "Plantation Futures." *Small Axe* 17, no. 3 (2013): 1–15.

McLagan, Elizabeth. *A Peculiar Paradise: A History of Blacks in Oregon, 1778–1940.* Portland: Georgian Press, 1980.

McMichael, Philip. "Slavery in Capitalism: The Rise and Demise of the U.S. Antebellum Cotton Culture." *Theory and Society* 20, no. 3 (1991): 321–49.

McNairn, Rosemarie M. "Baiting the British Bull: A Fiesta, Trials, and a Petition in Belize." *The Americas* 55, no. 2 (October 1998): 240–74.

McNally, David. *Global Slump: The Economics and Politics of Crisis and Resistance.* Oakland, Calif.: PM Press, 2011.

Meena, Hareet Kumar. "Famine in Late 19th Century India: Natural or Man-Made." *Journal of Human and Social Science Research* 6, no. 1 (2015): 35–44.

Mehrotra, S. R. "The British India Society and Its Bengal Branch, 1839–46." *Indian Economic and Social History Review* 4, no. 2 (1967): 131–54.

———. "The Landholders' Society, 1838–44." *Indian Economic and Social History Review* 3, no. 4 (1966): 358–77.

Melish, Joanne Pope. *Disowning Slavery: Gradual Emancipation and "Race" in New England, 1780–1860.* Ithaca: Cornell University Press, 1998.

Merrill, Walter M., ed. *The Letters of William Lloyd Garrison.* Vol. 3. Cambridge, Mass.: Harvard University Press, 1974.

Metcalf, Thomas R. *The Aftermath of Revolt: India, 1857–70.* Princeton: Princeton University Press, 1964.

———. *Ideologies of the Raj.* Cambridge: Cambridge University Press, 1994.

———. *Imperial Connections: India in the Indian Ocean Arena, 1860–1920.* Berkeley: University of California Press, 2007.

———. *Land, Landlords, and the British Raj: Northern India in the Nineteenth Century.* Berkeley: University of California Press, 1979.

Midgley, Clare. *Feminism and Empire: Women Activists in Imperial Britain, 1790–1865.* London: Routledge, 2007.

———, ed. *Gender and Imperialism.* Manchester: Manchester University Press, 1998.

Miles, Edwin Arthur. *Jacksonian Democracy in Mississippi.* Chapel Hill: University of North Carolina Press, 1960.

Mills, Brandon. "Exporting the Racial Republic: African Colonization, National Citizenship, and the Transformation of U.S. Expansion." Ph.D. diss., University of Illinois at Urbana-Champaign, 2011.

Millward, Jessica. "'The Relics of Slavery': Interracial Sex and Manumission in the American South." *Frontiers: A Journal of Women Studies* 31, no. 3 (2010): 22–30.

Misra, Maria. *Business, Race, and Politics in British India, c. 1850–1960.* Oxford: Clarendon Press, 1999.

Mitra, Debendra Bijoy. *Cotton Weavers of Bengal, 1757–1833*. Calcutta: Firma KLM Limited, 1978.

Moles, I. N. "The Indian Coolie Labour Issue in Queensland." *Historical Society of Queensland Journal* 5, no. 5 (1957): 1345–72.

Montgomery, David. *Beyond Equality: Labor and the Radical Republicans, 1862–72*. Urbana: University of Illinois Press, 1981.

Moore, John Hebron. *The Emergence of the Cotton Kingdom in the Old Southwest: Mississippi, 1770–1860*. Baton Rouge: Louisiana State University Press, 1988.

Moreton-Robinson, Aileen. *The White Possessive: Property, Power, and Indigenous Sovereignty*. Minneapolis: University of Minnesota Press, 2015.

Morgan, Jennifer. "Accounting for 'The Most Excruciating Torment': Gender, Slavery, and Trans-Atlantic Passages." *History of the Present* 6, no. 2 (2016): 184–207.

———. *Laboring Women: Reproduction and Gender in New World Slavery*. Philadelphia: University of Pennsylvania Press, 2004.

———. *"Partus sequitur ventrem*: Law, Race, and Reproduction in Colonial Slavery." *Small Axe* 22, no. 1 (2018): 1–17.

Morgan, K. "Mercantilism and the British Empire, 1688–1815." In Donald Winch and Patrick Karl O'Brien, *The Political Economy of British Historical Experience, 1688–1914*, 165–92. Oxford: Oxford University Press, 2002.

Morgan, Lynda J. *Emancipation in Virginia's Tobacco Belt, 1850–1870*. Athens: University of Georgia Press, 1992.

Morgan, Philip D. "Work and Culture: The Task System and the World of Lowcountry Blacks, 1700 to 1880." *William and Mary Quarterly* 39, no. 4 (1982): 563–99.

Morris, Thomas D. *Southern Slavery and the Law, 1619–1860*. Chapel Hill: University of North Carolina Press, 1999.

Morrison, James Ashley. "Before Hegemony: Adam Smith, American Independence, and the Origins of the First Era of Globalization." *International Organization* 66, no. 3 (2012): 395–428.

Moses, Dirk. "An Antipodean Genocide? The Origins of the Genocidal Moment in the Colonization of Australia." *Journal of Genocide Research* 2, no. 1 (2000): 89–106.

———, ed. *Genocide and Settler Society: Frontier Violence and Stolen Indigenous Children in Australia*. New York: Berghahn Books, 2004.

Moses, Wilson Jeremiah. *Creative Conflict in African American Thought: Frederick Douglass, Alexander Crummell, Booker T. Washington, W. E. B. Du Bois, and Marcus Garvey*. New York: Cambridge University Press, 2004.

Mukherjee, Mukul. "Impact of Modernisation on Women's Occupations: A Case Study of the Rice-Husking Industry of Bengal." *Indian Economic and Social History Review* 20, no. 1 (1983): 27–45.

Mukherjee, R. "The Azamgarh Proclamation and Some Questions on the Revolt of 1857 in the North Western Provinces." In *Essays in Honour of S. C. Sarkar*, edited by Barun De, 477–98. New Delhi: India People's Publishing House, 1976.

Muntsch, Albert. "Xaibe: A Mayan Enclave in Northern British Honduras." *Anthropological Quarterly* 34, no. 2 (1961): 121–26.

Nadri, Ghulam. *The Political Economy of Indigo in India, 1580–1930*. Leiden: Brill, 2016.

Naoroji, Dadabhai. *Dadabhai Naoroji: Selected Private Papers*. New Delhi: Oxford University Press, 2016.

Nash, R. C. "South Carolina Indigo, European Textiles, and the British Atlantic Economy in the Eighteenth Century." *Economic History Review* 63, no. 2 (2010): 362–92.

Naved, Shad. "The Colonial Encounter in Marxist Terms." *Social Scientist* 36, nos. 11/12 (2008): 33–46.

Nevius, Marcus. *City of Refuge: Slavery and Petit Marronage in the Great Dismal Swamp, 1763–1856*. Athens: University of Georgia Press, 2020.

Newman, Brooke. *Dark Inheritance: Blood, Race, and Sex in Colonial Jamaica*. New Haven: Yale University Press, 2018.

Ngai, Mae. "Chinese Miners, Headmen, and Protectors on the Victorian Goldfields, 1853–1863." *Australian Historical Studies* 42, no. 1 (2011): 10–24.

North, Douglass. *The Economic Growth of the United States*. New York: Norton, 1966.

———. "The Peculiar Fate of the Bourgeois Critique of Slavery." In *Slavery and the American South*, edited by Winthrop D. Jordan, 29–56. Jackson: University Press of Mississippi, 2003.

Oakes, James. *The Ruling Race: A History of American Slaveholders*. New York: Knopf, 1982.

Ochiai, Akiko. *Harvesting Freedom: African American Agrarianism in Civil War Era South Carolina*. Westport, Conn.: Praeger, 2004.

———. "The Port Royal Experiment Revisited: Northern Visions of Reconstruction and the Land Question." *New England Quarterly* 74, no. 1 (2001): 94–117.

Oddy, D. J. "Urban Famine in Nineteenth-Century Britain: The Effect of the Cotton Famine on Working-Class Diet and Health." *Economic History Review* 36, no. 1 (1983): 68–86.

Olmstead, Alan L. "Antebellum U.S. Cotton Production and Slavery in the Indian Mirror." *Agricultural History* 91, no. 1 (2017): 5–33.

Olmstead, Alan L., and Paul W. Rhodes. "Biological Innovation and Productivity in the Antebellum Cotton Economy." *Journal of Economic History* 68, no. 4 (2008): 1123–71.

Onuf, Peter S. "Every Generation Is an 'Independent Nation': Colonization, Miscegenation, and the Fate of Jefferson's Children." *William and Mary Quarterly* 57, no. 1 (2000): 153–70.

Ortiz, Fernando. *Cuban Counterpoint: Tobacco and Sugar*. New York: Knopf, 1947.

Ortiz, Paul. *An African American and Latinx History of the United States*. Boston: New Beacon Press, 2018.

———. *Emancipation Betrayed: The Hidden History of Black Organizing and White Violence in Florida from Reconstruction to the Bloody Election of 1920*. Berkeley: University of California Press, 2005.

Oubre, Claude F. *Forty Acres and a Mule*. Baton Rouge: Louisiana State University Press, 1978.

Owen, E. R. *Cotton and the Egyptian Economy, 1820–1914*. Oxford: Clarendon Press, 1969.

Page, Sebastian and Phillip Magness. *Colonization after Emancipation: Lincoln and the Movement for Black Resettlement*. Columbia: University of Missouri Press, 2011.

Pares, Richard. "The Economic Factors in the History of the Empire." *Economic History Review* 7, no. 2 (1937): 119–44.

Pargas, Damian Alan. *Slavery and Forced Migration in the Antebellum South*. New York: Cambridge University Press, 2015.

Park, K-Sue. "Money, Mortgages, and the Conquest of America." *Law and Society Inquiry* 41 (2016): 1006–35.

Parthasarathi, Prasannan. "The Great Divergence." *Past and Present* 176 (2002): 275–93.

———. *Why Europe Grew Rich and Asia Did Not: Global Economic Divergence, 1600–1850*. Cambridge: Cambridge University Press, 2014.

Patterson, Orlando. *Slavery and Social Death*. Cambridge, Mass.: Harvard University Press, 1982.

Pease, William H. "Three Years among the Freedmen: William C. Gannett and the Port Royal Experiment." *Journal of Negro History* 42, no. 2 (1957): 98–117.

Peck, Gunther. "White Slavery and Whiteness: A Transnational View of the Sources of Working-Class Radicalism and Racism." *Labor: Studies in Working-Class History of the Americas* 1, no. 2 (2004): 41–63.

Perelman, Michael. *Marx's Crises Theory: Scarcity, Labor, and Finance*. New York: Praeger, 1987.

Perrone, Giuliana. "What, to the Law, Is the Former Slave?" *Slavery and Abolition* 40, no. 2 (2019): 258–59.

Persky, Joseph. "Wage Slavery." *History of Political Economy* 30, no. 4 (1998): 627–50.

Peterson, Dawn. *Indians in the Family: Adoption and the Politics of Antebellum Expansion*. Cambridge, Mass.: Harvard University Press, 2017.

Phillips, Ulrich Bonnell. *Life and Labor in the Old South*. Boston: Little, Brown, 1929.

Pickering, Paul A., and Alex Tyrell. *The People's Bread: A History of the Anti-Corn Law League*. New York: Leicester University Press, 2000.

Polanyi, Karl. *The Great Transformation: The Political and Economic Origins of Our Time*. 1944. Reprint, Boston: Beacon Press, 2001.

Pomeranz, Kenneth. *The Great Divergence: China, Europe, and the Making of the Modern World Economy*. Princeton: Princeton University Press, 2000.

Pomeroy, Earl S. "French Substitutes for American Cotton, 1861–65." *Journal of Southern History* 9, no. 4 (1943): 555–60.

Pope, Christie Farnham. "Southern Homesteads for Negroes." *Agricultural History* 44, 2 (1970): 201–12.

Postone, Moishe. *Time, Labor, and Social Domination: A Reinterpretation of Marx's Critical Theory*. Cambridge: Cambridge University Press, 2006.

Prakash, Gyan. *Another Reason: Science and the Imagination of Modern India*. Princeton: Princeton University Press, 2002.

———. "Colonialism, Capitalism and the Discourse of Freedom." *International Review of Social History* 41 (1996): 9–25.

Pruneau, Leigh Ann. "All the Time Is Work Time: Gender and the Task System on Antebellum Low Country Rice Plantations." Ph.D. diss., University of Arizona, 1997.

Quarles, Benjamin. *Black Abolitionists*. New York: Da Capo Press, 1991.

Rabaka, Reiland. *Du Bois's Dialectics: Black Radical Politics and the Reconstruction of Critical Social Theory*. Lanham, Md.: Lexington Books, 2009.

Rabin, Dana. *Britain and Its Internal Others, 1750–1800*. Manchester: Manchester University Press, 2017.

———. " 'In a Country of Liberty?': Slavery, Villeinage and the Making of Whiteness in the Somerset Case (1772)." *History Workshop Journal* 72, no. 1 (2011): 5–29.

Ramusack, Barbara N., and Antoinette Burton. "Feminism, Imperialism and Race: A Dialogue between India and Britain." *Women's History Review* 3, no. 4 (1994): 469–81.

Rana, Aziz. *The Two Faces of American Freedom*. Cambridge, Mass.: Harvard University Press, 2010.

Ranade, Rekha. *Sir Bartle Frere and His Times: A Study of His Bombay Years, 1862–67*. New Delhi: Mittal Publications, 1990.

Randall, James G. *Constitutional Problems under Lincoln*. 1926. Rev. ed., Urbana: University of Illinois Press, 1951.

Randhawa, M. S. *A History of Agriculture in India*. Vol. 3. New Delhi: Indian Council of Agricultural Research, 1983.

Rao, Amiya, and B. G. Rao. *The Blue Devil: Indigo and Colonial Bengal*. Oxford: Oxford University Press, 1992.

Rapport, Sara. "The Freedmen's Bureau as a Legal Agent for Black Men and Women in Georgia: 1865–1868." *Georgia Historical Quarterly* 73 (1989): 26–53.

Ratcliffe, Barrie M., ed. *Great Britain and Her World, 1750–1914: Essays in Honour of W. O. Henderson*. Manchester: Manchester University Press, 1975.

Rawick, George. *From Sundown to Sunup: The Making of the Black Community*. Westport, Conn.: Greenwood, 1972.

Ray, Indrajit. *Bengal Industries and the British Industrial Revolution*. London: Routledge, 2011.

Ray, Rajat Kanta. "Asian Capital in the Age of European Domination: The Rise of the Bazaar." *Modern Asian Studies* 29, no. 3 (1995): 449–554.

———. *Entrepreneurship and Industry in India, 1800–1947*. Delhi: Oxford University Press, 1992.

Reckord, Mary. "The Jamaica Slave Rebellion of 1831." *Past and Present* 40 (July 1968): 108–25.

Rediker, Marcus. *The Amistad Rebellion: An Atlantic Odyssey of Slavery and Freedom*. New York: Viking, 2012.

———. *The Slave Ship: A Human History*. New York: Penguin Books, 2007.

Reynolds, Henry, and Dawn May. "Queensland." In *Contested Ground: Australian*

Aborigines under the British Crown, edited by Ann Mcgrath, 168–207. St. Leonards, NSW: Allen and Unwin, 1995.

Riddleberger, Patrick W. *George Washington Julian: Radical Republican.* Indianapolis: Indiana Historical Bureau, 1966.

———. "George W. Julian: Abolitionist Land Reformer." *Agricultural History* 29, no. 3 (1995): 108–15.

Riello, Giorgio. *Cotton: The Fabric that Made the Modern World.* Cambridge: Cambridge University Press, 2013.

Roark, James L. "George W. Julian: Radical Land Reformer." Indiana Magazine of History 64, no. 1 (1968): 25–38.

Robb, Peter. *Peasants, Political Economy, and Law.* Oxford: Oxford University Press, 2007.

———, ed. *Meanings of Agriculture: Essays in South Asian History and Economics.* Delhi: Oxford University Press, 1996.

Robbins, Hollis, and Henry Louis Gates Jr., eds. *The Portable Nineteenth-Century African American Women Writers.* New York: Penguin Books, 2017.

Robert, Joseph Clarke. "Rise of the Tobacco Warehouse Auction System in Virginia, 1800–1860." *Agricultural History* 4 (October 1933): 170–82.

Robinson, Cedric J. *Black Marxism: The Making of the Black Radical Tradition.* London: Zed Books, 1983.

———. "Capitalism, Marxism, and the Black Radical Tradition: An Interview with Cedric Robinson." *Perspectives on Anarchist Theory* 3, no. 1 (1999): 1, 6–8.

———. "Capitalism, Slavery and Bourgeois Historiography." *History Workshop Journal* 23, no. 1 (1987): 122–40.

Rockman, Seth. "What Makes the History of Capitalism Newsworthy?" *Journal of the Early Republic* 34, no. 3 (2014): 439–66.

Rodney, Walter. *History of the Guyanese Working People, 1881–1905.* Baltimore: Johns Hopkins University Press, 1981.

Roeckell, Lelia M. "Bonds over Bondage: British Opposition to the Annexation of Texas." *Journal of the Early Republic* 9, no. 2 (1999): 257–78.

Roediger, David. *Colored White: Transcending the Racial Past.* Berkeley: University of California Press, 2002.

———. *Seizing Freedom: Slave Emancipation and Liberty for All.* New York: Verso, 2014.

———. *The Wages of Whiteness: Race and the Making of the American Working Class.* New York: Verso, 1991.

Roediger, David, and Elizabeth Esch. *The Production of Difference.* Oxford: Oxford University Press, 2012.

Roediger, David, and Philip Foner. *On Our Own Time: A History of American Labour and the Working Day.* London: Verso, 1989.

Rogin, Michael. *Fathers and Children: Andrew Jackson and the Subjugation of the American Indian.* New Brunswick, N.J.: Transaction Publishers, 2000.

Roper, Laura Wood. "Frederick Law Olmsted and the Port Royal Experiment." *Journal of Southern History* 31, no. 3 (1965): 272–84.

Ropp, Stephen. "Chinese in Belize: An Examination of Nationalism, Development and Social Conflict." Master's thesis, UCLA, 1996.

Rosdolsky, Roman. *The Making of Marx's Capital*. London: Pluto Press, 1977.

Rose, Willie Lee. *Rehearsal for Reconstruction: The Port Royal Experiment*. New York: Oxford University Press, 1976.

Rosselli, John. *Lord William Bentinck: The Making of a Liberal Imperialist, 1774–1839*. Delhi: Thomson Press (India) Limited, 1974.

Rothman, Adam. *Slave Country: American Expansion and the Origins of the Deep South*. Cambridge, Mass.: Harvard University Press, 2009.

Rousseau, Peter L. "Jacksonian Monetary Policy, Specie Flows, and the Panic of 1837." *Journal of Economic History* 62, no. 2 (2002): 457–88.

Roy, Tirthankar. "Indigo and Law in Colonial India." *Economic History Review* 64 (2011): 60–75.

Rugemer, Edward. *The Problem of Emancipation: The Caribbean Roots of the American Civil War*. Baton Rouge: Louisiana State University Press, 2008.

Rungta, Radhe Shyam. *The Rise of Business Corporations in India, 1851–1900*. Cambridge: Cambridge University Press, 1970.

Said, Edward. *The World, the Text, and the Critic*. Cambridge, Mass.: Harvard University Press, 1983.

Sakai, J. *Settlers: The Mythology of the White Proletariat*. Chicago: Morningstar Press, 1989.

Sarkar, Susobhan, ed. *Rammohun Roy on Indian Economy*. Calcutta: Rare Book Publishing Syndicate, 1965.

Sarkar, Tanika. "The Hindu Wife and the Hindu Nation: Domesticity and Nationalism in Nineteenth Century Bengal." *Studies in History* 8, no. 2 (1992): 213–35.

Sartori, Andrew. *Bengal in Global Concept History: Culturalism in the Age of Capital*. Chicago: University of Chicago Press, 2008.

———. *Liberalism in Empire*. Oakland: University of California Press, 2014.

Satya, Laxman D. "British Imperial Railways in Nineteenth Century South Asia." *Economic and Political Weekly*, 22 November 2008, 69–77.

———. *Cotton and Famine in Berar, 1850–1900*. New Delhi: Manohar, 1997.

Saxton, Alexander. *The Rise and Fall of the White Republic*. London: Verso, 1990.

Scanlon, James E. "A Sudden Conceit: Jefferson and the Louisiana Government Bill of 1804." *Louisiana History* 9 (1968): 139–62.

Scarborough, William Kauffman. *The Allstons of Chicora Wood: Wealth, Honor, and Gentility in the South Carolina Lowcountry*. Baton Rouge: Louisiana State University Press, 2011.

Schermerhorn, Calvin. *The Business of Slavery and the Rise of American Capitalism, 1815–1860*. New Haven: Yale University Press, 2015.

Schnurr, Matthew A. "Cotton as Calamitous Commodity." *Canadian Journal of African Studies/Revue canadienne des études africaines* 47, no. 1 (2013): 115–32.

Schoen, Brian. *The Fragile Fabric of Union: Cotton, Federal Politics, and the Global Origins of the Civil War*. Baltimore: Johns Hopkins University Press.

Schwalm, Leslie A. *A Hard Fight for We: Women's Transition from Slavery to Freedom in South Carolina*. Urbana: University of Illinois Press, 1997.

Schweninger, Loren. *Families in Crisis in the Old South: Divorce, Slavery, and the Law*. Chapel Hill: University of North Carolina Press, 2012.

Scott, James C. *Domination and the Arts of Resistance: Hidden Transcripts*. New Haven: Yale University Press, 1990.

———. *Seeing Like a State: How Certain Schemes to Improve the Human Condition Have Failed*. New Haven: Yale University Press, 1999.

Sell, Zach. "Asian Indentured Labor in the Age of African American Emancipation." *International Labor and Working-Class History* 91 (April 2017): 8–27.

———. "White Overseers of the World." *Salvage* 3 (2016). http://salvage.zone/in-print/white-overseers-of-the-world/.

———. "Worst Conceivable Form: Race, Global Capital, and the Making of the English Working-Class." *Historical Reflections/Réflexions Historiques* 41, no. 1 (2015): 54–69.

Selleck, R. J. W. *James Kay-Shuttleworth: Journey of an Outsider*. Essex: Woburn Press, 1994.

Semmel, Bernard. *The Governor Eyre Controversy*. London: Macgibbon and Kee, 1962.

———. *The Rise of Free Trade Imperialism: Classical Political Economy; the Empire of Free Trade and Imperialism*. Cambridge: Cambridge University Press, 1970.

Sen, Sudipta. *Empire of Free Trade: The East India Company and the Making of the Colonial Marketplace*. Philadelphia: University of Pennsylvania Press, 1998.

Sengupta, Syamalendu. *A Conservative Hindu of Colonial India: Raja Radhakanta Deb and His Milieu*. New Delhi: Navrang, 1990.

Sharma, Jayeeta. "British Science, Chinese Skill and Assam Tea: Making Empire's Garden." *Indian Economic and Social History Review* 43, no. 4 (2006): 429–55.

———. *Empire's Garden: Assam and the Making of India*. Durham: Duke University Press, 2011.

Sharma, Sanjay. "The 1837–38 Famine in U.P.: Some Dimensions of Popular Action." *Indian Economic and Social History Review* 30, no. 3 (1993): 337–72.

———. *Famine, Philanthropy, and the Colonial State: North India in the Early Nineteenth Century*. New Delhi: Oxford University Press, 2001.

Sharrer, G. Terry. "The Indigo Bonanza in South Carolina, 1740–1790." *Technology and Culture* 12, no. 3 (1971): 447–55.

Shepherd, Verene. *Slavery without Sugar: Diversity in Caribbean Economy and Society since the 17th Century*. Gainesville: University Press of Florida, 2002.

Shing, C. "Central America and the Chinese." *Asia and the Americas* 43 (1943): 209–12.

Shoman, Assad, and O. Nigel Bolland. *Land in Belize, 1765–1871*. Mona, Jamaica: Institute of Social and Economic Research, University of the West Indies, 1977.

Shortall, Felton. *The Incomplete Marx*. Brookfield, Vt.: Avebury, 1994.

Siddiqi, Asiya. "The Business World of Jamsetjee Jeejeebhoy." *Indian Economic and Social History Review* 19, nos. 3–4 (1982): 301–24.

Silver, Arthur J. *Manchester Men and Indian Cotton, 1847–1872*. New York: Barnes and Noble, 1967.

Simkins, Francis Butler, and Robert Woody. *South Carolina during Reconstruction*. Chapel Hill: University of North Carolina Press, 1932.

Simmons, Donald C., Jr. *Confederate Settlement in British Honduras*. Jefferson, N.C.: McFarland, 2001.

Singh, Navtej. *Starvation and Colonialism: A Study of Famines in the Nineteenth*

Century British Punjab, 1858–1901. New Delhi: National Book Organisation, 1996.

Sinha-Kerkhoff, Kathinka. *Colonising Plants in Bihar (1760–1950)*. Delhi: Partridge Press, 2014.

Sloan, Herbert E. *Principle and Interest: Thomas Jefferson and the Problem of Debt*. New York: Oxford University Press, 1995.

Smallwood, Stephanie. *Saltwater Slavery: A Middle Passage from Africa to American Diaspora*. Cambridge, Mass.: Harvard University Press, 2008.

———. "What Slavery Tells Us about Marx." *Boston Review*, 21 February 2018. Available online at: http://bostonreview.net/forum/remake-world-slavery-racial -capitalism-and-justice/stephanie-smallwood-what-slavery-tells-us.

Smith, Hayden. "Rice Swamps and Rice Grounds: The Specialization of Inland Rice Culture in the South Carolina Lowcountry, 1670–1861." Ph.D. diss., University of Georgia, 2012.

Smith, Troy. "Nations Colliding: The Civil War Comes to Indian Territory." *Civil War History* 59, no. 3 (2013): 279–319.

Spillers, Hortense. "Mama's Baby, Papa's Maybe: An American Grammar Book." *Diacritics* 17, no. 2 (1987): 64–81.

Spivak, Gayatri. *A Critique of Postcolonial Reason: Toward a History of the Vanishing Present*. Cambridge: Harvard University Press, 2003.

———. "General Strike." *Rethinking Marxism* 26, no. 1 (2014): 9–14.

Srivastava, Hari Shanker. *The History of Indian Famines and Development of Famine Policy, 1858–1918*. Agra, India: Sri Ram Mehra and Co., 1968.

Stampp, Kenneth. *The Peculiar Institution: Slavery in the Ante-bellum South*. New York: Vintage Books, 1956.

Stampp, Kenneth, and Leon F. Litwack, eds. *Reconstruction: An Anthology of Revisionist Writings*. Baton Rouge: Louisiana State University Press, 1969.

Stanley, Amy Dru. "Histories of Capitalism and Sex Difference." *Journal of the Early Republic* 36, no. 2 (2016): 343–50.

Starobin, Robert. *Industrial Slavery in the Old South*. Oxford: Oxford University Press, 1970.

Stephenson, Wendell Holmes. *Isaac Franklin, Slave Trade and Planter*. Baton Rouge: Louisiana State University Press, 1938.

Stokes, Eric. "Agrarian Society and the *Pax Britannica* in Northern India in the Early Nineteenth Century." *Modern Asian Studies* 9, no. 4 (1975): 505–28.

———. *The English Utilitarians and India*. Oxford: Clarendon Press, 1959.

———. *The Peasant and the Raj: Studies in Agrarian Society and Peasant Rebellion in Colonial India*. Cambridge: Cambridge University Press, 1978.

Stoler, Ann Laura, ed. *Haunted by Empire: Geographies of Intimacy in North American History*. Durham: Duke University Press, 2006.

Stoler, Ann Laura, and Frederick Cooper. "Between Metropole and Colony: Rethinking a Research Agenda." In *Tensions of Empire: Colonial Cultures in a Bourgeois World*, edited by Frederick Cooper and Ann Laura Stoler, 1–56. Berkeley: University of California Press, 1997.

Stuckey, Sterling. *The Ideological Origins of Black Nationalism*. Boston: Beacon Press, 1972.

————. *Slave Culture: Nationalist Theory and the Foundations of Black America.* 1987. Reprint, Oxford: Oxford University Press, 2013.

Sturgis, James L. *John Bright and the Empire.* London: Athlone Press, 1969.

Subramanian, Lakshmi. *Three Merchants of Bombay: Trawadi Arjunji Nathi, Jamsetjee Jeejeebhoy, and Premchand Roychand.* New Delhi: Allen Lane, 2012.

Swan, Dale E. "The Structure and Profitability of the Antebellum Rice Industry, 1859." Ph.D. diss., University of North Carolina, 1972.

Sweeney, Shauna. "Black Women in Slavery and Freedom: Gendering the History of Racial Capitalism." *American Quarterly* 72, no. 1 (2020): 277–89.

Sweeney, Stuart. "Indian Railways and Famine, 1875–1914: Magic Wheels and Empty Stomachs." *Economic and Business History* 26 (2008): 141–57.

Syrett, John. *Civil War Confiscation Acts: Failing to Reconstruct the South.* New York: Fordham University Press, 2011.

Tadman, Michael. "The Demographic Cost of Sugar: Debates on Slave Societies and Natural Increase in the Americas. " *American Historical Review* 105, no. 5 (2000): 1534–75.

————. *Speculators and Slaves: Masters, Traders, and Slaves in the Old South.* Madison: University of Wisconsin Press, 1989.

Takaki, Ronald. "The Movement to Reopen the African Slave Trade in South Carolina." *South Carolina Historical Magazine* 66, no. 1 (1965): 38–54.

Tallie, T. J. *Queering Colonial Natal: Indigeneity and the Violence of Belonging in Southern Africa.* Minneapolis: University of Minnesota Press, 2019.

Taylor, A. A. "The Convention of 1868." *Journal of Negro History* 9, no. 4 (1924): 381–408.

Taylor, Amy Murrell. *Embattled Freedom: Journeys through the Civil War's Slave Refugee Camps.* Chapel Hill: University of North Carolina Press, 2018.

Taylor, Christopher. *Empire of Neglect: The West Indies in the Wake of British Liberalism.* Durham: Duke University Press, 2018.

Thapar, Romila. "Imagined Religious Communities? Ancient History and the Modern Search for a Hindu Identity." *Modern Asian Studies* 23, no. 2 (1989): 209–31.

Thompson, E. P. *The Making of the English Working Class.* New York: Vintage Books, 1963.

Toole, Janet. "Workers and Slaves: Class Relations in South Lancashire in the Time of the Cotton Famine." *Labour History Review* 63, no. 2 (1998): 160–81.

Toscano, Alberto, and Jeff Kinkle. *Cartographies of the Absolute.* Winchester, UK: Zero Books, 2015.

Tripathi, Amales. *Trade and Finance in the Bengal Presidency, 1793–1833.* Calcutta: Oxford University Press, 1979.

Tripathi, Dwijendra. "Opportunism of Free Trade: Lancashire Cotton Famine and Indian Cotton Cultivation." *Indian Economic and Social History Review* 4, no. 3 (1967): 255–63.

————. *Oxford History of Indian Business.* New York: Oxford University Press, 2004.

————, ed. *Business Communities of India.* New Delhi: Manohar, 1984.

Tripathi, Dwijendra, and Mehta Makrand. *Business Houses in Western India: A Study in Entrepreneurial Response, 1850–1956*. New Delhi: Manohar, 1990.

Tsing, Anna. *Friction: An Ethnography of Global Connection*. Princeton: Princeton University Press, 2005.

———. "On Nonscalability: The Living World Is Not Amenable to Precision-Nested Scales." *Common Knowledge* 18, no. 3 (2012): 505–24.

———. "Sorting Out Commodities: How Capitalist Value Is Made through Gifts." *HAU: Journal of Ethnographic Theory* 3, no. 1 (2013): 21–43.

———. "Supply Chains and the Human Condition." *Rethinking Marxism* 21, no. 2 (2009): 148–76.

Turley, David. *The Culture of English Antislavery, 1780–1860*. London: Routledge: 1991.

Turner, Mary. "The Jamaica Slave Rebellion of 1831." *Past and Present* 40 (1968): 108–25.

Tuteja, K. L. "Agricultural Technology in Gujarat: A Study of Exotic Seeds and Saw Gins, 1800–50." *Indian Historical Review* 18 (1990): 136–51.

———. "American Planters and the Cotton Improvement Programme in the Bombay Presidency in Nineteenth Century." *Indian Journal of American Studies* 28 (1998): 103–8.

Ullman, Victor. *Martin R. Delany: The Beginnings of Black Nationalism*. Boston: Beacon Press, 1971.

Veracini, Lorenzo. *Settler Colonialism: A Theoretical Overview*. Basingstoke: Palgrave Macmillan, 2010.

Viswanath, Rupa. *The Pariah Problem: Caste, Religion, and the Social in Modern India*. New York: Columbia University Press, 2015.

Voegeli, V. Jacque. "A Rejected Alternative: Union Policy and the Relocation of Southern 'Contrabands' at the Dawn of Emancipation." *Journal of Southern History* 69, no. 4 (2003): 765–90.

Vorenberg, Michael. "Abraham Lincoln and the Politics of Black Colonization." *Journal of the Abraham Lincoln Association* 14, no. 2 (1993): 22–45.

Waldstreicher, David. *Slavery's Constitution: From Revolution to Ratification*. New York: Farrar, Straus and Giroux, 2013.

Walker, Juliet E. K. *The History of Black Business in America: Capitalism, Race, Entrepreneurship*. New York: Macmillan, 1998.

Walton, John K. *Lancashire: A Social History*. Manchester: Manchester University Press, 1987.

Ward, Geoffrey, ed. *The Civil War: An Illustrated History*. New York: Knopf, 1990.

Washbrook, David. "South Asia, the World System and World Capitalism." In *South Asia and World Capitalism*, edited by Sugata Bose, 40–84. Oxford: Oxford University Press, 1990.

Wesley, Charles H. "Lincoln's Plan for Colonizing the Emancipated Negroes." *Journal of Negro History* 4, no. 1 (1919): 7–21.

Wiecek, William M. "Somerset: Lord Mansfield and the Legitimacy of Slavery in the Anglo-American World." *University of Chicago Law Review* 42, no. 1 (1974): 86–146.

Wiener, Joel. *Radicalism and Freethought in Nineteenth-Century Britain: The Life of Richard Carlile.* Westport, Conn.: Greenwood Press, 1983.

Wiener, Jonathan M. "Class Structure and Economic Development in the American South, 1865–1955." *American Historical Review* 84 (October 1979): 970–92.

Wilderson, Frank, III. "Gramsci's Black Marx: Whither the Slave in Civil Society?" *Social Identities* 9, no. 2 (2003): 225–40.

Williams, Eric. "The British West Indian Slave Trade after Its Abolition in 1807." *Journal of Negro History* 27 (1942): 175–91.

———. *Capitalism and Slavery.* Chapel Hill: University of North Carolina Press, 1945.

Williams, Robert Webb, Jr. "The Mississippi Career of Thomas Affleck." Ph.D. diss., Tulane University, 1954.

Williams, Wilson E. *Africa and the Rise of Capitalism.* 1938. Reprint, New York: AMS Press, 1975.

Wilson, Beckles. *John Slidell and the Confederates in Paris.* New York: Minton, Balch, 1932.

Wolfe, Patrick. "*Corpus Nullius*: The Exception of Indians and Other Aliens in U.S. Constitutional Discourse." *Postcolonial Studies* 10, no. 2 (2007): 127–51.

———. "Settler Colonialism and the Elimination of the Native." *Journal of Genocide Research* 8, no. 4 (2006): 387–409.

———. *Traces of History: Elementary Structures of Race.* London: Verso, 2016.

Wood, Betty. *Women's Work, Men's Work: The Informal Economies of Lowcountry Georgia.* Georgia: University of Georgia Press, 1995.

Wood, Marcus. "William Cobbett, John Thelwall, Radicalism, Racism and Slavery: A Study in Burkean Parodics." *Romanticism on the Net* 15 (1999). http://www.erudit.org/revue/ron/1999/v/n15/005873ar.html.

Wood, Peter. *Black Majority: Negroes in Colonial South Carolina from 1670 through the Stono Rebellion.* New York: Knopf, 1974.

Woodman, Harold. *King Cotton and His Retainers: Financing and Marketing the Cotton Crop of the South, 1800–1925.* Lexington: University of Kentucky Press, 1968.

Wright, Gavin. "Review of *River of Dark Dreams.*" *Journal of Economic History* 52, no. 3 (2014): 877–79.

Wynter, Sylvia. "Beyond the Categories of the Master Conception: The Counterdoctrine of Jamesian Poiesis." In *C. L. R. James's Caribbean*, edited by Paget Henry and Paul Buhle, 63–91. Durham: Duke University Press, 1996.

———. "Novel and History, Plot and Plantation." *Savacou* 5 (1971): 95–102.

Yagyu, Tomoko. "Slave Traders and Planters in the Expanding South: Entrepreneurial Strategies, Business Networks, and Western Migration in the Atlantic World, 1787–1859." Ph.D. diss., University of North Carolina at Chapel Hill, 2006.

Yang, Anand. *The Limited Raj: Agrarian Relations in Colonial India, Saran District, 1793–1920.* Berkeley: University of California Press, 1989.

Yokota, Kariann. *Unbecoming British: How Revolutionary America Became a Postcolonial Nation.* New York: Oxford University Press, 2014.

Zastoupil, Lynn. *John Stuart Mill and India*. Stanford: Stanford University Press, 1994.

Zimmerman, Andrew. *Alabama in Africa: Booker T. Washington, the German Empire, and the Globalization of the New South*. Princeton: Princeton University Press, 2010.

———. "Cotton Booms, Cotton Busts, and the Civil War in West Africa." *Journal of the Gilded Age and Progressive Era* 10 (2011): 454–63.

———. "Three Logics of Race: Theory and Exception in the Transnational History of Empire." *New Global Studies* 4, no. 1 (2010): 1–11.

Index

Page numbers in italics refer to illustrations.

Bowen, George, 154
Bowring, John, 73
boycotts, antislavery, 54
Brady, Wes, 130
Bram, as Denmark Vesey insurrectionist, 59
Brazil, 52, 61; sugar production in, 26, 30, 31, 32, 33, 63
Bright, John, 35, 94, 159, 247n42
Briscoe, E. C., 15
British and Foreign Anti-Slavery Society, 32, 242n17
British Empire, 3, 61, 163, 194, 224; cotton and textiles in, 11, 73, 94, 117, 119, 142, 157; imperialism of, 1–4, 62, 112; India and, 11, 36, 39, 117; liberalism and, 62, 88, 112; slavery and emancipation in, 1, 17–18, 62, 118, 145; United States and, 17, 209, 211; U.S. slaveholders and, 4, 34. *See also* Caribbean, British; Great Britain; *and names of colonies in*
British Guiana, 171, 223, 266n13
British Honduras, 4, 11–12, 167, 176, 187, 266n13; Chinese coolies in, 179–82, 268n62; emancipation in, 170–72, 266n14; former U.S. slaveholders in, 167–68; population of, 169, 265n7; white settlers in, 188–91
British Honduras Company, 168–69, 171, 176, 267n43
British India Society, 35, 72–73, 74
Brown, Francis Carnac, 39
Brown, Henry "Box," 23
Brown, John, raids Harpers Ferry, 87
Brown, William Wells, 54
Bulandshahr, 110
Buncombe County, N.C., 24, 25
Bundelkhand, 79
Burma, 52
Burroughs, Ga., as free town, 194, 200
Butler, Benjamin F., 195–96
Byrd, Jodi, 74

Calcutta, 65, *65*, 102, 138; cotton trade of, 35, 89, 92, 259n106; Manchester

goods and, 89, 96, 97; migrant labor from, 160, 163
Calhoun, John C., 28, 33, 34
Canada, 1, 209, 215
Canning, Charles John Canning, 1st Earl (Lord Canning), 111–12, 121–22
Cape Colony, 32, 215
capital, 6, 68, 144; convergence of empire and slavery with, 1–12; finance, 2, 3, 20; race and class and, 7, 105. *See also* accumulation of capital
Capital (3 vols.; Marx), 6–7, 221, 248n51; on colonialism, 83–84; on slavery, 222, 229n34
capitalism, 6, 50, 72, 172, 179, 228n34; American, 8, 194; colonialism and, 7, 41, 75, 83–84, 102; crises of and disasters within, 5, 90–96, 135, 245n15; history and, 8–9, 229n34, 229n50; industrial, 84, 92, 104, 112, 119; monopoly and, 30, 234n18; plantation, 17, 161, 189; race and racism and, 1, 2, 7, 50, 163; slavery and, 8, 41, 162; violence and, 2, 6, 62. *See also* capital; *Capital* (3 vols.; Marx); Marx, Karl
capitalists: British industrial, 75, 88, 124, 125, 248n43; U.S. slaveholders as, 2, 30, 47
Caribbean, 1, 4, 17, 216. *See also* Caribbean, British; *and names of islands of*
Caribbean, British, 28, 32, 214; after slavery, 31, 46; slavery and slave trade and, 8, 131; white racism and racists and, 47, 169, 170–79
Carlyle, Thomas, 144
Carolina rice. *See* rice and rice cultivation: Carolina rice
Carolinas. *See* North Carolina; South Carolina
Cartwright, Samuel, 84
caste (India), 63, 80
Caste War (Guerra de Castas; British Honduras), 169, 185, 186
Cen, Bel, 185

Central America, 74, 211. *See also* Belize; British Honduras; Guatemala; Panama

Central Provinces of India, 125–26, 129–31

Ceylon, 39

Cha-Jua, Sundiata, 201

Chalisa, famine of, 99

Chamber of Commerce, 33–34; of Bengal, 91, 96, 115, 135–36; of Manchester, 91, 93, 103, 105, 121, 134, 136, 137

chaos, capitalism and, 72

Charleston, S.C., 15–16, 46–47, 51, 58, 212

chattel slavery, 15–16, 230n10

chaudhari (head of cultivators), 81–83

Chelsea, 162

Chengalpattu, 69

Cherokee, 74, 210; dispossession of, 25, 72, 210

Cheshire, 114

Cheyenne, 207

Chickasaw, 72, 74, 122, 210

China, 163, 169, 171, 238n32; Britain and, 17, 89, 91. *See also* Asia; Chinese indentured labor, laborers; coolies

Chinese indentured labor, laborers, 11–12, 147, 153, 163, 177, 213; in British Honduras, 168–70, 179–82, 268n62, 268n80; Queensland and, 149, 153–55. *See also* Asia; China; coolies

Chiriquí, New Grenada (Panama), 172, 173

Chivington, John, 207

Choctaw, 210

Christmas, 186

Chunder, Bholanauth, 98

Citizenship Amendment Act (India, 2019), 9

Civil War (United States, 1861–65), 1, 3, 5, 28, 34, 52, 74, 87, 105, 130, 153–54, 162, 214; battles of, 178, 197; Britain and, 11, 88, 106, *107*, 120, 133, 174–75; causes of, 196–97; cotton scarcity during, 11, 90–95, 106, *107*, 133, 137,

254n5, 254–55n8, 257n56; freedpeople and, 168, 194–202, 267n41; fugitive slaves in, 144, 172–73; India and, 104, 125, 132; Lancashire Cotton Famine and, 11, 106, *107*, 133; Marx on, 105; U.S. slaveholders after, 167–68; West and, 207. *See also* Black freedom; emancipation, U.S.; Confederacy; Lincoln, Abraham; Union army in U.S. Civil War; Union blockade during U.S. Civil War

Clarkson, Thomas, 75

class, 105; struggles between, 217, 222. *See also* bourgeoisie; working class

Clay, Henry, 23

Cloud, Noah B., 214

Cobden, Richard, 30, 32, 154

coercion and coerced labor, 2, 9, 78, 119, 146, 161, 168, 179; debates over, 4–5, 154; economic, 64, 82; in India, 44, 76, 80, 81, 128. *See also* indentured labor; violence; *and "slavery" entries*

coffee, 39, 132

collateral, enslaved people as, 22–23

colonialism, 8, 49, 109, 116, 117; agrarianism and, 52, 79; British, 1, 3, 83, 104–5; capitalism and, 75, 139; exploitation and expropriation and, 72, 142; Marx on, 6, 7; slaveholders', 4, 202, 220; slavery and, 4, 169; U.S., 4, 23, 150, 220. *See also* British Empire; colonization; United States: as empire-state; *and "settler" entries*

colonization, 7, 148, 169; Black, 196, 210; of British Honduras, 167, 267n43; of Indian economy, 89, 100, 143. *See also* British Empire; colonialism; United States: as empire-state; *and "settler" entries*

Colorado Territory, 207

commensurability, 104, 115, 116

commodities, slavery-produced, 51, 61, 63, 121; demand for, 2, 52, 70; histories of, 8, 10, 40; southern U.S. plantations and, 42, 49, 118; Union blockade and, 5, 126, 245n8; U.S. exports of, 1,

3, 17, 28, 54. *See also names of particular commodities (e.g., cotton)*
communism, 7, 26
Communist Manifesto, The (Marx), 221
compensated emancipation, 31, 63
Compensation Act (United States, 1862), 178
Confederacy, 105, 174, 195, 197–98, 210, 271n70; blockade of ports of, 5, *107*, 126, 245n8; Second Confiscation Act and, 172–73. *See also* Civil War (United States, 1861–65)
confiscation of slaveholders' landed property and slavery, 195–96, 203, 205
Connolly, Nathan, 16
consignment, 89
contraband, contrabands: camps of., 171, 174–76, 178; formerly enslaved people as Civil War, 170, 173, 195–97
convergence of slavery, empire, and capital, 1–12
Coolie-nama, 223–24
coolies, 144, 218, 223; in British Honduras, 171, 181–82; enslaved people and, 145–46, 179–80; India and, 79–80, 82, 154; Queensland and, 153–54, 161; trade of, 92, 99, 180; U.S. slaveholders on, 4, 145. *See also* Asia; Asia: indented labor from; China; Chinese; Chinese indentured labor, laborers; indentured labor, laborers; racism, anti-Asian
Corn Laws (Britain), repeal of, 26, 30, 59–60
cotton, 17, 29, 34, 129, 201, 237n38, 248n51; in Australia, 147, 148; Marx on, 131; as slavery-produced commodity, 8, 10, 39, 41; taxes and duties on, 26, 136. *See also* India, cotton and; and other "cotton" entries
cotton, U.S., 3, 51, 63, 122, 145, 152, 161; disruptions in supply of, 88; India and, 72–84, 93, 117–43
cotton cultivation, 242n22; in Africa, 246n24; in Australia, 147, 260n122; British imperial projects for, 118; in

India, 35, 45, 76–84, 117–43, 240n75, 247n38, 247n42, 254–55n8, 254n5, 257n56, 258n84; in United States, 21, 146, 157, 242n23
Cotton Districts Emigration Society, 157
cotton famine, 5, 10–11, 244n2, 251n109, 254–55n8
Cotton Frauds Act (India, 1863), 134
Cotton Kingdom (Lower South), 72, 77
cotton plantations: in Queensland, 154, 161; in United States, 50–51, 126
cotton prices, 50, 51, 89, 95, 102, 117, 118, 123, 127–28, 135, 138, 142, 247n42, 254n5, 257n56
cotton production, 130, 132, 235n39, 245n8, 259n106; in India, 77–84, 126; machinery in, 124, 133, 242n23; in Manchester, 245n6; in New England, 34
cotton staples, 45, 71, 125, 132
Cotton Supply Association, 88, 103, 141
Couper, George, 113–14
Coventry, 157
Creek, 24, 210; dispossession of, 25, 72
crisis, crises, 245n8; of capitalism, 5, 10–11, 91, 221; displacement of, 134–39
Crosthwaite, Charles, 94
Cruzob, 185–86
Cuba, 95; slavery and slave owners in, 61, 63, 222; sugar in, 26, 30–33, 63, 168
Cubitt, William, 112–13

Dakota Sioux, 173, 207
Davis, Jefferson, 200
Davis, Joseph, 200
Davis Bend, Miss., plantations, 194, 200–202
Deb, Radhakanta, 64, 65, 240n75
De Bow, J. D. B., 214
De Bow's Review (journal), 45, 141, 145, 189
De Coin, Robert, 147
deeds, 25; U.S. slavery and, 21–22
Defoe, Daniel, 131
De Gruythers, Mr., 111–12

global economy, 32, 117; labor in, 100, 144; markets and trade of, 2, 33, 60, 67, 229n50; slavery and, 36, 45, 50–51, 70, 131; transformation of, 42–43. *See also* global capital and capitalism

Glymph, Thavolia, 177–78

gold mining in Australia, 155

Gorakhpur, 145

grain. *See* wheat and grains

Grant, J. P., 48

Grant, Ulysses S., 210

Graves, S. R., 113

Great Britain, 1, 3, 5, 9, 10–11, 52, 58, 65, 213, 216; anti-slavery in, 5–6; Royal Society of Arts in, 145–46; U.S. diplomatic relations with, 29–30, 171, 174–75; U.S. trade with, 3, 9, 26–36. *See also* British Empire; capitalists: British industrial; Ireland; manufacturing, British; metropolitan Britain; Scotland; *and names of British counties and cities*

Great Dismal Swamp, *108*

Great Lakes, 18

Great London Exhibition (1851), 54

Grossman, Henryk, 245n7, 246n26

Grundrisse (Marx), on slavery, 222–23

Guatemala, 185

Guerra de Castas (Caste War; British Honduras), 169, 185, 186

Guha, Ranajit, *A Rule of Property for Colonial Bengal*, 202

Guiana, Guianese, 92, 99, 223

gunny cloth, 35, 36, 235n39

Habib, Irfan, 89

Haiti, 20, 46, 173

Hammond, James Henry, 145, 211–12

Hampton, Wade, 45, 48

Hardy, J. F. E., 24

Harnetty, Peter, 248n44, 250n74

Harpers Ferry, 87

Hartman, Saidiya, 79

Haywood, Felix, 220

Haywood, G. R., 117–18, 123

Hazareesingh, Sandip, 130

Helper, Hinton Rohan, 211, 272n90

hemp, 35, 235n39

Henry, Patrick, 218

Herbert, Robert, 154

Heriot, Edward, 54–55

Hermitage plantation (Tenn.), 24

Hilton Head, S.C., 197

Hindustan, 96, 250n77

Hinganghat cotton, 93

Hobsbawm, Eric, 26–27

Hodge, John, 171–80, 184, 188

Homestead Act (United States, 1862), 106, 203, 206

Horry, Ben, 57

Houston, Sam, 26

Houston, Texas, 217

Howard, Oliver O., 198–99

Huddersfield Mutiny Fund, 112

humanitarianism, imperial, 113

Hume, Joseph, 32

Hyde, George, 190

Hyde riots in, 106

Illinois, 140, 176, 196, 215

immigration, 168, 211–12, 215, 218

Immigration Act (United States, 1861), 168

imperialism, 1, 8, 144; culture of, 47–49; of free trade, 3, 118, 261n130; world of, 2–6

incarceration, 64, 65, 69–70, 240n92

indentured labor, laborers, 4, 149, 169; from Asia, 5, 150; Chinese, 11–12, 179–82; as labor exploitation, 145, 156; in United States, 146, 171. *See also* coolies

India, 9, 34, 74, 76, 79, 96, 122, 149, 169, 209, 211; Agra famine in, 72, 79; British colonialism and, 3, 4, 6–7, 35–36, 62–72; free trade movement and, 34–35; indigo in, 4, 5, 10, 29, 34–35, 39–49, 61–64, 129; peasant smallholders in, 51, 61–62, 74; rice and, 52–71, 238n32; slavery and, 1,

of Commerce of, 91–93, 103–5, 121, 134–37; cotton and, 119–20, 254–55n8; India and, 72–73, 112, 120; manufacturing of, 2, 245n6; United States and, 88, 105. *See also other "Manchester" entries*

Manchester Cotton Company, 117–18, 121–22, 125, 139, 247n41; India projects of, 94, 123–25

Manchester Cotton Supply Association, 93–94, 120, 155, 260n122

Manchester Emigrants' Aid Committee, 159

Manchester goods, 136–39, 245n6, 245n15; in India, 97, 100, 117; social histories of, 89–96

Manchester Statistical Association, 115

Manchester Statistical Society, 143

Manila, 161

Manjapra, Kris, 8

manufacturers and factory owners, British, 9, 32, 44, 45, 93, 146, 228n22; India and, 11, 35, 244n4

manufacturing, British, 1, 2–3, 39, 73, 244n2; slavery and, 7, 10–11; United States and, 21, 87

manufacturing, manufacturers, U.S., 29, 34, 40, 198

market economy and markets, 17, 41, 51; discipline of, 61–63

Marx, Karl, 26, 90, 105, 131, 144, 224, 242n15, 245n8; *Capital* (3 vols.), 6–7, 83–84, 221–22, 229n34, 248n51; *Grundrisse*, 222–23; Postone on, 228–29n34; *Theories of Surplus Value*, 6

Maryland, 48, 211

Mathe, Antonio, 185

Mathura, 98

Mauritius, 1, 63; emigration to, 92, 99, 135, 249n69; sugar in, 39, 161

Maya, 185, 187; dispossession of, 168, 186; sovereignty of, 11–12, 169

McCutcheon, Samuel, 188–91

McDunn, Isaac, 24

McHenry, George, 247n38

McKittrick, Katherine, 22

McLeod, D., 113

mechanization: in cotton industry, 73; of rice production, 58–61. *See also* industrialization and industrial revolution; steam power

Melanesia, 149, 161

Menard, John Willis, 176

mercantilism, British, 27–28

Metcalf, Thomas, 102

metropolitan Britain, 1, 63, 129, 134; crises of capitalism in, 5, 91. *See also* London

Mexico, 26

Midwest United States, 163

migration, 11, 98; forced, 15, 72

Mill, John Stuart, 83, 152; *Principles of Political Economy*, 106

Milliken's Bend battle (U.S. Civil War, 1863), 178

Minnesota, 207

Mirzapur, 97

miscegenation, equality through, 204

Mississippi, 30, 140, 206, 214; freedpeoples' land struggles in, 194–95, 200–202; slaveholders and plantations in, 4, 15, 24, 67, 77, 215

Mississippi River, 18; cotton shipped down, 89, 122, 124; steamboats on, 140; valley of, 20–21, 33

Missouri, 54, 196

Mitra, Rajendrala, 5

Mobile, Ala., 50, 212, 219

Montgomery, Benjamin, 200–202

Montgomery, Robert, 111, 112

Moradabad, 110

Morant Bay Rebellion (Jamaica, 1865), 5, 105

Moreton-Robinson, Aileen, 158

Morgan, Jennifer, 8

Morrell, Z. N., 187–88

Morrill Tariff (United States, 1861), 245n8

Morris, James, 67–69, 74, 78

Moss, Gilbert W., *108*

racism, 31, 70, 116, 171, 220; colonial, 64, 104–5; in India, 77, 81, 112, 127; in Queensland, 148–49, 155; slur terms of, 31, 47–48, 104. *See also* white supremacy, supremacists

racism, anti-Asian, 147, 182–85. *See also* Chinese indentured labor, laborers; coolies

racism, anti-Black, 16, 32, 47, 52, 61–62, 70, 150, 214, 272n90; Black emancipation and, 1, 221–22; in Congressional debates over H.R. 85, 203–5; in Queensland, 155–61

railroads, 203, 206, 215; in India, 122, 124; investment in, 102, 103

raiyati, raiyats (smallholdinig cultivators and their tenure), 44, 76, 78–80, 83. See also *ryots*

Rajputana, 98, 109–10, 114–15

Rana, Aziz, 17

Rao, Shivdan Singh Raja, 114–15

raw materials, 2, 248n51

Rawtenstall, 133

real estate, white, 194–202

real estate principle, 9, 197; Du Bois on, 15–17, 140; enslaved African Americans and, 15–25, 29, 230n10

Reconstruction in United States, 207, 271n70

Redgrave, Alexander, 105–6

Regalia sugar plantation (British Honduras), 188–90

Remond, Charles Lenox, 75

Remond, Sarah Parker, 3

removal, 170–71, 206, 211. *See also* dispossession; Native Americans: dispossession of; race: separation of

republicanism, white settler, 149, 152, 156, 162

Republicans, U.S., 202, 211, 220; Black people and, 170–79, 194–95, 205; colonization and, 177–78, 207

resemblance (Marx), 6–7

Rhode Island, 35

rice and rice cultivation, 4, 17, 21, 29, 51, 53, 147, 238n32; in Africa, 57, 59; Carolina rice, 50–71; exports of, 34, 103; imperial culture and, 47–49; milling of, 52, 55, 57–61; as slavery-produced commodity, 3, 10, 28; in South Carolina, 50–61; threshing of, 57–58

Richard, in Denmark Vesey insurrection, 59

Richmond, Va., 212

riots during Lancashire cotton famine, 106

risk in cotton industry, 94–95, 119–20, 128

Rivett-Carnac, Henry, 130–31, 256n45

Robinson, Cedric, 7, 72

Rodney, Walter, 169

Roles, John, 177

Rose, William A., 114

Ross, John, 74, 210

Rotherhithe, 58

Roychand, Premchand, 126

Ruffin, Edmund, 145, 214

Rusk, Thomas, 26

Ryles, Josephine, 219–20

ryots (tenant cultivators), 48, 66, 120, 123, 128, 129. See also *raiyati, raiyats*

Sa'id Pasha, 123

Saint Domingue, 62

Saint Helena, 1, 63

Sampson, Theophilus, 181

San Pedro, 186

Sanskrit, 235n39

Santa Cruz Maya, 12, 185–88

Sattrah Akal, 99–100

Saunders, P., 129

Savannah, Ga., 67, 199

Savannah Colloquy (1865), 199

Saxton, Rufus B., 198, 199

Scandinavia, immigration from, 213

Schrottky, Eugene, *The Principles of Rational Agriculture* (1876), 142

Scotland, 159, 214, 216; labor imported from, 147–48, 151, 157–58, 214–15 peasant smallholders, 123; as India cotton producers, 124–25, 127, 131; as India rice planters and rice producers, 51, 62–63, 66, 68; perceived dishonesty of, 133–34

Peck, Nathaniel, 266n13

Peel, Robert, 30, 31

Peel, Thomas, 83–84

Permanent Relief Fund for the Population of India, 113

Permanent Settlement of 1793 (Bengal), 17

Peterson, Dawn, 24

Philbrick, Edward, 198

Phillips, Wendell, 41–42, 46, 49, 73–74, 197, 209–10

piece goods, 91, 245n6

piece work, 133

pieza framework of Atlantic slave trade, 16

Pilsbury, Charles A., 189

plantations, 4, 10, 29, 61, 72, 179, 185; in British Honduras, 182–85; development of, 169, 214; futures of, 22, 41; households of, 217, 219; in India, 5, 76, 79–81; management of, 45, 127, 214–15; racial regimes of, 9, 180; sugar, 145, 167; violence on, 190; in West Indies, 28, 266n14. *See also* overseers; plantations, southern U.S.

plantations, southern U.S., 15, 17, 24, 35, 40, 43, 67; Britain and, 2, 27, 89; cotton, 140; at Davis Bend, Miss., 200–202; rice, 55–61; violence and, 130, 190

planters, 31, 48, 153; southern U.S., 46, 54, 123, 130, 199, 212

Polanyi, Karl, *The Great Transformation*, 5

political power of U.S. slaveholders, 18–21, 26, 29

Pollard, Edward Alfred, 5

Pomeroy, Samuel C., 173

poor, able-bodied, 110

poor laws, 109, 114, 116

populism, authoritarian, 9

Port Gibson, Miss., 15–16

Port Hudson battle (American Civil War, 1863), 178

Port Royal, S.C., 194, 197–98

Port Royal battle (American Civil War), 197

possession, 21–23. *See also* dispossession

Postone, Moishe, 228–29n34

Potter, Edmund, 91; "manufacturers' manifesto" of, 158

Preston, 109

prices, 40, 51, 91, 167; of cotton, 50, 89, 117–18, 123, 127–28, 135, 138, 142, 245n6, 247n38, 247n42, 248n44, 254n5, 257n56; of enslaved African Americans, 51; of indigo, 41, 43, 46–47; of wheat and grains, 92, 97–98, 100, 102

Prigg v. Pennsylvania (1842), 19

primitive accumulation, 6

private property, 202

Proclamation of Amnesty and Reconstruction (United States), 271n70

Proctor, Jenny, 35

profits, 2, 63

property, personal, 15–16

property, rule of, 202–7

public lands, 202–3

Punjab, 98, 109–10, 113

Queensland, Australia, 118, 124, 213, 263n51; British emigration to, 154, 215; indentured Chinese laborers and, 149, 153–55, 161, 179; Lancashire workers as emigrants to, 108, 118, 150, 155, 157–61; white labor in, 151–52, 155–61; as white man's country, 159–61; white settler colonialism in, 11, 108, 118, 147, 170

race, 80, 215, 223; class and capital and, 105, 217; history of, 8, 33; imperial culture and, 47–49; management of, 4, 145; separation of, 172–79, 196–97, 265n10; sex between, 203, 204

racial capitalism, 7, 9, 156, 160

Sea Islands (South Carolina, Georgia, and Florida), 51, 197–98
Second Confiscation Act (United States, 1862), 172, 174, 196, 198
Sedashegar, 94, 118, 123–24
Seminole, 72, 210
settler colonialism and colonization, 40, 83, 123, 156, 194, 216; abolishing, 207–10; American Indian genocide through, 207–8; in Australia, 4, 6, 7, 12, 108; U.S., 2–3, 21, 62, 163; in U.S. South, 25, 118, 147; white supremacist, 9, 149, 156. *See also* settler slavery; settler slavery, U.S.
settler empire, United States as, 17, 23, 34, 209
settler slavery, 31, 51; demand for, 52–55; India and, 72, 75. *See also* settler slavery, U.S.
settler slavery, U.S., 3, 32, 36, 51, 66, 68–69, 96, 147, 191, 204, 223; agrarian conquest of India and, 74–75, 79, 84; colonial liberalism and, 63, 121; cotton economy and, 119, 122; end of, 149–50; Queensland colonization and, 156, 160. *See also* slaveholders, U.S.; slavery, U.S.
Seward, William, 173, 177
sex, interracial, 203, 204
Seymour, Frederick, 176
Shah, Firoz, 101
sharecropping, 218–20
Sharma, Jayeeta, 63–64
Sheridan, Philip, 207, 209
Sherman, William Tecumseh, 198–99, 209
silk, 102
Sioux Wars (United States, 1865), 207
slaveholders, U.S., 1, 10, 17, 18, 22, 25–26, 30, 42, 45, 55, 127, 167–68, 210; colonialism of, 202, 212, 214, 220; global markets and, 2, 47; indigo and, 40, 46–47; oppose European immigration, 211–12; power of, 2–3, 21, 29; as rice planters, 50, 60; in South Caro-

lina, 15, 145; tariff policies and, 9, 25, 34; in Virginia, 4–5. *See also* enslaved African Americans; enslavement; slavery, U.S.
slave rebellions and insurrections, 1, 5, 10, 87, 244n2
slavery, 31, 61, 74, 145, 229n34, 266n14; chattel, 15–16, 230n10; colonialism and, 4, 169; convergence of empire and capital with, 1–12; plantation, 19, 60–61, 229n50; racial, 6, 44, 50, 70, 130; regimes of, 5–6; violence of, 12, 40, 70. *See also* slavery, U.S.
slavery, U.S., 4, 9, 12, 19, 45, 49–51, 61, 131, 134, 212; Asian indentured labor and, 144–45; Britain and, 1–2, 26–27, 39, 63, 117, 132; cotton and, 125, 132; defense of, 54–55; diffusion of, 20, 232n43; Du Bois on, 15–17; expansion of, 1–3, 6–7, 10, 20–21, 26, 232n43; global impact of, 144, 191; India and, 45, 62, 75, 129–30; persistence and revitalization of, 59, 118; Queensland and, 149, 162; on rice plantations, 55, 63; trade liberalization and, 27–28; violence of, 55, 119, 172
Slavery Abolition Act (Britain, 1833), 63
slave ships, 18, 26
slave trade, Atlantic, 5–7, 16–20, 43, 118, 131, 215
slave trade, internal, 6–7, 15, 40, 118, 145, 237n5; enslaved families separated by, 50, 177, 219; Louisiana Purchase and, 20, 21; Upper South planters profit through, 50–51
slave traders, 15–17
Smith, John Benjamin, 94, 109, 244n4
Smith, Samuel, 125–30, 135, 257n56
Solomon Islands, 149
Somerset, James, 17–18
Somerset v. Stewart (1772), 17–18
songs of enslaved people, 12
sorghum, 145
So Tsing Whan, 190

trade liberalization in United States, 34
transportation infrastructure in India, 102–3, 118, 122–24
Treaty of 1866 (United States and Cherokee), 210
Treaty of New Echota (United States and Cherokee, 1837), 25
Trinidad, 171, 223, 266n13
"Trouble of the World" (slave song), 12, 224
Trumbull, Lyman, 196–97
Truth, Sojourner, 22

unemployment, 5, 9
Union army in U.S. Civil War: Black soldiers in, 174–79; freedpeople and, 194–99; land confiscations by, 200, 201
Union blockade during U.S. Civil War, 5, *107*, 126, 245n8
United States, 16, 34, 122, 169, 179; Black emancipation in, 1, 6, 11–12; Britain and, *3*, 26–36, 29–30, 89; cotton in, 242n23, 247n42; as empire-state, 2, 16, 18, 52, 207; free soil movement in, 155–56; racism of, 11, 154; as settler empire, 17, 25, 34; settler slavery in, 3, 6, 21, 26, 32, 36, 55; territorial expansion of, 18, 20, 26; 2008 financial crisis in, 8, 9. *See also* southern United States; *and names of regions, territories, states, and cities of*
Upper South, 50–51, 211
uprisings, 5; global, 9
U.S. Constitution: Fifteenth Amendment of, 203; Fugitive Slave Clause of, 18, 19; Sixteenth Amendment of, 203; slavery and Three-Fifths Compromise in, 18
U.S.-Dakota War (1862), 207
Usher, John, 173, 174
U.S. House of Representatives, 203–6
U.S.-Mexico War (1846–48), 26, 27, 30
U.S. Senate, 205
U.S. Supreme Court, 19
Utah, 215

Vanuata, 149
Veracini, Lorenzo, 21
Vesey, Denmark, insurrection of, 59
Victoria, Australia, 148, 153–55
violence, 20, 44, 48, 55, 57, 62, 70, 146, 148, 210; against Black people, 177–78; in British Empire, 173, 209, 234n18; against Chinese migrants, 18–85, 187; in India, 63, 65, 76–78, 80, 82, 103, 248n44; on plantations, 46, 172, 189–90; racial, 40, 218, 223; sexual, 24–25, 203, 205; of U.S. slavery, 12, 48, 55, 68, 70, 119, 130, 218–19
Virginia, 4–5, 18, 162, 173, 195–96; tobacco in, 29, 51
Viswanath, Rupa, 63
voting rights of African Americans, 195, 203
Vrindavan, 98

wage work, workers, 2–6, 145, 181, 197, 220, 242n15, 251n102; enslaved people and, 59, 61. *See also* factory workers; free labor
Walker, Robert J., 30
Walker, William, 171
Walker Tariff (United States, 1846), 26, 30, 59–60
Washington, D.C., 173, 176
Watie, Stand, 210
Watkins, James, 172
Watson, J. Forbes, *Textile Manufactures and the Costumes of the People of India* (1866), 138–39
Watts, John, 134
weavers, 100, 250n74; in Britain, 157–58; in India, 92–93, 249n69, 250n77; in Lancashire, 92, 106, 114–15, 133; in North-Western Provinces of India, 135, 139, 142; suffering of, 101, 117
Western Australia, 83–84
Western United States, 195, 207, 212, 215
West Indies, 28, 234n25, 266n14
West Point Mill (Charleston, S.C.), 58